NARRATIVE OF
MILITARY OPERATIONS
DURING THE
CIVIL WAR

J. E. Johnston

gift

NARRATIVE OF
MILITARY OPERATIONS
DURING THE
CIVIL WAR

GENERAL JOSEPH E. JOHNSTON

NEW INTRODUCTION BY
FRANK E. VANDIVER

A DA CAPO PAPERBACK

Library of Congress Cataloging in Publication Data

Johnston, Joseph E. (Joseph Eggleston), 1807-1891.
  [Narrative of military operations directed during the late War Between
the States]
  Narrative of military operations during the Civil War / by Joseph E.
Johnston; new introduction by Frank E. Vandiver.
     p.   cm. – (A Da Capo paperback)
  Reprint, with new index. Originally published: Narrative of military
operations directed during the late War Between the States. New York:
D. Appleteon, 1874.
  ISBN 0-306-80393-3
  1. United States – History – Civil War, 1861-1865 – Campaigns. 2. John-
ston, Joseph E. (Joseph Eggleston), 1807-1891. 3. Generals – Southern
States – Biography. 4. Confederate Statesof America. Army – Biography.
5. United States – History – Civil War, 1861-1865 – Personal narratives,
Confederate. I. Title.
E470.J73   1990
973.7'82 – dc20   89-49354
[B]   CIP

This Da Capo Press paperback edition of *Narrative of Military Operations During the Civil War* is an unabridged republication of the edition
published in 1874, here supplemented with an introduction and index by
Frank E. Vandiver, with the permission of Indiana University Press.

Published by Da Capo Press, Inc.
A Subsidiary of Plenum Publishing Corporation
233 Spring Street, New York, New York 10013

Manufactured in the United States of America

I offer these pages as my contribution of materials for the use of the future historian of the War between the States.

–JOSEPH E. JOHNSTON
General, C.S.A.

INTRODUCTION

Was Joseph E. Johnston a genius or a marplot? This question almost splintered the Confederacy, and still intrigues students of the Civil War. His partisans regard him as a brilliant strategist and sound field commander whose talents were stifled by a rancorous Chief Executive. They feel that had Jefferson Davis given Johnston proper opportunity and support, he would have rivaled Lee in achievement. Foes point to constant retreating, absence of victories, and a petty punctilio to illustrate an almost pathological unwillingness to make decisions and a basic personal insecurity. He was, they argue, temperamentally unsuited to be a general.

The enigma of Johnston has both attracted and repelled biographers. In 1891 Bradley T. Johnson, an old military associate, edited *A Memoir of the Life and Public Service of Joseph E. Johnston.* A polemical book, it accepted Johnston's prejudices and assumed his ability. The panegyric tone of Johnson's *Memoir* was imitated in Robert M. Hughes' *General Johnston,* published in 1897 as one of the Appleton "Great Commanders" series. After Hughes' book, sixty-five years were to pass before the publication of another biography. The long silence was prompted more by the difficulty of the subject than by lack of interest.

Part of the difficulty lay in Johnston's somewhat cavalier attitude toward his military papers, part in the welter of conflicting data appearing in the formidable *Official Records of the Union and Confederate Armies* and in the volumes of *Battles and Leaders of the Civil War*. But Johnston himself was the greatest difficulty. The external man could be easily sketched—his pride, his generosity toward subordinates, his feud with Davis, his broad military views, his plans and his battles. The usual biographical details were readily available: born in 1807; graduated from the United States Military Academy in 1829; served in the Black Hawk Expedition of 1832, in the Seminole War, on the United States-Texas Boundary Survey, in the Mexican War, in the Utah campaign of 1858, with the Artillery, Topographical Engineers, the Cavalry, and the Quartermaster Corps; rose to full general in the Confederate Army; served after the Civil War as Representative from Virginia, and Commissioner of Railroads; died in 1891. But the surface picture only tantalized the student.

What was he like? His early biographers knew him and what he was like and so concentrated on what he did. Since they took a partisan stand, motivation proved no problem—they had only one side to consider. Motivation became the great concern of later investigators, and still the answer appeared hidden in Johnston's puzzling personality.

He fared well at the hands of historians for some time, possibly, as one historian said, because Davis fared so badly. Gradually, though, the tide turned against him, and increasing evidence was marshaled to show that much of Davis's criticism had been valid. Davis contributed to the new trend with the publication, in 1881, of his two-volume

Rise and Fall of the Confederate Government. His carefully constructed case against Johnston had force and "ie ring of truth. In time, as Davis's historical rehabilitation continued, his views gained some acceptance.

Gradually Johnston faded from attention. He was ranked a first-rate second-rater, if not worse, by most Civil War scholars, and dismissed. His own *Narrative,* which had helped set his position, was regarded with lofty scholarly suspicion and pointed to as an example of the bad taste which characterized so many former Confederates in the period of the "Battle of the Books."

The popular view, however, was not completely satisfying, and in the 1920's the old controversy again erupted. In 1923 Thomas Robson Hay evaluated Johnston's strategy and tactics in the operations from Dalton to Atlanta, Georgia, in two articles entitled "The Atlanta Campaign," in the *Georgia Historical Quarterly,* VII, and in 1924 he re-examined the circumstances surrounding Johnston's removal from command of the Army of Tennessee on the eve of the battle for Atlanta in an article entitled "The Davis-Hood-Johnston Controversy of 1864," *Mississippi Valley Historical Review,* XI. His careful study of much new material, added to his studious detachment, enabled him to see virtue on both sides of the Atlanta questions. Johnston was not completely blameless, but neither was Davis. And though critical of some phases of Johnston's operations, Hay concluded that in general his Atlanta campaign had been well fought.

But the disagreements about the general were far from ended. In 1927, Professor Alfred P. James published an article entitled "General Joseph E. Johnston, Storm Center of the Confederate Army," in the *Mississippi Valley Historical Review*, XIV. Highly critical of the general's role in the internal politics of the Confederacy, James alleged that Johnston committed the unforgivable blunder of permitting himself to become the figurehead for a military junta opposed to the Administration, and that he was used as a counterpoise to the President. This was a grave offense, and since Johnston's loyalty to the South can hardly be doubted, it seems clear that he must have been politically juvenile.

In a way the critical tone of James's article indicated Johnston's future treatment at historians' hands. Although interest in the war developed rapidly in the 1930's, and biographies of prominent participants found wide audience, Johnston did not attract attention. Numerous students of the war, Douglas Southall Freeman among them, pointed to the need for a modern biography, but did no more than point. Johnston's military operations were reviewed in several broad studies of the war in Virginia and Tennessee, but the general himself still defied analysis.

In 1956 James W. Livingood and Gilbert Govan published the first full, scholarly biography of Johnston under the perceptive title of *A Different Valor*. Still the general won his own sort of victory over his biographers. Livingood and Govan brought sound research and modern biographical techniques to bear, and could do no more than write about their subject. They described him, sympathized with him, went with him into battle, and yet failed to understand him. Perhaps, after all, Johnston best understood himself, and because he was a mass of so many contradictions even he often understood imperfectly.

For a man well endowed with social graces—he was rated a good conversationalist, an interested

listener, and a dinner-table asset—Johnston seemed
curiously inarticulate about himself. Possibly he
had the natural reticence of an active man, but whatever the reason, his reserve helped obscure him to
history. Not vain in the normal sense, he kept no
diary, and his correspondence is rarely self-analyt-
ical. To a few he wrote frankly, and his letters to
the South Carolina-born Texan, Louis T. Wigfall,
are among the most revealing sources on his career.
But even in unguarded letters he is rarely autobio-
graphical. The student must read him into his views
on others. His biography must be built in a mosaic
of reflections, of shadings and interpretations. For
this reason, then, his *Narrative of Military Operations* deserves to rank at one of the most important
of Confederate memoirs.

Intensely partisan, the *Narrative* is on the surface
a dubious historical source. In reviewing military
decisions Johnston occasionally remembered events
to his own advantage and forgot with a purpose. His
accounts of battles offer little information not available elsewhere from more reliable sources, and he
rarely makes a character analysis. In addition, his
style is marred by bitterness and by painfully legal-
istic argument. A casual reading leaves the impression that his reputation would have benefited had
he suppressed so ill-tempered an account of personal
and military frustrations. Closer examination,
though, tends to temper the initial judgment.

Johnston's book received considerable attention
when it appeared in 1874, largely because he got
into the "War of the Reminiscences" early. Few
other Confederates had yet arranged their reputa-
tions for publication or developed literary enemies.
The general, however, had several old scores to
settle, and most of all he had to defend himself

before history from what he felt were the cruelly
unjust attacks of Jefferson Davis. During the war
he had collected evidence of the President's perfidy,
and he added to his ammunition during the postwar
years. His feelings toward Davis gave him a vil-
lain and a theme, and his own stoic endurance of
persecution gave him a hero.

Even with these ingredients, unfortunately, the
Narrative does not compare favorably with memoirs
of other war figures. Johnston is overmatched by
his old enemy William T. Sherman in military analysis, and is put to shame by Grant's elegantly frugal
style. James Longstreet, hardly a docile man, wrote
a less biased account of his Confederate career, and
Richard Taylor, one of Johnston's former subordinates, recounted his Confederate exploits with a
charm which caused Douglas Freeman to label him
"the one Confederate who possessed literary art that
approached first rank." Even Jefferson Davis out-
classed him with the breadth and comparative mod-
eration of his *Rise and Fall of the Confederate
Government*.

Structurally defective as literature, the *Narrative*
exhibits yet another defect. Preoccupation with
special pleading led Johnston to ignore the vital
"inside" information which he obviously possessed.
He held some of the most important commands in
the South and had entree into the highest councils,
but he rarely discusses Confederate grand strategy.
And unlike many reminiscers, he never pictures or
characterizes the great with whom he associated.
Perhaps this is because he was one of the great
himself, and so close to the others that they were
not unique.

Johnston's book, though, has many virtues. Chief
among them is the fact that he wrote it. In it he

gives unconscious insight into his strange personality, a personality with large effect on the course of the war. Because historians have scorned the *Narrative* on grounds of bias, they have missed its real significance. Careful and sympathetic reading offers a dual approach to understanding the author. He reveals something of himself by argumentation. What he chooses to argue reveals more, as does his capacity to marshal fancied fact. More than piecemeal characterization can be gleaned from the book. In its pages Johnston paints a clear physical self-portrait.

"Gamecock" was the word often used to describe him and it seems apt. Short, stiffly straight from familiarity with the saddle, easy to meet and pleasant in conversation, the general had a high, studious forehead and his prominent brows accented thoughtful eyes. He wore sideburns, a carefully tended moustache, and a small vandyke. Around him always seemed to cling an air of natural neatness, attested by the brushed and pressed gray uniform which gave his small figure a tailored elegance. He liked people, and friendships for him were lasting. So were enmities. His marriage to Lydia, the daughter of Louis McLane, diplomat and cabinet member, gave Johnston social position and helped make him popular in the United States and Confederate armies. Position and popularity he bore as befitted a Virginia gentleman, but he knew how to use these advantages. Command came naturally to him—it was almost a caste mark—and his subordinates generally were his loyal admirers. It was otherwise with equals or superiors.

A curious species of pride caused many of Johnston's troubles in the Confederacy, a pride which frequently was mistaken for contentiousness.

The Johnstons had long been influential in Virginia affairs, and Joseph remained keenly conscious of his father's Revolutionary War record. Heroism ran in the family, along with a tradition of gentility. On first acquaintance Johnston's gentility could not be missed, but his pride usually lay hidden beneath a cloak of courtesy. His looks and manners confirmed his refinement but belied his spirit and ambition.

Pride demanded that Johnston write the *Narrative* to defend his honor; refinement dictated that it be detached, aloof in tone. An urge to prove Davis's rancor occasionally mars Johnston's detachment, however, and serves to guide the organization of his book. The central theme, his own loyalty in the face of Davis's perfidy, logically divided at four crises: first, the crisis arising over questions of rank; second, that resulting from the retreat of Johnston's troops from Centreville, Virginia, and his conduct of the Battle of Seven Pines; third, the crisis produced by his failure in departmental command and the loss of Vicksburg; fourth, the Atlanta campaign. Johnston's laborious examination of these crises shows that each had a direct and cumulative effect on the next and that together they reveal much of the general's personality.

The special Johnston vanity showed itself in close concern for prerogative, and contributed to the first serious breach with Jefferson Davis. In the late summer of 1861 President Davis, acting under a law passed in May, nominated five full generals for approval by Congress. As Johnston understood Confederate military policy, all former United States Army officers who joined the Southern cause would hold their old position in the army or be promoted according to original date of rank. If this were true, then he had reason to consider himself the senior general in the Confederacy, for he had been brigadier general and Quartermaster General of the "Old Army," and no other fellow-Confederate had achieved rank beyond brevet brigadier in the United States service.

Virtually certain of seniority, Johnston was shocked to read the President's list: Samuel Cooper stood first, followed by Albert Sidney Johnston, Robert E. Lee, Joseph E. Johnston, and P. G. T. Beauregard. The list was arranged in order of rank, and since Johnston's demotion from first to fourth place was obviously illegal, it must represent a studied insult. Honor demanded a protest. Unfortunately Johnston protested by letter, and he wrote in the heat of resentment. With sentences bristling, he reviewed his past military service, avowed his loyalty to the Southern cause, and lamented the undeserved stain on his reputation resulting from reduction in rank without due process of military law. He summed up his feelings in a characteristic declamation:

I repeat, my right to my rank as general is established by the act of Congress of the 14th of March, 1861, and the 16th of May, 1861, and not by the nomination and confirmation of the 31st of August, 1861. To deprive me of that rank it was necessary of Congress to repeal those laws. That could be done by express legislative act alone. It was not done, it could not be done by a mere vote in secret session upon a list of nominations.

Davis thought the letter insubordinate and his answer was a model of acid brevity. General Johnston's language, said the President, seemed unusual and his arguments "utterly one-sided, and . . . [his] insinuations as unfounded as they are unbecoming." Obviously there would be no change in rank. Davis

misconstrued Johnston's pride as pretension, and
the general, who doubtless was right in his claim
to rank, saw deliberate persecution in an instance
of presidential weakness.

By the time Johnston abandoned his positions
near Centreville in March, 1862, mutual distrust had
become entrenched, and Davis found it relatively
easy to believe reports of profligate waste of matériel
during the retreat. Persistent reminders from Johnston that too much food, ammunition, and baggage
had been sent to his Manassas railhead were forgotten, and the President paid no attention to the
fact that fifteen days had been consumed in moving
vast quantities of stores to new depots before Johnston pulled back. Statistics indicted the general.
He had destroyed or left behind 1,434,316 pounds
of precious foodstuffs and had burned a meat-packing plant at Thoroughfare Gap. The situation was
made worse by Johnston's failure to keep the Administration informed of his activities through the first
two weeks of March. Consequently Richmond had
to rely on rumor for any information from the army,
even for word of the retreat. Such isolation must
have been a relief to Johnston, but it left him open
to criticism.

Then, too, he failed to explain that the abandonment of mounds of personal baggage had been necessary to strip the army for field operations. He
complained in his *Narrative* that since the "amount
of . . . [soldier's] baggage had not been limited,
consequently a trunk had come with each volunteer,"
and in correspondence that "this army had accumulated a supply of baggage like that of Xerxes' myr-
iads." Enough had been explained before the
retreat began, he thought, to inform Davis of the
logistical snarl facing the army. If the President

chose to ignore several February letters describing the fantastic, sprawling depots, Johnston would not press the matter.

But this incident, when combined with later dissatisfaction with Johnston's efforts to halt General George B. McClellan's advance up the Virginia Peninsula, bolstered Davis's growing contempt for his general's ability. Johnston seemed careless about details, and apparently lacked sound logistical sense. The Manassas madhouse got beyond him and he all but lost control of his supplies. But he did not, as Davis appeared to think, race southward without any concern for what was lost; his actions were dictated by clear military necessity.

Disagreement on matters of strategy further alienated Davis and Johnston. The general, logically enough, thought that purely military problems would be left in his hands; the President, who never forgot his Mexican War record or that he had been Franklin Pierce's Secretary of War, frequently exercised his constitutional right to command. When he proposed plans for halting McClellan in April, 1862, he clashed with Johnston on the question of strategy. Johnston, as anxious as Davis to protect Richmond, wanted to avoid fighting McClellan on the Peninsula. The James and York rivers would give the Federal general too good a chance to use the United States Navy to land troops behind the Confederate lines. A line close to Richmond would reduce the danger of flanking and offer opportunities for effective attack.

Davis believed that the best way to secure the capital would be to fight a battle as far away as possible. If McClellan could not be beaten at Yorktown or Williamsburg, his progress up the Peninsula ought to be contested inch by inch. Confederate ground could not be yielded without desperate defense. Johnston correctly grasped the fact that McClellan's army was the main objective; the tactical defense of Richmond and precious Southern acres were secondary considerations. If all available Confederate troops were collected at Richmond and the army protected on its flanks, the pressure would be on the Yankees—a point which the afternoon strategists in the lobby of the Spotswood Hotel failed to appreciate. As the Federals advanced from their base, their gunboats would be left behind, the Peninsula would grow wider, and finally their expanding front would be bisected by the treacherous Chickahominy River.

Although initially overruled, Johnston had the satisfaction of seeing his theories proved sound. Confederate lines at Yorktown, Williamsburg, and Eltham's Landing were turned, and the Union Navy shifted McClellan's prodigious city of supplies to West Point on the Richmond and York River Railroad. When this happened, the wisdom of Johnston's plans must have been clear to all: as the Confederates retired on their Richmond base and contracted their lines, McClellan had to move away from his own base into hostile and unfamiliar country, extend his front, and straddle a sizable stream. The Federal general's situation was further confounded by the fact that he hoped to join with General Irvin McDowell's army, marching south from the Fredericksburg sector.

Johnston knew he must strike before the junction took place if he hoped to beat "Little Mac," but he refused to panic. Although McClellan was careful, his awkward position might force him into a mistake. It did. To broaden his front and cover his left flank, McClellan sent two corps south of the Chickahominy River. By May 31, 1862, persistent and incredible rains had turned that river into a booming torrent and McClellan's two corps were neatly cut off. Johnston had waited for such a chance, and hit the stray Yankee units near Seven Pines.

Tactically his battle plan was good—a turning movement by the Confederate right around the Union left—but his unconcern for details, plus the greenness of his men, undid him. The battle ideally should have been fought by masses; instead, the grayclads went into action in bits and dribbles. Only the greater demoralization of the bluecoats enabled Johnston's men to shove them back. At the height of the battle, while trying for more coordination of his confused units, Johnston was unhorsed by a severe wound.

The President, on the field, rode to the general's side and expressed sincere solicitude. Obviously he would be incapacitated for some time; the army must have a new commander. General Lee took command; he soon found that Johnston's battle had gone to pieces with the general's disability and abandoned hope of following up the small advantage gained at Seven Pines. Always Johnston believed that victory had been snatched from him at the crucial moment. Had the battle been resumed the next day, the Confederates' "advantage of position and superiority of numbers would have enabled them to defeat" the enemy.

Seven Pines could not be rated a success. The action began slowly with consequent loss of the element of surprise. Johnston's subordinates were uncertain of who commanded on what part of the field—his fault, certainly—and coordination of several large bodies of men appeared beyond the capacity of inexperienced generals and staff officers. Much

confusion could have been avoided had Johnston
taken the time to issue precise orders and to make
certain that they were carefully distributed. Instead
he relied on his friends among the generals to see
that everyone knew his plan. Since he did not make
clear the chain of command, he ignored the very
point which had most confused him in the Battle
of Manassas. And there was some indication that
in the heat of this essentially well planned but inde-
cisive action he lost control of various parts of the
battle.

The disabled general found refuge in a Richmond
house, where for almost six months he fretted
through convalescence. Lee's smashing victories
pleased him, but gave him twinges of jealousy. Long
before Seven Pines he had urged heavy reinforcements for his army so that he could fight with some
slight chance of superiority. Help came, but tanta-
lizingly little. With Lee in command, troops seemed
to pour into Richmond from all directions. "As
soon as I had lost command of the Army of Virginia by wounds in battle," lamented Johnston in
his *Narrative*, "my suggestion was adopted. In that
way the largest Confederate army that ever fought,
was formed in the month of June, by strengthening
the forces near Richmond with troops from North
and South Carolina and Georgia."

Enforced inactivity ought to have improved relations between the Johnston and Davis families,
especially since Lydia and Varina were close com-
panions. Not so, however, for frustration and bitterness, plus leisure hours, made Johnston easy prey
to a growing anti-administration cabal. This group
had a dual appeal. Not only were many of them
old friends—especially Louis T. Wigfall—but they
said the right things against Davis. Doubtless en-

couraged by his discontented comrades, Johnston
grew more resentful about being neglected and mis-
treated by the President, and as his anger mounted
the feud spread to Lydia and Varina. Their animosity soon crackled with that refined venom re-
served to ladies, and each presided over a circle of
loyal wives. Had there been any inclination on the
part of either the general or the President to for-
give, the ladies prevented their forgetting.

Wigfall, a former Confederate general, and now
a Senator from Texas, helped organize a pro-John-
ston faction in Congress which continually urged
the general for important posts. Davis, though
unhappy with his past performances, still had some
respect for a man who commanded the good will
of so many. And Johnston was one of the most
experienced and highest ranking officers in the South.

A seasoned veteran was badly needed for an
experiment which the changing nature of the war
forced upon Davis. Although he cherished the prospect of directing all Confederate military operations, the conflict had grown to such gigantic proportions and had spread to such remote areas that
he recognized the need for a modern command system. Some of his responsibility had to be decen-
tralized. Davis hated to delegate any of his pre-
rogatives and had no precedent upon which to build
a new army organization. But after much delibera-
tion and debate with Secretaries of War George W.
Randolph and James A. Seddon, he decided to create a large geographical—or theater—command in
the West. Something of the sort had evolved in
Virginia under Lee and it worked well. Lee could
not be spared from the Army of Northern Virginia
and Johnston seemed the only other qualified choice
for the post.

As Davis conceived the new organization, Johnston would have over-all charge of the Department of the West, an area embracing "a portion of Western North Carolina, and Northern Georgia, the States of Tennessee, Alabama and Mississippi, and that portion of the State of Louisiana east of the Mississippi River." In this huge domain were several Confederate armies—those of Bragg in Tennessee, Pemberton at Vicksburg, Gardner at Port Hudson, plus the forces in East Tennessee, and at Mobile, Alabama—which would be under Johnston's control.

No more important command could have been given Johnston, nor one which should have been more to the liking of so stanch an advocate of coordination. In the realm entrusted to him he could do almost anything he wished with his several armies —combine them, coordinate their separate activities, depose their commanders—and he had absolute logistical authority to support his operations. He accepted the assignment in November, 1862, and journeyed to Chattanooga to establish Department Headquarters. Although he plunged into work with characteristic energy it soon appeared that something had gone wrong. The true nature of his post, the fulness of his powers, apparently escaped him. "I have been very busy for some time looking for something to do, to little purpose," he confided to Wigfall in February, 1863:

each of the three departments assigned to me has its general, & there is no room for two, & I can't remove him appointed by the Pres. for the precise place [so] nothing but the part of inspector general is left to me. I wrote the President on the subject, trying to explain that I am virtually laid upon the shelf with the responsibility of command, but he has not replied, perhaps because he has no better place for me. I should much prefer the *command* of fifty men.

Revealing indeed is the remark about *"command."*
It shows clearly that he never fully appreciated the
possibilities of geographical departments and that
he was unable to make intelligent and systematic
use of his authority. Letters to Wigfall and others
show that Johnston sought to defend his inactivity
with reasonable military arguments, and the *Narrative* continues the deception. He tried to bring
the army of General Theophilus H. Holmes across
the Mississippi from Arkansas, but when this was
rejected for political reasons, Johnston felt that no
other combinations could succeed. Bragg's and
Pemberton's armies could not be combined because
of distance and poor transportation. Once he had
voiced these convictions he took refuge in the belief
that "my command was little more than nominal."
When the danger to Vicksburg reached a peak in
April and May, 1863, no amount of cajoling from
an exasperated Secretary of War or critical President could induce the department commander to
violate a basic military principle by taking personal
charge of Pemberton's army. His reasons are out-
lined in the *Narrative* (pp. 242-243) :

While commanding one army in Mississippi, in the presence
of the much more powerful one of General Grant, it was
impossible for me to direct the operations of another far off
in Tennessee, also greatly outnumbered by its enemy. That
a general should command but one army, and that every
army should have its general present with it, are maxims
observed by all governments—because the world has produced few men competent to command a large army when
present with it, and none capable of directing the operations
of one hundreds of miles off; still less one capable of doing
both at the same time.

Even when relieved of over-all departmental command, Johnston still refused to take control of
Pemberton's army. Instead he remained at Jackson,

Mississippi, urging Pemberton to evacuate Vicksburg and avoid a siege. The loss of Vicksburg, attributed by Davis to Johnston's failures, confirmed his every suspicion concerning the general.

The incredibly complicated problems which Johnston faced in Mississippi were not appreciated by Davis, and once again the two failed to understand each other's views. Davis could see only the desperate need to hold the Mississippi bastion; Johnston could see only the necessity to save Pemberton's army. Politically the President was on sound ground; militarily the general was right.

But by that time questions of right and wrong were academic. Vicksburg was gone, and with it virtually all contact with the trans-Mississippi Confederacy. The events leading to this disaster had all occurred while Johnston supposedly commanded the defending forces, and the Southern people wrathfully blamed him. More bitter, though, than popular condemnation must have been Johnston's self-disillusionment. In a moment of high tragedy he must have realized that there were inescapable flaws in his character—flaws which stood revealed only at times of decision. He might seek to share the blame with Davis, might later recite excuses, but the truth he knew within himself.

The months following the loss of Vicksburg were filled with black recrimination. The anti-Davis group, now grown to huge proportions and organized both in and out of Congress, charged the President with grossly interfering in military matters. This hostile faction complained that while Johnston had urged the evacuation of Pemberton's army in order to combine it with his own small force near Jackson, Davis had hysterically ordered Pemberton to hold Vicksburg to the last. Had he left the campaign in Johnston's hands, all would have been well. Some of the general's Congressional friends, notably Wigfall, agitated for a full investigation of events in the West. If the whole story could be brought out, they felt that Davis and Pemberton would appear in a far dimmer light than "Old Joe." So general did this feeling become that the Johnstons found themselves basking in martyrdom. The general's quiet acceptance of a small, unimpressive command in Mississippi won friends and added to his hero's lustre.

With few infantry and over-ridden cavalry, Johnston did his best to protect the area from the Georgia-Alabama line to the Mississippi River. But Grant made no serious effort to control this territory, even though Sherman's troopers ranged destructively on foraging expeditions, and Johnston obviously had been cast out to pasture.

In this quiet sector the only fighting of consequence was with the President, who inflicted on Johnston a fifteen-page "bill of indictment" written in typically glacial style. All the disasters in the Mississippi area were ascribed to the general's incompetence. This inexcusably insulting communication goaded Johnston into an equally lengthy review of his case. Both of these curious documents are printed in the *Narrative*.

Post-Vicksburg reaction waned rapidly—other crises occupied the public attention—and pressure on Johnston eased. He might well have served the duration in Mississippi had not friend Braxton Bragg muffed the aftermath of the victory at Chickamauga. After his men panicked at Missionary Ridge and bolted into northern Georgia, even Davis had to concede that Bragg seemed to have lost the confidence of the Army of Tennessee. Removal of the

presidential favorite posed a serious problem: who
could succeed him? General William J. Hardee,
competent, hard-hitting, and a logical selection, professed his inability to command, and was willing to
serve only in caretaker capacity. At this critical
moment Davis received an avalanche of requests to
appoint his old foe. So agonizing a prospect burned
into the President's memory, and his misgivings he
could recount with relish months later. "After relieving General Bragg," he wrote in February, 1865,

of our five generals, Lee and Beauregard were the only
officers of that grade in the field except General Johnston.
Neither of the first two could properly be withdrawn from
the position occupied by him, and General Johnston thus
remained the only officer of the rank superior to that of
Lieut. General who was available. . . . There seemed to be
scarcely a choice left; but my reluctance to risk the disasters
which I feared would result from General Johnston's assignment to this command could with difficulty be surmounted.
Very pressing requests were made to me by members of
Congress. The assignment of this commander was said to
be demanded by the common voice of the Army, the press
and the people; and, finally, some of my advisors in the
Cabinet represented, that it might well be the case, that this
assignment with the disasters apprehended from it, would
be less calamitous than the injury arising from an apparent
indifference to the wishes and opinion of officers of State
Governments, of many members of Congress and of other
prominent citizens. I committed the error of yielding to
these suggestions against my own deliberate convictions. . . .

Lydia, enjoying quiet civilian life, urged Joseph
to quit the army rather than continue service under
a "wicked man." Another assignment, she felt,
would result only in further trouble. But Joseph
wanted the Army of Tennessee. Although always
professing satisfaction with any military position
in defense of the South, he desired army command

more than anything else. If it could not be the Army of Northern Virginia, then the second most important field force in the Confederacy would do.

He found his army in camps around Dalton, Georgia, and assumed command on December 27, 1863. Conditions were not good. Not only was Dalton militarily weak, but also the men were dispirited, worn, hungry, and glad for the relative safety of winter quarters. These morale problems were familiar ones, and could be handled with rigid discipline and attention to such things as dry socks, new trousers, and better rations. More practiced now in the science of logistics, Johnston saw that the army got these things, and in turn it gave its heart to "Old Joe." A veteran army it was, one cursed with a succession of bad leaders and abortive battles. It knew when it had a general and for Johnston it would try anything. For his part, Johnston was in his element. Commanding an army was to him the natural function of a general and it was the post for which he was thoroughly qualified by temperament, training, inclination, and experience.

Soon aware that Richmond's promises of reinforcements were "air castles," Johnston made ready as best he could to oppose Sherman's huge aggregation. Although anxious to attack, Johnston refused to take suicidal risks with inadequate numbers and, again, his caution impressed Davis as cowardice. Without substantial aid he could do nothing more than retire before the Yankee advance which began in early May, 1864, but his retreat from Dalton to Atlanta stands as a model of operational strategy. In almost constant contact for over seventy days with an army at least twice the size of his own, Johnston contested every mile, deftly eluded Sherman's flankers, avoided general combat unless he had advantage of ground, struck as he saw a chance, and conserved men and equipment with a parsimony reminiscent of Stonewall Jackson.

Sherman's superior numbers enabled him to continue inching toward Atlanta, but he understood clearly when he crossed the Chattahoochee and approached heavy Rebel works that as long as Johnston's army held those lines the campaign had failed. Both the Confederate army and its Atlanta base were still intact.

Comfortably entrenched, and readying an attack on Sherman as he ventured across Peachtree Creek, Johnston suddenly received peremptory orders to turn over command to one of his subordinates, General John B. Hood. On July 18, 1864, Johnston left the army. His removal may well have been Davis's greatest single blunder of the war.

Davis's reasons for installing the "dealer of manly blows," as Johnston called Hood, had some validity. Despite the brilliance of his Fabian campaign, Johnston again had failed to keep the Chief Executive informed of his plans. Rumors persisted that Atlanta would be given up by "Retreatin' Joe," and he did not deny them. Nothing could be learned about what he would do if he did give up the city. Would he retreat to the sea? To Davis it seemed likely.

In his *Narrative* Johnston clearly indicates that he intended to hold Atlanta "forever," but he did not say so at the time. Not even to General Bragg, sent by the President as a sort of spy to Johnston's headquarters, did he give a definite promise of defense. It is probable that he had not firmly decided on a plan when the Army of Tennessee occupied the Atlanta lines. He had nothing but contempt for Davis's dedication to ground and doubtless would have evacuated the city if strategy so dictated.

Removal from command and apparent retirement may have been almost a relief, for now Johnston could take with him something of his old confidence. Everything had been done on the retreat to Atlanta that could have been done, and there need be no self-doubt. With this inner satisfaction the six months of exile were borne with patience. Finally, in February, 1865, Johnston left the comforts of civil life at the behest of General Lee, belatedly created General-in-Chief of the remnants passing for Confederate "armies." Hood had failed utterly and Johnston once again took command of the Army of Tennessee, reduced now to a hard core of iron men.

Sherman still was the foe—a foe flushed with successes from Atlanta to the sea, and on into North Carolina. Against his large and rugged blue horde Johnston's handful could offer little resistance as they retreated toward Durham Station, North Carolina. For a brief moment at Bentonville in March the old spirit flashed again, but it was an afterglow. Lee's surrender doomed the Army of Tennessee and on April 26, 1865, Johnston surrendered it to his old enemy.

Unlike most fellow-Rebels, Johnston's war was not over. Although he looked to the future and refused to bemoan a Lost Cause, he still fought with Jefferson Davis. While the ex-President languished in Federal prison, the general learned much about the depths of Davis's hatred for him. Information unavailable during the war showed that the former Chief Executive had maligned him at every opportunity.

Such viciousness—some of it fancied—could not go unanswered, and Johnston made full reply in the *Narrative*. In this reply he offered an indirect self-estimate. Misunderstood and subjected to the slurs of a superior maddened by a senseless vendetta, the general nonetheless did always what was right. He was virtually a Horatius, standing alone and undaunted, destined for vindication by history.

But history has judged Johnston pretty much as did his contemporaries. The controversy over his ability continues, and the consensus remains essentially negative. Undeniably he lacked the human understanding of a Napoleon, the pliability and inventiveness of a Jackson, Grant, or Lee. These deficiencies sparked his troubles with Davis and led to his failure in department command. They narrowed his military vision and prevented his grasping the changing grand strategy of total war.

Still, many advocates claim he had real strategical sense, and they are partly right. Strategy is an art which may be practiced at two levels, and on the secondary level Johnston had few equals. No better example of operational strategy can be cited than his brilliant Atlanta Campaign. Unfortunately an estimate of Johnston as a general cannot be based solely upon the Atlanta Campaign. Splendid as it was, it does not offset instances of mediocrity, even of incompetence, which force the conclusion that though he became a superb army commander, he lacked the mentality and personality for greatness.

Readers of the *Narrative* will find that the author exhibits some defects of the general. Details occasionally are wrong. Statistics seem to have been especially bothersome to Johnston, who frequently committed the human error of overestimating enemy strength and undercounting his own. A few of his generalizations might have been modified had he troubled to check his memory and to temper emotion with fact. His own confusion sometimes confuses recollected events; particularly is this true of affairs in the Mississippi basin in late 1862 and early 1863.

These defects are, however, amply counterbalanced by virtues. Far more than an intriguing self-portrait can be found in Johnston's book. As a vital exhibit in the Johnston-Davis feud, it ranks as a primer of intrigue as well as one of the important Confederate sources. Its value is enhanced by a chapter of the general's guesses on why the Confederacy lost and by an extensive appendix containing some documents of importance unavailable elsewhere.

More than is true of most memoirs, the *Narrative* bears the mark of its author. It puzzles, irritates, lulls, and charms; it misinforms in one passage and enlightens in the next, and from it comes a glimpse into an enigma and an insight into a war.

The editor wishes to thank his wife, Susie, and Mr. and Mrs. Archie P. McDonald for their painstaking help with the index.

FRANK E. VANDIVER
Texas A & M University
College Station, Texas

CONTENTS.

CHAPTER I.

Passage of Ordinance of Secession by Virginia Convention.—Resign office of Quartermaster - General of the United States.—Defense of West Point Officers, who resigned, from Unjust Attack.—Assigned to Duty of organizing Virginia Troops.—Ordered by President Davis to take command at Harper's Ferry.—Convinced, on Examination, that it was untenable.—Correspondence, on the Subject, with General Lee and the Confederate Authorities.—General Beauregard assigned to command of Confederate Army at Manassas.—Movements of General Patterson.—Withdrawal from Harper's Ferry.—Affair near Romney.—General Patterson again marches on Martinsburg.—Battle offered at Darkesville.—General McDowell advances on Manassas.—Precautions preparatory to assisting General Beauregard   PAGE 9

CHAPTER II.

Movement of Troops to Manassas.—Discouragements of the March.—Arrival at Manassas.—President Davis's Telegram.—General Beauregard's Proposed Plan of Attack approved.—General McDowell anticipates it.—Battle of Manassas.—Arrival of President Davis.—Reasons why an Advance on Washington was impracticable   36

CHAPTER III.

The Summer spent in observing the Enemy and preparing for Active Service.— Mason's and Munson's Hills occupied.—Colonel J. E. B. Stuart.—General McClellan in command of the Federal Forces.—Consequences of Want of Preparation for the Struggle beginning to be seriously felt.—The President appoints Five Generals.—Correspondence with him on the Subject.—Organization of the Confederate Army.—President invited to Headquarters of the Army for Consultation.—He visits Fairfax Court-House.—Account of the Conference and its Result.—Battle of Leesburg.—Affair at Drainsville.— Effective Total of the Confederate Army at the End of the Year 1861.—Allusion to Events in the West   69

CHAPTER IV.

General Jackson proposes to resign.—Interference of Secretary Benjamin with the Army.—Proposition to exchange Prisoners.—Summoned to Richmond for Conference.—Preparations for withdrawal from Manassas.—Secretary Benjamin continues his Interference with the Discipline of the Army.— Movement to the Rappahannock.—Orders to General Jackson.—Battle of

Kernstown.—Army moved to the Rapidan.—Appointment of General Randolph Secretary of War.—Movements of General McClellan.—Another Conference with the President.—Its Result   .   .   .   .   .   PAGE 87

CHAPTER V.

Take Command on the Peninsula.—General Magruder's Defensive Preparations.
—Inform War Department of Intention to abandon Yorktown.—Battle of
Williamsburg.—Affair near Eltham.—No further Interruption to the March.
—Army withdrawn across the Chickahominy.—Disposition of the Confed-
erate Forces in Virginia at this Time.—Advance of General McClellan.—
Reported Movement of McDowell.—Battle of Seven Pines   .   .   117

CHAPTER VI.

Report for Service at the War-Office.—Received Orders on November 24th.—
Correspondence with the War Department.—Colonel Morgan's Achievement
at Hartsville.—Meet the President at Chattanooga, and accompany him to
Mississippi.—Battle of Murfreesboro'.—Van Dorn attacked at Franklin.—
While en route to Mississippi, ordered to take direct Command of General
Bragg's Army.—Events in Mississippi.—General Pemberton's Dispatches.
—Battle near Port Gibson.—Ordered to Mississippi to take "Chief Com-
mand"   147

CHAPTER VII.

Start for Mississippi.—Dispatch from General Pemberton.—Arrival at Jackson.
—Movements of the Enemy.—Orders to General Pemberton.—Battle of
Baker's Creek.—Retreat of General Pemberton across the Big Black to
Vicksburg. — Letter from General Pemberton.—Order him to evacuate
Vicksburg.—Investment of Vicksburg by the Enemy.—Port Hudson in-
vested.—Siege of Vicksburg.—Telegraphic Correspondence with the Presi-
dent and Secretary of War.—Move to the Relief of General Pemberton.—
Receive News of the Fall of Vicksburg.—Army retires to Jackson   174

CHAPTER VIII.

General Sherman advances on Jackson with Large Force.—Dispositions made
for its Defense.—Correspondence by Telegraph with the President.—Daily
Skirmishing.—Enemy expected to attack.—Instead of attacking, begin a
Siege.—Evacuation of Jackson. — Army withdrawn to Morton.—Enemy,
after burning much of Jackson, retire to Vicksburg.—Relieved of Command of Department of Tennessee.—General Bragg's Telegram; Suggestion
too late.—Review of the Mississippi Campaign.—Visit Mobile to examine
its Defenses.—Letter from the President, commenting harshly on my Military Conduct.—My Reply to it.—Congress calls for the Correspondence.—
My Letter not furnished.—Both Letters.—Events during the Fall.—Ordered
to take Command of the Army at Dalton.—Arrive on 26th and assume
Command on 27th of December   205

CHAPTER IX.

Find Letter of Instruction from Secretary of War at Dalton.—My Reply.—Letter from the President.—Mine in reply.—Condition of the Army.—General
Hardee ordered to Mississippi to repel General Sherman's Advance.—

Movements of the Enemy in our Front.—Dispositions to meet them.—General Hardee and his Troops return to Dalton.—Correspondence with General Bragg.—Effective Strength of the Army of Tennessee.—Advance of General Sherman . . . . PAGE 262

CHAPTER X.

Disposition of the Confederate Troops.—Affair at Dug Gap.—Cavalry Fight at Varnell's Station. — Fighting at Resaca. — General Wheeler encounters Stoneman's Cavalry.—Army withdrawn to Resaca to meet Flanking Movement of the Enemy 287

CHAPTER XI.

Skirmishing at Resaca along our whole Lines.—The Enemy cross the Oostenaula.—Our Army put in Position to meet this Movement.—Causes of leaving Dalton.—The Dispositions there of the Confederate Army.—The Army at Cassville.—The Position a strong one.—In Line of Battle.—Generals Hood and Polk urge Abandonment of Positions, stating their Inability to hold their Ground.—General Hardee remonstrates.—Position abandoned, and Army crosses the Etowah.—Losses up to Date.—Affairs near New Hope Church.—Manœuvring of Federal Troops.—Kenesaw.—General Assault.—Battle of Kenesaw.—Army crosses the Chattahoochee.—Visit of General Brown.—Relieved from Command of the Army of Tennessee.—Explain my Plans to General Hood.—Review of the Campaign.—Grounds of my Removal —Discussion of them.—General Cobb's Defense of Macon . . 304

CHAPTER XII.·

Again ordered to the Command of the Army of Tennessee in North Carolina.—Interview with General Beauregard.—Movement of the Federal Forces in North Carolina.—General Bragg attacks the Enemy successfully near Kinston. —General Hardee attacked by Two Corps near Averysboro'.—Battle of Bentonville.—Events in Virginia.—Evacuation of Richmond, and Surrender of General Lee's Army.—Negotiations begun with General Sherman.—Details of the Conference.—Armistice and Convention agreed on.—The latter represented by Washington Authorities.—The Army surrenders.—Farewell Order to the Confederate Troops 371

CHAPTER XIII.

Causes of Failure.—Misapplication of Means.—Inefficient Financial System.—Bad Impressment Laws.—No Want of Zeal or Patriotism.—Refutation of Charges against Secretary Floyd.—Facts of the Case.—Deficiency of Small-Arms at the South 421

CHAPTER XIV.

Mr. Davis's Unsent Message.—Letters of Governor Humphreys and Major Mims.—Synopsis of Unsent Message.—Reply to Unsent Message . 430

APPENDIX 469

INDEX 605

LIST OF MAPS AND PORTRAITS.

PAGE

MAP OF RICHMOND AND THE PENINSULA . . . following 117

MAP OF MISSISSIPPI CAMPAIGN (VICKSBURG) . facing 169

MAP OF CAMPAIGN IN NORTH GEORGIA,
No. 1 (DALTON) . . . . . . " 277

MAP OF CAMPAIGN IN NORTH GEORGIA,
No. 2 (ADAIRSVILLE) . . . . . " 321

MAP OF CAMPAIGN IN NORTH GEORGIA,
No. 3 (MARIETTA) . . . . . . " 327

MAP OF ATLANTA AND VICINITY . . . . " 347

GENERAL JOSEPH E. JOHNSTON . . . . Frontispiece.

GENERAL P. G. T. BEAUREGARD . . . . facing 38

MAJOR-GENERAL IRWIN MCDOWELL . . . . " 42

LIEUTENANT-GENERAL T. J. JACKSON . . . " 106

GENERAL GEORGE B. MCCLELLAN . . . . " 110

LIEUTENANT-GENERAL JAMES LONGSTREET . . " 120

LIEUTENANT-GENERAL R. S. EWELL . . . . " 128

GENERAL BRAXTON BRAGG . . . . . " 148

LIEUTENANT-GENERAL WILLIAM J. HARDEE . . " 156

LIEUTENANT-GENERAL LEONIDAS POLK . . . " 158

LIEUTENANT-GENERAL U. S. GRANT . . . . " 166

MAJOR-GENERAL W. T. SHERMAN . . . . " 302

GENERAL JOHN B. HOOD . . . . . . " 306

LIEUTENANT-GENERAL A. P. STEWART . . . " 328

LIEUTENANT-GENERAL WADE HAMPTON . . . " 390

NARRATIVE OF
MILITARY OPERATIONS

JOHNSTON'S NARRATIVE.

CHAPTER I.

Passage of Ordinance of Secession by Virginia Convention.—Resign Office of Quartermaster-General of the United States. — Defense of West Point Officers, who resigned, from Unjust Attack.—Assigned to Duty of organizing Virginia Troops.—Ordered by President Davis to take command at Harper's Ferry.—Convinced, on Examination, that it was untenable.—Correspondence, on the Subject, with General Lee and the Confederate Authorities.—General Beauregard assigned to command of Confederate Army at Manassas.—Movements of General Patterson.—Withdrawal from Harper's Ferry.—Affair near Romney.—General Patterson again marches on Martinsburg.—Battle offered at Darkesville.—General McDowell advances on Manassas.—Precautions preparatory to assisting General Beauregard.

THE composition of the convention assembled in Richmond in the spring of 1861, to consider the question of secession, proved that the people of Virginia did not regard Mr. Lincoln's election as a sufficient cause for that measure, for at least two-thirds of its members were elected as "Union men." And they and their constituents continued to be so, until the determination to "coerce" the seceded States was proclaimed by the President of the United States, and Virginia required to furnish her quota of the troops to be organized for the purpose. War being then inevitable, and the convention compelled to decide whether the State should aid in the subju-

gation of the other Southern States, or join them in
the defense of principles it had professed since 1789
—belong to the invading party, or to that standing
on the defensive—it chose the latter, and passed its
ordinance of secession. The people confirmed that
choice by an overwhelming vote.

The passage of that ordinance, in secret session
on the 17th of April, was not known in Washington, where, as Quartermaster-General of the United
States Army, I was then stationed, until the 19th.
I believed, like most others, that the division of the
country would be permanent; and that, apart from
any right of secession, the revolution begun was
justified by the maxims so often repeated by Ameri-
cans, that free government is founded on the consent of the governed, and that every community
strong enough to establish and maintain its independence has a right to assert it. Having been educated in such opinions, I naturally determined to return to the State of which I was a native, join the
people among whom I was born, and live with my
kindred, and, if necessary, fight in their defense.

Accordingly, the resignation of my commission,
written on Saturday, was offered to the Secretary of
War Monday morning. That gentleman was requested, at the same time, to instruct the Adjutant-
General, who had kindly accompanied me, to write
the order announcing its acceptance, immediately.

No other officer of the United States Army of
equal rank, that of brigadier-general, relinquished
his position in it to join the Southern Confederacy.

Many officers of that army, of Southern birth,
had previously resigned their commissions, to return

to the States of which they were citizens, and many others did so later. Their objects in quitting the United States Army, and their intentions to enter the service of the seceded States, were well known in the War Department. Yet no evidence of disapproval of these intentions was given by the Federal Administration, nor efforts made by it to prevent their execution. This seems to me strong proof that they were not then considered criminal.

Northern editors and political speakers accuse those who thus left the service of the United States for that of the Southern Confederacy, of perjury, in breaking their oaths of allegiance. It is impossible that the inventors and propagators of this charge can be ignorant that it is false. The acceptance of an officer's resignation absolves him from the obligations of his military oath as completely as it releases the government from that of giving him the pay of the grade he held. An officer is bound by that oath to allegiance to the United States, and obedience to the officers they may set over him. When the contract between the government and himself is dissolved by mutual consent, as in the cases in question, he is no more bound, *under his oath*, to allegiance to the government, than to obedience to his former commander. These two obligations are in force only during tenure of office. The individual who was an officer has, when he becomes a citizen, exactly the same obligations to the United States as other citizens.

This principle was always acted upon by the United States. Whenever a military officer received a new appointment, either of a higher grade, or of an equal one in another corps, he was required to repeat the oath of office, because the previous one, including of course that of allegiance, was held to have expired with the previous office, although the individual had not ceased to be an officer of the army. When he left the army, as well as a particular office in it, the case was certainly stronger.

Leaving all my property but personal arms and clothing, I set off to Richmond with my family, on Tuesday. In consequence of railroad accidents, however, we did not reach that place until daybreak, Thursday.

General Lee had been appointed commander-in-chief, with the rank of major-general. There were, however, several other officers of that grade. A few hours after my arrival, Governor Letcher gave me the appointment of major-general.

The commander-in-chief assigned me to the service of organizing and instructing the volunteers then just beginning to assemble at the call of the Governor. He himself was then selecting the points to be occupied by these troops for the protection of the State, and determining the number to be assigned to each. Norfolk, a point near Yorktown, another in front of Fredericksburg, Manassas Junction, Harper's Ferry, and Grafton, seemed to be regarded by him as the most important positions, for they were to be occupied in greatest force.

I was assisted in my duties by Lieutenant-Colonel Pemberton, Majors Jackson and Gilham, and Captain T. L. Preston. Near the end of April, however, the second named was promoted to a colonelcy and assigned to the command of Harper's Ferry, held until then by Colonel Kenton Harper.

I was employed in this way about two weeks. Then, Virginia having acceded to the Southern Confederacy, the government of which assumed the direction of military affairs, I accepted a brigadier-generalcy offered me by telegraph by the President. It was then the highest grade in the Confederate army. The offer had been made in one or two previous telegrams sent to General Lee, for me, but not delivered. The Virginia Convention had abolished my office in the State service, and offered me the next lower. But, as it was certain that the war would be conducted by the Confederate Government, and its officers had precedence of those having like State grades, I preferred the Confederate commission.

The President had me called to Montgomery to receive instructions, and there assigned me to the command of Harper's Ferry.

In my journeys from Washington to Richmond, from Richmond to Montgomery, and thence to Harper's Ferry, I saw in the crowds assembled at all the railroad-stations the appearance of great enthusiasm for the war against subjugation—so much as to give me the impression that all of the population fit for military service might have been brought into the field, if the Confederate Government could have furnished them with arms and ammunition—which, unfortunately, it had not provided. That government depended for arms, for the war then imminent, mainly upon those found in the arsenals at Fayetteville, Charleston, Augusta, Mount Vernon, and Baton Rouge; United States muskets and rifles of discarded pattern, the number supposed to be about seventy-five thousand; above forty thousand muskets belonging to the State of Virginia in course of rapid conversion from "flint" to "percussion lock" by Governor Letcher's orders; and twenty thousand lately procured for the State of Georgia, by Governor Brown.

I reached Harper's Ferry soon after noon of the 23d of May, accompanied by Colonel E. Kirby Smith,[1] acting adjutant-general, Major W. H. C. Whiting,[2] of the Engineer Corps, Major E. McLean, of the Quartermaster's Department, and Captain T. L. Preston, assistant adjutant-general. Within an hour the commanding officer, Colonel Jackson,[3] visited me; learned the object of my coming, and read the order of the War Department, assigning me to the command he had been exercising. My order announcing the change of commanders, made by the President's authority, was sent to him next morning, with the request that he would have the proper number of copies made and distributed to the troops, as I had no office as yet. He replied very courteously, in writing, that he did not "feel at liberty to transfer his command to another without further instructions from Governor Letcher or General Lee;" but offered me, in the mean while, every facility in his power for obtaining information relating to the post. Major Whiting, who had been his school-fellow, saw him at my request, and convinced him very soon that the President's authority was paramount in military affairs, and his action in the

---

[1] Afterward lieutenant-general.
[2] Who fell at Fort Fisher, a major-general.
[3] Who became so celebrated as lieutenant-general.

case in accordance with military usage.   This misun-derstanding of military custom produced little more delay than the time consumed by the messenger in bringing me Colonel Jackson's note, and by Major Whiting in going to that officer's quarters from mine.

This little affair is mentioned, only because what seems to me a very exaggerated account of it has been published.[1]

Governor Letcher had taken possession of Har-per's Ferry as soon as possible, and had it occupied by a body of troops commanded by Colonel Kenton Harper—not soon enough, however, to prevent the destruction of the small-arms stored in the armory. The Federal commanding officer, when compelled by the approach of the Virginia troops to abandon the place, set fire to the buildings containing these arms,[2] to destroy what he could not save for his govern-ment.   Soon after being appointed commander-in-chief of the forces of the State, General Lee increased the garrison of Harper's Ferry, and placed Colonel Jackson in command there.   On extending its control of military affairs over Virginia, the Confederate Gov-ernment, as if equally impressed with the importance of the position, made another addition to the troops assembled there—of three regiments and two bat-talions of infantry.   I was also instructed in Mont-gomery to "take Lynchburg in my route, and to make arrangements there for sending forward to Har-per's Ferry 'such force' as I might deem necessary to strengthen my command."   I found no available "force" there, however.

---

[1] In Dabney's "Life of Jackson."

[2] It was said that there were about seventeen thousand of them.

The forces thus assembled were, the Second, Fourth, Fifth, Tenth, Thirteenth, and Twenty-seventh Virginia, Second and Eleventh Mississippi and Fourth Alabama regiments of infantry, and a Maryland and a Kentucky battalion; four companies of artillery (Virginia), with four guns each, but without caissons, horses, or harness; and the First Regiment of Virginia Cavalry—of about two hundred and fifty men, including Captain Turner Ashby's company, temporarily attached to it by Colonel Jackson—in all, about five thousand two hundred effective men. Among the superior officers were several who subsequently rose to high distinction : "Stonewall" Jackson ; A. P. Hill, who won the grade of lieutenant-general ; Stuart, matchless as commander of outposts ; and Pendleton, General Lee's commander of artillery.

These troops were undisciplined, of course. They were also badly armed and equipped—several regiments being without accoutrements—and were almost destitute of ammunition, and, like all new troops assembled in large bodies, they were suffering very much from sickness ; nearly forty per cent.[1] of the "total" being in the hospitals there or elsewhere, from the effects of measles and mumps.

General Lee's command in Virginia, as major-general in the State service, was continued until Richmond became the Confederate seat of government. The law converting the Confederate brigadier-generals into generals, approved May 16th, had not been published to the army in orders, by the War Department, but was known to be in existence, for it had appeared in the newspapers.

---

[1] This proportion is given from memory.

My conversations with General Lee in Richmond, and the President's oral instructions to me in Montgomery, had informed me distinctly that they regarded Harper's Ferry as a natural fortress—commanding the entrance into the Valley of Virginia from Pennsylvania and Maryland—and that it was occupied in that idea, and my command not that of a military district and active army, but of a fortress and its garrison. Maps, and intelligent persons of the neighborhood, told me that the principal route into "the Valley" from Pennsylvania crosses the Potomac at Williamsport, and the railroad at Martinsburg, at least twenty miles west of this garrison, and of course beyond its control. A careful examination of the position and its environs, made on the 25th, with the assistance of an engineer of great ability, Major Whiting, convinced me that it could not be held against equal numbers by such a force as then occupied it.

Harper's Ferry is untenable against an army by any force not strong enough to hold the neighboring heights north of the Potomac and east of the Shenandoah, as well as the place itself. It is a triangle formed by the Potomac, Shenandoah, and Furnace Ridge, the latter extending from river to river, a mile and a half above their junction. Artillery on the heights above mentioned to the north and east could sweep every part of this space. As the rivers are fordable at various points, it was easy to turn or invest the place, or assail it on the west (Furnace Ridge) side.

Two main routes lead from Maryland and Pennsylvania into the Valley of Virginia, meeting at Winchester : one passing through Frederick, and crossing the Potomac at Harper's Ferry ; the other leading through Chambersburg, Williamsport (where it crosses the Potomac), and Martinsburg. These roads are met at Winchester by the principal one from Northwestern Virginia into " the Valley," and also by a good and direct one from Manassas Junction, through Ashby's Gap, which, east of the Blue Ridge, had the advantage of easy communication with the Manassas Gap Railroad. This road is, perhaps, little shorter than that from Manassas Junction to Harper's Ferry ; but there were insuperable objections to the latter. Near Harper's Ferry it follows the course of the Potomac, and could be completely swept by artillery on the north bank of the river, so that it might have been closed to us by a few Federal batteries ; and, even if our troops following it escaped that danger, they might have been intercepted near Centreville by the Federal army.

The United States had, at that time, three armies threatening Virginia. The principal one at Washington, commanded by Major-General McDowell; the second at Chambersburg, under Major-General Patterson's command ; and the third in Northwestern Virginia, under that of Major-General McClellan.

We supposed that these armies would coöperate with each other, and that the Federal general-in-chief would direct their combined forces against Richmond. This supposition was partially sustained by our scouts and friends in Maryland, who reported that the armies of Generals Patterson and McClellan were to unite at Winchester; and this report was confirmed by the Northern press.

It was necessary, of course, that the Confederate troops in the Valley should always be ready to meet this invasion, as well as to unite quickly with the army at Manassas Junction, whenever it might be threatened by General McDowell's. At Harper's Ferry, they were manifestly out of position for either object, for Patterson's route from Chambersburg lay through Williamsport and Martinsburg—a long day's march to the west; and the only direct road thence to Manassas Junction was completely under the enemy's control. Winchester was obnoxious to neither objection, but, on the contrary, fulfilled the conditions desired better than any other point. The commanders on both sides, in the subsequent military operations in that region, seem to have appreciated its importance, and to have estimated its value as I did, except those who disposed the forces of the United States in September, 1862, when eleven thousand men, placed at Harper's Ferry as a garrison, were captured, almost without resistance, by General Lee's troops, *coming from Maryland.*

My objections to Harper's Ferry as a position, and to the idea of making a garrison instead of an active force of the troops intrusted with the defense of that district, were expressed to the proper authorities in letters dated May 26th and 28th, and June 6th, and replied to by General Lee [1] on the 1st and 7th of June. These letters of his express the

---

[1] After Richmond became the seat of the Confederate Government, General Lee performed a part of the duties of the Secretary of War, and of the Adjutant-General.

dissent of the authorities from my views, and their opinion that the maintenance of the existing arrangement was necessary to enable us to retain the command of the Valley of Virginia, and our communications with Maryland, held to be very important.

General Lee wrote in his letter of June 1st: "I received, on my return from Manassas Junction, your communications of the 25th and 28th ult., in reference to your position at Harper's Ferry. The difficulties which surround it have been felt from the beginning of its occupation, and I am aware of the obstacles to its maintenance with your present force. Every effort has been made to remove them, and will be continued. But, with similar necessities pressing on every side, you need not be informed of the difficulty of providing against them. . . ." And in that of the 7th: "I have had the honor to receive your letter of the 6th inst. The importance of the subject has induced me to lay it before the President, that he may be informed of your views. He places great value upon the retention of the command of the Shenandoah Valley, and the position at Harper's Ferry. The evacuation of the latter would interrupt our communication with Maryland, and injure our cause in that State. . . ."

The objects of the Confederate Government, expressed in these letters, were not to be accomplished by the concentration of its forces at Harper's Ferry; for General Patterson's invasion was to be from Chambersburg, and therefore by Williamsport and Martinsburg, a route beyond the control of Harper's Ferry.

Notwithstanding this determination on the part

of the Executive, I resolved not to continue to occupy the place after the purposes for which the troops were sent to it should require them elsewhere.

About the 9th of June, however, I again repre- sented to the Government the objections to its plan, and urged it to change the character of my command.[1]

General Beauregard came to Manassas Junction and assumed command on that frontier, a week after my arrival at Harper's Ferry. We communicated with each other at once, and agreed that the first attacked should be aided by the other to his utmost. We were convinced of our mutual dependence, and agreed in the opinion that the safety of the Confed- eracy depended on the coöperation of the armies we commanded.

In the mean time the Potomac was observed by the cavalry from the Point of Rocks to the western part of the county of Berkeley, as had been done un- der my predecessor. The manufacture of cartridge- boxes and belts was ordered in the neighboring towns and villages. Cartridges were made of powder fur- nished by Governor Letcher, and lead found at the place, or procured in the neighborhood. Caps (in small quantities only) were smuggled from Baltimore. Cais- sons were constructed at Captain Pendleton's sugges- tion, by fixing roughly-made ammunition-chests on the running-parts of farm-wagons. Horses, and harness of various kinds, for the artillery, and wagons and

---

[1] In my report of the military operations, ending in the battle of Manassas, published by the Government, I briefly reminded the War Department of these views, and of the expression of them by me at the time, and that " the continued occupation of the place was deemed by it indispensable." (*See* fourth and fifth paragraphs of that report.)

teams for field-transportation, were collected in the surrounding country; and the work of removing the machinery of the armory, begun by Governor Letcher's orders, was continued. Two heavy guns on naval carriages, that had been placed in battery on the west side of the village by Colonel Jackson's direction, were mounted on Furnace Ridge. My predecessors had constructed two very slight outworks, one on the summit of the mountain on the Maryland side of the Potomac, the other on the Loudon Heights.

Before the end of the first week in June the Seventh and Eighth Georgia and Second Tennessee regiments had arrived.

About the 10th of the month, General Patterson, who had been organizing and instructing his troops at Chambersburg, advanced from that place to Hagerstown. According to the information we could obtain from scouts and intelligent people of the country, they amounted to about eighteen thousand men. The organization of this army, as published in a newspaper of Hagerstown, corresponded very well with this estimate; for twenty-four regiments of infantry were enumerated in it, and several small bodies of regular artillery and cavalry.[1]

The garrison of Harper's Ferry had then been increased to almost seven thousand men of all arms.

At sunrise on the 13th the Hon. James M. Mason brought from Winchester intelligence, received there the night before, that two thousand Federal troops, supposed to be the advanced guard of General McClellan's army, had marched into Romney the day before. That place is forty-three miles west of

[1] This statement is from memory.

Winchester. As this information had come from the most respectable sources, it was believed, and Colonel A. P. Hill immediately dispatched to Winchester with his own (Thirteenth) and Colonel Gibbons's (Tenth Virginia) regiments on trains provided by Mr. Mason's forethought. Colonel Hill was instructed to add Colonel Vaughn's (Third Tennessee) regiment, which had just reached the town, to his detachment, and to move on toward Romney without delay, and to take the best measures in his power to retard the progress of the Federal troops, if they should be approaching "the Valley."

During that day and the next the heavy baggage of the troops (almost every private soldier had a trunk), the property of the quartermaster's and subsistence departments, and the remaining machinery of the armory, were removed to Winchester by railroad, whence the machinery was transported over the turnpike to Strasburg, on the Manassas Gap Railroad, and the bridges over the Potomac were destroyed from the Point of Rocks to Shepardstown.

The troops followed on the morning of the 15th, by the Berryville road, and bivouacked for the night three or four miles beyond Charlestown.

Before the time for resuming the march next morning, intelligence was received from the cavalry outposts that General Patterson's army had crossed the Potomac below Williamsport, and was marching toward Martinsburg. I determined at once to oppose its advance on that road; and directed the march of the Confederate troops across the country to Bunker's Hill, midway between Martinsburg and Winchester, to prevent the junction of Patterson's and McClellan's forces.

While we were waiting for a guide to lead us by the best road to Bunker's Hill, a courier from Richmond brought me a letter[1] from General Cooper,[2] dated June 13th, giving me the President's authority to abandon Harper's Ferry and retire toward Winchester in such a contingency as the present, in the following passages: " . . . You will consider yourself authorized, whenever the position of the enemy shall convince you that he is about to turn your position, to destroy every thing at Harper's Ferry which could serve the purposes of the enemy, and retire upon the railroad toward Winchester. . . . Should you not be sustained by the population of 'the Valley,' so as to enable you to turn upon the enemy before reaching Winchester, you will continue to retire slowly to the Manassas road, in some of the passes of which, it is hoped, you will be able to make an effective stand, even against a very superior force. . . . Should you move so far as to make a junction with General Beauregard, the enemy would be free immediately to occupy the Valley of Virginia, and to pass to the rear of Manassas Junction. . . ."

We moved at nine o'clock, and, passing through Smithfield, reached the turnpike at Bunker's Hill in the afternoon, and bivouacked on the banks of the stream that flows through the hamlet.

Next morning the troops were formed on the high ground on the Martinsburg side, which offered a favorable position for battle, to await the approach of

---

[1] In reply to mine of the 9th.

[2] The Adjutant-General of the Confederate States army.

the Federal army. About noon, however, information that it had recrossed the Potomac was received—
we supposed in consequence of this movement of
ours. It was really because some of General Patterson's best troops had just been taken from him.

In pursuance of my original design, the army
marched toward Winchester, and bivouacked some
three miles from the town, and on the 18th was disposed in camps in its immediate vicinity, on the Martinsburg front, except the cavalry, which was replaced in observation along the Potomac; its colonel
had already won its full confidence, and mine.

In the night of the 18th Colonel Hill, then at
Romney, detached Colonel Vaughn with two companies of his regiment (Third Tennessee), and two of
the Thirteenth Virginia, to destroy the bridge of the
Baltimore and Ohio Railroad over New Creek. Colonel Vaughn learned, when near the bridge, that a
small body of Federal troops—two hundred and fifty
infantry and two field-pieces—was near it, on the
other side of the Potomac. He crossed the river at
sunrise in their presence,[1] put them to flight, and
captured their cannon and colors; the guns were
found loaded, and spiked.

As it had become certain that no considerable
body of United States troops was approaching from
the west, Colonel Hill's detachment was called back
to Winchester.

It being ascertained that some of the public property (rough gun-stocks) had been left at Harper's
Ferry, Lieutenant-Colonel G. H. Stewart was sent
with his Maryland Battalion to bring it away, which

---

[1] Colonel Vaughn's official report to Colonel Hill.

was done in about a day. Nothing worth removing was left.

In a letter dated the 18th, addressed to me at Winchester, giving the President's further instructions, General Cooper wrote: ". . . You are expected to act as circumstances may require, only keeping in mind the general purpose to resist invasion as far as may be practicable, and seek to repel the invaders whenever and however it may be done.

"In order that all dispositions may be made to meet your wants, it is necessary that you write frequently and fully as to your position, and the movements that may be contemplated by you. Since the date of my last letter reënforcements have been steadily sent forward to the camp at Manassas Junction, and others will be added to that place and to yours, as the current of events may determine us to advance on one line or the other. . . .

"Reënforcements will be sent to you of such character and numbers as you may require and our means will enable us to afford. . . . "

In another, written on the 19th, he added: " A large supply of ammunition for your command left here this morning, including eighty thousand percussion caps. An additional supply will be forwarded by to-morrow morning's train. Every effort will be made to support and sustain you, to the extent of our means. . . .

"The movements of the enemy indicate the importance he attaches to the possession of the Valley of Virginia, and that he has probably seen the power he would acquire if left free to do so, by advancing as far as Staunton and distributing his forces so as to cut off our communication with the west and south, as well as to operate against our Army of the Potomac, by movements upon its lines of communications, or attacking upon the reverse, supplying himself at the same time with all the provisions he may acquire in the Valley of the Shenandoah, enabling him to dispense with his long line of transportation from Pennsylvania. Every thing should be destroyed which would facilitate his movements through 'the Valley.'"

In a few days the army was strengthened by the accession of Brigadier-General Bee, Colonel Elzey, and the Ninth Georgia regiment. It was then re-organized. Jackson's brigade was formed of the Second, Fourth, Fifth, and Twenty-seventh Virginia regiments, and Pendleton's battery; Bee's of the Second and Eleventh Mississippi, Fourth Alabama, and Second Tennessee regiments, and Imboden's battery; Elzey's of the Tenth and Thirteenth Virginia, Third Tennessee and Maryland regiments, and Groves's battery; and Bartow's of the Seventh, Eighth, and Ninth Georgia regiments, the Kentucky Battalion, and Alburtis's battery.

As the intelligence obtained from Maryland indicated that General Patterson was preparing to cross the Potomac again, Colonel Jackson was sent with his brigade to the vicinity of Martinsburg to support the cavalry. He was instructed also to protect and aid an agent of the Government, appointed for the work, in removing such of the rolling-stock of the Baltimore and Ohio Railroad as he might select for the use of the Confederacy, or as much of it as practicable. It was to be transported to the railroad at

Strasburg, on the turnpike through Winchester. The orders of the Government required the destruction of all that could not be brought away.

It has been said[1] somewhat hastily, and I think harshly, that those who had the power to seize and remove this property committed a gross blunder by failing to send it to Winchester by railroad from Harper's Ferry before the evacuation of that place. This charge falls upon the Executives of the State and of the Confederacy, and the military commanders, General Jackson and myself. I presume that all were governed by the same considerations—those that directed my course. It would have been criminal as well as impolitic on our part to commit such an act of war against citizens of Maryland, when we were receiving aid from the State then, and hoping for its accession to the Confederacy. The seizure of that property by us could have been justified only by the probability of its military use by the enemy. Such a probability did not appear, of course, until after our evacuation of Harper's Ferry. Besides, at the time in question, the Winchester Railroad and its rolling-stock were required exclusively for the transportation of property far more valuable to the Confederacy than engines and cars—the machinery of the armory. There was another cogent reason, the engines of the Baltimore and Ohio Railroad were too heavy for use on the other, or even to pass over it, especially near the Shenandoah, where it rests on trestles. While at Harper's Ferry I was prevented from attempting to use them in the removal of the machinery by the remonstrances of the engineers of

[1] In Dabney's "Life of Jackson."

both roads, founded on their opinions that the heavier engines of the Baltimore and Ohio Railroad would crush the trestle-work of the Winchester road if brought upon it.

Mr. Davis wrote to me in a letter dated 22d : " I congratulate you on the brilliant movement of Colonel Vaughn's command.   To break the line of the Baltimore and Ohio Railroad was essential to our operations, and if the bridge at Cheat River and the Grand Tunnel could be destroyed so as to prevent the use of that railroad for the duration of the war the effect upon public opinion in Western Virginia would doubtless be of immediate and great advantage to our cause.

" If the enemy has withdrawn from your front to attack on the east side of the mountain, it may be that an attempt will be made to advance from Leesburg to seize the Manassas Gap road and to turn Beauregard's position. . . . In that event, if your scouts give you accurate and timely information, an opportunity will be offered to you by the roads through the mountain-passes to make a flank attack in conjunction with Beauregard's column, and with God's blessing to achieve a victory alike glorious and beneficial. . . . I wish you would write whenever your convenience will permit, and give me fully both information and suggestions."

Twenty-five hundred militia, called out in Frederick and the surrounding counties, were assembling at Winchester under Brigadier-Generals Carson and Meem ; and, especially to increase their value, Major Whiting was directed to have a few light defensive works constructed on the most commanding positions

on the northeast side of the town, and to have some
very ineffective heavy guns, on ship-carriages found
there, mounted in them.

On the 2d, General Patterson's army, which had
been strongly reënforced, again crossed the Potomac and marched toward Martinsburg, driving before it the little body of cavalry that Stuart was able
to gather. Colonel Jackson directed his brigade to
retire, according to the instructions he had received;
and with the rear-guard, composed of three hundred
and eighty men of Colonel Harper's (Fifth Virginia)
regiment and a field-piece,[1] which Stuart joined with his
little detachment, engaged the enemy's leading troops
near Falling Waters. By taking a position in which
the smallness of his force was concealed, he was able
to keep the greatly superior Federal numbers in check
for a considerable time, long enough for his object,
the safety of his baggage, and retired only when his
position was about to be turned. He lost in this
affair[2] two men killed and six or eight wounded, and
brought off forty-five prisoners, besides inflicting
other loss; two brigades were engaged with this
little rear-guard.[3]

On this intelligence, received at sunset, the army
was ordered forward, and met Jackson's brigade retiring, at Darksville, six or seven miles from Martinsburg, soon after daybreak. We bivouacked there
in order of battle, as the Federal army was supposed
to be advancing to attack us. We waited in this position four days, expecting to be attacked, because we

---

[1] Commanded by Captain Pendleton himself.
[2] General Jackson's report.
[3] General Patterson's report.

did not doubt that General Patterson had invaded
Virginia for that purpose. But, unwilling to assail
greatly superior numbers in a town so defensible as
Martinsburg, with its solid buildings and inclosures
of masonry, and convinced, at length, that we were
waiting to no purpose, I ordered the troops to return
to Winchester, much to their disappointment, for they
were eager to fight.

Our effective force, then, was not quite nin ͻ thousand men, of all arms. General Patterson's was
about twenty thousand, I believe, instead of thirty-
two thousand, the estimate of the people of Martinsburg at the time. We overrated each other's strength
greatly, as was generally done by the opposing commanders during the war—probably from the feeling
in Gil Blas, which made his antagonist's sword seem
" d'une longueur excessive."

In a letter, dated July 10th, the President said:
" . . . . Your letter found me trying by every method
to hasten reënforcements to you. . . .

" Colonel Forney's regiment will, I suppose, get
off in the morning, if not this evening, and more shall
follow as fast as the railroad will permit. . . ."

And in another, dated the 13th: " . . . . Another
(regiment) for the war came yesterday. It was fully
equipped, and to-day has gone to your column. . . .
I could get twenty thousand from Mississippi, who
impatiently wait for notice that they can be armed.
In Georgia, numerous tenders are made to serve for
any time, at any place, and to these and other offers
I am still constrained to answer, ' I have not arms to
supply you.' . . ."

The rich country around us furnished abundant

supplies of provision and forage, which the farmers and millers willingly sold on credit to the quartermasters and commissaries of the army. We neither received nor required assistance from the Commissary Department at Richmond, except for the articles of coffee and sugar, which were then parts of the Confederate soldier's ration. The army was so fortunate as to have Major Kersley for its chief commissary, a gentleman of sense and vigor, well acquainted with that district and its resources. Under his administration of the commissariat, "the Valley" could have supplied abundantly an army four times as large as ours.

It was not so easy to procure ammunition: no large quantity had been imported; and the Ordnance Department, then not fully organized, had neither time nor means to prepare half the amount required. The very small supply brought from Harper's Ferry was increased, however, by applications to the chief of the department at Richmond, and by sending officers elsewhere for caps as well as cartridges.

On the 15th, Colonel Stuart reported that the Federal army had advanced from Martinsburg to Bunker's Hill. It remained there on the 16th, and on the 17th moved by its left flank a few miles to Smithfield. This gave the impression that General Patterson's design was to continue this movement through Berryville, to interpose his army between the Confederate forces at Winchester and those at Manassas Junction, while the latter should be assailed by McDowell, or perhaps to attack Winchester from the south, thus avoiding the slight intrenchments.

Since the return of the army from Darksville,

the Thirty-third Virginia regiment, organized by Colonel A. C. Cummings, had been added to Jackson's brigade; the Sixth North Carolina to Bee's; the Eleventh Georgia to Bartow's;[1] and a fifth brigade formed, for Brigadier-General E. Kirby Smith, just promoted, of the Nineteenth Mississippi, Eighth, Ninth, Tenth, and Eleventh Alabama regiments, and Stannard's Battery. Measles, mumps, and other diseases, to which new troops are subject, had been so prevalent, that the average effective strength of the regiments of this army did not much exceed five hundred men.

About one o'clock A. M., on the 18th, I received the following telegram from General Cooper, Adjutant and Inspector-General: " General Béauregard is attacked; to strike the enemy a decisive blow, a junction of all your effective force will be needed. If practicable, make the movement, sending your sick and baggage to Culpepper Court-House either by railroad or by Warrenton. In all the arrangement, exercise your discretion." A half-hour later, a telegram from General Beauregard informed me of his urgent need of the aid I had promised him in such an emergency. This intelligence, dispatched to me by him when he reported to the War Department, had been unaccountably delayed.

Being confident that the troops under my command could render no service in " the Valley," so important to the Confederacy as that of preventing a Federal victory at Manassas Junction, I decided, without hesitation, to hasten to that point with my

---

[1] The Ninth Georgia had joined it soon after the troops reached Winchester.

whole force. The only question was, whether to attempt to defeat or to elude General Patterson. The latter, if practicable, was to be preferred, as quickest and safest. Stuart's first report was expected to give the means of judging of its practicability, while the troops were preparing to move. Although the Federal cavalry had greatly the advantage of the Confederate in arms and discipline, it was not in the habit, like ours, of leaving the protection of the infantry. This enabled Stuart to maintain his outposts near the enemy's camps, and his scouts near their columns, learning their movements quickly, and concealing our own.

Stuart's expected report showed that the Federal army had not *advanced* from Smithfield at nine o'clock. It was certainly too far from our road, therefore, to be able to prevent or delay our march. This information left no doubt of the expediency of moving as soon as possible.

The order to send the sick to Culpepper Court-House was not obeyed, because obedience would have caused a delay of several days, when hours were precious,[1] for it would have involved their transportation in wagons eighteen miles to Strasburg, and

[1] There were about seventeen hundred of them. In my report of the battle of Manassas, as published by the Administration, this sentence does not appear : " The delay of sending our sick, seventeen hundred in number, to Culpepper Court-House, would have made it impossible to arrive at Manassas in time ; they were, therefore, provided for in Winchester." And this one is in its place: " Our sick, seventeen hundred in number, were provided for in Winchester." The original is in possession of the Government in Washington. In an indorsement on it, by Mr. Davis, I am accused of reporting his telegram to me inaccurately. I did not profess to quote his words, but to give their meaning, which was done correctly.

none were available for the purpose but those that
had been procured for the troops, and were absolutely necessary for the march. Therefore they were
provided for in Winchester, comfortably and quickly.
The brigades (militia) of Generals Carson and Meem
were left to defend the place and district, for which
their strength was quite sufficient; for it could
scarcely be doubted that General Patterson would
follow the movement to Manassas Junction with his
main force, at least, as soon as he discovered it. To
delay this discovery as long as possible, Colonel
Stuart was instructed to establish as perfect a cordon
as his regiment could make, and as near the Federal
army as practicable, to prevent access to it from the
side of Winchester and Berryville, and to maintain
it until night; then to follow the army through Ashby's Gap.

CHAPTER II.

Movement of Troops to Manassas.—Discouragements of the March.—Arrival at Manassas.—President Davis's Telegram.—General Beauregard's Proposed Plan of Attack approved.—General McDowell anticipates it.—Battle of Manassas.—Arrival of President Davis.—Reasons why an Advance on Washington was impracticable.

THE troops left their camps about noon, Jackson's brigade leading. After the march was fairly begun, and the rear had left Winchester a mile or two, the different regiments were informed, at the same time, of the important object in view, of the necessity of a forced march, and exhorted to strive to reach the field in time to take part in the great battle then imminent.

The discouragement of that day's march to one accustomed, like myself, to the steady gait of regular soldiers, is indescribable. The views of military command and obedience, then taken both by officers and privates, confined those duties and obligations almost exclusively to the drill-ground and guards. In camps and marches they were scarcely known. Consequently, frequent and unreasonable delays caused so slow a rate of marching as to make me despair of joining General Beauregard in time to aid him. Major Whiting was therefore dispatched to the nearest station of the Manassas Gap Railroad, Piedmont, to ascertain if trains, capable of transporting the troops to their destination more quickly than they were likely to reach it on foot, could be provided there, and, if so, to make the necessary arrangements. That officer met me at Paris, after executing his instructions, with a report so favorable as to give me reason to expect that the transportation of the infantry over the thirty-four miles between Piedmont and Manassas Junction would be accomplished easily in twenty-four hours.

Jackson's brigade, his leading men, that is to say, reached Paris, seventeen miles from Winchester, about two hours after dark. The four others halted for the night on the Shenandoah, having marched thirteen miles; Jackson's brigade marched the six miles from Paris to Piedmont before eight o'clock, Friday morning; and, as trains enough for its transportation were found there, it moved in an hour or two. The other brigades came up separately in the afternoon—Bartow's first. Other trains, capable of transporting two regiments, being in readiness about three o'clock, the Seventh and Eighth Georgia regiments were dispatched in them. No other infantry had the means of moving that day, although the president of the railroad company had promised that the last regiment should reach Manassas Junction Saturday morning—nine thousand men—before sunrise.

The artillery and cavalry were directed to continue their march by the wagon-road, under Colonels Stuart and Pendleton.

At night, Captain Chisholm, an officer of General Beauregard's staff, arrived, bringing a suggestion from him to me, to march by Aldie and fall upon the rear of the Federal right, at Centreville, while his troops, advancing from Bull Run, assailed that army in front. I did not agree to the plan, because, ordinarily, it is impracticable to direct the movements of troops so distant from each other, by roads so far separated, in such a manner as to combine their action on a field of battle. It would have been impossible, in my opinion, to calculate when our undisciplined volunteers would reach any distant point that might be indicated. I preferred the junction of the two armies at the earliest time possible, as the first measure to secure success.

Enough of the cars, sent down in the morning to convey about two regiments, were brought back before midnight, but the conductors and engineers disappeared immediately, to pass the night probably in sleep, instead of on the road. And it was not until seven or eight o'clock Saturday morning that the trains could be put in motion, carrying the Fourth Alabama and Second Mississippi regiments, with two companies of the Eleventh. General Bee and myself accompanied these troops. Brigadier-General E. Kirby Smith was left at Piedmont to expedite the transportation of the remaining brigades—about three-fifths of the army.

We reached General Beauregard's position about noon. The Seventh and Eighth Georgia regiments were united to the detachment just arrived, to form a temporary brigade for General Bee.

As the army had not been informed, in the usual way, of the promotion of Generals Cooper, Lee, and myself, to the grade of general, I had, after leaving Winchester, requested the President, by telegraph, to

GENERAL P. G. T. BEAUREGARD

state what my rank in the army was, to prevent the possibility of a doubt of the relative rank of General Beauregard and myself in the mind of the former. His reply was received on the 20th. His excellency said, in his telegram: "You are a general in the Confederate army, possessed of all the powers attaching to that rank."

The position occupied by the Confederate army was too extensive, and the ground, much of it, too broken, thickly wooded, and intricate, to be studied to any purpose in the brief space of time at my disposal; for I had come impressed with the opinion that it was necessary to attack the enemy next morning, to decide the event before the arrival of General Patterson's forces. Meanwhile, it might reasonably be expected all of ours would be united. Delay was dangerous, because it was not to be hoped that our movement from Winchester could be concealed from General Patterson more than twenty-four hours; or that, after learning it, he would fail to follow the movement, and march promptly to join McDowell. Battle being inevitable, it was certainly our part to bring it on before the arrival of so great an addition to the number of our enemies. My intention, and these reasons for it, were expressed to General Beauregard at once. He had formed the same opinion, as I had expected.

He then showed me, on a map prepared by his engineer officers, the position of his own troops, and that of the Federal army near Centreville. Unfortunately, this map only represented the roads and streams, without expressing the configuration of the ground.

He had chosen the southern bank of Bull Run for his defensive line; and, on information communicated by spies, to the effect that Lieutenant-General Scott had ordered the Federal army to advance from Centreville by roads eastward of that leading directly to Manassas Junction, which crosses Bull Run at Mitchell's Ford, he had posted his main force below (to the east of) that ford: Ewell's brigade on the right, at Union Mills, D. R. Jones's at McLean's Ford, Longstreet's at Blackburn's, and Bonham's at Mitchell's. Holmes's and Early's were in the second line, the former on the right. The remaining brigade, Colonel Cocke's, was at Ball's Ford, four miles above Mitchell's. Fourteen companies and a battery belonging to that brigade, under Colonel Evans, guarded " the Stone Bridge " (by which the Warrenton turnpike crosses Bull Run) a half-mile above, and a farm-ford a thousand yards still farther up the stream. Jackson's and Bee's brigades, as they arrived, had been placed near Bonham's and Longstreet's by General Beauregard's orders.

Some slight field-works constructed for the defense of the depot at Manassas Junction were armed with fourteen or fifteen old twenty-four-pounders on naval carriages, and occupied by two thousand men. The heavy artillery was under the command of naval officers.

General Beauregard pointed out, on his map, five roads converging to Centreville from different points of his front, and proposed an order of march on these roads, by which the army should be concentrated near the Federal camps. It was accepted without hesitation; and, having had no opportunity to sleep in either of the three nights immediately preceding, I requested him to draw up this order of march and have the number of copies necessary written by our staff-officers and brought to me in time for distribution that evening, while I was preparing, by rest, for the impending battle.

These papers were not ready for distribution that evening, nor until the next morning (21st), when I was able to sign them by the light of day in the grove where I had slept. They were not in the form usual in the United States Army, being written by General Beauregard's adjutant-general in his name,[1] my sanction to be written on each copy. This was too immaterial to be worth correction; but, even if it had not been so, it was now too late to make such a correction, for the troops should then have been in motion.

Soon after sunrise, and before the distribution of these orders could have been completed, a light cannonade was opened upon our troops at the Stone Bridge, and a little later a similar demonstration was made in General Bonham's front. At half-past five o'clock a report was received from Colonel Evans that a body of Federal infantry, with a long line of skirmishers deployed before it, was visible on the opposite side of the valley of Bull Run. I had previously requested General Beauregard to send orders for me to Bee and Jackson to move their brigades to the left and place them near the Stone Bridge. He also ordered Colonel Hampton with the infantry of his legion, just arrived at Manassas, to hasten to the same locality.

[1] *See* copy of this order, Appendix.

The plan of operations adopted the day before was now, apparently, made impracticable by the enemy's advance against our left. It was abandoned, therefore, and another adopted—suggested by General Beauregard. This was, a change of front to the left, and a vigorous attack on the left flank of the troops assailing our left, by the six brigades of our centre and right, while Cocke's, Jackson's, and Bee's brigades, and Hampton's legion, were meeting their assault. The orders for this, like those preceding them, were distributed by General Beauregard's staff-officers, because they were addressed to his troops, and my staff knew neither the positions of the different brigades, nor the paths leading to them. Want of promptness in the delivery of these orders frustrated this plan—perhaps fortunately.

Scouts, sent forward in the mean time by Generals Longstreet and D. R. Jones, reported strong bodies of Federal troops on the wooded heights in front of their brigades. From their reports it seemed to be as probable that McDowell was forming his main force in front of *our* main body, as that he was directing it against our left. At nine o'clock, Captain Alexander, of the Engineer Corps, who was also chief signal-officer, reported that large bodies of Federal troops could be seen from one of his signal-stations, crossing the valley of Bull Run, about two miles above our extreme left. When these troops were first observed, the head of the column had passed the open ground, in which they were visible. Their number, consequently, could not be estimated. He called our attention, soon after, to a heavy cloud of dust, such as the marching of an army might raise,

MAJOR-GENERAL IRVIN McDOWELL

about ten miles from us, to the north-northwest—
the direction of the road from Harper's Ferry. This
excited apprehensions of the near approach of General
Patterson's army.

General McDowell had marched from the Potomac
with instructions from the general-in-chief to
turn the right of the Confederate army and seize its
line of communication with Richmond. Before involving
himself in such an enterprise, the Federal
general bestowed three days upon the examination
of the ground before him. In this way he learned
that the region into which he would have been led,
by obedience to his instructions, was altogether unfavorable
to the more numerous assailing army, and
advantageous to the smaller force standing on the
defensive; for it is rugged, and covered with thick
woods, and the Occoquan, a stream to be crossed, is
large enough to be a serious obstacle; while to the
west the country is open, the hills gentle, and Bull
Run almost everywhere fordable. He therefore decided,
judiciously, to attempt to turn the Confederate
line by moving through the open and favorable
ground on his right, instead of involving his army
in the thick woods and rugged hills on his left. The
best argument for this change of plan, however, was
the object explained by General McDowell—" to
break up the communication between the two Confederate
armies," an object which might have been
accomplished by prompt action.

For some unexplained purpose, one Federal division,
Runyon's, had been left between the Potomac
and Centreville, near Vienna. Leaving another,
Miles's, at Centreville, to divert attention from the

movements of his main body by demonstrations in front of the Confederate right and centre, General McDowell had marched at daybreak with Tyler's, Hunter's, and Heintzelman's divisions, to cross Bull Run at Sudley Ford, two miles and a half above the Warrenton Turnpike, seize that road, and, as he expresses it, "send out a force to destroy the railroad at or near Gainesville, and thus break up the communication between the enemy's forces at Manassas and those in the Valley of Virginia." [1]

The Federal army followed the Warrenton Turnpike three miles, and then turned to the right into a country-road by which it reached Sudley Ford and Church. There it entered, at right angles, a road crossing the turnpike a mile and a half from the Stone Bridge, and leading, though not very directly, to Manassas Junction. Before the column turned out of the turnpike, the leading brigade and a battery were sent forward and formed near the Stone Bridge, to conceal the movement around the Confederate left.

This movement was reported to Colonel Evans, by his detachment stationed above the bridge. On receiving the intelligence, he moved rapidly to the left and rear with eleven companies and two field-pieces, to endeavor to check or delay the progress of the enemy, having left three companies and two field-pieces to prevent the passage of the bridge by the body of troops he had been observing in front of it. Following the base of the hill on the north of Young's Branch, he threw himself in the enemy's way a little in advance of the intersection of the

[1] General McDowell's report.

turnpike and Sudley road, and formed his small
force under cover of a detached wood. Here he was
soon assailed by greatly superior and continually-
increasing numbers, against which he and his little
band held their ground bravely. The change of direction at Sudley Ford was so strong that the portion
of the column beyond the stream, when the firing
commenced, was almost parallel with the line of
battle. This greatly expedited the deployment of
the Federal army. Burnside's brigade, leading the
march, attacked first, and was soon joined by a part
of Porter's and one of Heintzelman's regiments.

The noise and smoke of the fight were distinctly
heard and seen by General Beauregard and myself
near Mitchell's Ford, five miles off; but, in its earlier
stages, they indicated no force of the enemy that the
troops on the ground and those of Bee, Hampton, and
Jackson, that we could see hastening toward the
firing in the order given, were not competent to cope
with.

Bee, who was much in advance of the others, saw
the strength and dispositions of the combatants, and
the character of the ground around and before him,
from the summit of the hill south of Young's Branch;
and, seeing the advantage given to this position by
its greater elevation than that of the opposite ridge,
on which the enemy stood, by its broad, level top,
and by the extent of open ground before it, he formed
his brigade, including Bartow's two regiments and
Imboden's battery, there; but, being appealed to for
aid by Evans, then fully engaged, and seeing that his
troops, that had suffered much in the unequal contest, were about to be overwhelmed, he moved for-

ward to disengage him, and, crossing the valley under the fire of the Federal artillery, formed on the right, and in advance of his line.

Although, even after this accession, the Confederate force was less than that of a Federal brigade, Bee maintained the fight for some time with such appearance of equality as to inspire in him the hope, apparently, of holding his ground until effective aid could reach him. At length, however, finding himself engaged with fivefold numbers in Burnside's, Porter's, Sherman's, and Keyes's brigades, and in danger of being enveloped by the coming into action of Heintzelman's division, he fell back to the position he had first chosen; crossing the broad, open valley, closely pressed by the Federal army.

Fortunately Hampton, hastening up with his legion, had reached the valley when the retrograde movement began. He promptly formed his battalion and joined in the action, and, by his courage and admirable soldiership, seconded by the excellent conduct of the gentlemen he had assembled in his legion, contributed greatly to the maintenance of order in the retreat. His lieutenant-colonel, Johnson, fell while gallantly aiding him. Imboden rendered excellent service with his battery in this difficult operation.

On the ground where he intended to reform, Bee met Jackson at the head of his brigade, and they began, the one to reform, and the other to deploy, simultaneously; Jackson on the left.

In the mean time, I had waited with General Beauregard, on an eminence near the centre, where my headquarters had been fixed at eight o'clock, the

full development of General McDowell's designs.
The violence of the firing on the left indicated a battle, but the heavy forces, reported by chosen scouts
to be in front of our centre and right, kept me in uncertainty. At length, near eleven o'clock, reports that
those forces were felling trees gave me the impression that they were preparing for defense, not attack;
and new clouds of dust showed that a large body of
Federal troops was arriving on the field, and about
to take part in the action. These indications convinced me that the great effort was in progress against
our left. This conviction was expressed to General
Beauregard as well as the consequent necessity of
strengthening that wing as much and as soon as possible, and my intention to hurry to it. Orders were
accordingly dispatched at once to General Holmes
and Colonel Early to march with their brigades as
rapidly as possible to the scene of conflict marked
by the firing; and to General Bonham, to send up
two of his regiments and a battery; he, Longstreet,
and D. R. Jones, were also directed to feel the enemy
in their front.

It was now evident that a battle was to be fought
entirely different, in place and circumstances, from
either of the two plans previously adopted. Events
just related had prevented us from attacking the
Federal army near Centreville; or, later, engaging it
between that place and Bull Run, according to the
second plan, suggested by General Beauregard. Instead of taking the initiative and operating in front of
our line, we were now compelled to fight on the defensive, a mile and a half behind that line, and at right
angles to it, on a new and unsurveyed field, with no

other plans than those suggested by the changing events of battle.

As soon as the necessary orders had been dispatched, I set out at a rapid gallop, accompanied by General Beauregard, to give such aid as we could to our troops engaged four miles off. Passing Colonel Pendleton, chief of artillery, with his former battery and Alburtis's, I desired him to follow with them as fast as possible.

We came upon the field not a moment too soon. The long contest against great odds, and the heavy losses, especially of field-officers, had discouraged Bee's troops, and destroyed or dispersed those of Evans— for we found him apparently without a command. The Fourth Alabama Regiment, of Bee's brigade, had lost all its field-officers, and was without a commander. Colonel S. R. Gist,[1] a volunteer on General Bee's staff, was requested to take command of it.

Our presence with the troops under fire, and the assurance it gave of more material aid, had the happiest effect on their spirits. Order was easily and quickly restored, and the battle well reëstablished. It was during the efforts for this that Jackson and his brigade are said to have acquired the name they have since borne—by Bee's calling to his men to observe how Jackson and his brigade[2] stood "like a stone-wall," a name made still more glorious in every battle in which general and brigade afterward fought.

After assigning General Beauregard to the com-

---

[1] Distinguished in the Army of Tennessee, as brigadier-general, and fell at Franklin.

[2] Those in sight of Bee's troops were lying down by Jackson's order, to avoid the enemy's artillery.

mand of the troops immediately engaged, which he properly suggested belonged to the second in rank, not to the commander of the army, I returned to the supervision of the whole field. The aspect of affairs was not encouraging, yet I had strong hope that Beauregard's capacity and courage, the high soldierly qualities of Bee and Jackson, and the patriotic enthusiasm of our Southern volunteers, would maintain the fight until adequate reënforcements could be brought to their aid.

Urgent messages were sent to Bonham, Holmes, and Early, to hasten the march of their troops; and Ewell was directed to follow them with his brigade as quickly as possible. Colonel Hunton with his regiment, and Colonel (Governor) Smith with his battalion, both detached from Cocke's brigade, were sent to Bee's support. Many of the broken troops, individual stragglers as well as fragments of companies, were reorganized and led back into the fight with the help of my own staff and a part of General Beauregard's. The largest of these bodies, about equal to four companies, and so organized, having no field-officer with it, was placed under the command of Colonel F. J. Thomas, chief ordnance-officer, who fell while gallantly leading it against the enemy. These troops were all sent to the right to strengthen and encourage the regiments that had been weakened in the previous contest.

Cocke's brigade was held in rear of the right of our line, to observe a strong body of Federal troops, on the north side of Bull Run, in a position from which it could have struck Bee in flank in a few minutes.

After these additions to the forces engaged, we had nine regiments and two companies of infantry, two hundred and fifty cavalry, and five field-batteries (twenty guns) of the Army of the Shenandoah, and twenty-seven companies of infantry, six companies of cavalry, and six pieces of artillery of the Army of the Potomac, contending with three divisions of the United States army and superior forces of cavalry and artillery; yet the brave Southern volunteers lost not a foot of ground, but repelled the repeated attacks of the heavy masses of the enemy, whose numbers enabled them to bring forward fresh troops after each repulse. Colonel Stuart contributed materially to one of these repulses, by a well-timed and vigorous charge upon the Federal right flank with two of his companies, those of Captains Welby Carter and J. B. Hoge.

It must not be supposed that such successful resistance by the Southern troops was due in any degree to want of prowess in their assailants. The army they fought belonged to a people who had often contended on the field on *at least* equal terms with the nation that had long claimed to be the most martial in Europe. The Northern army had the disadvantage, a great one to such undisciplined troops as were engaged on both sides, of being the assailants, and advancing under fire to the attack, which can be well done only by trained soldiers. They were much more liable to confusion, therefore, than the generally stationary ranks of the Confederates.

About two o'clock an officer of General Beauregard's adjutant-general's office galloped from Manassas Junction to report to me that a Federal army had reached the Manassas Gap Railroad, was marching toward us, and was then but three or four miles from our left flank. Although it seemed to me impossible that General Patterson could have come up so soon, and from that direction, I fixed on a new field upon which to concentrate our whole force should the report prove to be true—one nearly equidistant from Manassas Junction, the troops engaged, and those on the right—and sent orders to the commanders of the latter to gather their respective brigades south of the stream, that they might be ready to move to it promptly.

On the appearance of Fisher's (Sixth North Carolina) regiment soon after (at half-past two o'clock), approaching from the direction of Manassas Junction, Colonel Cocke was desired to lead his brigade into action on the right; which he did with alacrity. When Fisher's regiment came up, the Federal general seemed to be strengthening his right. It was ordered to the left, therefore. Kershaw's and Cash's regiments of Bonham's brigade, then in sight, received similar orders on arriving.

Soon after three o'clock, while General McDowell seemed to be striving, by strengthening his right, to drive back our left, and thus separate us from Manassas Junction, Brigadier-General Kirby Smith, hastening with Elzey's brigade from that railroad-station, arrived by the route Fisher had followed. He was instructed, by a staff-officer sent forward to meet him, to form on the left of the line, with his left thrown forward, and to assail the enemy's right flank. At his request I joined him, directed his march, and gave these instructions in person. Before the formation was completed, he fell, severely wounded, directing, while falling from his horse, Colonel Elzey to take command of the brigade. That officer, who understood and appreciated the manœuvre, executed it well. General Beauregard promptly seized the opportunity thus afforded, and threw forward his whole line. The enemy was driven from the long-contested hill, but rallied in the valley, upon a very strong reserve; and the united force, much stronger than any previously engaged at one time, was formed for another attack.

In the mean time Colonel Early came upon the field with his brigade, by the route on which we had first seen Fisher's and Kirby Smith's troops. He was instructed by me to move around our left, to form facing the Federal right flank, and fall upon it. On the way he was reënforced by five companies of cavalry, commanded by Colonel Stuart, and a battery under Lieutenant Beckham. He reached the position intended just when the Federal army, reformed, was apparently about to resume the offensive, and assailed its exposed flank. The attack was conducted with too much skill and courage to be for a moment doubtful. The Federal right was at once thrown into confusion. A general advance of the Confederate line, directed by General Beauregard, completed our success, and terminated the battle. The right of the Federal army fled in wild confusion from the field toward Sudley Ford, while the centre and left marched off hastily by the turnpike toward Centreville.

It was then twenty minutes before five o'clock. Instructions were immediately sent to General Bonham, through Lieutenant-Colonel Lay of his staff, who happened to be with me, to march with his own and Longstreet's brigades by the quickest route to the turnpike, and form them across it to intercept the retreating enemy. Colonel Radford, with two squadrons that had been held in reserve near me, was directed to cross Bull Run at Ball's Ford, and strike that column in flank, on the turnpike; and Stuart, with the cavalry he had in hand and Beckham's battery, pursued the fugitives on the Sudley road. The number of prisoners taken by·these little bodies of cavalry greatly exceeded their own force, but they were too weak to make any serious impression upon an *army*, even a defeated one.

The body of troops that had passed the day near the Stone Bridge and beyond the stream made a demonstration toward the rear of our right, when the retreat commenced; it was quickly met and repelled by Holmes's brigade just arriving, principally by his artillery, Captain Lindsay Walker's battery

When General Bonham saw the Federal column on the turnpike, its appearance presented so little indication of rout that he thought the execution of the instructions he had received impracticable;[1] he therefore ordered the two brigades to march back to their camps.

Some half-hour after the termination of the battle, the President rode upon the field, conducted from Manassas Station by Lieutenant-Colonel Jordan. He had arrived there from Richmond when the struggle had just closed, and had, doubtless, hurried out to take part in it. The crowd of fugitives he had seen

---

[1] Reports (verbal) of staff-officers; no others were received.

from his railroad-car, before reaching the station, had so strongly impressed upon his mind the idea that we were defeated, that it was not immediately removed by the appearance of the field. I judged so, at least, from his first words, while we were shaking hands: "How has the battle gone?"

In Alfriend's "Life of Jefferson Davis" it is asserted (p. 305) that the President reached " the battle-field while the struggle was still in progress;" that " to the troops his name and bearing were the symbols of victory;" that "while the victory was assured, but by no means complete, he urged that the enemy, still on the field (Heintzelman's troops, as subsequently appeared), be warmly pursued, as was successfully done" (p. 313).

These are fancies. He arrived upon the field after the last armed enemy had left it, when none were within cannon-shot, or south of Bull Run, when the victory was "complete" as well as "assured," and no opportunity left for the influence of "his name and bearing."

General Ewell reported to me for orders soon after the firing ceased, and informed me that his brigade, then probably about four miles from us, was hurrying on as fast as possible. He had ridden forward to study the part of the field to which he might be assigned, to prepare to act intelligently in the battle. He was told that it would not be wanted, and desired to lead it back to its camp; General Holmes was requested to do likewise; their immediate commander, General Beauregard, was requested to give them orders, however.

The preceding narrative shows how great were

the odds against which the Southern volunteers contended in the early stages of this action; their numbers engaged, gradually increasing, amounted at its
close to about thirteen thousand men of all arms.
But two of the superior officers of General McDowell's army gave in their reports the numbers of their
troops, General Heintzelman and Colonel Porter: the
former led nine thousand five hundred men into battle that day, in his division, and the latter three
thousand seven hundred in his brigade. From these
indications it may reasonably be inferred that the
three Federal divisions on the field were about
two to one compared with the Confederates, at four
o'clock, and four to one at noon; at eleven o'clock
the disparity of numbers was much greater.

Considering the length of time in which the troops
were engaged at short range, the losses were small in
relation to their numbers. That of the Confederates
was: in the Army of the Shenandoah two hundred
and seventy killed, nine hundred and seventy-nine
wounded, eighteen missing; in that of the Potomac,
one hundred and eight killed, five hundred and ten
wounded, twelve missing: total, three hundred and
seventy-eight killed, fourteen hundred and eighty-
nine wounded, thirty missing.

That of the Federal army could not be ascertained by us accurately. Including prisoners, it must
have been about four thousand.

Twenty-eight pieces of artillery, four thousand
five hundred muskets, almost half a million cartridges, a garrison-flag, and ten regimental colors,
were taken on the field, or near it in the pursuit, besides sixty-four artillery-horses with their harness,

twenty-six wagons, and camp-equipage, clothing, and other military property.

The Southern infantry had great advantage over the Northern in their greater familiarity with fire-arms. It was the reverse, however, in relation to the artillery; for that of the South had had neither time nor ammunition for practice, while much of that of the North belonged to the regular service. Still, ours, directed principally by Colonel Pendleton, was more effective even than the regular batteries of the United States army, in that battle.

The pursuit was pressed as long as it was effective. But when the main column of retreating infantry was encountered, after the parties in its rear and on the flanks had been dispersed or captured, our cavalry found itself too weak to make any serious impression, and returned with the prisoners already taken. The infantry was not required to pursue far from the field, because by doing so it would have been harassed to no purpose. It is well known that infantry, unencumbered by baggage-trains, can easily escape pursuing infantry.

The victory was as complete as one gained by infantry and artillery only can be.

The Army of the Potomac, exclusive of the garrison of the intrenched position at Manassas Junction, amounted then to about nineteen thousand men of all arms. A large proportion of it was not engaged in the battle. This was a great fault on my part. When Bee's and Jackson's brigades were ordered to the vicinity of the Stone Bridge, those of Holmes and Early should have been moved to the left also, and placed in the interval on Bonham's left

—if not then, certainly at nine o'clock, when a Federal column was seen turning our left; and, when it seemed certain that General McDowell's great effort was to be made there, Bonham's, Longstreet's, Jones's, and Ewell's brigades, leaving a few regiments and their cavalry to impose on Miles's division, should have been hurried to the left to join in the battle.

If the tactics of the Federals had been equal to their strategy, we should have been beaten. If, instead of being brought into action in detail, their troops had been formed in two lines with a proper reserve, and had assailed Bee and Jackson in that order, the two Southern brigades must have been swept from the field in a few minutes, or enveloped. General McDowell would have made such a formation, probably, had he not greatly under-estimated the strength of his enemy.

It was not until the 22d that any of the troops left at Piedmont by General Kirby Smith rejoined the army. All came on that day, however.

In the biography referred to, on page 12, it is asserted that "General Jackson's infantry was placed upon trains there (at Piedmont) on the forenoon of Friday (the 19th July); . . . . but, by a collision, which was with great appearance of reason attributed to treachery, the track was obstructed, and all the remaining troops detained, without any provision for their subsistence, for two successive days. Had they been provided with food, and ordered to continue their forced march, their zeal would have brought the whole to the field long before the commencement of the battle."

Three brigades of the Army of the Shenandoah

were engaged in the battle, not General Jackson's alone, as is stated in the above extract.[1] The only collision in the transportation of these troops from the Piedmont to the Manassas Station, occurred Saturday night or Sunday morning, of a train bearing Colonel Fisher's (Sixth North Carolina) regiment, with an empty one returning. It "obstructed" the track so little, that the regiment was carried on, reached its destination Sunday morning, and took part in the battle. Elzey's brigade, following on another train, passed over the place of collision soon after the occurrence, and arrived upon the field but an hour later than Fisher's regiment. The detention, that kept "all the remaining troops" out of the battle, was due to miserable mismanagement of the railroad trains, such as could neither have been foreseen nor apprehended by those who directed this movement.

The troops[2] had been nine or ten hours in marching from Winchester to the Shenandoah—thirteen miles. It was therefore certain that they would not accomplish the forty-four still before them in less than three days, or before Sunday evening. We met, at Paris, intelligence of the affair of the 18th, showing that the Federal army was in the immediate presence of that of General Beauregard, so that a battle on Friday was probable—its occurrence later than Saturday very unlikely. It was evident, therefore, from such experience as we had, that there was no hope of reaching the field in time, but by the railroad.

[1] *See* previous Narrative, and Johnston's and Beauregard's reports.
[2] Except Jackson's.

The troops were provided with rations for five days, before leaving Winchester.¹ If any of them were without food at Piedmont, it must have been because they had thrown away their rations, then not unusual on a march.

The President remained at Manassas Junction until nine or ten o'clock A. M., on the 23d, employed chiefly in matters of military organization. When I recommended to him General Beauregard's promotion to the grade of general in the Confederate army, he informed me that the nomination had already been written, or determined on. He also promoted Colonel Elzey, Lieutenant-Colonel S. Jones, and Major W. H. C. Whiting, to brigadier-generalcies. He offered me the command in Western Virginia, subsequently conferred on General Lee, promising to increase the forces there adequately from the army around us. In replying, I expressed the opinion that the Government of the United States would organize a great army near Washington, which would be ready for offensive operations before the end of the fall, when we might expect another invasion, on a much larger scale than that just defeated. Being in position to command against it, I was unwilling to be removed to a much less important though more immediate service.

If the tone of the press indicated public opinion and feeling in the South, my failure to capture Washington received strong and general condemnation. Many erroneously attributed it to the President's prohibition; but he gave no orders, and expressed

¹ The rich neighborhood of Piedmont Station could have furnished food, if it had been needed.

neither wish nor opinion on the subject, that ever came to my knowledge. Considering the relative strength of the belligerents on the field, the Southern people could not reasonably have expected greater results from their victory than those accomplished: the defeat of the invasion of Virginia, and the preservation of the capital of the Confederacy.

All the military conditions, we knew, forbade an attempt on Washington. The Confederate army was more disorganized by victory than that of the United States by defeat. The Southern volunteers believed that the objects of the war had been accomplished by their victory, and that they had achieved all that their country required of them. Many, therefore, in ignorance of their military obligations, left the army —not to return. Some hastened home to exhibit the trophies picked up on the field; others left their regiments without ceremony to attend to wounded friends, frequently accompanying them to hospitals in distant towns. Such were the reports of general and staff officers, and railroad officials. Exaggerated ideas of the victory, prevailing among our troops, cost us more men than the Federal army lost by defeat.

Besides this condition of our army, the reasons for the course condemned by the non-combatant military critics were:

The unfitness of our raw troops for marching, or assailing intrenchments.

The want of the necessary supplies of food and ammunition, and means of transporting them. Until near the 10th of August, we never had rations for more than two days, and sometimes none; nor half enough ammunition for a battle.

The fortifications upon which skillful engineers, commanding the resources of the United States, had been engaged since April, manned by at least fifty thousand Federal troops,[1] half of whom had not suffered defeat.

The Potomac, a mile wide, bearing United States vessels-of-war, the heavy guns of which commanded the wooden bridges and southern shore.

The Confederate army would have been two days in marching from Bull Run to the Federal intrenchments, with less than two days' rations, or not more.[2] It is asserted that the country, teeming with grain and cattle, could have furnished food and forage in abundance. Those who make the assertion forget that a large Federal army had passed *twice* over the route in question. Many of the Southern people have seen tracts of country along which a Federal army has passed once; they can judge, therefore, of the abundance left where it has passed twice. As we had none of the means of besieging, an immediate assault upon the forts would have been unavoidable; it would have been repelled, inevitably, and our half supply of ammunition exhausted; and the enemy, previously increased to seventy thousand men by the army from Harper's Ferry, and become the victorious party, could and would have resumed their march to Richmond without fear of further opposition.

And, if we had miraculously been successful in our assault, the Potomac would have protected

---

[1] Mansfield's, Miles's, and Runyon's divisions, and eleven thousand men sent from camps in Pennsylvania, July 22d.

[2] Dabney's "Life of Jackson."

Washington, and rendered our further progress impossible.

It is certain that the Federal Government and generals did not regard the capture of Washington by us as practicable, like the non-combatant authors of the criticisms to which I refer. The fact that the army at Harper's Ferry was left idle there instead of being brought to Washington, is conclusive on that point. I have never doubted the correctness of my course on that occasion. Had I done so, the results of the invasions made subsequently by disciplined and much more numerous armies, properly equipped and provided, and commanded by the best soldiers who appeared in that war, would have reassured me. The first of these expeditions was after General Lee's victory over Pope, and those of Majors-General Jackson and Ewell over Fremont, Banks, and Shields, in 1862; the second, when the way was supposed to have been opened by the effect of General Lee's victory at Chancellorsville, in 1863.

The armies defeated on those occasions were four times as numerous as that repulsed on the 21st of July, 1861, and their losses much greater in proportion to numbers; yet the spirit of the Northern people was so roused by these invasions of their country, that their armies, previously defeated on our soil, met ours on their own at Sharpsburg and Gettysburg so strong in numbers and in courage as to send back the war into Virginia from each of those battle-fields. The failure of those invasions, directed by Lee, aided by Longstreet and Jackson, with troops inured to marches and manœuvres as well as to battle, and attempted under the most favorable circumstances of the war, proves that the Confederacy was too weak for offensive warfare, and is very strong evidence in favor of the course against which Southern writers have declaimed vehemently.

The authors of Alfriend's "Life of Jefferson Davis" seem to regard this tone of the Southern press as evidence of Southern opinion on this question, and claim that "Mr. Davis was far from approving the inaction which followed Manassas. He confidently expected a different use of the victory.... Indeed, before leaving Manassas, President Davis favored the most vigorous pursuit practicable.... The evidences of disorganization upon which General Johnston dwells with such force and emphasis were indeed palpable, but Mr. Davis confidently believed that an efficient pursuit might be made by such commands as were in comparatively good condition. Such were his impressions then; and that he contemplated immediate activity, as the sequel of Manassas, is a matter of indisputable record" (pp. 812–314).

These assertions are accompanied by no proofs, by no orders, nor even suggestions to the commander of the army by the President while he was at Manassas Junction, nor correspondence on the subject after his return to Richmond. The author cannot assume for him, as he does for Jackson, that "his sense of official propriety sealed his lips." He came to the army as President—to give instructions—and, if necessary, orders in such a crisis.

If he had been "far from approving the inaction that followed Manassas," he would have required action.

If he had "expected a different use of victory," he would have compelled me to attempt to fulfil that expectation. He came to control both general and army.

If he thought that "an advance" would secure "immediate and consecutive triumphs," and the certainty of "even more glorious and valuable achievements," he violated his duty and his oath, by neglecting to compel an aggressive movement by the army, to accomplish such results.

He was with the army about forty hours—quite long enough to see what had been accomplished, and to learn if more could be done, but expressed none of the "views" and opinions ascribed to him in the biography, and gave me no orders for movements of troops, and discussed no matters concerning the army, except such as related to administration. The fact that he gave no instructions in relation to the employment of the army, nor orders to make any aggressive movement nor even suggested such, proves conclusively that he thought none expedient, and was satisfied with the victory as it was. His dispatch of Sunday night, and the speech at the depot of the Central Railroad in Richmond, express that satisfaction, and it only.

The President approved the course pursued after the victory at Manassas, because he knew the discouragements of a march without sufficient food, the utterly inadequate supply of ammunition, the hopelessness of assailing a far more numerous enemy in strong intrenchments, and that the Potomac was impassable. At that time, too, defensive war was regarded by the Southern leaders as our best policy,

as, it was apprehended, invasion by us would unite
all the people of the North, Democrats and Republicans, in the defense of their country. It is certain
that either country could have raised armies stronger,
both in numbers and in spirit, for defensive than for
offensive war.

The President could have expected no "different
use of victory," because he [1] knew that I thought that
the next important service of that army would be
near the end of October, against the invasion of a
much greater Federal army than McDowell's; and
he proposed, the day after the battle, to send me,
with a part of the army at Manassas, to Western
Virginia.

Our own dead were buried without unnecessary
delay; but the expectation on our part that General
McDowell would send a party of his own soldiers to
perform that duty to their late comrades, left the
Federal dead unburied several days, until we found
it necessary to inter them.

After the troops had been somewhat reorganized,
new positions were assigned to them. Among the
charges against me, is that of exposing the army at
the same time to the stench of the battle-field, [1] and
the miasma of the August heat, and thus producing
" camp-fevers tenfold more fatal than the bullets of
the enemy."

Those who have seen large bodies of new troops
know that they are sickly in all climates. Our Southern volunteers were peculiarly so, being attacked in
the early part of their camp-life by measles and

---

[1] *See* page 36.

[2] Dabney's " Life of Jackson," p. 234.

mumps—epidemics to which adults of thickly-inhabited regions, like the Northern States, are not liable. The former was often followed by pneumonia or typhoid fever. The ignorant attributed the prevalence of inevitable disease to extraordinary causes. The troops of the Army of the Shenandoah suffered as much in the healthy climate of the Valley as they and others did at Centreville and Fairfax Court-House.

I have said that the dead were all buried as soon as it appeared that General McDowell intended to leave his share of that duty to us. Before their burial, the nearest troops, a mile or mile and a half from the field, were not incommoded by its neighborhood; they were Whiting's (late Bee's) and Evans's brigades. I say this from personal observation, having been in their camps daily. After the interments were all made, parties of ladies visited the ground without inconvenience. The camp of Whiting's brigade was removed to the neighborhood of Bristow, on account of complaints of bad water—not of stench or tainted air; and Evans's was sent to Leesburg as an outpost. Longstreet's, D. R. Jones's, Cocke's, and Forney's brigades, were placed near and beyond Centreville; those of Ewell, S. Jones, and Early, were encamped from seven to nine miles from the places of burial. Jackson's camp,[1] the nearest to them, was about four miles off. The headquarters of the army were at the same distance. On the 29th of July the surgeons of Jackson's brigade reported that the number of its sick was increasing. Upon that information General Jackson was requested to choose

_____

[1] After the removal of Whiting's and Evans's.

the most convenient and healthy position for his
camp that could be found. He selected one a mile
from Centreville, on the road to Fairfax Court-House,
on which he established his camp on the 1st or 2d of
August. The cavalry was in advance of Fairfax
Court-House, supported by Elzey's brigade. The
positions described above, except Jackson's, were
occupied by the troops on the 23d or 24th of July.

Although we were near the rich Piedmont region,
and on a railroad leading from the Valley of the
Shenandoah, complaints of scarcity, even absolute
want of food, were not unfrequent. Until the 10th
of August we never had a supply for more than two
days, somtimes none. The chief commissary of the
army, Lieutenant-Colonel R. B. Lee, an officer of capacity and experience, and a tried soldier, was not permitted by the chief of his department to purchase the more
important articles of food for the troops—products
of the country—but was required to apply for them
to a commissary in Richmond; so the flour sent to us
in one week had, in most cases, passed by our depot
on its way to Richmond the previous one. The effects
of this system were delay and irregularity in receiving this important article, and an addition of at least
twenty-five per cent. to its price. Efforts were made
by General Beauregard and myself, by correspondence
with the Government, to bring about a change of
system for the sake of economy, regularity of supply,
and the military object of anticipating the Federal
army in the consumption of the beef and flour of
the rich and exposed counties of Loudon, Jefferson,
and Frederick.

These efforts had no effect, unless they caused

the loss to the army of its excellent chief commissary, who was summarily removed. He had no other part in them than furnishing, at my orders, information from his office for my use in the correspondence.

CHAPTER III.

The Summer spent in observing the Enemy and preparing for Active Service.—Mason's and Munson's Hills occupied.—Colonel J. E. B. Stuart.—General McClellan in command of the Federal Forces.—Consequences of Want of Preparation for the Struggle beginning to be seriously felt.—The President appoints Five Generals.—Correspondence with him on the Subject.—Organization of the Confederate Army.—President invited to Headquarters of the Army for Consultation.—He visits Fairfax Court-House.—Account of the Conference and its Result.—Battle of Leesburg.—Affair at Drainsville.—Effective Total of the Confederate Army at the End of the Year 1861.—Allusion to Events in the West.

No military event deserving notice occurred on our part of the frontier during the remainder of the summer. We were employed in observing the enemy and preparing our troops for active service by diligent instruction. The captured material enabled Colonel Pendleton to increase and improve our artillery very much.

At the beginning of September the army was encamped about Fairfax Court-House, with strong outposts at Munson's and Mason's Hills, with the cavalry on their flanks. Stuart, who commanded it, had already impressed those who had opportunity to observe him, with the sagacity and courage that qualified him so admirably for the command of outposts. As had been his previous practice, his pickets were always near the enemy, while the Federal cavalry rarely ventured beyond the protection of infantry.

The Federal intrenchments, in front of which General McClellan had encamped his army, had been greatly extended by him, and they covered the heights on the Virginia side of the Potomac from a point above Georgetown to the hill south of Alexandria.

The accessions to the army since July 21st had been the excellent brigade of Georgians formed and brought to Virginia by General Toombs, two regiments from Mississippi, and one each from North Carolina, South Carolina, Alabama, and Texas.[1]

The consequences of neglect on the part of the Government of the Confederate States to prepare for a great war before its actual commencement, were now severely felt. While the United States was organizing an army of half a million of men, almost half of whom were assembling in front of Washington, we, with a population far more eager to defend their country than that of the Northern States to invade it, were able to add but ten regiments, averaging little more than five hundred men, to our principal army. If arms and ammunition could have been furnished then, hands to use them would have been offered promptly, and the Confederate army would have outnumbered that which the Federal Government was forming for our subjugation.

It was reported, about the end of August, that General A. S. Johnston, coming from California by the southern (land) route, had entered the Confederacy; and, on the 31st of the month, the President nominated five persons to be generals in the Confederate army: First, S. Cooper, to rank from May 16th, the date of the law creating the grade; second, A. S.

[1] This statement is from memory.

Johnston, to rank from May 28th; third, R. E. Lee, from June 14th; fourth, J. E. Johnston, from July 4th; and, fifth, G. T. Beauregard, from July 21st, the date of the appointment previously conferred upon him.[1]

This action was altogether illegal, and contrary to all the laws enacted to regulate the rank of the class of officers concerned. Those laws were:

1. The act of March 6th, fixing the military establishment of the Confederacy, and providing for four brigadier-generals, that being the highest grade created.

2. The act of March 14th, adding a fifth brigadier-general, and authorizing the President to assign one of the five to the duties of adjutant and inspector-general; and, 3. Enacting further, "that in all cases of officers who have resigned, or who may, within six months, tender their resignations from the army of the United States, and who have been, or may be appointed to original vacancies in the army of the Confederate States, the commissions issued shall bear one and the same date, so that the relative rank of officers of each grade shall be determined by their former commissions in the United States army, held anterior to the secession of these Confederate States from the United States."

4. The act of May 16th: "That the five general officers, provided by existing laws for the Confederate States, shall have the rank and denomination of general, instead of brigadier-general, which shall be the highest military grade known to the Confederate States. . . . Appointments to the rank of general,

___

[1] *See* the President's telegrams on p. 21.

after the army is organized, shall be made by selection from the army."

Under the first act, S. Cooper, R. E. Lee, and myself, were brigadiers-general on the 16th of May, when the fourth was approved; and under the third ranked relatively, as we had done in the United States army before secession, when I was brigadier-general, General Cooper colonel, and General Lee lieutenant-colonel in that army. The passage of the fourth act made us generals, and, according to military rule, without affecting this relative rank. It also abolished the grade of brigadier-general in the army to which we belonged. General Cooper, General Lee, and myself, had no commissions if we were not generals. If we were generals, executive action could not give our commissions new dates. The order of rank established by *law* was—first, J. E. Johnston (brigadier-general U. S. A.); second, S. Cooper (colonel U. S. A.); third, A. S. Johnston (colonel U. S. A.); fourth, R. E. Lee (lieutenant-colonel U. S. A.); G. T. Beauregard (captain U. S. A.). The change in the legal arrangement was made by my removal from the first place on the list to the fourth.

Information of these nominations, and their confirmation, came to me at the same time. On receiving it, I wrote to the President such a statement as the preceding, and also expressed my sense of the wrong done me. But, in order that sense of injury might not betray me into the use of language improper from an officer to the President, I laid aside the letter for two days, and then examined it dispassionately, I believe; and was confident that what it

contained was not improper to be said by a soldier
to the President, nor improperly said. The letter
was, therefore, dispatched.

It is said that it irritated him greatly, and that
his irritation was freely expressed. The animosity
against me that he is known to have entertained ever
since was attributed, by my acquaintances in public
life, in Richmond at the time, to this letter.

On the 11th Colonel Stuart ascertained that a
body of Federal troops had advanced to Lewinsville.
To prevent it from holding the position by intrenching itself there, which would have annoyed us very
much, he determined to attack it with three hundred
and five infantry (Thirteenth Virginia), under Major
Terrill, a section of Rosser's battery, and Captain
Patrick's company of cavalry. He conducted the
march of his party so adroitly as to surprise the enemy completely, and by a bold attack drove them
off in confusion. It was the escort of a reconnoitring officer [1]—a brigade of infantry, a battery of
eight guns, and a detachment of cavalry.

At this time such an organization of the army as
that completed a year later was proposed to the Administration—the formation of corps and divisions
as well as brigades, and the creation of the grades
of lieutenant-general and major-general. It was partially adopted then, and four divisions formed of the
thirteen brigades of the army. E. Van Dorn, G. W.
Smith, J. Longstreet, and T. J. Jackson, were appointed majors-general to command them. Bonham's, Early's, and Rodes's brigades, formed Van
Dorn's division; D. R. Jones's, Ewell's, and Cocke's,

[1] Stuart's report.

joined Longstreet's; those of S. Jones, Toombs, and Wilcox, G. W. Smith's; and Jackson's was composed of his former brigade, Elzey's, Crittenden's, and Walker's.

No army composed of new troops ever had general officers of more merit than those just enumerated. This fact, and the admirable character of the troops themselves, justified me in the belief that it was practicable for us to hold our position against such a force even as General McClellan was supposed to command. It was important to do so, to avoid the discouragement that would have been caused by falling back to the line of the Rappahannock, to protect so many more of our people, and to retain for the Confederate armies the use of the products of the valley of the Shenandoah, and of the counties of Loudon and Fauquier. But, that we might be prepared for the possible necessity of withdrawing from this position, Colonel Williamson, of the Engineer Department, was then engaged in the construction of field-works on the Rappahannock, to improve that line, naturally much stronger than the present one. Early in September the construction of batteries at Evansport was begun under the direction of Brigadier-General Trimble, by order of the War Department, to prevent the navigation of the Potomac by vessels of the United States.

About the 20th of the month I became convinced that the increasing strength and efficiency of the Federal army were rendering the position of the outposts at Munson's and Mason's Hills more hazardous daily, and therefore had them withdrawn.

We had been hoping, since the battle of Manassas,

that the effective strength of the army would be so increased as to justify us in assuming the offensive, If such a change of policy was to be adopted, there was no time to lose, for the end of the season for active operations was near. I determined, therefore, to suggest it to the President, in the hope that he might regard many of the troops stationed in unthreatened parts of country as available for such a purpose. With that view the subject was put before him in a letter addressed by me to the Secretary of War, on the 26th, in which it was proposed that the President himself should come to the headquarters of the army, then at Fairfax Court-House, to decide this question, after conference with such officers as he might select, or send the Secretary of War, or some other confidential officer. Mr. Davis preferred the former course, and came himself, promptly, arriving on the last day of September (I think). He had a conference of several hours on the matter in question, the evening of the next day, in General Beauregard's quarters, with that officer, Major-General G. W. Smith, and myself.

It was conceded that no decisive success could be gained by attacking General McClellan's army in its position under the guns of a long line of forts. It was agreed, too, that decisive action before the winter was important to us; for it was certain that without it, when the spring campaign opened, the effective strength of the United States army would be much increased by additional numbers and better discipline. Ours, on the contrary, could not be materially increased; for the Confederacy had no arms but those in the hands of the volunteers, and twenty-five hundred of those captured on the 21st of July, which were in the ordnance-store of the army, at Fairfax Court-House.

Under these circumstances, the three military officers proposed, as the course offering the best chance of success, the concentration there of all the available forces of the Confederate States; crossing the Potomac, into Maryland, at the nearest ford with this army, and placing it in rear of Washington. This, we thought, would compel McClellan to fight with the chances of battle against him. Success would bring Maryland into the Confederacy, we thought, and enable us to transfer the war to the northern border of that State, where the defensive should be resumed. In our opinion, Confederate troops could not be employed advantageously then in any other part of the South. And we supposed that North and South Carolina and Georgia, which were unthreatened, could easily furnish the necessary reënforcements. The President asked us, beginning with General Smith, what was the smallest number of men with which such a campaign might be commenced. He replied, "Fifty thousand soldiers." General Beauregard answered, "Sixty thousand;" and I the same number. Each of the three explained that he meant such soldiers as formed the army around us. We also explained to the President that large additions to our supply of ammunition and means of transportation would be required; for we had not then enough of either for our present force.

The President replied that no such reënforcements as we asked for could be furnished to the army; that the whole country was applying for arms and troops; that he could take none from other points for that army, and could do no more to increase its strength than send it as many recruits as there were arms in our ordnance-store—twenty-five hundred. This, of course decided the question of active operations *then*.

Mr. Davis then proposed some operations of a partisan character, especially an expedition, by a detachment, against Hooker's division, in Maryland, opposite to Evansport. I objected to this proposition, because we had no means of transporting any sufficient body of men to the Maryland shore quickly; and the Potomac being controlled by Federal vessels-of-war, such a body, if thrown into Maryland, would inevitably be captured or destroyed in attempting to return, even if successful against the land forces. Upon my declining such an enterprise, the conference terminated.

The army had advanced to Fairfax Court-House, for the contingency of being made strong enough to assume the offensive while General McClellan's was still unprepared to take the field. The semicircular course of the Potomac, and roads converging from different points on it to our position, made it easy for the Federal army to turn either of our flanks without exposing its own communications. As that great army became capable of manœuvring, the position of ours, of course, became more hazardous. On the 19th of October, therefore, it was drawn back to Centreville—a position much stronger in front, as well as less easily and safely turned. Van Dorn's and Longstreet's divisions occupied the ground between Union Mills and the village of Centreville—the former on the right; G. W. Smith's formed on the left, thrown back on the heights nearly parallel to and north of the Warrenton Turnpike; and Jackson's, constituting the reserve, was posted in rear of Centreville. The engineers were directed to fortify the summit of the hill near this village—that, by holding it, the strongest and salient point of the position, with two or three thousand men, the army itself might be free to manœuvre. As we had not artillery enough for their works and for the army fighting elsewhere, at the same time, rough wooden imitations of guns were made, and kept near the embrasures, in readiness for exhibition in them. To conceal the absence of carriages, the embrasures were covered with sheds made of bushes. These were the quaker guns afterward noticed in Northern papers.

The President's visit to the army seems to have suggested to him its reorganization in such a manner, as far as practicable, as to put the regiments of each State into the same brigades and divisions. The organization then existing had been made by General Beauregard and myself, necessarily without reference to States. The four or five regiments arriving first formed the first brigade, the next four or five the second, and so on. As the regiments united in this manner soon became attached to each other and to their commanders, it had been thought impolitic, generally, to disturb this arrangement. Soon after the President's return to Richmond, orders were issued directing me to organize the troops anew, so that each brigade should be formed of regiments belonging to the same State. I was instructed to do this, however, *only when it might be done safely.*[1]

As the enemy was nearer to our centre than that centre to either flank of the army, and another advance upon us by the Federal army not improbable on any day, it seemed to me unsafe to make the reorganization then; for it would have exposed the army to the danger of being attacked by the enemy while in the confusion incident to a general change of position by our regiments, when most of them would be unable to take their places in the line of battle.

Although displeased by the delay, the President did not take from me the discretion as to selection of time, previously given. While expressing dissatisfaction, he repeated his order in the terms in which it had first been given: to make the reorganization[2] when it could be done without exposing the army to danger.

It is asserted in the "Rebellion Record," that, on the 16th of October, General Geary ascertained that the Eighth Virginia and Thirteenth and Eighteenth Mississippi infantry, and Ashby's cavalry regiments, were at Harper's Ferry, and, crossing the Potomac at that point with ten companies of Federal infantry, attacked, defeated, and drove them off. Ashby was not under my command, so that I cannot assert that his regiment was not at Harper's Ferry at the time specified; but the three infantry

---

[1] The underscoring and phraseology are mine.

[2] "To be executed as early as in your discretion it could be safely done."—Letter of Mr. Benjamin, acting Secretary of War, December 9, 1861.

regiments named belonged to Evans's brigade, of the army I commanded, and to my certain knowledge were no nearer Harper's Ferry on the 16th than on the 21st of October. If Ashby was *ever* defeated at Harper's Ferry, I believe that he died unconscious of the fact; and, under the circumstances, Confederate soldiers may reasonably doubt the occurrence, not merely of the victory claimed, but of any serious engagement.

On the 21st, Evans's brigade, near Leesburg, was attacked by a detachment of Federal troops, commanded by Colonel Baker. Four Federal regiments crossed the Potomac at Edwards's Ferry, and were held in check by Colonel Barksdale's (Thirteenth) Mississippi regiment. Five others, under Colonel Baker's immediate direction, crossed the river at the same time at Ball's Bluff, and were met by Hunton's (Eighth Virginia), Featherston's (Seventeenth Mississippi), and Burt's (Eighteenth Mississippi) regiments, and after an obstinate contest driven over Ball's Bluff in such a panic that numbers rushed into the river and were drowned. Colonel Baker had fallen on the field.

Brigadier-General Evans reported that the Confederate loss was thirty-six killed, including the gallant Colonel Burt, one hundred and seventeen wounded, and two captured; and that of the enemy, thirteen hundred killed, wounded, and drowned, and seven hundred and ten prisoners.

Colonel Barksdale attacked a superior force next day in advance of Edwards's Ferry, and drove it back to the river, which it recrossed in the night.

At the end of October the "effective total" of

the army (by the return in my possession) was
twenty-seven thousand infantry and artillery, and
twenty-four hundred cavalry, at and in front of Centreville, twenty-two hundred at Manassas Junction,
six thousand seven hundred between Dumfries and
the Occoquan, and twenty-seven hundred at Leesburg
—in all forty-one thousand capable of going into battle. According to the information given us by spies,
the effective force of the Federal army opposed to us
was a hundred and fifty thousand.

About the 1st of November a new military arrangement was made on the northern frontier of Virginia, by which my command was extended to the
Alleghany on one side and the Chesapeake on the
other, by the formation of " the Department of Northern Virginia." It was composed of " the Valley district," lying between the Alleghany and Blue Ridge,
commanded by Major-General Jackson; " the District
of the Potomac," commanded by General Beauregard,
and extending from the Blue Ridge to the Quantico;
and that of the Acquia, lying between the Quantico
and the Chesapeake, commanded by Major-General
Holmes.

" The Stonewall Brigade " was transferred with
General Jackson to the Valley district. Brigadier-
General R. B. Garnett, who joined the army soon
after, was sent to Winchester, where General Jackson's headquarters were established, to command it.
Major-General E. Kirby Smith, who had recovered
from his wound, and rejoined the army just then,
succeeded General Jackson in the command of the
reserve.

The Texan Brigade, ever after so distinguished in the Army of Northern Virginia, had then been completed by Brigadier-General Wigfall.

A trifling circumstance that occurred at this time was the foundation of a grave accusation, said to have been frequently made against me orally, by Mr. Benjamin, then acting Secretary of War.

Major-General Van Dorn reported to me that he had information, from an excellent source, that the left Federal division (General Heintzelman) had advanced so far on the Occoquan road as to be entirely separated from the army—so far that it might be beaten by a prompt attack, before aid could reach it. He proposed that we should take advantage of this exposure, and attack it. I had daily intelligence that contradicted this, but desired General Van Dorn to send one of our best scouts, who belonged to his division, to obtain accurate information, promising that he should make the attempt he suggested should the intelligence brought justify it. A day or two after this General Van Dorn told me that the scout's report had satisfied him that the report he had previously made to me was incorrect, and that there had been no forward movement of the Federal left. Gentlemen coming to the army from Richmond, at different times during the earlier part of the winter, stated that the acting Secretary of War had repeatedly, in conversation, accused me of having neglected to destroy a body of some twelve thousand men which the Federal general had left long exposed. This charge had no better foundation than the incidents just related.

At the end of November the " effective total " of

the troops of the Department of Northern Virginia was forty-seven thousand two hundred, of whom four thousand eight hundred belonged to the Acquia district, and three thousand seven hundred to that of the Valley.[1] Brigadier-General D. H. Hill had succeeded Brigadier-General Evans in the command of the troops near Leesburg, the latter being transferred to South Carolina.

Early in December, Major Blair, the chief commissary of the army, was compelled by ill health to leave that position. He was succeeded in it by Major R. G. Cole, who assumed its duties about the 20th of the month, and continued to perform them until the end of the war. He was desired to have the stock of provision for the army increased to a supply for fifteen days, and to have that quantity kept on hand; and also to establish a reserve-depot at Culpepper Court-House. This measure was a preparation for the contingency of our finding it necessary or expedient to fall back from Centreville to the line of the Rappahannock.

On the 20th, Brigadier-General Stuart was sent to forage in the southeastern part of the county of Loudon, with an escort of sixteen hundred infantry and Cutts's battery. To protect the party gathering forage, he placed his escort at Drainsville, between that party and the Federal army. In taking that position, he encountered the escort of a Federal foraging-party. Finding this body of troops much stronger than his own, he thought it necessary to draw off his foraging-party, and, to cover its withdrawal, attacked the enemy, and kept them engaged

---

[1] The figures are taken from the return in my possession.

until his trains were safe, when he fell back with his escort. He was undisturbed in this movement, and his adversary withdrew also very soon after. Cutts's battery did excellent service in this affair.

Three brigades under Brigadier-General Loring, transferred from Western Virginia to the Valley district, reported to Major-General Jackson in December: the first, commanded by Colonel Taliaferro, early in the month; the two others, Brigadier-General S. R. Anderson's and Colonel Gilham's, near its close.

In the course of the month two regiments were received in the Potomac district, which completed Hampton's brigade; that officer's military merit procured his assignment to this command, but I was unable to induce the Administration to give him corresponding rank.

At the end of the year, the effective total of the troops belonging to the departments was fifty seven thousand three hundred and thirty-seven—ten thousand two hundred and forty-one in the Valley district, forty thousand eight hundred and thirty-nine in that of the Potomac, and six thousand two hundred and fifty-seven in the Acquia district.

Although the great Federal army was so near, our military exercises had never been interrupted. No demonstrations were made by the troops of that army, except the occasional driving in of a Confederate cavalry-picket by a large mixed force. The Federal cavalry rarely ventured beyond the protection of infantry, and the ground between the two armies had been less free to it than to that of the Confederate army. Until the end of December, military operations were practicable; but, from that time

to the beginning of spring, the condition of the country south of the Potomac and east of the Blue Ridge
would have made them extremely difficult—indeed,
almost impossible. The quantity of rain that fell,
and of snow, always melting quickly, made a depth
of mud rarely equaled.

The Confederate troops fought bravely and well
wherever they encountered those of the United
States, in 1861.   At Bethel, under Magruder and D.
H. Hill; at Oakhill, under Price and McCulloch; on
the Gauley, under Floyd; on the Greenbrier, under
H. R. Jackson; on Santa Rosa Island, under R. H.
Anderson; at Belmont, under Polk and Pillow; on
the Alleghany, under Edward Johnson, and at Chas-
tenallah, under McIntosh.   On all these occasions
they were superior to their adversaries, from greater
zeal and more familiarity with the use of fire-arms.
The thorough system of instruction introduced into
the United States army gradually established equality in the use of fire-arms, and our greater zeal finally
encountered better discipline.

Had the Confederate troops in Arkansas been
united under a competent, or even a merely respectable commander, their fighting would have been
effective, and valuable to the Southern cause.   I
might have gained the powerful state of Missouri to
the Confederacy, and brought sixty thousand of its
martial inhabitants into the Southern armies.   Such
an accession to the Southern Confederacy might, and
probably would, have made the northern and eastern
borders of that State the seat of war, instead of Mississippi and Tennessee.

Among the measures to hold Tennessee and gain

Kentucky were intrenched camps, made at Columbus, Island No. 10, Forts Henry and Donelson, and Bowling Green; each of which required an army to hold it; and, consequently, a respectable army divided among them, gave each one a force utterly inadequate to its defense. Regular forts, each requiring a garrison of one or two thousand men, and constructed with much less labor than the intrenched camps, would have held the ground much better, and made it practicable to form an active army at the same time, capable of facing those of Buell and Grant, one after the other. As it was, the Confederates were alike weak at every point, and, when the Federal armies advanced, they were captured, or abandoned the country precipitately, after much misdirected labor had been expended in preparations to defend it.

CHAPTER IV.

General Jackson proposes to resign.—Interference of Secretary Benjamin with the Army.—Proposition to exchange Prisoners.—Summoned to Richmond for Conference.—Preparations for Withdrawal from Manassas.—Secretary Benjamin continues his Interference with the Discipline of the Army.— Movement to the Rappahannock.—Orders to General Jackson.—Battle of Kernstown.—Army moved to the Rapidan.—Appointment of General Randolph Secretary of War.—Movements of General McClellan.—Another Conference with the President.—Its Result.

In the beginning of the year, General Jackson moved from Winchester with four brigades of infantry and a regiment of cavalry, to drive the Federal troops, then in the northern part of his district, across the Potomac. Their number being inconsiderable, he succeeded in ten days, without serious fighting. His men suffered very much, however, from cold, and hard marches.

In the distribution of the troops of the district, agreed upon by General Jackson and myself, General Loring's three brigades were stationed near Romney, General Meem's brigade of militia at Martinsburg, General Carson's at Bath, and the militia regiments of Colonels Monroe, McDonald, Harness, and Johnson, occupied Moorfield, and different points on a curved line thence, in advance of Romney, to Bath.

A week or two after these dispositions were completed, General Jackson received the following order from Mr. Benjamin, acting Secretary of War: "Our news indicates that a movement is being made to cut off General Loring's command. Order him back to Winchester immediately." After I had received from General Jackson information of this singular interference, it seemed to occur to Mr. Benjamin that his order should have been sent directly to me, for a copy came to my office then.

General Jackson thought himself so much wronged, officially, by this procedure of the acting Secretary of War that, immediately after obeying the order, he sent me a letter addressed to that officer, for transmission to him, asking to be relieved of his command, either by restoration to his professorship in the Virginia Military Institute, or by the acceptance of the resignation of his commission in the Confederate army. I retained the letter, and wrote him this remonstrance: "My dear friend, I have just read, with profound regret, your letter to the Secretary of War, asking to be relieved from your present command, either by an order to the Virginia Military Institute, or the acceptance of your resignation.

"Let me beg you to reconsider this matter. Under ordinary circumstances, a due sense of one's own dignity, as well as care for professional character and official rights, would demand such a course as yours. But the character of this war, the great energy exhibited by the Government of the United States, the danger in which our very existence as an independent people lies, require sacrifices from us all who have been educated as soldiers. I receive my information of the order of which you have such cause to complain, from your letter. Is not that as great an official wrong to me as the order itself to you? Let us dispassionately reason with the Government on this subject of command, and, if we fail to influence its practice, then ask to be relieved from positions, the authority of which is exercised by the War Department, while the responsibilities are left to us.

"I have taken the liberty to detain your letter, to make this appeal to your patriotism, not merely from warm feelings of personal regard, but from the official opinion which makes me regard you as necessary to the service of the country in your present position."

He agreed, ultimately, to remain in the army.

I wrote to the President on this subject on the 5th: "I have just received from Major-General Jackson a copy of the letter of the Secretary of War to him, directing the evacuation of Romney, and withdrawal of our troops to Winchester.

"On a former occasion I ventured to appeal to your excellency against such exercise of military command by the Secretary of War. Permit me now to suggest the separation of the Valley district from my command, on the ground that it is necessary for the public interest. A collision of the authority of the Hon. Secretary of War with mine might occur at a critical moment; in such an event disaster would be inevitable.

"The responsibility of the command has been imposed upon me; your excellency's known sense of justice will not hold me to that responsibility while the corresponding control is not in my hands.

"Let me assure your excellency that I am

prompted in this matter by no love of privileges of position, or of official rights, as such, but by a firm belief that, under the circumstances, what I propose is necessary to the safety of our troops and cause."

The suggestion made in this letter was not accepted. Early in the month the army lost Major-General Van Dorn, and in the latter part of it General Beauregard, who held the first place in the estimation of much the larger number of the troops; both were sent by the Government to the valley of the Mississippi.

What was known in the army as the bounty and furlough law went into effect on the first day of the year. It was intended to encourage reëngagement in the service by those who had volunteered for but one year. Either from defects in the law itself, or faults in the manner in which it was administered, it had the effect of weakening the army by its immediate operation, without adding to its strength subsequently. Its numbers were greatly reduced before the end of the month by furloughs under the recent law, given directly by the acting Secretary of War. It was further weakened, and its discipline very much impaired, by Mr. Benjamin's daily interference in its administration and interior management. That officer was in the habit of granting leaves of absence, furloughs, and discharges, accepting resignations, and detailing soldiers to labor for contractors, or on nominal service, taking them out of the army upon applications made directly to himself, without the knowledge of the officers whose duty it was to look to the interests of the Government in such cases. He also granted indiscriminately to officers, private soldiers, and civilians, authority to raise companies of cavalry and artillery, especially the latter, from our excellent infantry regiments, in some instances for merely local service. Although the artillery of the army already exceeded the European proportion, many additional batteries were thus authorized. Fortunately the Ordnance Department was unable to arm and equip them; otherwise the army would have been deprived of several regiments of excellent infantry, and encumbered with artillery that could not have been taken into battle without danger of capture, for want of infantry to protect it. In all this the Honorable Secretary did more mischief by impairing the discipline of the army than by reducing its numbers.[1] My respectful remonstrances were written to him on the 1st, as follows:

"Your letter of the 25th, in reply to mine of the 18th, did not reach me until yesterday.

"In entering upon the delicate and difficult work assigned to me, I shall keep in view your advice 'to go to the extreme verge of prudence in tempting my twelve-months men, by liberal furloughs, to reënlist.' It is, however, indispensable to the success of the undertaking, that you should remove certain difficulties which not only embarrass the execution of these particular orders, but are also causing great confusion and an approach to demoralization in the army. They result from a practice of giving orders to the army in matters of military detail which should only

[1] There was such a want of arms at this time, that I was directed by the acting Secretary of War to send those of all soldiers "sick in hospital" to Richmond (see Appendix; in this way the army lost six thousand muskets.

come from the commanding officers present. It is
impossible to specify in detail all these orders, as
many of them are brought incidentally to my knowledge by the difficulties attending their execution. I
allude especially to those granting furloughs, leaves of
absence, discharges, and acceptances of resignations,
made directly by yourself, without giving the officers
concerned a hearing; detailing mechanics and other
soldiers to labor for contractors ; ordering troops into
this department and from it without consulting me,
or even informing me of the fact; and removing companies from point to point within it. Two of these
companies were at Manassas—having been selected
to man some heavy batteries there ; they had become
well instructed in that service, and, of course, were
unpractised as infantry. The companies that take
their places will for weeks be worthless as artillery,
as they are as infantry. Our organization being
incomplete, I am compelled thus to select troops for
special service; and, if, as general, I cannot control
such matters, our heavy guns are useless expense.

"The matters above mentioned are purely military, and, I respectfully submit, should be left under
the control of military officers.

"I have been informed that you have already
granted furloughs to four entire companies, but have
received only one of the orders. They are, it is said,
enlisted as artillery ; we shall thus lose good infantry, and gain artillery having no other advantage over
recruits than that of being inured to camp-life. This
increases the difficulty of inducing reënlistment of
infantry as such. You will perceive readily that, while
you are granting furloughs on such a scale at Rich-

mond, I cannot safely grant them at all. To execute these orders consistently and advisedly, there must be a system; if the War Department continues to grant these furloughs without reference to the plan determined on here, confusion and disorganizing collisions must be the result.

"I have been greatly surprised to-day to receive an order from the War Office, detailing a private for a working-party here. I hazard nothing in saying that a Secretary of War never before, in time of war, made such a detail.

"In calling your attention to the mischiefs resulting from the orders alluded to above, I assure you I am making no point upon mere official propriety; they are practical evils which are weighing heavily upon this army. Officers, laboring under the impressions that I am in some way responsible for the changes they direct, complain that they are made without consulting their wishes, and in opposition to their plans. The discipline of the army cannot be maintained under such circumstances. The direct tendency of such orders is to insulate the commanding general from his army, to impair his authority with his troops, to diminish his moral as well as his official control over them, and to harass him with the constant fear that his most matured plans may be contravened by orders from the Government which it is impossible for him to anticipate.

"I respectfully request that you will forbear the exercise of your power upon these points. You have seen proper to intrust to 'my skill and judgment,' as you kindly express it, a work full of hazards and difficulties: may I not ask that you will extend your confidence in me to those matters of minor detail which legitimately belong to my position?

"I appreciate fully the demands upon your attention by the great pressure upon all our lines of defense, which you so vividly present in your letter of the 25th ult. By leaving to me the exclusive control of the military arrangements appertaining to my command here, you will be relieved of much that must divert your mind from that general supervision which your exalted station requires.

"I have written, sir, in no spirit of captiousness, but with perfect frankness, in order to remove any causes of misunderstanding, and to secure concert of action between us. From all I can learn, the disposition to reënlist is not very general. I will do what I can to stimulate it into activity. Care must be taken, however, not to reduce the army to such an extent as to make its very feebleness the inducement to the enemy's attack."

The Secretary took no notice of this letter, and in no degree abated his irregular course remonstrated against; and gave furloughs under the "bounty and furlough law" as lavishly as if he had not especially delegated its execution to me.

About the end of January the Confederate Government desired the adoption of measures for the exchange of all prisoners taken by the armies of the belligerents, and the Secretary of War instructed me to propose to General McClellan the proper arrangements for that object.

These instructions were obeyed on the 1st of February, by transmitting the following letter of that date to General McClellan, by the hands of

Lieutenant-Colonel Julian Harrison, of the Virginia cavalry, who was selected to bear it on account of the interest attaching to the subject, and its importance.

"SIR: I am instructed by the Secretary of War of the Confederate States to propose to you to enter into arrangements for a general exchange of prisoners of war, on terms in accordance with the usages of civilized warfare.

"This proposition is intended to be general—to embrace not merely the prisoners of war taken by armies near the Potomac, but to apply to those captured by all the forces of either belligerent.

"The terms of exchange, which seem to me appropriate, are those which have been established in modern war—equal exchange of those having similar rank; equivalent values when there is not equality of rank.

"In the hope that your answer will be favorable, and that we may thus together take at least one step to diminish the sufferings produced by the war, I am," etc.

As this proposition was not entertained nor the letter noticed, the matter is introduced here only to show how early in the war the Confederate Government attempted to lessen the sufferings of prisoners of war by shortening their terms of confinement, and how little of that spirit was exhibited by the Federal Administration.

When the Department of East Tennessee was constituted, Major-General E. Kirby Smith was selected to command it. Maney's, Bate's, and Vaughn's Tennessee regiments were transferred with him to that department. Major-General R. S. Ewell, just promoted, succeeded to the command of General E. K. Smith's division.

Soon after the middle of this month, I was summoned to Richmond by the President, who wished to confer with me on a subject in which secrecy was so important that he could not venture, he said, to commit it to paper, and the mail. I arrived in Richmond on the 20th, early enough to reach the President's office two hours before noon. The cabinet was in session, and I was summoned into the room. The President explained that he had sent for me to discuss the question of withdrawing the army to a less exposed position. I replied that, although the withdrawal of the army from Centreville would be necessary before McClellan's invasion, which might be expected as soon as the country should be in condition for the marching of armies, it was impossible then, without much suffering by the troops, and great sacrifice of military property, including baggage. On that account, I thought the measure should be postponed until the end of the winter, and represented that the artillery-horses could not then draw field-pieces with their ammunition-chests, nor loaded caissons. This brought on a long discussion of the best mode of bringing off the guns of the Evansport batteries, which prolonged the conference until near sunset. It terminated without the giving of orders, but with the understanding on my part that the army was to fall back as soon as practicable.

The discussion was understood to be strictly confidential; yet, on reaching the hotel, going directly from the President's office, I was asked by Colonel Pender, Sixth North Carolina regiment, just arrived in the city on his way to the army, after leave of absence, if I had heard a report that he had found in that house, that the cabinet had been discussing that day the question of withdrawing the army from the line then occupied. On my way back to Centreville next day, I met an acquaintance from the county of Fauquier, too deaf to hear conversation not intended for his ear, who gave me the same information that he had heard, he said, the evening before.

This extraordinary proof of the indiscretion of the members of the cabinet, or of some one of them, might have taught the danger of intrusting to that body any design the success of which depended upon secrecy.

On the 22d orders were given to the chiefs of the quartermaster's and subsistence departments to remove the military property in the depots at Manassas Junction and its dependencies, to Gordonsville, as quickly as possible; and the president and superintendent of the Orange and Alexandria Railroad were requested to work it to its utmost capacity for that object. To expedite the operation, as well as for the probability of their being required near that point, Colonel Cole was instructed to have a portion of his stores deposited at Orange Court-House. A supply for ten days had been placed previously at Culpepper Court-House, for the contingency of the occupation of the line of the Rappahannock by the army.

An enormous quantity of military property had been accumulated at Manassas Junction, besides that of the Confederate Government in the hands of its officers of the quartermaster's and subsistence departments. There were large stores of provisions and clothing belonging to States, and under the charge of State agents; there was also such a quantity of baggage as no such army had ever before collected together. As the different regiments had been brought from their homes to Manassas Junction by railroad, the amount of their baggage had not been limited, consequently a trunk had come with each volunteer.

The arrangements of the commissary department, made without reference to probable military operations, or the views of the commander of the army, added still more to the great quantity of public property depending on the troops for protection. Major R. G. Cole,[1] chief commissary of the army, had

[1] In a letter to me on this subject, dated February 7, 1871, Colonel R. G. Cole states: " By your direction I requested the commissary-general to increase the supply of provisions to an amount sufficient for fifteen days' rations for the army. In a short time I discovered that the accumulation was too large, and reported the fact to you, and by your direction I telegraphed, on the 4th of January, 1862, to the Commissary-General, that you desired all stores sent from Richmond stopped at Culpepper Court-House. At this place I had, by your orders, established a reserve depot. Supplies continued to come from Richmond, Lynchburg, Staunton, and Fredericksburg. I requested the commissary-general by telegraph, on the 16th of January, to have the shipments to Manassas stopped. On the 29th I repeated the request, indicating that the amount at Manassas was nearly double that required. . . .

" The gross weight of supplies at Manassas was three million two hundred and forty thousand three hundred and fifty-four pounds. In addition, there was, in the packing-establishment at Thoroughfare, the rise of two million, mostly of salt meat; the gross weight of provision necessary for the army was one million five hundred and thirty-seven

endeavored, under my instructions, to limit the quantity of provisions in his storehouses to a supply for fifteen days—in weight about fifteen hundred thousand pounds. But the subsistence department, disregarding his repeated representations of my views, had collected there more than three million pounds. It had also located a meat-curing establishment for the Confederate armies at Thoroughfare Gap, on the Manassas Gap Railroad, without my knowledge. In this establishment there were more than two million pounds of meat, cured and in the process, besides large herds of cattle and hogs: so that the subsistence department, contrary to my expressed wishes and opinion, had encumbered the army with above five million pounds of its property, more than three hundred and fifty car-loads; while by my system there would have been about a million and a half pounds, a hundred car-loads, for removal.

In the mean time the Secretary of War continued to pursue the course against which I had remonstrated on the 1st of February, to the great injury

thousand two hundred and fifty-four pounds. The gross weight of supplies abandoned was one million four hundred and thirty-four thousand three hundred and sixteen pounds. Of these stores, fifty thousand seven hundred and fifteen pounds of vinegar, two hundred and forty-six thousand three hundred and seventy-one of hard bread, and one hundred and forty-six thousand eight hundred and ninety-eight of flour, were damaged by exposure to the weather, owing to want of shelter, and totally unfit for issue."

By this statement of the best authority, not much more than a sixth of the food recklessly brought from the interior to the frontier was lost, exclusive of that spoiled. In spite of the accumulation at Manassas, every thing would have been saved but for the establishment of the meat-packery of the Confederate armies on that frontier; as if our troops were maintained to protect this establishment, not to meet the movements of the enemy.

of the army.   I therefore asked the President's intervention, on the 1st of March, as follows:

"I ask permission to call your attention to practices prevailing at the War Department, which are disorganizing in their effects upon this army, and destructive to its discipline.

"Orders of the War Department are received daily, granting leaves of absence and furloughs, and detailing soldiers for some service away from their companies, based upon applications made directly to the Hon. Secretary of War, without the knowledge of commanding officers, and in violation of the army regulations on this subject.   The object of this wholesome rule, which was to give the Government the right to be heard through its officers, is defeated, the Department acting upon mere *ex-parte* statements.   This is especially the case in reference to furloughs, their arrival being, usually, the first intimation of an application. . . .

"My object in writing to your excellency on this subject is, to invoke your protection of the discipline and organization of this army.   My position makes me responsible for the former, but the corresponding authority has been taken from me.   Let me urge its restoration.   The course of the Secretary of War has not only impaired discipline, but deprived me of the influence in the army without which there can be little hope of success.

"I have respectfully remonstrated with the Hon. Secretary, but without securing his notice. . . ."

His excellency's reply gave me reason to suppose that he would not interfere; for he assured me, in his answer to my appeal, that I had been imposed

upon by spurious orders; saying, in explanation:
"The Secretary of War informs me that he has not
granted leaves of absence or furloughs to soldiers of
your command for a month past." The adjutant-
general, Major T. G. Rhett, to whom I read the letter
on account of this statement, told me that a large
package of the orders in question had been received
by the mail in which that letter had come! Mr.
Benjamin's removal from the War Department, soon
after, implied that the President thought less poorly
of my intelligence than the language of his letter
indicated.

In writing to the President on the 22d of February, I had requested him to have the assignment
of officers of engineers expedited; such an assignment had been applied for early in the month. Captain Powhatan Robinson reported to me, with three
or four lieutenants, in the first two or three days of
March. He was directed, with his party, to examine
the two roads leading from our camps to the Rappahannock near the railroad-bridge. He reported, on
the 6th, that they were practicable, but made difficult by deep mud. On the 7th he was sent to the
Rappahannock, to have the railroad-bridge made
practicable for wagons.

We had to regard four routes to Richmond as
practicable for the Federal army: that chosen in
the previous July; another east of the Potomac to
the mouth of Potomac Creek, and thence by Fredericksburg; the third and fourth by water, the one to
the Lower Rappahannock, the other to Fort Monroe;
and from those points respectively by direct roads.

As the Confederate troops in Virginia were dis-

posed, it seemed to me that invasion by the second
route would be the most difficult to meet; for, as the
march in Maryland would be covered by the Potomac, the Federal general might hope to conceal it
from us until the passage of the river was begun, and
so place himself at least two days' march nearer to
Richmond than the Army of Northern Virginia, on
Bull Run. I did not doubt, therefore, that this route
would be taken by General McClellan. The opinion
was first suggested by the location of a division of
the United States army [1] on it, opposite to Dumfries.

On the 5th, information from Brigadier-General
Whiting, of unusual activity in the division opposite
to him—that referred to above—suggested that the
Federal army was about to take the field; so I determined to move to the position already prepared for
such an emergency—the south bank of the Rappahannock—strengthened by field-works, and provided
with a depot of food; for in it we should be better
able to resist the Federal army advancing by Manassas, and near enough to Fredericksburg to meet the
enemy there, should he take that route; as well as to
unite with any Confederate forces that might be sent
to oppose him should he move by the Lower Rappahannock or Fort Monroe.

Brigadier-Generals Whiting and D. H. Hill were
ordered to march on the morning of the 7th: the
first from the Lower Occoquan and neighborhood of
Dumfries, with his own, Wigfall's, and Hampton's
brigades, to Fredericksburg, where Major-General
Holmes was directed to concentrate his troops;
and the second from Leesburg by Thoroughfare and

---

[1] General Hooker's.

Warrenton to the south side of the Rappahannock.
The troops near Centreville and Manassas Junction
were directed to march on the morning of the 8th;
Smith's and Longstreet's divisions and Pendleton's
reserve artillery by the Turnpike—to the south side
of the Rappahannock—by the bridge near the Warrenton Springs; and Ewell's and Early's (late
Bonham's) to the south side of that river near the
railroad-bridge—one part taking the road following the railroad, and the other that to the south of
it, through Brentsville. In all cases artillery and
wagons were to precede troops. It was found necessary to transport the ammunition-chests of the artillery—those of the caissons as well as of the pieces—
by railroad.

So much property was still remaining in the depots on the morning of the 8th, that the commanders
of the divisions at Centreville and Bull Run were
directed to keep their positions. They remained in
them until the evening of the 9th, when they
marched to rejoin their baggage—the trains having
moved the day before. Much provision was left
at Manassas, and salt meat at Thoroughfare. The
country people were invited to divide this meat
among themselves, as soon as Hill's brigade, in passing, had taken as much of it as it could transport.

General Stuart occupied the line of Bull Run
with the cavalry, during the night of the 9th, and
at ten o'clock next morning set fire to the abandoned
storehouses. Early on the 11th all the infantry
and artillery crossed the Rappahannock. Ewell's
and Early's divisions encamped near the river, on
both sides of the railroad, and Smith and Long-

street marched on to Culpepper Court-House, as no
enemy appeared on the turnpike. The cavalry occupied Warrenton Junction, with pickets on Cedar
Run and the turnpike. My headquarters were near
the Rappahannock Station, but south of the river.

The authors of Alfriend's "Life of Jefferson
Davis" assert that "the destruction of valuable material, including an extensive meat-curing establishment containing large supplies of meat, and established by the Government, which ensued upon the
evacuation of Manassas, elicited much exasperated
censure."

The censure elicited by this "destruction" should
have been directed at those who located the great
meat-curing establishment of the Government on the
frontier, instead of in the interior of the country;
this, too, without the knowledge of the commander
on that frontier; and who burdened the army, besides, with more than three millions of rations,
when the general protested against a supply of more
than fifteen hundred thousand pounds.[1] Fifteen days
(from the 23d of February to the 9th of March, inclusive) were devoted by the army to the work of
removing the property in question, quite long enough
to subordinate the operations of an army to the protection of commissary stores exposed against the
wishes and remonstrances of the general.

Orders to remove the enormous accumulation of
public property were given by me at Manassas on
the 22d. The work was begun next morning, and
continued fifteen days. During that time I called
the President's attention, five times, to unavoidable

[1] *See* Colonel R. G. Cole's statement, Appendix.

delays in the preparations for our change of position, in the following passages of letters: February 22d: " .... The condition of the country is even worse than I described it to be, and rain is falling fast. I fear that field artillery near the Potomac cannot be removed soon." .... February 23d: " In the present condition of the country, the orders you have given me cannot be executed promptly, if at all. Well-mounted officers from the neighborhood of Dumfries report that they could ride no faster than at the rate of twelve miles in six hours and a half." .... February 25th: " .... They" (the roads) "are not now practicable for field artillery with our teams of four horses .... The accumulation of subsistence stores at Manassas is now a great evil. The commissary-general was requested, more than once, to suspend those supplies. A very extensive meat-packing establishment near Thoroughfare is also a great encumbrance. .... The vast quantities of personal property in our camps is a still greater one. Much of both kinds of property must be sacrificed in the contemplated movement." .... February 28th: " I regret to be unable to make a favorable report of the progress of our preparations to execute your plan. .... As I remarked to you orally,[1] the measure must be attended with great sacrifice of property, and perhaps much suffering " .... March 3d: " Your orders for moving cannot be executed now, on account of the condition of roads and streams. .... It is evident that a large quantity of it" (public property) " must be sacrificed. ... In conversation with you,[2]

[1] In the " consultation," February 20th.
[2] February 20th.

and before the cabinet, I did not exaggerate the difficulties of marching in that region. The sufferings and sickness that would be produced can hardly be exaggerated."

These passages, written after the "falling back" of the army had been authorized in the consultation, indicate a strong disposition on my part to postpone it, on account of the difficulties and hardships of marching at that season. They proved, too, that the President was reminded of these difficulties when we were discussing the measure in his office, with his cabinet.

After it had become evident that the Valley was to be invaded by an army too strong to be encountered by Jackson's division, that officer was instructed to endeavor to employ the invaders in the Valley, but without exposing himself to the danger of defeat, by keeping so near the enemy as to prevent him from making any considerable detachment to reënforce McClellan, but not so near that he might be compelled to fight.

Under these instructions, when General Banks, approaching with a Federal force greatly superior to his own, was within four miles of Winchester, General Jackson [1] fell back slowly before him to Strasburg—marching that distance, of eighteen miles, in two days. After remaining there undisturbed until the 16th, finding that the Federal army was again advancing, he fell back to Mount Jackson, twenty-four miles, his adversary halting at Strasburg.

General Jackson's report, showing these relative

[1] March 12th.

LIEUTENANT-GENERAL T. J. JACKSON

positions, made with his usual promptness, was received on the 19th, when I suggested to him that his
distance from the Federal army was too great for the
object in view. In the note acknowledging this, dispatched on the 21st, he wrote that he was about to
move his headquarters to Woodstock, twelve miles
from the enemy's camp; and at half-past 6 A. M., on
the 23d, at Strasburg, he expressed the hope that he
should be near Winchester that afternoon; and at
ten o'clock that night he wrote, in his brief manner,
that he attacked the Federal army at Kernstown
at 4 P. M. and was repulsed by it at dusk. In his
formal report, written on the 29th of April, he reported that his force on the field was three thousand
and eighty-seven infantry, two hundred and ninety
cavalry, and twenty-seven pieces of artillery. He estimated that of the enemy at eleven thousand. The
Confederate loss was eighty killed, three hundred
and forty-two wounded, and two hundred and thirty
prisoners; he supposed that of the Federal army to
have been three times as great. On the 24th and
25th he returned to Mount Jackson.

In the Federal report of this action, General
Shields's force is set down at seven thousand, and
his loss at seven hundred and eighteen, that of the
Confederate army at five hundred killed and a thousand wounded.

After remaining seven days in the positions to
which they had marched from Manassas, the troops
crossed the Rapidan and encamped between Orange
Court-House and the railroad-bridge. Ewell's division, however, was left in its position near the Rappahannock, with Stuart's cavalry, in observation of

a Federal division that had followed our march to Cedar Run, where it halted.

The line of the Rappahannock had been taken temporarily, in preference to that of the Rapidan, be-. cause it is nearer Bull Run, and covered more of the country; the river being deeper, protected the troops better, and we wished to use the provision then in its rich valley, as well as to deprive the enemy of it. On the 18th it had become evident that the activity reported in Maryland, two weeks before, was connected with no advance of the enemy on the Fredericksburg route. This made the selection of one of the eastern routes by the Federal general seem to me more probable than I had before thought it. The army was, therefore, ordered to move to the south side of the Rapidan, where it was in better position to unite with the Confederate forces between Richmond and the invading army. Ewell's division and Stuart's brigade remained on the Rappahannock, in observation.

Before the end of the month, General Randolph was appointed Secretary of War, which enabled the military officers to reëstablish the discipline of the army; and the expiration of furloughs, and a draft of about thirty thousand Virginians, made by Governor Letcher, made it stronger in numbers than it had ever been before.

From the 25th to the 29th of the month, our scouts, observing the Potomac, reported steam transports, loaded with Federal troops and military material, passing down the river continually. By their estimates of the number of men carried by each boat and their count of the number of trips, an army of one hundred and forty thousand men was conveyed in this way to some point beyond the mouth of the Potomac, probably Fort Monroe, as no reports of such vessels entering the Rappahannock were received. Reports of the Adjutant-General of the United States Army, published subsequently, show that it amounted to one hundred and twenty-one thousand men, and two hundred and forty field-pieces; it was joined, not long after, by a division of twelve thousand men.

The President was uncertain whether this army was destined for Fort Monroe, to invade Virginia by the peninsula, or for the invasion of North Carolina. I learned this at Gordonsville, where he summoned me to meet him to decide upon some measure of preparation for either event. The result was, an order to me to send two brigades to Richmond, to be held in reserve there under his direction. Brigadier-General John G. Walker's was sent from Fredericksburg, and that of Brigadier-General Wilcox from the Rapidan; neither was permitted to pause in Richmond, however, the first being sent on to join the Confederate forces in North Carolina, and the second to Magruder's army near Yorktown.

Major-General Holmes having been assigned to the command of the Confederate forces in North Carolina, I transferred Major-General Smith to Fredericksburg, to command the troops there. Brigadier-General D. R. Jones was promoted to command Smith's division.

When it was ascertained, about the 5th of April, that the Federal army was marching from Fort Monroe toward Yorktown, D. H. Hill's, D. R. Jones's, and Early's divisions, were transferred from the Army of

Northern Virginia to that of the Peninsula. The former was thus reduced to four divisions : Jackson's at Mount Jackson, Ewell's on the Rappahannock, Longstreet's at Orange Court-House, and G. W. Smith's at Fredericksburg.

Before the 10th, the President was convinced, by Major-General Magruder's reports, that the entire army just brought down the Potomac from Alexandria, by General McClellan, was then on the Peninsula, to move upon Richmond by that route. He therefore directed me to make such defensive arrangements as might be necessary in the Department of Northern Virginia, and put my remaining troops in march for Richmond, and then to report to him for further instructions. In obedience to these orders, Major-General Ewell was left with his division and a regiment of cavalry, in observation on the Upper Rappahannock; and Major-General Longstreet was directed to march with his to Richmond. Major-General Jackson was left in the Valley to oppose greatly superior Federal forces, and authorized to call Ewell's division to his assistance in case of necessity; and General Ewell was instructed to comply with such a call. Major-General Smith was instructed to leave a mixed force, equal to a brigade, in front of Fredericksburg, and move towards Richmond with all his remaining troops.

On reporting to the President, I was informed by him that my command was to be extended over the Departments of the Peninsula and Norfolk; and his excellency desired me to visit those departments immediately, to ascertain their military condition, before assuming the command.

GENERAL GEORGE B. McCLELLAN

I went to the Peninsula as soon as possible, reaching General Magruder's headquarters early in the morning; and passed the day in examining his works with the assistance of General Whiting, who accompanied me for the purpose, and in obtaining all the pertinent information General Magruder could give.

That officer had estimated the importance of at least *delaying* the invaders until an army capable of coping with them could be formed; and opposed them with about a tenth of their number,[1] on a line of which Yorktown, intrenched, made the left flank. This boldness imposed upon the Federal general, and made him halt to besiege instead of assailing the Confederate position. This resolute and judicious course on the part of General Magruder was of incalculable value. It saved Richmond, and gave the Confederate Government time to swell that officer's handful to an army.

His defensive line was Warwick River, a tidewater branch of the James; a system of inundations along Warwick Creek, the stream of which the river is the estuary, extending to the bend in its course opposite to Yorktown, and a line of field-works just begun, to connect the inundations with the intrenchments of the village. Gloucester Point, on the north bank of York River, and directly opposite to Yorktown, was also intrenched. Water-batteries had been established at both places, to command the channel between them. General Magruder had placed his left there, because it is the only point where the river could be commanded by such guns as ours. Everywhere else it is about two miles

---

[1] Thirteen thousand effective men.

wide, there less than one. The works had been constructed under the direction of engineers without experience in war or engineering. They were then held by about thirty-five thousand men; but the Federal army threatening them amounted to a hundred and thirty-three thousand.[1] This army was provided with an artillery proportionally formidable, including a hundred Parrott guns of the largest calibre, and at least thirty siege-mortars, besides a full proportion of field-batteries.

Before nightfall I was convinced that we could do no more on the Peninsula than delay General McClellan's progress toward Richmond, and that, if he found our intrenchments too strong to be carried certainly and soon, he could pass around them by crossing York River. It seemed to me the more probable, however, that he would open York River to his vessels by demolishing our water-batteries, and passing us by water, unless tempted, by discovering the weakness of our unfinished works between Yorktown and the head of the inundations, to force his way through our line there. For these reasons I thought it of great importance that a different plan of operations should be adopted without delay; and, leaving General Magruder's headquarters at nightfall, I hastened back to Richmond to suggest such a one, and arrived next morning early enough to see the President in his office as soon as he entered it.

After describing to him Magruder's position and the character of his defensive arrangements, I endeavored to show that, although they were the most judicious that that officer could have adopted when

---

[1] Report of Congress on the conduct of the war.

he devised them, they would not enable us to defeat McClellan; and called his attention to the great length of the line compared to the number of troops occupying it; the still unfortified space between Yorktown and the head of the inundations; the fact that these inundations protected the Federal troops as well as the Confederate; the certainty that the Federal rifled cannon, mounted out of range of our obsolete "smooth-bore" guns, could destroy the batteries of Yorktown and Gloucester Point; and the very strong probability that General McClellan's plan was to open York River to his fleet by demolishing those batteries with his powerful artillery. That being done, we could not prevent him from turning our position, by transporting his army up the river and landing in our rear, or by going on to Richmond and taking possession there.

Instead of only delaying the Federal army in its approach, I proposed that it should be encountered in front of Richmond by one quite as numerous, formed by uniting there all the available forces of the Confederacy in North Carolina, South Carolina, and Georgia, with those at Norfolk, on the Peninsula, and then near Richmond, including Smith's and Longstreet's divisions, which had arrived. The great army thus formed, surprising that of the United States by an attack when it was expecting to besiege Richmond, would be almost certain to win; and the enemy, defeated a hundred miles from Fort Monroe, their place of refuge, could scarcely escape destruction. Such a victory would decide not only the campaign, but the war, while the present plan could produce no decisive result.

The President, who had heard me with apparent interest, replied that the question was so important that he would hear it fully discussed before making his decision, and desired me to meet General Randolph (Secretary of War) and General Lee, in his office, at an appointed time, for the purpose; at my suggestion, he authorized me to invite Major-Generals Smith and Longstreet to the conference. I was confident of the support of the former, for at Fairfax Court-House and Centreville we had discussed the general question, and agreed that the Confederate Government ought to meet McClellan's invasion with all its available forces. In giving the invitation to General Smith, I explained to him the object of the conference, after which we agreed perfectly upon the course to be advocated.

The conference began more than an hour before noon, by my describing,[1] at the President's request, General Magruder's defensive arrangements, as I had done to him, and representing that General McClellan's probable design of molesting our batteries at Gloucester Point and Yorktown, and turning our position by transporting his army up the river, could not be prevented, so that the adoption of a new plan was necessary.

Major-General Smith was then asked by the President to give his opinion, and suggested the course we had agreed upon: the assembling all the Confederate forces available for the purpose, near Richmond—Magruder's troops, and Huger's from Norfolk, to arrive among the last—and assail the Federal army when, following Magruder, it came within reach.

[1] And exhibiting the memorandum in the Appendix.

In the discussion that followed, General Ran-dolph, who had been a naval officer, objected to the plan proposed, because it included at least the tem-porary abandonment of Norfolk, which would in-volve the probable loss of the materials for many vessels-of-war, contained in the navy-yard there. General Lee opposed it, because he thought that the withdrawal from South Carolina and Georgia of any considerable number of troops would expose the important seaports of Charleston and Savannah to the danger of capture. He thought, too, that the Peninsula had excellent fields of battle for a small army contending with a great one, and that we should for that reason make the contest with McClel-lan's army there. General Longstreet took little part, which I attributed to his deafness. I main-tained that all to be accomplished, by any success attainable on the Peninsula, would be to delay the enemy two or three weeks in his march to Richmond, for the reasons already given ; and that success would soon give us back every thing temporarily abandoned to achieve it, and would be decisive of the war, as well as of the campaign.

At six o'clock the conference was adjourned by the President, to meet in his house at seven. The discussion was continued there, although languidly, until 1 A. M., when it ceased, and the President, who previously had expressed no opinion on the question, announced his decision in favor of General Lee's opinion, and directed that Smith's and Longstreet's divisions should join the Army of the Peninsula, and ordered me to go there and take command, the

Departments of Norfolk and the Peninsula being added to that of Northern Virginia.

The belief that events on the Peninsula would soon compel the Confederate Government to adopt my method of opposing the Federal army, reconciled me somewhat to the necessity of obeying the President's order.

CHAPTER V.

Take Command on the Peninsula.—General Magruder's Defensive Preparations.
—Inform War Department of Intention to abandon Yorktown.—Battle of
Williamsburg.—Affair near Eltham.—No further Interruption to the March.
—Army withdrawn across the Chickahominy.—Disposition of the Confed-
erate Forces in Virginia at this Time.—Advance of General McClellan.—
Reported Movement of McDowell.—Battle of Seven Pines.

I ASSUMED my new command on the 17th. The
arrival of Smith's and Longstreet's divisions increased
the army on the Peninsula to about fifty-three thousand men, including three thousand sick. It was
opposed to a hundred and thirty-three thousand Federal soldiers.[1] Magruder's division formed the Confederate right wing, Longstreet's the centre, D. H.
Hill's the left, and Smith's the reserve. The field-
works at Gloucester Point and Yorktown, on the left
flank, and Mulberry Point, on the right, were occupied by eight thousand men.

In this position we had nothing to do but to finish the works begun, between Yorktown and the
head of the inundations, and observe the enemy's
operations. They were limited to a little skirmishing at long range, and daily cannonading, generally
directed at Magruder's left, or Longstreet's right,
and the construction of a long line of batteries in

[1] Franklin's division, of twelve thousand men, was kept on board
of transports, in readiness to move up York River.

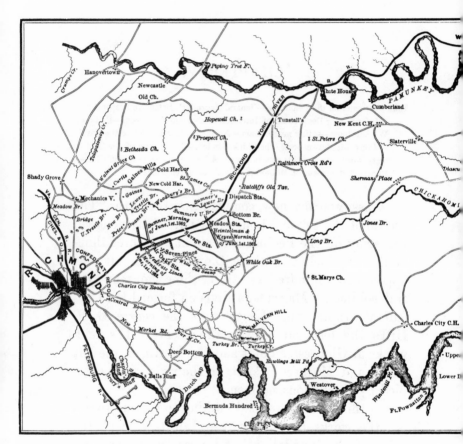

RICHMOND AND THE PENINSULA.

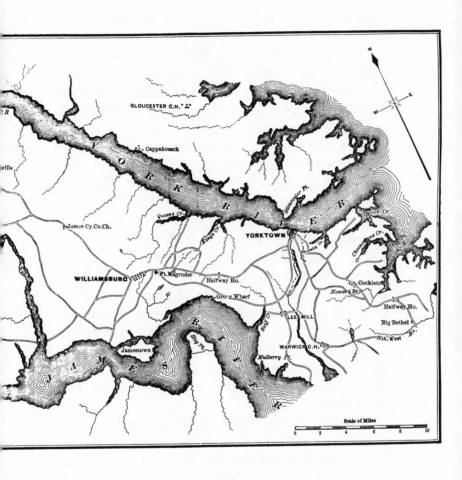

front of Yorktown, and beyond the range of our old-fashioned ship-guns. These batteries, our scouts reported, were for about one hundred of the heaviest Parrott guns, and above thirty mortars. A battery on the shore, three miles (pilot's distance) below Yorktown, received the first guns mounted. Shots of the first volley, fired to get the range of the Confederate works, fell in the camp of the reserve, a mile and a half beyond the village.

It was evident that the enemy was pursuing the course predicted, and preparing to demolish our batteries on York River. The greater range of his guns would have enabled him to do it without exposure, and at the same time to inflict great loss upon our garrisons. I could see no other object in holding the position than that of delaying the enemy's progress, to gain time in which arms might be received and troops organized. But, as the additional day or two to be gained by enduring a cannonade would have been dearly bought in blood, I determined to remain in the position only so long as it could be done without exposing our troops to the powerful artillery which, I doubted not, would soon be brought to bear upon them.

Finding, on the 27th, that the Federal batteries would be ready for action in five or six days, I informed the War Department of the fact, and of my intention to abandon Yorktown and the Warwick, before the fire of that artillery should be opened upon our troops. The suggestion made in the conference in the President's office was also repeated: to form a powerful army near Richmond, of all the available forces of the Confederacy, to fall upon McClellan's army when it should come within reach. Major-General Huger was instructed, at the same time, to prepare to evacuate Norfolk, and Captain S. S. Lee, commanding the navy-yard at Gosport, to remove to a place of safety as much of the valuable property it contained as he could.

On Saturday, the 3d of May, the army was ordered to fall back, on information that the Federal batteries would be ready for service in a day or two; Longstreet's and Magruder's divisions by the Warwick road, through Williamsburg, and G. W. Smith's and D. H. Hill's by that from Yorktown—the movement to begin at midnight, and the rear-guard, of cavalry, to follow at daybreak. Information of this was sent to Commodore Tatnall, commanding the iron-clad Virginia, and Captain Lee, at the navy-yard, and instructions were sent to Major-General Huger to march to Richmond.

The four divisions were assembled at Williamsburg about noon of the 4th. Magruder's division, temporarily commanded by Brigadier-General D. R. Jones, was ordered to move on in the afternoon, by the " New Kent road," and to turn off at the " Burnt Ordinary," toward the Diascund Bridge; to be followed, at two o'clock next morning, by G. W. Smith's, which was to keep the New Kent road. The baggage was to move next, in rear of which D. H. Hill's and Longstreet's divisions were to march.[1]

About four o'clock P. M., the cavalry rear-guard, on the Yorktown road, was driven in, and rapidly followed by the enemy. Brigadier-General McLaws

---

[1] This order of march was based on the idea that a part of the Federal army might pass us by the river.

was sent with the two brigades nearest, Kershaw's and Semmes's, to support the rear-guard. He met the enemy near and beyond Fort Magruder, made his dispositions with prompt skill and courage, and quickly drove the Federal troops from the field, taking a piece of artillery. At sunset a rearguard of two brigades of Longstreet's division—Anderson's and Pryor's, commanded by General Anderson—occupied Fort Magruder and four of the little redoubts on its right, and two of those on the left.

At daybreak on the 5th, Smith's division and the baggage-train marched in a heavy rain and deep mud. An hour or two later, the enemy appeared again in front of Fort Magruder, and opened a light cannonade, and a brisk fire of skirmishers upon Anderson's brigade. Both gradually increased, and at ten o'clock Wilcox's and A. P. Hill's brigades were sent to the assistance of the troops engaged, and, as the Federal force on the field continued to increase, Pickett's and Colston's brigades also reënforced ours.

At noon the fighting was reported by Longstreet and Stuart to be so sharp, that D. H. Hill's division, which had marched several miles, was ordered back to Williamsburg, and I returned myself; for at ten o'clock, when the action had lasted more than four hours, there seemed to be so little vigor in the enemy's conduct, that I became convinced that it was a mere demonstration, intended to delay our march—that the Federal army might pass us by water—and had ridden forward to join the leading troops. At three o'clock General Longstreet reported that the enemy was threatening to turn his left. I therefore directed

LIEUTENANT-GENERAL JAMES LONGSTREET

General Hill to move toward Longstreet's left, and rode to the field myself, to take command whenever more than Longstreet's division should be engaged on the Confederate side.

Until ten o'clock the fighting had been limited to the fire of artillery and skirmishers upon Fort Magruder, returned by the eight field-pieces belonging to General R. H. Anderson's command. That officer, observing that a division[1] of Federal troops had entered the wood a thousand yards to the right of Fort Magruder, placed Wilcox's brigade before it; being further reënforced by A. P. Hill's and Pickett's brigades, he determined to attack the Federal division, and formed the newly-arrived brigades and a part of Pryor's from the redoubts in rear, on Wilcox's right, and ordered all to advance. This was done with such regularity and vigor that the Federal troops were driven back, after a spirited contest of several hours, into the open fields in rear, west and southwest of the point where the Warwick road enters this open ground—the southeastern part of that in which Williamsburg stands. The contest was just leaving the wood and entering the open ground when I first saw it. Here Colston's brigade joined the Confederate, and Kearney's division the Federal troops engaged. But in the open ground the Confederates were more rapidly successful than in the earlier part of the affair, and drove the enemy into the forest on the east of the scene of conflict. When the combatants were near it, I cautioned General Longstreet against permitting his division to attempt to enter the forest, but to be content to hold the open field,

[1] Hooker's.

as the enemy was in force in front as well as to the left of Fort Magruder.

About five o'clock General Early sent an officer to report that a battery, that had been firing upon Fort Magruder and the troops near it, was near in his front, and asked permission to attack it. The message was delivered to General Longstreet in my presence, and he referred it to me. I authorized the attempt, but enjoined caution in it. Early's brigade advanced in two equal detachments, commanded, one by Major-General Hill, and the other by himself. They were separated in a thick wood, and General Early, in issuing from it, found a redoubt near and in front of him. He attempted an assault, in which he was severely wounded, after which his two regiments were quickly defeated, with a loss of nearly four hundred men.

In the mean time Longstreet had driven the enemy before him, out of the open ground, which there extends a mile from the position of our rear-guard, where it began.

This terminated what deserved to be called an action; although firing of field-pieces and skirmishing were continued until after sunset, without attempt, on the Federal part, to recover the lost ground. The remainder of the afternoon and the evening were devoted to burying the dead and providing for the comfort of our wounded, who, with many of those of the Federal army, who had been captured, were placed in hospitals and private residences in Williamsburg. Longstreet's and Hill's divisions slept on the field.

The Confederate loss was about twelve hundred

killed and wounded.   The proportion of the former
was unusually small; but it included Colonel Mott,
Nineteenth Mississippi, and Colonel Ward, Second
Florida regiment.   The Confederate officers, who
saw the ground upon which the dead and wounded
of both parties lay, supposed that of the enemy to be
from three to five times greater than ours.   General
Hooker, on oath before the committee on the conduct of the war, said that his division alone lost
seventeen hundred men.   About four hundred un-
wounded prisoners, ten colors, and twelve field-
pieces, were taken from the enemy.   We had the
means of bringing off but five of these guns.   The
carriages of five were cut to pieces with an axe, and
two were left in another part of the field uninjured,
because the captors had no axe.

Five Confederate guns without equipments, found
at the College Creek wharf, where they had probably
passed the winter, had been hauled to Williamsburg
that morning, by Major Barbour's orders.   As we
had no more spare horses and harness than those appropriated to five of the captured guns, these pieces
were necessarily left in the road where we found
them.

Longstreet reported nine thousand men of his
division engaged with Hooker's and Kearney's divisions on the right.   General Sumner, the ranking
Federal officer on the field, stated that two-thirds of
Smith's division and Peck's brigade were also engaged; and General Couch complimented his division,
in orders, for its conduct in the battle.   As the Federal army, except Franklin's division, had marched

but nine miles to the field the day before, by two roads, one cannot understand why four, or even six divisions, if necessary, were not brought into action. The smallness of the force engaged on this occasion greatly strengthened my suspicion that the army itself was moving up York River in transports.

We fought for no other purpose than to hold the ground long enough to enable our baggage-trains to get out of the way of the troops. This object was accomplished without difficulty. There was no time during the day when the slightest uncertainty appeared. I rode from the field a little before dark, because the action, except desultory firing of skirmishers, had ceased nearly two hours before. The occupation of a redoubt beyond our left by a Federal brigade did not affect us, otherwise than by the loss of some four hundred men by the two Confederate regiments that attacked it—an attack due to the fact that its existence was unknown to us, until General Early, issuing from a wood, came upon it suddenly.

The army had no ambulances, and the wagons had moved on in the morning. We were compelled, therefore, to leave all the wounded unable to march. At eleven o'clock at night, when all had been cared for, Dr. Cullen, General Longstreet's chief surgeon, reported that the number was about four hundred.

In the Federal reports, a victory is claimed at Williamsburg. The proofs against that claim are:

That what deserves to be called fighting, ceased two hours before dark, yet the Confederates held the field until the next morning, when they resumed their march.

That they fought only to protect their trains and artillery, and accomplished that object.

That, although they marched but twelve miles the day after the action, the rear-guard saw no indications of pursuit; unless the appearance of a scouting-party, once, may be so called.

That they inflicted a loss twice as great as that they suffered.

And in the ten days following the battle they marched but thirty-seven miles from the field, and then moved to the neighborhood of Richmond, only because the Federal gun-boats had possession of James River.

It is true that they left four hundred wounded in Williamsburg, because they had no means of transporting them; but an equal number of *un*-wounded Federal soldiers was brought off, with colors and cannon—the best evidences of successful fighting, except that already mentioned—sleeping on the field of battle.

Magruder's division, then commanded by Brigadier-General D. R. Jones in consequence of the illness of the major-general, passed the night of the 5th at Diascund Bridge; that of Major-General Smith at Barhamsville, twelve miles from New Kent Court-House; those of Longstreet and D. H. Hill, with the cavalry, at Williamsburg, as has been said.

In Federal dispatches of the 6th many prisoners are claimed to have been taken. The Confederate officers were conscious of no other losses of the kind than the captures made by Hancock, from the Fifth North Carolina and Twenty-fourth Virginia regiments. The cavalry rear-guard, following all the by-roads and paths parallel to the main road, found no lurkers or stragglers from Longstreet's and Hill's divisions.

The day after the action those troops marched at daybreak, and Stuart's at sunrise, and encamped soon after noon at the Burnt Ordinary, twelve miles from Williamsburg; Smith's and Magruder's divisions were stationary; Colonel Fitzhugh Lee, who was observing York River with his regiment of cavalry, reported a Federal fleet of vessels-of-war and transports, passing up toward West Point.

In the evening Major-General Smith sent me intelligence, to the Burnt Ordinary, that a large body of United States troops had landed at Eltham's, and nearly opposite to West Point, on the southern shore of York River. Early next morning the army was concentrated near Barhamsville. In the mean time General Smith had ascertained that the enemy was occupying a thick wood between the New Kent road and Etham's Landing. The security of our march required that he should be dislodged, and General Smith was intrusted with this service. He performed it very handsomely with Hampton's and Hood's brigades, under Whiting, driving the enemy, in about two hours, a mile and a half through the wood, to the protection of their vessels-of-war. General Smith's two brigades sustained a trifling loss in killed and wounded. If statements published in Northern newspapers are accurate, their loss was ten times as great as ours.

The way being thus cleared, the march was resumed. Smith's and Magruder's divisions followed the road by New Kent Court-House, and Longstreet's and Hill's that by the Long Bridges. In these marches the right column reached the Baltimore Cross-roads, nineteen miles from Barhamsville, and the left the Long Bridges. The army remained five days in this position, in line facing to the east, Longstreet's right covering the Long Bridges, and Magruder's left the York River Railroad; it was easily and regularly supplied by the railroad, and could no longer be turned by water.

It will be remembered that in reporting to the Government, on the 27th of April, my intention to withdraw the army from the Peninsula, I repeated the suggestion made to the President in Richmond twelve days before, to concentrate all his available forces before McClellan's army. In making the suggestion on this second occasion, I had no doubt of its adoption, for the Federal forces on the Peninsula were to ours at least in the ratio of five to two; the expediency, even necessity, of this concentration, was much greater at that time than in June, when the measure was adopted, for the ratio had been reduced then to about eleven to seven. In my correspondence with the Administration in May, this suggestion was repeated more than once, but was never noticed in the replies to my letters.

Intelligence of the destruction of the iron-clad Virginia was received on the 14th. I had predicted that its gallant commander, Commodore Tatnall, would never permit the vessel to fall into the hands of the enemy. The possession of James River by the naval forces of the United States, consequent upon this event, and their attack upon the Confederate battery at Drury's Bluff, suggested the necessity of

being ready to meet an advance upon Richmond up
the river, as well as from the direction of West Point.
The Confederate forces were, in consequence, ordered
to cross the Chickahominy on the 15th. And Colonel Goode Bryan, with his regiment of Georgia rifle-
men, was sent to aid in the defense of Drury's Bluff,
by occupying the wooded bluff on the north side of
the river, and immediately below the battery. On
this height his rifles could easily have commanded
the decks of vessels in the river below. On the 17th,
the army encamped about three miles from Richmond, in front of the line of redoubts constructed in
1861. Hill's division in the centre, formed across the
Williamsburg road; Longstreet's on the right, covering the river road; Magruder's on the left, crossing
the Nine-miles road; and Smith's in reserve, behind
Hill's left and Magruder's right.

Generals Jackson and Ewell, the former commanding as senior officer, were then opposing General Banks, in the Valley of the Shenandoah, still
under my direction. The President had placed Brigadier-General J. R. Anderson, with nine thousand
men, in observation of General McDowell, who was
at Fredericksburg with forty-two thousand men;
Brigadier-General Branch, with four or five thousand,
at Gordonsville; and had halted Huger's division at
Petersburg, when on its way to Richmond, under my
orders. That division, estimated by the Secretary of
War and General Lee at eighteen thousand a month
before, was then reduced to nine thousand by detachments to Branch and J. R. Anderson.

On leaving the Rapidan, I had requested Generals Jackson and Ewell to send their letters to me

LIEUTENANT-GENERAL R. S. EWELL

through the Adjutant-General's office.   These papers must have been acted upon in Richmond, for none were forwarded to me until the army had reached the neighborhood of the Chickahominy.   Then, one from General Jackson, written soon after his return from McDowell, was delivered to me.   In it he described the position of the Federal army, near Strasburg, and asked instructions.   These were given at once, and were to advance and attack, unless he found the enemy too strongly intrenched.

Instead of moving directly on Strasburg, General Jackson took the road by Front Royal, to turn the Federal army.   His movement was so prompt as to surprise the enemy completely.   Ewell, who was leading, captured most of the troops at Front Royal, and pressed on to Winchester, by the direct road, with his troops, while Jackson, turning across to that from Strasburg, struck the main Federal column in flank, and drove a large part of it back toward Strasburg.   The pursuit was pressed to Winchester, but the Federal troops continued their flight into Maryland.   Two thousand prisoners were taken in this pursuit.

After reaching the Chickahominy, General McClellan's troops advanced very slowly.   Sumner's, Franklin's, and Porter's corps, were on and above the railroad, and Heintzelman's and Keyes's below it, and on the Williamsburg road.   The last two, after crossing the stream, at Bottom's Bridge, on the 22d, were stationary, apparently, for several days, constructing a line of intrenchments two miles in advance of the bridge.   They then advanced, step by step, forming four lines, each of a division, in advancing. I hoped that their advance would give us an opportunity to make a successful attack upon these two corps, by increasing the interval between them and the larger portion of their army remaining beyond the Chickahominy.

On the 24th their leading troops encountered Hatton's Tennessee brigade, of Smith's division, within three miles of Seven Pines, and were driven back by it, after a sharp skirmish. It was proposed that we should prepare to hold the position then occupied by Hatton's brigade, to stop the advance of the enemy there. But it seemed to me more judicious to await a better opportunity, which the further advance of the Federal troops would certainly give, by increasing the interval between them and the three corps beyond the Chickahominy.

On the same day, Federal troops drove our cavalry out of Mechanicsville and occupied the village. This extension to the west by the Federal right made me apprehend the separation of the detachments near Fredericksburg and Gordonsville, from the army, and induced me to order them to fall back and unite where the Fredericksburg road crosses the Chickahominy. Near Hanover Court-House, on the 27th, Branch's brigade was attacked by Porter's corps, and suffered severely in the encounter. It was united with Anderson's on the same day, however, at the point designated for their junction. There a division was formed of these troops, to the command of which General A. P. Hill, just promoted, was assigned.

In the afternoon a party of cavalry left near Fredericksburg by General Anderson, to observe McDowell's movements, reported that his troops were marching southward. As the expediency of the junction of this large corps with the principal army was manifest, the object of the march could not be doubted. Accordingly, I determined to attack that army before it could receive so great an accession.

For this object, Huger's division,[1] now reduced to three brigades,[1] was called to the army from Petersburg. A. P. Hill's division was ordered to march by the left bank of the Chickahominy to Meadow's Bridge, and to remain on that side of the stream. General Smith was directed to place his division on the left of Magruder's—on the Mechanicsville turnpike — that he, the second officer of the army in rank, might be in position to command on the left. Longstreet's division was placed on the left of that of D. H. Hill, and Huger's in rear of the interval between the two last-named.

It was intended that Major-General Smith, with his own division and that of A. P. Hill, should move against the extreme right of the Federal army, and that Magruder's and Huger's, crossing by the New Bridge, should form between the left wing and the Chickahominy, while Longstreet's and D. H. Hill's divisions, their left thrown forward, assailed the right flank of the two corps on the Williamsburg road, and on the Richmond side of the stream. I supposed that the bridges and fords of the little river would furnish means of sufficient communication between the two parts of the Confederate army.

At night, when the major-generals were with me to receive instructions for the expected battle, Gen-

[1] One had been transferred to Drury's Bluff by the Government.

eral Stuart, who had a small body of cavalry observing McDowell's corps, reported that the troops that had been marching southward from Fredericksburg had returned. This indicated, of course, that the intention of uniting the two Federal armies was no longer entertained.

As the expediency to us of an immediate general engagement depended on the probability of so great an accession to McClellan's force as McDowell could bring, this intelligence induced me to abandon the intention of attacking, and made me fall back upon my first design—that of assailing Heintzelman's and Keyes's corps as soon as, by advancing, they should sufficiently increase the interval between themselves and the three corps beyond the Chickahominy. Such an opportunity was soon offered.

On the morning of the 30th, armed reconnaissances were made under General D. H. Hill's direction—on the Charles City road by Brigadier-General Rhodes, and on the Williamsburg road by Brigadier-General Garland. No enemy was found by General Rhodes; but General Garland encountered Federal outposts more than two miles west of Seven Pines, in such strength as indicated the presence of a corps at least. This fact was reported to me by General Hill soon after noon. He was informed, in reply, that he would lead an attack upon this enemy next morning.

An hour or two later, orders were given for the concentration of twenty-three of our twenty-seven brigades against McClellan's left wing—about two-fifths of his army. The four others were observing the river, from the New Bridge up to Meadow

Bridge. Longstreet and Huger were directed to conduct their brigades to D. H. Hill's position, as early
as they could next morning; and Smith to march
with his to the point of meeting of the New Bridge
and Nine-miles roads, near which Magruder had five
brigades.

Longstreet, as ranking officer of the three divisions to be united near Hill's camp, was instructed,
verbally, to form his own and Hill's division in two
lines crossing the Williamsburg road at right angles,
and to advance to the attack in that order; while
Huger's division should march along the Charles City
road by the right flank, to fall upon the enemy's left
flank as soon as our troops became engaged with
them in front. It was understood that abatis, or
earthworks, that might be encountered, should be
turned. General Smith was to engage any troops
that might cross the Chickahominy to assist Heintzelman's and Keyes's corps; or, if none came, he was to
fall upon the right flanks of those troops engaged
with Longstreet. The accident of location prevented
the assignment of this officer to the command of the
principal attack, to which he was entitled by his
rank. As his division was on the left of all those to
be engaged, it was apprehended that its transfer to
the right might cause a serious loss of time.

The rain began to fall violently in the afternoon,
and continued all night; and, in the morning, the little streams near our camps were so much swollen as
to make it seem probable that the Chickahominy was
overflowing its banks, and cutting the communication
between the two parts of the Federal army.

Being confident that Longstreet and Hill, with

their forces united, would be successful in the earlier part of the action against an enemy formed in several lines, with wide intervals between them, I left the immediate control, on the Williamsburg road, to them, under general instructions, and placed myself on the left, where I could soonest learn the approach of Federal reënforcements from beyond the Chickahominy. From this point scouts and reconnoitering parties were sent forward to detect such movements, should they be made.

An unexpected delay in the forward movement on the right disappointed me greatly, and led to interchanges of messages between General Longstreet and myself for several hours.

Although the condition of the ground and little streams had delayed the troops in their movements, those of Smith and Longstreet were in position quite early enough. But the soldiers from Norfolk, who had seen garrison service only, and were unaccustomed to the incidents of a campaign, were unnecessarily stopped in their march by a swollen rivulet, which, unfortunately, flowed between them and their destination.

After waiting in vain for this division until two o'clock, Longstreet put his own and Hill's in motion toward the enemy, in order of battle, the latter forming the first line, with the centre on the Williamsburg road; three of Longstreet's brigades constituting the second line, two advancing on the Charles City road on the right, and one along the York River Railroad on the left.

At three o'clock the Federal advanced troops were encountered. They were a long line of skirmishers supported by five or six regiments of infantry, covered by abatis. The ardor and greatly superior numbers of the Confederates soon overcame their resistance, and drove them back to the main position of the first line of Keyes's corps—Casey's division. It occupied a line of rifle-pits, strengthened by a redoubt, and covered by abatis. Here the resistance was obstinate; for the Federal troops, commanded by an officer of tried courage, fought as soldiers usually do under good leaders, and time and vigorous efforts were required to drive them from their position. But the resolution of Garland's and George B. Anderson's brigades, that pressed forward on the left through an open field, under a destructive fire; the admirable service of Carter's and Bondurant's batteries, and a skillfully combined attack upon the Federal left, under General Hill's direction, by Rodes's brigade in front, and that of Rains in flank, were finally successful, and the enemy abandoned their intrenchments. Just then reënforcements were received from their second line, and they turned to recover their lost position. But to no purpose—they were driven back, fighting, upon their second line—Couch's division at Seven Pines. R. H. Anderson's brigade, transferred by Longstreet to the first line, after the capture of Casey's position, bore a prominent part in the last contest.

Keyes's corps, united in this second position, was assailed with such spirit by the Confederate troops that, although reënforced by Kearney's division of Heintzelman's corps, it was broken, divided, and driven from its ground—the greater part along the

Williamsburg road, to General Heintzelman's intrenched line, two miles from Bottom's Bridge, and
two brigades to the southeast into White-oak
Swamp.

General Hill pursued the enemy toward Bottom's Bridge, more than a mile; then, night being
near, he gathered his troops and re-formed them, facing to the east, as they had been fighting. The line
thus formed crossed the Williamsburg road at
right angles. The left, however, was thrown back
to face Sumner's corps at Fair Oaks. In an
hour or two Longstreet's and Huger's division,
whom it had not been necessary to bring into
action, came into this line under General Longstreet's
orders.

When the action began on the right, the musketry was not heard at my position on the Nine-miles
road, from the unfavorable condition of the air to
sound. I supposed, therefore, that the fight had not
begun, and that we were hearing an artillery duel.
However, a staff-officer was sent to ascertain the fact.
He returned at four o'clock, with intelligence that
our infantry as well as artillery had been engaged
for an hour, and that our troops were pressing forward with vigor. As no approach of Federal troops
from the other side of the Chickahominy had been
discovered or was suspected, I hoped strongly that
the bridges were impassable. It seemed to me idle,
therefore, to keep General Smith longer out of action, for a contingency so remote as the coming of
reënforcements from the Federal right. He was desired, therefore, to direct his division against the
right flank of Longstreet's adversaries. I thought it

prudent, however, to leave Magruder's division in reserve. It was under arms, near.

General Smith moved promptly along the Nine-miles road. His leading regiment, the Sixth North Carolina, soon became engaged with the Federal skirmishers and their reserves, and in a few minutes drove them off entirely. On my way to Longstreet's left, to combine the action of the two bodies of Confederate troops, I passed the head of General Smith's column near Fair Oaks, and saw the camp of a body of infantry of the strength of three or four regiments, apparently in the northern angle between the York River Railroad and the Nine-miles road, and the rear of a body of infantry moving in quick time from that point toward the Chickahominy, by the road to the Grape-vine Ford. A few minutes after this, a battery, at the point where this infantry had disappeared, opened its fire upon the head of the Confederate column. A regiment sent against it was received with a volley of musketry, as well as canister, and recoiled. The leading brigade, commanded by Colonel Law, then advanced, and so much strength was developed by the enemy, that General Smith formed his other brigades and brought them into battle on the left of Law's. An obstinate contest began, and was maintained on equal terms; although the Confederates engaged superior numbers in a position of their own choosing.

I had passed the railroad some little distance with Hood's brigade, when the action commenced, and stopped to see its termination. But, being confident that the Federal troops opposing ours were those whose camps I had just seen, and therefore not more than a brigade, I did not doubt that General Smith was quite strong enough to cope with them. General Hood was desired to go forward, therefore, and, connecting his right with Longstreet's left, to fall upon the right flank of his enemy. The direction of the firing was then (near five o'clock) decidedly to the right of Seven Pines. It was probably at Casey's intrenched position.

The firing at Fair Oaks soon increased, and I rode back to that field—still unconvinced, however, that General Smith was fighting more than a brigade, and thinking it injudicious to engage Magruder's division yet, as it was the only reserve. While waiting the conclusion of this struggle, my intercourse with Longstreet was maintained through staff-officers. The most favorable accounts of his progress were from time to time received from them.

The contest on the left was continued with equal determination by the two parties, each holding the ground on which it had begun to fight.

This condition of affairs existed on the left at half-past six o'clock, and the firing on the right seemed then to be about Seven Pines. It was evident, therefore, that the battle would not be terminated that day. So I announced to my staff-officers that each regiment must sleep where it might be standing when the contest ceased for the night, to be ready to renew it at dawn next morning.

About seven o'clock I received a slight wound in the right shoulder from a musket-shot, and, a few moments after, was unhorsed by a heavy fragment of shell which struck my breast. Those around had me borne from the field in an ambulance; not, however, before the President, who was with General Lee, not far in the rear, had heard of the accident, and visited me, manifesting great concern, as he continued to do until I was out of danger.

The firing ceased, terminated by *darkness only*, before I had been carried a mile from the field.

As next in rank, Major-General G. W. Smith succeeded to the command of the army.

His division remained in the immediate presence of the enemy during the night, its right resting on the railroad, where it joined Longstreet's left. Magruder's division was within supporting distance.

Next morning, Brigadier-General Pickett, whose brigade was near the left of Longstreet's and Hill's line, learned that a strong body of Federal troops was before him and near. He moved forward and attacked it, driving it from that ground. Very soon, being reënforced apparently, the Federals (several brigades) assumed the offensive, and attacked him. In the mean time General Hill had sent two regiments of Colston's brigade to him. Although largely outnumbered, Pickett met this attack with great resolution, and after a brisk but short action repulsed the enemy, who disappeared, to molest him no more. I have seen no Confederate officer who was conscious of any other serious fighting, by the troops of those armies, on Sunday. A strong proof of that fact is, that during the day Hill had almost seven thousand small-arms gathered from the field, which was covered by his line of troops, and much other military property; proof, also, that the Confederates were not even threatened.

About noon General Lee was assigned to the command of the Army of Northern Virginia, by the President; and at night the troops were ordered by him to return to their camps near Richmond, which they did soon after daybreak, Monday.

The operations of the Confederate troops in this battle were very much retarded by the dense woods and thickets that covered the ground, and by the deep mud and broad ponds of rain-water, in many places more than knee-deep, through which they had to struggle.

The loss in Longstreet's and Hill's divisions was about three thousand;[1] among the killed were Colonels Lomax, Jones, and Moore, of Alabama. About five-sixths of the loss was in the latter division, upon which the weight of the fighting on the right fell. The officers of those troops, who followed the enemy over all the ground on which they fought, and saw the dead and wounded of both parties on the field, were confident that the Federal loss was more than three times as great as ours. It was published in Northern papers as from ten to twelve thousand.

General Smith reported a loss of twelve hundred and thirty-three in his division, including Brigadier-General Hatton, of Tennessee, killed; and General Sumner's was twelve hundred and twenty-three, according to General McClellan's report.

Three hundred and fifty prisoners,[2] ten pieces of artillery, six thousand seven hundred muskets and

---

[1] Longstreet's report. General McClellan adds Hill's loss, twenty-five hundred, to the sum, of which it already made five-sixths, thus counting it twice—making the total six thousand seven hundred and thirty-three, instead of four thousand two hundred and thirty-three.

[2] *See* General D. H. Hill's report.

rifles in excellent condition, a garrison-flag and four regimental colors, medical, commissary, quartermaster's and ordnance stores, tents, and sutlers' property, were captured and secured.

The troops in position to renew the battle on Sunday were, at Fair Oaks, on the Federal side, two divisions and a brigade; one of the divisions, Richardson's, had not been engaged, having come upon the field about, or after, nightfall. On the Confederate side, ten brigades in Smith's and Magruder's divisions, six of which were fresh, not having fired a shot. On the Williamsburg road four Federal divisions, three of which had fought and been thoroughly beaten—one, Casey's, almost destroyed. On the Confederate side, thirteen brigades, but five of which had been engaged on Saturday—when they defeated the three Federal divisions that were brought against them successively. After nightfall, Saturday, the two bodies of Federal troops were completely separated from the two corps of their right, beyond the Chickahominy, by the swollen stream, which had swept away their bridges, and Sumner's corps at Fair Oaks was six miles [1] from those of Heintzelman and Keyes, which were near Bottom's Bridge; but the Confederate forces were united [1] on the front and left flank of Sumner's corps. Such advantage of position and superiority of numbers would have enabled them to defeat that corps had the engagement been renewed on Sunday morning, before any aid could have come from Heintzelman, after which his troops, in the condition to which the action of the day before had reduced them, could not have made effectual resistance.

[1] *See* map.

I was eager to fight on the 31st, from the belief that the flood in the Chickahominy would be at its height that day, and the two parts of the Federal army completely separated by it: it was too soon, however. We should have gained the advantage fully by a day's delay. This would also have given us an accession of about eight thousand men that arrived from the south next morning, under Major-General Holmes and Brigadier-General Ripley; they had been ordered to Richmond without my knowledge, nor was I informed of their approach.[1]

After this battle of Seven Pines—or Fair Oaks, as the Northern people prefer to call it—General McClellan made no step forward, but employed his troops industriously in intrenching themselves.

I had repeatedly suggested to the Administration the formation of a great army to repel McClellan's invasion, by assembling all the Confederate forces, available for the object, near Richmond. As soon as I had lost the command of the Army of Virginia by wounds in battle, my suggestion was adopted. In that way, the largest Confederate army that ever fought, was formed in the month of June, by strengthening the forces near Richmond with troops from North and South Carolina and Georgia. But, while the Confederate Government was forming this great army, the Federal general was, with equal industry, employed in making defensive arrangements; so that in the "seven days' fighting" his intrenchments so covered the operation of "change of base," that it was attended with little loss, considering the close proximity and repeated engagements of two

[1] Such information would have induced me to postpone the attack.

such armies. Had ours been so strengthened in time to attack that of the United States when it reached the Chickahominy, and before being intrenched, results might and ought to have been decisive; still, that army, as led by its distinguished commander, compelled the Federal general to abandon his plan of operations, and reduced him to the defensive, and carried back the war to Northern Virginia.

No action of the war has been so little understood as that of Seven Pines; the Southern people have felt no interest in it, because, being unfinished in consequence of the disabling of the commander, they saw no advantage derived from it; and the Federal commanders claimed the victory because the Confederate forces did not renew the battle on Sunday, and fell back to their camps on Monday.

General Sumner stated to the committee on the conduct of the war, that he had, in the battle of Fair Oaks, five or six thousand men in Sedgwick's division, part of Couch's, and a battery, and that, after the firing had continued some time, six regiments which he had in hand on the left of the battery charged directly into the woods; the enemy then fled, and the battle was over for that day.

General Heintzelman, before the same committee, claimed the victory at Seven Pines, upon no other ground that I can perceive, than the withdrawal of the Confederates to their camps on Monday, although his statement shows clearly that all his troops and Keyes's [1] that fought there were defeated, and driven back six or seven miles to the shelter of intrenchments previously prepared by his forethought; and

---

[1] Kearney's division; Hooker's was not engaged.

that they remained Sunday under the protection of these intrenchments while Hill was gathering the arms scattered in woods and thickets, more than two miles in extent.

The proofs against these claims are, that General McClellan, who had been advancing, although cautiously, up to the time of this battle, made no step forward after it, but employed his troops industriously in intrenching themselves, and that both of his subordinates—the commanders at Fair Oaks and on the Williamsburg road—stood on the defensive the day after the battle, while the Confederate right covered all the ground on which it fought the day before, and had leisure and confidence enough to devote much of the day to gathering the valuable military property, including arms, won the day before; and Smith's division, prolonging the line beyond the railroad and Fair Oaks, was confronting Sumner's corps.

General Sumner's extravagant statement, that six of his regiments charged and put to flight Smith's whole division, needs no comment. His estimate of his force on Saturday is not more accurate. According to it, there were in Sedgwick's division, which constituted half of his corps, less than five thousand men; consequently, his corps must have had in it less than ten thousand; and McClellan's army, of which that corps was a fifth, less than fifty thousand. As that army numbered a hundred and fifteen thousand men a month before, its number could not have been less than one hundred thousand, nor that of Sumner's corps less than twenty thousand; nor his force on Saturday, at Fair Oaks, less than thirteen or fourteen thousand.

General Sumner's corps was united at Fair Oaks Saturday evening. If he had driven Smith's division from the field in flight, it is not to be imagined that with at least twenty thousand men on the flank of the remaining Confederate troops, Longstreet's and Hill's, he would have failed to attack and destroy them on Sunday; for, being ranking officer, he could have united Heintzelman's and Keyes's corps to his own, and attacked the Confederates both in front and flank.

The claims of the same officers to decided successes on Sunday are disproved by what immediately precedes, and the reports of Generals Hill and Pickett. The chances of success on that day were all in favor of the Confederates. The numbers of the opposing forces were nearly equal. But three of the six Federal divisions had, successively, been thoroughly beaten the day before by five Confederate brigades.

The authors of Alfriend's "Life of Jefferson Davis," and some other biographers, represent, to my disparagement, that the army with which General Lee fought in "the seven days" was only that which I had commanded. It is very far from the truth. General Lee did not attack the enemy until the 26th of June, because he was employed, from the 1st until then, in forming a great army, by bringing, to that which I had commanded, fifteen thousand[1] men from North Carolina, under Major-General Holmes,[2] twenty-

---

[1] General Holmes told me in General Lee's presence, just before the fight began on the 31st, that he had that force ready to join me when the President should give the order. I have also the written testimony of Colonel Archer Anderson, then of General Holmes's staff, that he brought that number into General Lee's army.

[2] General Ripley gave me this number. He brought the first bri-

two thousand from South Carolina and Georgia, and above sixteen thousand from "the Valley" in the divisions of Jackson and Ewell, which the victories of Cross Keys and Port Republic had rendered disposable.

gade—five thousand men. General Lawton told me that his was six thousand, General Drayton that his was seven thousand; there was another brigade, of which I do not know the strength.

CHAPTER VI.

Report for Service at the War-Office.—Received Orders on November 24th.—
Correspondence with the War Department.—Colonel Morgan's Achievement
at Hartsville.—Meet the President at Chattanooga, and accompany him to
Mississippi.—Battle of Murfreesboro'.—Van Dorn attacked at Franklin.—
While *en route* to Mississippi, ordered to take direct Command of General
Bragg's Army.—Events in Mississippi.—General Pemberton's Dispatches.
—Battle near Port Gibson.—Ordered to Mississippi to take "Chief Com-
mand."

THE effects of the wounds received at Seven Pines
made me unfit for active military service until about
the 12th of November, when I reported for duty at
the war-office.

At that time General Lee's army had been reorganized, and was in high condition, and much
stronger than when it fought in Maryland; but that
to which it was opposed was much stronger in numbers. General Bragg had returned from his expedition into Kentucky, and was placing at Murfreesboro' the army he had received at Tupelo—outnumbered greatly, however, by the Federal forces in and
near Nashville, commanded by Major-General Rosecrans. Lieutenant-General Pemberton, recently appointed to command the Department of Mississippi
and East Louisiana, had garrisons thought to be
adequate, in Vicksburg and Port Hudson, and an active army of twenty-three thousand men[1] on the Tal-

[1] Lieutenant-General Pemberton's reports to me.

lahatchie, observing the Federal army of forty-five thousand men under Major-General Grant, between that river and Holly Springs.[1] In Arkansas, Lieutenant-General Holmes, who commanded the Trans-Mississippi Department, had a large army, supposed to amount to fifty-five thousand men, the main body, near Little Rock, opposed to no enemy, except garrisons at Helena, and perhaps one or two other points on the Mississippi.

Without actual assignment, I was told, on reporting, that the Government intended to place the Departments of Tennessee and Mississippi under my direction. This intimation justified me, I thought, in suggesting to the Secretary of War, General Randolph, that, as the Federal troops invading the Valley of the Mississippi were united under one commander, our armies for its defense should also be united, east of the Mississippi. By this junction, we should bring above seventy thousand men against forty-five thousand, and secure all the chances of victory, and even the destruction of the Federal army; which, defeated so far from its base, could have little chance of escape. That success would enable us to overwhelm Rosecrans, by joining General Bragg with the victorious army, and transfer the war to the Ohio River, and to the State of Missouri, in which the best part of the population was friendly to us. I visited him in his office for this purpose, and began to explain myself. Before I had finished, he asked me, with a smile, to listen to a few lines on the subject; and, opening a large letter-book, he read me a letter to Lieutenant-General Holmes, in which he directed

[1] Lieutenant-General Pemberton's reports to me.

GENERAL BRAXTON BRAGG

that officer to cross the Mississippi with his forces, and unite them with those of Lieutenant-General Pemberton. He then read me a note from the President, directing him to countermand his instructions to Lieutenant-General Holmes. A day or two after this, General Randolph retired from the War Department, to the great injury of the Confederacy.

On the 24th, I received orders of that date, assigning me to the command of the departments of General Bragg, Lieutenant-General E. Kirby Smith, and Lieutenant-General Pemberton.

I replied, on the same day: "I had the honor, this afternoon, to receive special orders, No. 225, of this date.

"If I have been correctly informed, the forces which it places under my command are greatly inferior in number to those of the enemy opposed to them, while in the Trans-Mississippi Department our army is very much larger than that of the United States. Our two armies on this side of the Mississippi have the disadvantage of being separated by the Tennessee River, and a Federal army (that of Major-General Grant) larger, probably, than either of them.

"Under such circumstances, it seems to me that our best course would be to fall upon Major-General Grant with the forces of Lieutenant-Generals Holmes and Pemberton, united for the purpose; those of General Bragg coöperating, if practicable.

"The defeat of General Grant would enable us to hold the Mississippi, and permit Lieutenant-General Holmes to move into Missouri.

"As our troops are now distributed, Vicksburg is in danger."

This suggestion was not adopted, nor noticed.

Several railroad accidents delayed me in my journey to Chattanooga—the location for my headquarters chosen by the War Department—so that I did not reach that place until the morning of the 4th of December.

A telegram from General Cooper, found there, informed me that Lieutenant-General Pemberton was falling back before superior forces, and that Lieutenant-General Holmes had been "peremptorily ordered" to reënforce him; but that, as Lieutenant-General Holmes's troops might be too late, the President urged upon me the importance of sending a sufficient force from General Bragg's command to Lieutenant-General Pemberton's aid.

I replied immediately, by telegraph as well as by mail, that the troops near Little Rock could join General Pemberton sooner than those in Middle Tennessee; and requested General Bragg, by telegraph, to detach a large body of cavalry to operate in General Grant's rear and cut his communications. On the following day, the 5th, at Murfreesboro', I again wrote to General Cooper by mail and by telegraph, giving him General Bragg's estimates of his own force and that of General Rosecrans, and endeavoring to show that he could not give adequate aid to General Pemberton without giving up Tennessee, adding, that troops from Arkansas could reach the scene of action in Mississippi much sooner than General Bragg's; and saying, besides, that I would not weaken the Army of Tennessee without express orders to do so. He was also informed that two thousand cavalry would be detached to break the Louisville and Nashville Railroad, and four thousand to operate on General Grant's communications.

On the 7th, Colonel J. H. Morgan achieved a very handsome feat of arms at Hartsville, where, with a portion of his cavalry and two regiments of Kentucky infantry, in all not much above fifteen hundred men, he attacked and defeated almost twice his number of Federal troops, taking eighteen hundred prisoners. In reporting this action on the 8th, I recommended his appointment to the grade of brigadier-general.

While engaged in acquainting myself with the condition of General Bragg's army, I was summoned by telegraph to Chattanooga to meet the President. On doing so, I found that the object of this meeting, on his part, was to confer with me in relation to transferring a strong body of troops from the Army of Tennessee to that of Mississippi. As the expression of my opinion, a copy of my letter to General Cooper from Murfreesboro', was given to him. Apparently he was not satisfied by it, for he went on to Murfreesboro' and consulted General Bragg, and determined to transfer nine thousand infantry and artillery of that army to Lieutenant-General Pemberton's command.

The President returned to Chattanooga in a few days, and directed me to give the orders necessary to carry his wishes into effect. Under those directions,[1] Major-General C. L. Stevenson was ordered to move by railroad, without delay, to Jackson, with his own division increased by a brigade of Major-General McCown's. These troops were named to me by his

[1] The order was given in the President's name, being his own act.

excellency himself. As soon as these orders had been given, he set off for Mississippi, desiring me to accompany him.

He arrived in Jackson in the morning of the 19th. Governor Pettus had just convened the Legislature, in order that the whole military force of the State might be brought out and added to the Confederate forces under Lieutenant-General Pemberton, which were utterly inadequate to the defense of the State, or to hold the Mississippi River. On the 20th, he went to Vicksburg, and was occupied there two days in examining the extensive but very slight intrenchments of the place. The usual error of Confederate engineering had been committed there. An immense intrenched camp, requiring an army to hold it, had been made instead of a fort requiring only a small garrison. In like manner the water-batteries had been planned to prevent the bombardment of the town, instead of to close the navigation of the river to the enemy; consequently the small number of heavy guns had been distributed along a front of two miles, instead of being so placed that their fire might be concentrated on a single vessel. As attack was supposed to be imminent, such errors could not be corrected.

It was reported in Vicksburg, the day of the President's arrival, that a division of General Holmes's army, of ten thousand men, was approaching from Little Rock. According to the estimate of Major-General M. L. Smith, a garrison of twelve thousand men was necessary to hold the place. He then had about half the number. From a map of Port Hudson which he showed me, that place seemed

to require a force almost as great to defend it. I
therefore proposed to the President that General
Holmes should be instructed to send twenty thousand of his troops to Mississippi, instead of the ten
thousand supposed to be on the way, because such
an additional force would have enabled us to put
adequate garrisons into Vicksburg and Port Hudson, by which we held the part of the Mississippi
between them, and to oppose General Grant with
an active force of forty thousand men. In writing
to the President on this subject, however, I expressed
again the opinion that Holmes's and Pemberton's
troops should be concentrated in Mississippi. The
President suggested to General Holmes, but did not
order him, to send the twenty thousand men asked
for. General Holmes, very properly, waited for orders.

From Vicksburg the President visited Lieutenant-General Pemberton's army, near Grenada, where
it was constructing intrenchments to contest the
passage of the Yallabusha River by the Federal
army. The front was so extensive, however, that it
is probably fortunate that the practicability of defending it was never tested. In conversing before
the President in relation to the defense of his department, Lieutenant-General Pemberton and myself
differed widely as to the mode of warfare best adapt-
ed to our circumstances.

On the 25th the President returned to Jackson,
accompanied by Lieutenant-General Pemberton as
well as myself.

On the 27th Major-General Loring, who was commanding at Grenada, reported that General Grant's

army, which had been advancing, was retiring, and in a few hours the immediate cause became known —the destruction of the Federal depot at Holly Springs, by Major-General Van Dorn. That officer, with three thousand cavalry, surprised the garrison at daybreak, took two thousand prisoners, and destroyed the large stores of provision and ammunition, and six thousand muskets.

The approach of the expedition against Vicksburg, under Major-General Sherman's command, being reported by Lieutenant-General Pemberton's scouts, the detachments of Stevenson's division were sent to that place as they arrived by railroad. The last of them did not reach Jackson until the 7th of January, although the management of the railroad trains was at least as good as usual in such cases.

After exhorting the Legislature, in a fervent address, to take all the measures necessary to enable the Governor to bring out the whole remaining military force of the State to aid the Confederate troops in the defense of its soil, Mr. Davis returned to Richmond.

Being convinced, before he left Jackson, that my command was little more than nominal, I so represented it to him, and asked to be assigned to a different one, on the ground that two armies far apart, like those of Mississippi and Tennessee, having different objects, and opposed to adversaries having different objects, could not be commanded by the same general. After reflection, he replied that the seat of government was so distant from the two theatres of war, that he thought it necessary to have an officer nearer, with authority to transfer troops from one army to the other in an emergency. If such an officer was needed, I certainly was not the proper selection; for I had already expressed the opinion distinctly that such transfers were impracticable, because each of the two armies was greatly inferior to its antagonist; and they were too far from each other for such mutual dependence. The length of time consumed in the transportation of Stevenson's division without artillery or wagons, from Tennessee to Mississippi, fully sustained this opinion. That time was more than three weeks.

Brigadier-General Forrest, who was detached by General Bragg to operate on Major-General Grant's rear, was very successful in breaking railroads in West Tennessee. After destroying large quantities of military stores also, and paroling twelve hundred prisoners, he was pressed back into Middle Tennessee by weight of numbers. At the same time, a body of Federal cavalry under Brigadier-General Carter, supposed to be fifteen hundred, burned the Holston and Watauga railroad bridges near Bristol.

As soon as Major-General Rosecrans was informed of the large detachment from the Confederate army of Tennessee to that of Mississippi, he prepared to take advantage of it, and on the 26th of December marched from Nashville toward Murfreesboro'. On his approach this movement was promptly reported to General Bragg by Brigadier-General Wheeler, who commanded his cavalry. In consequence of this intelligence the Confederate army was immediately concentrated in front of Murfreesboro'. It numbered about thirty thousand infantry and artillery in five divisions, and five thousand mounted troops.

On the 28th General Bragg reported to me by telegraph: "The enemy stationary within ten miles; my troops all ready and confident." And on the 30th: "Artillery firing at intervals, and heavy skirmishing all day. Enemy very cautious, and declining a general engagement. Both armies in line of battle within sight."

These lines were at right angles to the Nashville road. The Federal left rested on Stone's River. The Confederate right, Breckenridge's division, faced this left, and was separated from Polk's corps, forming the centre, by the little river, the course of which there crossed General Bragg's line obliquely. Hardee's corps constituted the left wing. Both armies were drawn up in two lines. The Federal, much the more numerous, had a strong reserve.

Both generals determined to attack in the morning of the 31st, and their plans of attack were similar—General Bragg's, to advance in echelon by his left, to drive the Federal right and centre behind their left and to the east of the Nashville road, and seize that line of retreat; and that of Major-General Rosecrans, to operate with his left leading, to drive the Confederate army to the west of the Murfreesboro' road, with a similar object.

Lieutenant-General Hardee's corps was in motion at dawn, and his attack made at sunrise by McCown's division, his first line; his second, Cleburne's division, coming up on its right and engaging the enemy soon after. The Federal troops, surprised and assailed with the skill and vigor that Hardee never failed to

LIEUTENANT-GENERAL WILLIAM J. HARDEE

exhibit in battle, were driven back, although formed in two lines, while the assailants were in but one. Their commander called for aid, and, very soon after, reported his wing being driven—"a fact that was but too manifest by the rapid movement of the noise of battle towards the north."[1]   The attack was taken up by the brigades of Polk's corps successively, from left to right, but they encountered a more determined resistance, and the success they obtained was won after an obstinate contest, and at the price of much blood.   When the right brigade of Polk's corps had become fully engaged, the Federal right and centre, except the left brigade,[2] had been driven back in the manner intended.   They were succored by Rousseau's and Van Cleve's divisions, however, and rallied on a new line perpendicular to the original one; their left joining the right of the brigade that still held its first position.   The Confederate troops could make no impression upon this new and stronger line which was covered by a railroad-cut, and the contest ceased, except at the angle where the new and old lines met. The brigade there, with the aid of several batteries and the advantages of a strong position and an ex- cellent commander,[3] repelled the successive attacks of two detachments of two brigades each, drawn from the Confederate right.[4]

The fight was not renewed.   On the 1st of Jan- uary it was found that the position assailed and de- fended so bravely, the previous afternoon, had been abandoned by the Federals.

[1] General Rosecrans's report.
[2] The left brigade of Palmer's division.
[3] Brigadier-General Hazen.   [4] Lieutenant-General Polk's report.

On the 2d, a division of the Federal left crossed Stone's River and took possession of a hill in front of the Confederate right, that commanded the right of Lieutenant-General Polk's position. Major-General Breckenridge was directed to drive the enemy from it with his division. He did so with less difficulty than might have been expected, although his troops in advancing to the attack were exposed to a well-directed fire of artillery while marching five or six hundred yards in open ground. They were not checked, however, by this cannonade, and closed with the Federal infantry with a spirit that drove them very soon down the hill and across the stream. But fresh troops in much stronger bodies, especially on the right, supported by as many batteries, apparently, as could be brought to bear, then advanced against the Confederates. The unequal struggle that ensued was soon ended by the defeat of the latter with severe loss, and the recovery of the contested hill by the enemy. Breckenridge's division resumed its former position at dusk.

During this engagement, the ground occupied on the 31st by Hazen's brigade was recovered by the enemy. In the morning of the 3d of January it was retaken by a detachment formed from Coltart's and White's brigades. A vigorous but ineffectual effort to dislodge this detachment was made by the Federals.

The armies faced each other without serious fighting during the remainder of the day. General Bragg was employed all the afternoon in sending his trains to the rear, and in other preparations to retire. The army was put in motion about mid-

LIEUTENANT-GENERAL LEONIDAS POLK

night, and marched quietly across Duck River, Polk's corps halting opposite to Shelbyville, and Hardee's at Tullahoma.

General Bragg estimates his force at thirty thousand infantry and artillery, and five thousand cavalry, and his loss at more than ten thousand, including twelve hundred severely wounded and three hundred sick, left in Murfreesboro'. He claims to have captured "over thirty pieces of artillery, six thousand prisoners, six thousand small-arms, nine colors, ambulances and other valuable property," and to have destroyed eight hundred loaded wagons.

Major-General Rosecrans reports that he had in his army forty-three thousand four hundred infantry and artillery, and three thousand three hundred cavalry; of whom nine thousand two hundred and sixty-seven were killed and wounded, and three thousand four hundred and fifty made prisoners—in all, twelve thousand seven hundred and seventeen.

While these events were occurring in Middle Tennessee, Major-General Sherman was operating against Vicksburg. He had embarked an army, estimated at thirty thousand men by Lieutenant-General Pemberton's scouts, on transports at Memphis, and, descending the Mississippi, ascended the Yazoo a few miles, and landed his troops on the southern shore on the 26th of December. Lieutenant-General Pemberton reported, the day after, that his lines had been attacked at four different points, and each attacking party handsomely repulsed. As his loss amounted to but five killed and fifteen wounded, these were probably reconnoissances rather than serious assaults. On the 29th, however, a real assault was made by a body of several thousand Federal troops, near Chickasaw Bayou, where Brigadier-General S. D. Lee commanded. That gallant soldier was successful in defeating the attempt with his brigade, inflicting a loss of eleven hundred upon the enemy, while his own was but a hundred and fifty.

On the 2d of January General Sherman reëmbarked and ran up to Milliken's Bend. His fleet of transports disappeared soon after.

Mississippi was thus apparently free from invasion, General Grant's forces having already reached the northern border of the State. The condition of the country was such, too, as to make military operations on a large scale in it impracticable; and the most intelligent class of the inhabitants supposed that it would remain in that condition until the middle of the spring. In Tennessee, on the contrary, after the most effective fighting made by either party up to that time, our army had lost much ground, and was in danger of further disaster. For, while the United States Government was sending such reënforcements as reëstablished the strength of its army, the Confederate War Department made no answer to General Bragg's calls for twenty thousand additional troops, which he required, he said, to enable him to hold the southern part of Middle Tennessee, which was still in his possession.

At this time Lieutenant-General Pemberton had some six thousand cavalry near Grenada, unemployed, and almost unorganized. Under the circumstances described, Major-General Van Dorn was directed to form a division of two-thirds of these troops, and to move into Tennessee, after preparing

it for the field. When there he was either to assist
General Bragg in holding his new position, or cover
the country near Columbia, upon which the army
depended for food. These troops were so poorly
equipped, and the difficulty of supplying deficiencies
so great, that the division was not ready for actual
service until February, nor able to cross the Tennessee until the middle of the month. It was directed to Columbia, and, by occupying that neighborhood, enabled General Bragg to feed his army in
Middle Tennessee. Without such aid he could not
have done this, and would have been compelled to
abandon the country north of the Tennessee River.

In the middle of January General Wheeler made
an expedition with the principal part of the cavalry
of the Army of Tennessee, to interrupt the Federal
communications. After burning the railroad-bridge
over Mill Creek, nine miles from Nashville, he went
on to the Cumberland and captured there four loaded
transports, three of which, with their cargoes, were
destroyed, and the fourth bonded to carry home four
hundred paroled prisoners. A gunboat which pursued the party was also captured with its armament.
General Wheeler then crossed the swollen stream,
the horses swimming through floating ice, and at the
landing-place near Harpeth Shoals destroyed a great
quantity of provisions in wagons, ready for transportation to Nashville.

While inspecting the defenses of Mobile on the
22d of January, I received a telegram from the President, directing me to proceed, "with the least delay,
to the headquarters of General Bragg's army," and
informing me that "an explanatory letter would be

found at Chattanooga." The object of this visit, as explained in the letter found in Chattanooga, was to ascertain the feeling toward the general entertained by the army—"whether he had so far lost its confidence as to impair his usefulness in his present position;" to obtain such information as would enable me "to decide what the best interests of the service required;" and "to give the President the advice which he needed at that juncture." Mr. Davis remarked, in this letter, that his own confidence in General Bragg was unshaken.

I bestowed three weeks upon this investigation, and then advised against General Bragg's removal, because the field-officers of the army represented that their men were in high spirits, and as ready as ever for fight; such a condition seeming to me incompatible with the alleged want of confidence in their general's ability.

On the 24th a fleet of transports, bearing the united forces of Generals Grant and Sherman, descending the Mississippi from Memphis, appeared near Vicksburg. This army did not repeat the attack upon the place from the Yazoo, but landed on the west side of the river, and commenced the excavation of a canal through the point of land opposite the town.

No military event worth mentioning occurred in either department in February. On the 5th of March Van Dorn's division was attacked, seven or eight miles south of Franklin, by the Federal garrison of that place, but repulsed the assailants, taking twenty-two hundred prisoners. Four or five days after this, however, this division was driven back to Columbia by the same troops largely reënforced; it escaped with difficulty, Duck River being considerably swollen.

As there were no indications of intention on the part of the Federal commander in Tennessee to take the offensive soon, and my presence seemed to me more proper in Mississippi than in Tennessee, I left Chattanooga for Jackson, on the 9th, and at Mobile, when continuing on the 12th the inspection interrupted by the President's telegram on the 22d of January, I received the following dispatch from the Secretary of War, dated March 9th: "Order General Bragg to report to the War Department here, for conference; assume yourself direct charge of the army in Middle Tennessee." In obedience to these instructions I returned immediately to Tennessee, and reached Tullahoma on the 18th, and there, without the publication of a formal order on the subject, assumed the duties of commander of the army. In consequence of information that the general was devoting himself to Mrs. Bragg, who was supposed to be at the point of death, I postponed the communication of the order of the Secretary of War to him, and reported the postponement, and the cause, to the Secretary.

The day after my arrival, dispatches from Lieutenant-General Pemberton informed me that the United States naval officers on the Lower Mississippi had ascertained the practicability of passing the Confederate batteries at Port Hudson with their iron-clad gunboats; two of them, the Hartford and Albatross, having passed those batteries on the 15th, while they were engaged with the other vessels of Admiral

Farragut's squadron. The success of this attempt greatly reduced the value of the two posts, Vicksburg and Port Hudson, by which we had been hoping to retain the command of the part of the river between them.

I soon found myself too feeble to command an army, and in a few days became seriously sick; so that, when the state of General Bragg's domestic affairs permitted him to return to military duty, I was unfit for it. He, therefore, resumed the position of commander of the Army of Tennessee.

In the latter part of the winter Lieutenant-General Pemberton had reason to apprehend that the enemy would attempt to approach Vicksburg through the Yazoo Pass, Coldwater, Tallahatchie, and Yazoo, and directed Major-General Loring, with an adequate body of troops, to select and intrench a position to frustrate such an attempt. That officer constructed Fort Pemberton in consequence of these orders, very judiciously located near the junction of the Yallobusha with the Tallahatchie,[1] with the usual accessory, a raft to obstruct the channel of the latter.

On the 11th the Federal flotilla appeared, descending the Tallahatchie.—nine gunboats, two of which, the Chillicothe and De Kalb, were iron-clads, and twenty transports bearing four thousand five hundred infantry and artillery. The gunboats opened their fire upon the Confederate works very soon and continued it for several hours. The 12th was devoted by the enemy to the construction of a battery on land, and on the 13th a spirited cannonade was maintained against Fort Pemberton by this battery

[1] Major-General Loring's report.

and the gunboats. It was resumed next morning, but ceased in half an hour. The contest was renewed on the 16th, and continued until night, when it ceased finally. The enemy was inactive until the 20th, probably repairing the damages their vessels had suffered. The flotilla then withdrew and returned to the Mississippi.

Until the end of the month Lieutenant-General Pemberton's dispatches represented that General Grant's troops were at work industriously digging a canal opposite to Vicksburg; his design being, evidently, to turn the Confederate batteries in that way, and reach a landing-place below the town, to attack it from the south. On the 3d of April, however, he reported that the Federal army was preparing for reëmbarkation; the object of which, he thought, might be to reënforce General Rosecrans in Middle Tennessee. In the reply to this dispatch, he was instructed to return Stevenson's division, or send an equal number of other troops to General Bragg, should he discover that his surmise was correct.

On the 11th General Pemberton expressed the opinion that "most of General Grant's forces were being withdrawn to Memphis;" and said that he was assembling troops at Jackson; and was then ready to send four thousand to Tennessee. This dispatch was received on the 13th, and on the same day he was desired to send forward the troops. In another telegram of that date, after announcing that he would send General Bragg eight thousand men, he added, "I am satisfied that Rosecrans will be reënforced from General Grant's army."

On the 16th, however, General Pemberton expressed the belief that no large part of Grant's army would be sent away. For that reason he thought it proper to transfer then but two brigades from his army to that of Tennessee. His dispatches, of the 17th, gave intelligence of the return of the Federal army [1] to its former position, and resumption of its operations against Vicksburg. He also reported that a body of Federal troops occupied New Carthage, and that there were nine gun-boats, of the two Federal fleets, between Port Hudson and Vicksburg.

In consequence of this information, the two brigades of infantry, under General Buford, on the way from Mississippi to Tennessee, were ordered to return.

The only activity apparent in either of the principal armies, before the end of March, was exhibited by that of General Grant, in its efforts to open a way by water around Vicksburg, to some point on the river, below the town. But in the beginning of April this enterprise was abandoned, and General Grant decided that his troops should march to a point selected, on the west bank of the Mississippi, and that the vessels-of-war and transports should run down to that point, passing the Confederate batteries at night. McClernand's corps (Thirteenth) led in the march, followed, at some distance, by McPherson's (Seventeenth).

About the middle of the month a Federal detachment of five regiments of cavalry, and two of infantry, with two field-batteries, moved from Corinth along the railroad towards Tuscumbia. Colonel Rod-

---

[1] Probably Sherman's corps, left to divert General Pemberton's attention from the movement towards Grand Gulf.

LIEUTENANT-GENERAL U. S. GRANT

dy, who had just been transferred from General
Bragg's to General Pemberton's command, met it
with his brigade, on the 18th, near Bear Creek, on
the Alabama side, and, in skirmishes, which continued most of the day, captured above a hundred prisoners, and a field-piece and caisson, with their horses.

The enemy waited until the next day for reënforcements, which increased their force to three full
brigades, under General Dodge, and resumed their
movement towards Tuscumbia, opposed at every step
by Roddy, who skirmished so effectively with the
head of the column as to make the rate of marching
not more than five miles a day; until the 25th, when
Tuscumbia was reached.

In the mean time a body of Federal troops landed
at Eastport, on the south bank of the Tennessee, and
burned the little town and several plantation-houses
in the neighborhood.

General Dodge's division moved on slowly, pressing back Roddy to Town Creek, where, on the 28th,
Forrest, with his brigade, joined Roddy. Near that
place the Federal forces divided; the cavalry, under
Colonel Streight, turning off to the south, towards
Moulton, and the main body, under General Dodge,
halting, and then marching back. Leaving Roddy
to observe Dodge, Forrest pursued Streight's party
with three regiments, and captured it within twenty
miles of Rome, after a chase of five days, and repeated
fights, in which he killed and wounded three hundred of the enemy. Fourteen hundred and sixty or
seventy officers and privates surrendered to him, a
number much exceeding that of the victors.

In writing to the President on the 10th of the

month, I informed him of my continued illness and inability to serve in the field, and added, " General Bragg is therefore necessary here." A similar report of the condition of my health was made on the 28th, to the Secretary of War.

While Forrest and Roddy were engaged with Dodge and Streight, Colonel Grierson made a raid entirely through Mississippi. Leaving Lagrange April 17th, with a brigade of cavalry, and passing through Pontotoc and Decatur, he reached the Southern Railroad at Newton on the 24th, where he destroyed some cars and engines, and small bridges. Crossing Pearl River at Georgetown, he struck the New Orleans and Jackson Railroad at Hazelhurst, where cars were destroyed, and some ammunition. At Brookhaven, the railroad-depot and more cars were burned, and the party arrived at Baton Rouge May 2d.

In the night of April 16th the Federal fleet, of gunboats and three transports towing barges, passed the batteries of Vicksburg, and ran down to " Hard Times," where the land-forces were; and in the night of the 22d six more transports and barges followed. The whole effect of the artillery of the batteries on the two occasions was the burning of one transport, sinking of another, and rendering six barges unserviceable.

General Grant's design seems to have been to take Grand Gulf by a combined military and naval attack, and operate against Vicksburg from that point. The squadron, under Admiral Porter, opened its fire upon the Confederate intrenchments at 8 A. M. on the 29th, and the Thirteenth Corps was held in

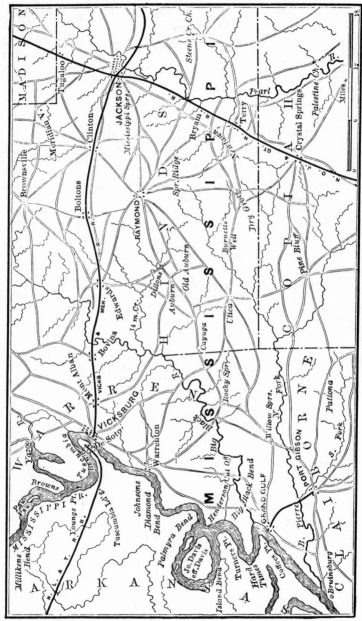

CAMPAIGN IN MISSISSIPPI.

readiness to land and storm them as soon as their
guns should be silenced. As that object had not
been accomplished at six o'clock in the afternoon,
General Grant abandoned the attempt, and determined to land at Bruinsburg. For this purpose
the troops debarked at Hard Times, and marched
to the plain below Grand Gulf; and the gunboats
and transports, passing that place in the night, as
they had done at Vicksburg, were in readiness at
daybreak next morning to ferry the troops to Bruinsburg, six miles. The number of vessels was sufficient
to transport a division at a time.

General Pemberton reported to me, by telegraph,
that day: "The enemy is at Hard Times in large
force, with barges and transports, indicating a purpose to attack Grand Gulf, with a view to Vicksburg.
Very heavy firing at Grand Gulf; enemy shelling
our batteries from above and below."

At that time, according to General Pemberton's
reports to me, more than twenty vessels, most of them
gunboats, had passed the Confederate batteries, and
were ready to aid the Federal army in its passage of
the river.

Brigadier-General Bowen, who commanded at
Grand Gulf, observing the movement of the Federal
forces down the river, and their landing at Bruinsburg, placed Green's and Tracy's brigades on the
route from that point into the interior, four miles in
advance of Port Gibson. Here they were encountered and attacked early in the morning of the 1st of
May, by the four divisions of McClernand's corps,
which had crossed the river in the day and night of
the 30th of April, and at once moved forward.

Although outnumbered five to one, Bowen was enabled to hold his ground until late in the afternoon, ten hours, by his own skill and courage, and the excellent conduct of Brigadier-Generals Tracy and Green, and the firmness of their troops—aided greatly, it is true, by the strength of the position, intersected by deep ravines and covered with fallen timber, and bushes interlaced with vines. He then began to fall back, but, being reënforced by Baldwin's brigade, which had marched twenty miles to join him, he halted and again formed for battle, supposing, probably, that the whole Confederate army was advancing to meet the enemy, but the Federal commander did not renew the engagement.

General Bowen reported that his loss in this action was severe in killed and wounded, but slight in prisoners; among the first was the gallant Tracy, whose death was much regretted by the army.

While the troops were engaged, General Pemberton telegraphed to me: "A furious battle has been going on since daylight, just below Port Gibson. . . . General Bowen says he is outnumbered trebly. . . . Enemy can cross all his army from Hard Times to Bruinsburg. . . . I should have large reënforcements. . . . Enemy's success in passing our batteries has completely changed character of defense." In the reply, dispatched immediately, he was told: "If General Grant's army lands on this side of the river, the safety of the Mississippi depends on beating it. For that object you should unite your whole force." In a telegram, dispatched to him next day, the instruction was repeated: "If Grant's army crosses, unite all your troops to beat him; success will give you back what was abandoned to win it."

General Pemberton's call for large reënforcements was transmitted by telegraph to the War Department forthwith, and I added, " They cannot be sent from here without giving up Tennessee."

On the 2d Bowen was pressed back through Port Gibson, but in perfect order; and returned to his post—Grand Gulf. On the 3d, however, finding his position turned, he abandoned it, after spiking his guns and blowing up his magazine, and marched to Hankinson's Ferry, to cross the Big Black there. General Loring, coming to his assistance with a division from Jackson, by Edwards's Depot, sent a detachment to hold Grindstone Ford, and turned to join him at the ferry. All their troops crossed the river that day unmolested, and rejoined General Pemberton.

To divert General Pemberton's attention from his real design, General Grant had left the Fifteenth Corps and a division at Milliken's Bend, under General Sherman, to make a demonstration against Vicksburg from the side of the Yazoo. This was executed by a slight attack upon Haynes's Bluff on the 30th of April, repeated next morning; after which General Sherman returned to Milliken's Bend, and marched from that point to rejoin the army.

The union of the Thirteenth and Seventeenth Corps was completed on the 3d, near Willow Spring, where they waited for Sherman's troops until the 8th. The army then moved forward on two parallel roads, the Thirteenth on one, the Seventeenth on the other, abreast, the Fifteenth following on both; the Thirteenth turned into the road to Edwards's Depot, however, while the Seventeenth kept that to Jackson, followed at an interval of a few miles by the Thir. teenth.

On the 5th, as Lieutenant-General Pemberton's dispatches subsequent to that of the 1st had contained no reference to the movements of the Federal army, nor to the result of the battle near Port Gib-son, I asked him to give me information on the two points. His reply, written on the 6th or 7th, contained no allusion to General Grant's forces, but gave his own positions, in cipher, so that they were imperfectly understood. He informed me, however, that General Bowen had been driven from the field with a loss of six or seven hundred men. I was thus left uncertain whether or not any but a detach-ment of the Federal forces had crossed the Missis-sippi.

On the 9th, in the evening, I received, at Tulla-homa, the following dispatch of that date from the Secretary of War: " Proceed at once to Mississippi and take chief command of the forces there, giving to those in the field, as far as practicable, the encour-agement and benefit of your personal direction. Ar-range to take for temporary service with you, or to be followed without delay, three thousand good troops who will be substituted in General Bragg's army by a large number of prisoners returned from the Arkansas Post capture, and reorganized, now on their way to General Pemberton. Stop them at the point most convenient to General Bragg.

" You will find reënforcements from General Beau-regard to General Pemberton, and more may be ex-

pected. Acknowledge receipt." I replied at once:
" Your dispatch of this morning received. I shall
go immediately, although unfit for field-service."

I had been prevented, by the orders of the Administration, from giving my personal attention to
military affairs in Mississippi [1] at any time since the
22d of January. On the contrary, those orders had
required my presence in Tennessee during the whole
of that period

[1] The reader's attention is called to this fact, because I have been
accused of neglecting Mississippi, to give my time to Tennessee.

CHAPTER VII.

Start for Mississippi.—Dispatch from General Pemberton.—Arrival at Jackson.
—Movements of the Enemy.—Orders to General Pemberton.—Battle of
Baker's Creek.—Retreat of General Pemberton across the Big Black to
Vicksburg. — Letter from General Pemberton.—Order him to evacuate
Vicksburg.—Investment of Vicksburg by the Enemy.—Port Hudson in-
vested.—Siege of Vicksburg.—Telegraphic Correspondence with the Presi-
dent and Secretary of War.—Move to the Relief of General Pemberton.—
Receive News of the Fall of Vicksburg.—Army retires to Jackson.

I SET out for Mississippi on the first train that left
Tullahoma, after the order of the Secretary of War was
received. It was in the morning of the 10th of May.

The intelligence of the assassination of the gal-
lant Van Dorn had been received, and General
Bragg and myself joined in recommending General
Forrest as his successor.

At Lake Station, in Mississippi, on the 13th, a
dispatch from Lieutenant-General Pemberton, dated
Vicksburg, May 12th, was sent to me from the telegraph-office.

I was informed in it that " the enemy is apparently moving in heavy force toward Edwards's
Depot, on Southern Railroad.[1] With my limited
force I will do all I can to meet him. That will be
the battle-field, if I can carry forward sufficient force,
leaving troops enough to secure the safety of this

[1] McClernand's Thirteenth Corps was apparently mistaken for the
" heavy force."

place. Reënforcements are arriving very slowly—
only fifteen hundred having arrived as yet. I
urgently ask that more be sent. Also that three
thousand cavalry be at once sent to operate on this
line. I urge this as a positive necessity. The enemy largely outnumbers me; and I am obliged to
keep a considerable force on either flank of Vicksburg out of supporting distance."

This telegram contained the first mention of the
Federal army made to me by Lieutenant-General
Pemberton, since that he dispatched while the con-
test at Port Gibson was going on.

In the mean time, Lieutenant-General Pemberton
had ordered Gregg's brigade coming from Port Hudson to Raymond, and W. H. T. Walker's, just arrived at Jackson, from General Beauregard's department, to join him there. On the 12th, McPherson
with his corps encountered Gregg near Raymond,
and drove him back, after a spirited resistance, considering that it was made by a brigade against a
corps.[1] He fell back to Jackson, in conformity to
General Pemberton's instructions for such a case,
accompanied by Walker, whom he met at Mississippi
Springs. They reached the place with their brigades on the evening of the 13th.

General Gregg, the senior of the two, reported
to me on my arrival at night.[2] He informed me
that he had learned from Colonel Wirt Adams, who

---

[1] In the Northern official statement, this affair is greatly exaggerated. Its effects were trifling, on the numbers as well as on the spirits of
Gregg's brigade, which joined me less than two days after it. The loss
of Colonel Randal McGavock, Tenth Tennessee regiment, who fell gallantly in this action, was much regretted.

[2] *See* telegram to Secretary of War, Appendix.

with his cavalry was observing the enemy's movements, that Lieutenant-General Pemberton's active forces were at Edwards's Depot, and his headquarters at Bovina; that McPherson's corps had marched from Raymond to Clinton; and was thus interposed between the Army of Mississippi and ourselves, and but ten miles from us. General Maxey's brigade, he added, was expected to reach Jackson in the course of the next day, from Port Hudson. I had learned, on the way, that reënforcements were coming from General Beauregard's department, and that the foremost of them, under Brigadier-General Gist, might join us next day, and, with Maxey's brigade, would raise the force at Jackson to eleven or twelve thousand men.

Under the impression given me by General Pemberton's dispatch of the 12th, that the main body of General Grant's army was to the south of Edwards's Depot, I inferred that McPherson's corps had been *detached* to Clinton to hold the Confederate line of communication, and prevent the junction of reënforcements with the army. I therefore sent a note[1] to that officer by Captain Yerger, who happened to be in Jackson and volunteered to bear it, informing him of the position of McPherson's corps between us at Clinton; urging the importance of reëstablishing his communications, that reënforcements might join his army, and ordering, "if practicable come up on his rear at once. To beat such a detachment would be of immense value. The troops here could coöperate. All the force you can quickly assemble should be brought. Time is all-important."

[1] *See* the note in Appendix.

Early next morning it was reported that another Federal corps, Sherman's, was on the Raymond road, twelve miles from Jackson; and, soon after, intelligence was received that both it and McPherson's were marching toward the place, one on each road. A brigade was sent forward to meet each corps, to delay the enemy's approach by skirmishing with the heads of the two columns. The resistance offered in this way so impeded the progress of the Federal troops as to give ample time for the evacuation of the place, and the removal of such military property as we had the means of transporting.[1] Fortunately, Major Mims, the chief quartermaster of the department, was in Jackson; and, foreseeing, from the intelligence received the day before, that a movement was inevitable, had begun at once to prepare for it.

Orders were sent to Brigadier-Generals Gist and Maxey, for the security of the troops under their respective commands. The train, loaded, left the town by the Canton road before two o'clock; and the two brigades were called in, and followed it, and encamped about five miles from the town. This road was chosen because its direction was more favorable than that of any other for effecting a junction with the Army of Mississippi.

While Sherman's and McPherson's corps were moving upon Jackson, McClernand's divisions were

[1] In the Federal official report, their skirmishing with Gregg's and Walker's brigades is exaggerated into a heavy engagement of two hours, in which the Confederate main body was badly beaten and pursued until night. On the contrary, the skirmishing was trifling, and there was nothing like pursuit—into Jackson even. And no body of Federal soldiers was discovered by our rear-guard and reconnoitring-party between Jackson and our camp.

ordered to Raymond, Mississippi Springs, and Clinton.

From the events of the 14th, I supposed that General Grant intended to occupy Jackson and hold it, to prevent the troops then there, and those coming from the East, from joining Lieutenant-General Pemberton's army. That army, including the garrison of Vicksburg, was probably about thirty-two thousand men.

In the evening of that day a letter was addressed to General Pemberton, to inform him of the events of the day, and of the instructions given to Brigadier-Generals Gist and Maxey. The hope was also expressed in it that those troops would be able to prevent General Grant's forces, in Jackson, from obtaining supplies from the East; and that the troops on the Canton road might keep those of the country to the north from them. He was asked if he could close their communication with the Mississippi, and, above all, if he could beat them, should they be compelled, by want of supplies, to fall back. He was told, also, that prisoners reported that the force in Jackson constituted half of Grant's army, and that it would decide the campaign to beat it; which could be done only by concentrating, especially when the troops expected from the East should arrive.

This letter was not answered. I found the explanation of this in Lieutenant-General Pemberton's report. It was not delivered to him until after the battle of Baker's Creek—too late to influence his action.

On the 15th the march of Gregg's and Walker's troops was continued ten miles, to Calhoun Station.

While on the way, at ten o'clock A. M., a letter to me, from General Pemberton, was delivered by Captain Yerger. It was dated Edwards's Depot, 5.40 P. M., May 14th, and contained no reference to mine of the 13th, carried to him by that gentleman, and delivered, he told me, about 7 A. M., on the 14th. In this note General Pemberton announced that he would "move as early as practicable on the 15th, with a column of seventeen thousand men, to Dillon's, on the main road from Jackson to Port Gibson, "for the purpose of" cutting the enemy's communications," and compelling them to attack him, as he did not think his force sufficient to justify him in attacking.

The fact that this letter was written almost eleven hours after my order had been delivered, and announced continued inaction for many more, when every hour was so important, was very discouraging, especially when the movement for which the preparations seemed to be made so deliberately would greatly increase the difficulty of our junction. In a reply, written and dispatched without delay, General Pemberton was told that the only mode by which we could unite was by his moving directly to Clinton and informing me, that I might meet him there with about six thousand men.

As the brigadier-generals represented that their troops required rest after the fatigue they had undergone in the skirmishes and marches of the last five or six days, and we wanted such intelligence from General Pemberton as would enable us to meet him, we were stationary on the 16th.

In the afternoon of that day, a reply to my first dispatch to General Pemberton was received, dated

Bovina, 9.10 o'clock A. M., of the 14th. It was to inform me that he would move at once, in obedience to my order, with his whole available force. He said, in conclusion : "In directing this move, I do not think you fully comprehend the position that Vicksburg will be left in.¹ But I comply at once with your order." General Pemberton's letter of a later date, received the day before, showed that my order, referred to, had been set aside.

In the evening, a reply to my dispatch of the 15th was received from General Pemberton, dated four miles south of Edwards's Depot, eight o'clock A. M., May 16th, saying that my note was received at 6.30 A. M., and that it found the army on the middle road to Raymond, and that the order to counter-march had been given. Then followed a minute and clear description of the route he intended to take, to direct my course in marching to meet him. He added, in a postscript, "Heavy skirmishing is now going on in our front."

General Grant had been told in Jackson, on the 14th, that Lieutenant-General Pemberton had been ordered peremptorily to march from Edwards's Depot to attack him in rear. He determined, therefore, to concentrate his own forces and fall upon General Pemberton's. For that object, McPherson with two divisions at Jackson, McClernand with three at Raymond, Hovey with one at Clinton, and Blair with one at New Auburn, were ordered, on the 15th, to march to Bolton's Depot, eight miles from Edwards's.

¹ It had a garrison of more than two divisions, quite sufficient to make it safe, while a Confederate army was employing that of General Grant, and was between it and Vicksburg.

After receiving, at Bovina, early in the morning of the 14th, my order of the night before, directing him to march upon Clinton, General Pemberton rode to the camp of his army just south of Edwards's Depot, and convened a council of war, composed of his general officers, to which he exhibited my note, making a long argument against obedience to the order expressed in it.[1] A majority of the members of the council voted for moving upon Clinton in obedience to orders. A minority advocated a plan for seizing the enemy's communications by placing the army on the road from Jackson and Raymond to Port Gibson, to compel General Grant to attack it. Although averse to both opinions, General Pemberton adopted that of the minority of his council,[2] and determined to execute a measure which he disapproved, which his council of war opposed, and which was in violation of the orders of his commander.

Twenty-four hours after the adoption of this resolution, in the afternoon of the 15th, the army commenced its march, and, after crossing Baker's Creek, encamped near Champion Hill, some three miles from the ground it had left. It had been compelled to march twice as far, however, by the destruction of a bridge by a flood in Baker's Creek.

General Pemberton was informed at night, that the camp of a strong body of Federal troops was near, in the direction of Bolton.[3] The fires were distinctly visible. It was that of Hovey's division, of the Thirteenth Corps.

Early in the morning of the 16th, Lieutenant-

---

[1] Lieutenant-General Pemberton's official report.   [2] Ibid.
[3] Ibid.

General Pemberton received my order of the day before, and prepared to obey it[1] by directing Major-General Stevenson to have the baggage-train turned and moved as rapidly as possible across Baker's Creek on the road by which they had advanced the day before. While the troops were waiting for the clearing of the road by this movement, that they might take the same direction, Colonel Wirt Adams's cavalry-pickets were attacked by the skirmishers of the Federal division; upon which Lieutenant-General Pemberton formed his three divisions for battle on a line extending from the Raymond to the Clinton road—Loring's division on the right, Bowen's in the centre, and Stevenson's on the left.

In this position the Confederate troops remained passive before a single division of the enemy some five hours[2]—until near noon—when they were attacked by General Grant, who had then completed the concentration of his forces, uninterrupted by his adversary.

When McPherson, with two divisions, had come up, and McClernand with four, including Blair's of Sherman's corps, was within an hour's march of the field, the action was begun by Hovey's division, which assailed the left and centre of Stevenson's. Logan's division, moving by the right of Hovey's, passed the left of Stevenson's line as if to take it in reverse. Stevenson transferred Barton's brigade from his right to the left rear to meet this movement, while with Cumming's and Lee's he opposed Hovey's attack.

[1] At sunrise. (*See* General Stevenson's report.)
[2] General Grant says the action commenced at eleven o'clock—Lieutenant-General Pemberton says about noon.

This opposition was so effective that General Hovey
called for aid, and McPherson's other division, Quimby's, was sent to his assistance. In the mean time
Logan had engaged Barton, and Stevenson's three
brigades were forced back by the three Federal
divisions; and at two o'clock they had lost the
ground on which they had just stood, many men,
and much of their artillery. Lieutenant-General
Pemberton restored the fight by bringing Bowen's
division, unemployed till then, to the assistance of
Stevenson's.

In the mean time, General McClernand, with his
four divisions, had been confronting Loring—not ven-
turing to attack, on account of the strength of the
Confederate position, while Loring felt himself well
employed in holding four divisions of the enemy in
check with his single one.

After bringing Bowen's troops into action, General
Pemberton directed Loring to join in it with at least
a part of his. That officer, for some time, did not
obey, from the consideration that his movement
would be followed by that of the corps that he had
been keeping out of action, and our defeat thus made
certain.

Stevenson's and Bowen's troops, and the reserve
artillery, well placed and served under the direction
of Colonel W. E. Withers, its commander, maintained
the contest until four o'clock; then the battle seemed
to be so completely lost that retreat was ordered.
The withdrawal of the troops that had been engaged
was covered by Loring with his division; Featherston's and Buford's brigades protecting Stevenson's
and Bowen's divisions in their retreat; and Tilgh-

man's resisting the advance of the enemy by the Raymond road. Tilghman himself fell in this duty, while encouraging his troops, when hardest pressed, by his brave example.

By the time that Stevenson's and Bowen's divisions had crossed Baker's Creek, the Federal troops were so near the stream as to render its passage by Loring's division impracticable; so that officer marched southward, and, after passing entirely beyond the enemy's left, turned to the east and led his division to Jackson.

Lieutenant-General Pemberton directed the retreat of Stevenson's division across the Big Black to Bovina, near which it bivouacked about one o'clock; but he halted Bowen's troops at a line of rifle-pits, three-quarters of a mile in advance of the railroad-bridge; this line had been occupied for several days by Vaughn's brigade, which Bowen's troops found in it.

The object of this measure was to defend the bridge to enable Loring's division to cross the Big Black.

In the morning of the 17th the Confederates were attacked in these lines by General Grant, with McPherson's and McClernand's corps. His vigorous assault was scarcely resisted, either because the Confederates had become disheartened by recent events; or else, feeling the danger of fighting a victorious enemy with a river behind them, each was eager to secure his own escape by being the first to reach the bridge. Sixteen or eighteen field-pieces were abandoned. After crossing the river on the railroad-bridge and a temporary one near it, these troops were conducted to Vicksburg by Major-General Stevenson, with his own division. They left the west bank of the Big Black about ten o'clock A. M., after destroying the bridges. This was by Lieutenant-General Pemberton's command.

The Federal army crossed the river on the 18th; McPherson's and McClernand's corps on floating-bridges, constructed by them near the railroad, and Sherman's, which left Jackson on the 16th, on a pontoon-bridge laid at Bridgeport. Its advanced troops skirmished in the afternoon with those in the field-works of Vicksburg,[1] and the investment of the place was completed on the 19th.[2]

On the 17th the two brigades with me marched fifteen or eighteen miles in the direction pointed out in Lieutenant-General Pemberton's note of the day before, and bivouacked on the road leading from Livingston to Edwards's Depot. Supposing that the Army of Mississippi had marched the day before by the route the general had described, I was confident that we should meet it that day, or early in the next. At night, however, Captain Henderson, who was the commander of General Pemberton's scouts, brought me a letter from that officer, written at Bovina in the morning, in which he said: "I notified you, on the morning of the 14th, of the receipt of your instructions to move and attack the enemy toward Clinton. I deemed the movement very hazardous, preferring to remain in position behind the Big Black, and near to Vicksburg. I called a council of war composed of all the general officers who were then with my movable army, and, placing the

[1] General Grant's report.   [2] Ibid.

subject before them (including your instructions) in every view in which it appeared to me, asked their opinions respectively. A majority of the officers expressed themselves favorable to the movement indicated by you. The others, including Major-Generals Loring and Stevenson, preferred a movement by which this army might endeavor to cut off the enemy's supplies from the Mississippi. My own views were expressed as unfavorable to any movement which would remove me from my base, which was, and is, Vicksburg. I did not, however, see fit to place my own judgment and opinions so far in opposition as to prevent the movement altogether; but, believing the only possibility of success to be in the plan proposed, of cutting off the enemy's supplies, I directed all my disposable force, say seventeen thousand five hundred, toward Raymond or Dillon's, encamping on the night of the 15th at Mrs. Ellison's, on the main Raymond and Edwards's Depot road, at a fork from which I could advance either to Raymond or Dillon's." Then came a brief account of the circumstances of the battle of Baker's Creek, and his retreat to the Big Black River, after which he continued: "I am, for the present, holding the Big Black bridge, where a heavy cannonading is now going on. There are so many points by which I can be flanked that I fear I shall be compelled to withdraw; if so, the position at Snyder's Mill will also be untenable. General Tilghman was killed yesterday. I have about sixty days' rations in Vicksburg and Snyder's Mill. I respectfully await your orders."

Soon after reading this letter, I received, from good but unofficial sources, intelligence that the army had abandoned the line of the Big Black River, and fallen back to Vicksburg. On this information my fourth order to Lieutenant-General Pemberton was dispatched. It was this: " If Haynes's Bluff is untenable, Vicksburg is of no value and cannot be held ; if, therefore, you are invested in Vicksburg you must ultimately surrender. Under such circumstances, instead of losing both troops and place, we must, if possible, save the troops. If it is not too late, evacuate Vicksburg and its dependencies, and march to the northeast."

I should have joined Lieutenant-General Pemberton's " movable army," and taken command of it, if at any time after my arrival in Jackson I had been strong enough to attempt such a ride.

In the hope that my order for the evacuation of Vicksburg would be obeyed, I directed that the two brigades with me should move to the northwest, to expedite their junction with Lieutenant-General Pemberton's troops. When about to mount my horse next morning, for the day's march, I received a dispatch from General Pemberton, dated Vicksburg, May 17th, in which he reported that the army had been driven from its position on the Big Black River, "owing to the demoralization consequent upon the retreat of yesterday," and "fallen back to the line of intrenchments around Vicksburg." In concluding his note the writer said: "I greatly regret that I felt compelled to make the advance beyond the Big Black, which has proved so disastrous in its results." This sentence, and the similar one in his previous dispatch of the same day, seemed designed to convey the impression that I " compelled him to cross the Big

Black River from the west. His telegram of the 12th,[1] dispatched before I entered Mississippi, and his official report,[2] prove that before I reached Jackson, where my first order to him was written, he had established his "movable army" six or seven miles "beyond" the river; and a large detachment (two brigades) near Raymond, twelve or fourteen miles still farther east. Those papers prove, also, that he had crossed the Big Black to give battle to the enemy, and expected Edwards's Depot to be the battle-field.

Early on the 19th, when near Vernon, I received Lieutenant-General Pemberton's reply to my note, conveying to him the order to evacuate Vicksburg. It was dated May 18th. After acknowledging the receipt of that order, General Pemberton said : " On the receipt of your communication, I immediately assembled a council of war of the general officers of this command, and having laid your instructions before them, asked the free expression of their opinions as to the practicability of carrying them out. The opinion was unanimously expressed that it was impossible to withdraw the army from this position with such *morale* and material as to be of further use to the Confederacy. While the council of war was assembled, the guns of the enemy opened on the works. . . . I have decided to hold Vicksburg as long as possible, with the firm hope that the Government may yet be able to assist me in keeping this obstruction to the enemy's free navigation of the Mississippi River. I still conceive it to be the most important point in the Confederacy."

Such an estimate of the military value of Vicks-

---

[1] *See* page 174.   [2] *See* General Pemberton's report, page 33.

burg, expressed five or six weeks earlier, might not have seemed unreasonable; for then the commanders of the United States squadrons believed, apparently, that its batteries were too formidable to be passed by their vessels-of-war. But, when Lieutenant-General Pemberton wrote the letter quoted from, those batteries had been proved to be ineffective, for Admiral Porter's squadron had passed them, and in that way had made "the severance of the Confederacy," before the end of April, that General Pemberton apprehended would be permitted, if he obeyed my order, to save his army by withdrawing it to the northeast, on the 18th of May.

In my reply to this letter, dispatched promptly, I said: "I am trying to gather a force which may attempt to relieve you. Hold out."

On the same day instructions were sent to Major-General Gardner, both by telegraph and by courier, to evacuate Port Hudson, and march toward Jackson.

After General Pemberton's investment in Vicksburg, there was no longer an object for moving to the northwest; Gregg's and Walker's brigades were, therefore, ordered to march to Canton, that they might be joined by the reënforcements expected from the East, and where, while being equipped for the field, they might have the advantage of railroad transportation.

On the 20th and 21st, Gist's brigade, sent by General Beauregard, and Ector's and McNair's, from General Bragg's army, joined me. Loring's division, separated from the army in the retreat, after the battle of Baker's Creek, reached Jackson on the

20th, and Maxey's brigade, from Port Hudson, on the 23d. On the 3d of June we had been reënforced, in addition to these, by Evans's brigade from South Carolina, and Breckenridge's division, and about two thousand cavalry from the Army of Tennessee.[1] This body of cavalry was commanded by Brigadier-General W. H. Jackson.

The Federal army was receiving considerable additions in the mean time, estimated by our scouts at not less than twenty thousand men.

The Confederate forces enumerated above, not equal to a third of the Federal army, were almost without artillery and field transportation, and deficient in ammunition for all arms; and could not, therefore, have been moved, with any hope of success, against that powerful army, already protected by lines of counter and circumvallation.

All the supplies that had been collected in the department were, of course, with the troops in Vicksburg and Port Hudson.

The troops coming from the East, by railroad, had brought neither artillery nor wagons. Frequent drafts upon the country had so much reduced the number of horses and mules, that it was not until near the end of June that artillery and wagons, and draught-animals enough for them, could be procured, generally from long distances—most of the artillery and wagons from Georgia. Some twelve pieces, found without carriages, were mounted on such as could be made in Canton.

There was no want of provision and forage in the department, but they were still to be collected;

[1] General Bragg's report.

and we had small means of collecting them, and none of transporting them with a moving army.

On the 23d, a dispatch was received from Major-General Gardner, dated 21st, informing me that all the Federal forces that had been assembled at Baton Rouge were now before Port Hudson, and asking for reënforcements. In reply to this, I repeated my order to him to evacuate the place, informed him that he could not be reënforced, and told him to march toward Jackson. This dispatch was never delivered, Port Hudson being invested before the arrival of the courier who bore it.

On the 24th such demonstrations were made by the enemy, beyond the Big Black and along the Yazoo, that Walker was sent with his division to Yazoo City, with orders to fortify that point. And these demonstrations being repeated, Loring's division was sent to Benton on the 31st. In order to superintend the preparation necessary to enable the troops to march as far as to the position of the army investing Vicksburg, and at the same time be ready for military operations near the Yazoo, I divided each day between Jackson and Canton.

I can give no better account of the siege of Vicksburg than that contained in Lieutenant-General Pemberton's dispatches to me during its operations, of which I had ten, and occasional verbal messages by the officers who bore them.

On the 24th two were received, dated the 20th and 21st. In the first he wrote: "The enemy assaulted our intrenched lines yesterday at two points, centre and left, and was repulsed with heavy loss. Our loss small. I cannot estimate the enemy's force now engaged around Vicksburg at less than sixty thousand It is probably more. At this hour (8 A. M.) he is briskly cannonading with long-range guns. That we may save ammunition, his fire is rarely returned. At present, our main necessity is musket-caps. Can you not send them to me by hands of couriers and citizens? An army will be necessary to relieve Vicksburg, and that quickly. Will it not be sent?" The bearer of the note gave a verbal message to the effect that a million caps were required.

In the second dispatch General Pemberton wrote: "The enemy kept up incessant sharp-shooting all yesterday, on the left and centre, and picked off our officers and men whenever they showed themselves. Their artillery-fire was very heavy—ploughed up our works considerably, and dismounted two guns in the centre. The works were repaired and the guns replaced last night. The great question is ammunition. The men credit, and are encouraged by, a report that you are near with a strong force. They are fighting in good spirits, and their organization is complete." At two o'clock he added: "Brisk musketry and artillery fire to-day on centre. Three guns dismounted. These will be replaced as far as possible. . . . Incessant mortar-firing from the river, and last night three gunboats engaged our lower batteries."

I wrote to General Pemberton on the 25th: "My last note was brought back by the messenger. Two hundred thousand caps have been sent. It will be continued as they arrive. Bragg is sending a division. When it comes I will move to you. Which do you think the best route? How and where is the enemy encamped? What is your force?" It was supposed then that artillery and means of transportation would be procured before the arrival of those troops. I wrote on the 29th: "I am too weak to save Vicksburg. Can do no more than attempt to save you and your garrison. It will be impossible to extricate you unless you coöperate, and we make mutually-supporting movements. Communicate your plans and suggestions, if possible."

Lieutenant-General Pemberton replied on the 3d of June: "Have not heard from you since the 29th; enemy continues to work on his intrenchments, and very close to our lines; is very vigilant. I can get no information from outside as to your position and strength, and very little in regard to the enemy. I have heard that ten messengers with caps have been captured. In what direction will you move, and when? I hope north of the Jackson road."

In replying to this dispatch on the 7th, I said: "Coöperation is absolutely necessary. Tell us how to effect it, and by what routes to approach."

Lieutenant-General Pemberton wrote on the same day: "I am still without information from you, or of you, later than your dispatch of the 25th. The enemy continues to intrench his position around Vicksburg. I have sent out couriers to you almost daily. The same men are in the trenches constantly, but are in good spirits, expecting your approach. The enemy is so vigilant that it is impossible to obtain reliable information. When may I expect you to move, and in what direction? My subsistence may be put down for about twenty days."

On the 10th General Pemberton wrote: "The

enemy bombards the city day and night from seven mortars on opposite side of peninsula; he also keeps up constant fire on our lines with artillery and sharp-shooters; we are losing many officers and men. I am waiting most anxiously to know your intentions. Have heard nothing from you nor of you since 25th of May. I shall endeavor to hold out as long as we have any thing to eat. ... " On the 12th he said in a brief note : ". . . . Very heavy firing yesterday, from mortars and on lines," and on the 15th: "The ene-my has placed several very heavy guns in position against our works, and is approaching them very nearly. His firing is almost continuous. Our men are becoming much fatigued, but are still in pretty good spirits. I think your movement should be made as soon as possible. The enemy is receiving reënforcements. We are living on greatly-reduced rations, but, I think, sufficient for twenty days."

In dispatches dated 14th and 15th I told General Pemberton that our joint forces could not compel the enemy to raise the siege of Vicksburg, and there-fore that we could attempt no more than to save the garrison, but that for this exact coöperation was in-dispensable; that my communications could best be preserved by my operating north of the railroad; and inquired where an attack upon the enemy by me would be most favorable to him. He was also informed that Major-General Taylor, with eight thousand men, would endeavor to open communi-cations with him from Richmond, Louisiana.

He replied on the 21st: " .... I suggest that, giv-ing me full information in time to act, you move by the north of the railroad, drive in the enemy's pickets at night, and at daylight next morning engage him heavily with skirmishers, occupying him during the entire day; and that on that night I move by the Warrenton road by Hankinson's Ferry; to which point you should previously send a brigade of cavalry, with two field-batteries, to build a bridge there and hold that ferry; also Hall's and Baldwin's, to cover my crossing at Hankinson's. I shall not be able to move with my artillery and wagons.

"I suggest this as the best plan, because all the other roads are too strongly intrenched, and the enemy in too heavy force for reasonable prospect of success, unless you move in sufficient force to compel him to abandon his communication with Snyder's Mill, which I still hope we may be able to do. . . ." Captain Saunders, who brought the dispatch, told me that he was directed to say, from Lieutenant-General Pemberton, that I ought to attempt nothing with less than forty thousand men.

This dispatch was answered on the 22d : "General Taylor is sent by General E. K. Smith to coöperate with you from the west bank of the river, to throw in supplies, and to cross with his forces if expedient and practicable. I will have the means of moving toward the enemy in a day or two, and will try to make a diversion in your favor ; and, if possible, communicate with you, though I fear my force is too small to effect the latter. I have only two-thirds of the force you told Captain Saunders to tell me is the least with which I ought to make an attempt. If I can do nothing to relieve you, rather than surrender the garrison, endeavor to cross the river at the last moment, if you and General Taylor communicate."

In a dispatch dated 22d, Lieutenant-General Pemberton suggested that I should propose terms to General Grant, the surrender of the place but not of the troops, adding, however: "I still renew my hope of your being, by force of arms, enabled to act with me to hold out, if there is hope of our ultimate relief, for fifteen days longer. . . . Federals opened all their batteries on our lines about half after three this morning, and continued the heaviest fire we have yet sustained, until eight o'clock; but did not assault our works. . . . The enemy's works are within twenty-five feet of our redan, and also very close on the Jackson and Baldwin's Ferry roads. I hope you will advance with the least possible delay. My men have been thirty-four days and nights in the trenches without relief, and the enemy is within conversation distance. We are living on very reduced rations. . . ."

In replying, on the 27th, to Lieutenant-General Pemberton's last dispatch, I said that the determination manifested by him, and General E. K. Smith's expected coöperation, encouraged me to hope that something might yet be done to save Vicksburg; but that if it should become necessary to make propositions to General Grant, they must be made by him, as my making them would be an impolitic confession of weakness.

Whatever may have been written subsequently by Lieutenant-General Pemberton, was intercepted or lost. The last dispatch received from him while in Vicksburg was that of the 22d.

The only intelligence I received from Port Hudson, during the siege, was given by a dispatch from

Major-General Gardner, dated June 10th : "I have repulsed the enemy in several attacks, but am still closely invested. I am getting short of provisions and ammunition of all kinds, and should be speedily reënforced." This was received in Jackson on the 15th. In my reply, he was informed that we had not the means of relieving the place ; that General Taylor, on the opposite side of the Mississippi, would give him all the assistance in his power, and that it was of the greatest importance that Port Hudson should hold out as long as possible, to keep General Banks's army employed in the South. This was repeated on the 20th.

In the mean time, my telegraphic correspondence with the President and Secretary of War had kept them informed of the condition of military affairs in Mississippi, especially of the inadequacy of the forces they had collected to break the investment of Vicksburg. In a telegram of the 24th of May, the President said : " . . . . I hope you will soon be able to break the investment, make a junction, and carry in munitions. . . . " I replied on the 27th : ". . . . General Pemberton estimates Grant's force at not less than sixty thousand. When all reënforcements arrive, I shall have about twenty-three thousand. Tell me if additional troops can be furnished."

On the 28th he wrote by telegraph : " The reënforcements sent you exceed, by say seven thousand, the estimate of your dispatch of the 27th instant. We withheld nothing which it is practicable to give. . . . " And on the 30th : " . . . . Added to the forces you have from Pemberton's army, he" (the Secretary of War) "states your whole force to be thirty-four thousand exclusive of militia." [1]   I replied on the 1st of June: "The Secretary of War is greatly mistaken in his numbers. By their own returns, the troops at my disposal available against Grant are: of Pemberton's, nine thousand seven hundred; of Bragg's, eight thousand four hundred; of Beauregard's, six thousand; not including irregular cavalry, nor Jackson's command [2] (cavalry), the strength of which I do not know. . . ." In a telegram to Mr. Seddon (Secretary of War), dated June 2d, I said: "Your letter of the 25th, and a telegram from the President, show that you are misinformed as to the force at my disposal. The effective force, infantry and artillery, is, from Lieutenant-General Pemberton, nine thousand eight hundred and thirty-one; from General Bragg, seven thousand nine hundred and thirty-nine; from General Beauregard, six thousand two hundred and eighty-three. Brigadier-General Jackson's cavalry not arrived, and irregular troops protecting Northern and Southern frontiers, not included. Grant is receiving continual accessions. Tell me if it is your intention to make up the number you gave the President as my force, or if I may expect more troops. With the present force we cannot succeed, without great blunders by the enemy."

In a telegram of the 3d, Mr. Seddon explained his estimate of my force; asked what his mistake was; expressed great anxiety concerning my "plans," and desired me to inform him of them as far as I

---

[1] I had no militia, and supposed that the State had none; for the Confederate military laws put the whole population fit to bear arms under the President's control.

[2] About two thousand, by General Bragg's report.

might think it safe to do so. To this I replied on the 4th: "The mistake on your part is, that all your numbers are too large; in reference to General Beauregard, nearly as ten to six. The troops you mention, including Jackson's, just arrived, are less than twenty-six thousand. My only plan is to relieve Vicksburg. My force is too small for the purpose. Tell me if you can increase it, and how much. Grant is receiving reënforcements. Port Hudson is closely invested. The great object of the enemy in this campaign is to acquire possession of the Mississippi. Can you collect here a force sufficient to defeat this object?"

In Mr. Seddon's next dispatch, dated June 5th, he said: ". . . . I regret my inability to promise more troops, as we have drained resources even to the danger of several points. You know best concerning General Bragg's army, but I fear to withdraw more. We are too far outnumbered in *it*[1] to spare any. You must rely on what you have, and the irregular forces Mississippi can afford." On the 8th he asked, on the same subject, "Do you advise more reënforcements from General Bragg?" I replied on the 10th: "I have not at my disposal half the number of troops necessary. It is for the Government to determine what department, if any, can furnish the reënforcements required." The Secretary's dispatch, in cipher, could be only partially deciphered. On the 12th, something more being understood, the answer was continued: "To take from Bragg a force that would make this army fit to oppose Grant's, would involve yielding Tennessee. It is for the Government to de-

---

[1] In Mr. Davis's quotation, in his letter of July 15th, this word is "Virginia." In the dispatch to me it is a word of two letters.

cide between this State and Tennessee." A duplicate of this dispatch of the 8th was deciphered and answered on the 15th : " I cannot advise as to the points
from which troops can best be taken, having no means
of knowing. Nor is it for me to judge which it is
best to hold, Mississippi or Tennessee—that is for
the Government to determine. Without some great
blunder of the enemy, we cannot hold both. The
odds against me are much greater than those you
express (two to one). I consider saving Vicksburg
hopeless."

Mr. Seddon replied on the 16th : "Your telegram
grieves and alarms me. Vicksburg must not be lost
without a desperate struggle. The interest and honor
of the Confederacy forbid it. I rely on you still to
avert the loss. If better resources do not offer, you
must attack. It may be made in concert with the
garrison, if practicable, but otherwise, without—by
day or night, as you think best."

I wrote in answer to this on the 19th : "I think
that you do not appreciate the difficulties in the course
you direct, nor the probability and consequences of
failure. Grant's position, naturally very strong, is
intrenched, and protected by powerful artillery, and
the roads obstructed. His reënforcements have been
at least equal to my whole force. The Big Black
covers him from attack, and would cut off our retreat
if defeated. We cannot combine operations with
General Pemberton, from uncertain and slow communication. The defeat of this little army would at
once open Mississippi and Alabama to Grant. I will
do all I can, without hope of doing more than aid to
extricate the garrison."

Mr. Seddon rejoined on the 21st: "Consequences are realized and difficulties recognized as being very great. But I still think, other means failing, the course recommended should be hazarded. The aim, in my judgment, justifies any risk, and all probable consequences." In another telegram of the same date, he added: "Only my conviction of almost imperative necessity for action, induces the official dispatch I have just sent you. On every ground I have great deference for your superior knowledge of the position, your judgment, and military genius, but feel it right to share—if need be, to take—the responsibility, and leave you free to follow the most desperate course the occasion may demand. Rely upon it, the eyes and hopes of the whole Confederacy are upon you, with the full confidence that you will act, and with the sentiment that it is better to fail nobly daring, than, through prudence even, to be inactive. I look to attack in the last resort, but rely on your resources of generalship to suggest less desperate modes of relief. I can scarce dare to suggest, but might it not be possible to strike Banks first, and unite the garrison of Port Hudson with you, or to secure sufficient coöperation from General Smith, or to practically besiege Grant by operations with artillery, from the swamps, now dry, on the north side of the Yazoo, below Haynes's Bluff? I rely upon you for all possible to save Vicksburg."

I explained, on the 24th: "There has been no voluntary inaction. When I came, all military materials of the department were in Vicksburg and Port Hudson. Artillery had to be brought from the East; horses for it, and field transportation, procured in an exhausted country; much from Georgia, brought over wretched railroads; and provision collected. I have not had the means of moving. We cannot contend with the enemy north of the Yazoo. He can place a large force there in a few hours—we, a small one, in ten or twelve days. We cannot relieve Port Hudson without giving up Jackson, by which we should lose Mississippi. . . ."

The want of field-transportation was then delaying an expedition toward Vicksburg. That want made it impossible, then, to march the much longer distance to Port Hudson, even if it had been expedient to do so. But such an expedition, by us, would have enabled General Grant to destroy our army, for, by the help of his strong lines, two-thirds of his forces could have been sent to intercept us, while the other maintained the investment of Vicksburg.

On the 28th, the necessary supplies and field transportation having been procured, the equipment of the artillery completed, and a serviceable floating-bridge finished (the first constructed having proved a failure), the army [1] was ordered to march next morning toward the Big Black River. In the afternoon of July 1st, Loring's, French's, and Walker's divisions bivouacked near Birdsong's Ferry, on that river, and Breckenridge's, with the floating-bridge, near Edwards's Depot. The cavalry, under General W. H. Jackson, was placed in observation along the river.

This expedition was not undertaken in the wild spirit that dictated the dispatches from the War Department, of the 16th and 21st of June. I did not

[1] The "effective force" was a little above twenty thousand infantry and artillery, and two thousand cavalry.

indulge in "the sentiment" that it was better for me to waste the lives and blood of brave soldiers, "than, through prudence even," to spare them; and therefore intended to make such close and careful examination of the enemy's lines as might enable me to estimate the probability of our being able to break them; and, should the chances of success seem to justify it, attack in the hope of breaking them, and rescuing the army invested in Vicksburg. There was no hope of saving the place by raising the siege.

In providing the means necessary for this expedition, I had looked to the employment of at least three days in reconnaissance, and thought it necessary to provide food and wagons for the Vicksburg troops, who, if the attempt to extricate them should prove successful, might be expected to join us with no other supplies than the ammunition in their cartridge-boxes.

Reconnaissances, to which the 2d, 3d, and 4th of July were devoted, convinced me that no attack upon the Federal position, north of the railroad, was practicable. They confirmed the previous reports of our scouts, that the besieging army was covered by a line of field-works, extending from the railroad-bridge to the Yazoo; that the roads leading to this line had all been obstructed with felled trees, and that strong bodies of Federal infantry and cavalry observed and guarded the river. This observation of ours, however, was not extended below the railroad.

I determined to move on the morning of the 5th, by Edwards's Depot, to the south of the road—thinking, from the reports of the officers who had reconnoitred on that side, that the Federal works there were less strong, and the river unguarded, and the chances of success, therefore, much better on that side; although the consequences of defeat would have been more disastrous, as General Sherman's troops, in the line between the bridge and Yazoo, might have intercepted retreat.

On the 3d a courier from Vicksburg arrived, but without dispatches from General Pemberton. He had been in such danger of capture, he said, as to think it necessary to destroy the letter he was bringing. He had left Vicksburg on the 28th of June, and the letter had that date. In a note dispatched at night General Pemberton was informed of this; and told that we were about to attempt to create a diversion, to enable him to cut his way out of the place, and hoped to attack the enemy, for this object, on the 7th.

But, in the evening of the 4th, intelligence of the surrender of Vicksburg was received; in consequence of which the army fell back to Jackson, which it reached on the afternoon of the 7th.

CHAPTER VIII.

General Sherman advances on Jackson with Large Force.—Dispositions made
for its Defense.—Correspondence by Telegraph with the President.—Daily
Skirmishing.—Enemy expected to attack.—Instead of attacking, begin a
Siege.—Evacuation of Jackson. — Army withdrawn to Morton.—Enemy,
after burning much of Jackson, retire to Vicksburg.—Relieved of Command of Department of Tennessee.—General Bragg's Telegram; Suggestion
too late.—Review of the Mississippi Campaign.—Visit Mobile to examine
its Defenses.—Letter from the President, commenting harshly on my Military Conduct.—My Reply to it.—Congress calls for the Correspondence.—
My Letter not furnished.—Both Letters.—Events during the Fall.—Ordered
to take Command of the Army at Dalton.—Arrive on 26th and assume
Command on 27th of December.

ABOUT seven o'clock in the morning of the 9th
of July General Sherman, with three corps of the
Federal army, appeared before the slight line of field-
works thrown up for the defense of Jackson by General Pemberton's orders. These works, consisting of
a very light line of rifle-pits, with low embankments
at intervals to cover field-pieces, extended from a
point north of the town, and a little east of the Canton road, to one south of it within a short distance
of Pearl River, and covered the approaches to the
place west of the river. These intrenchments were
very badly located and constructed, and offered very
slight obstacle to a vigorous assault.

The commanding officers of the comparatively
small bodies of our troops that had encamped near
Jackson in May and June, had reported that no oth-

er supply of water for troops was to be found than that of Pearl River. This led me to believe that the Federal army, which, as General Jackson reported, advanced from Clinton in a deep order of battle, could not besiege us, but would be compelled to make an immediate assault. This army consisted of three corps and a division. Notwithstanding the great superiority of numbers against them, the spirit and confidence manifested by the Confederate troops were so great, that I felt assured that, with the advantage given by our intrenchments, weak as they were, they would repel any assault certainly and decisively.

On the appearance of the enemy, our troops took the positions in the line of defense assigned to them the day before, in expectation of an immediate attack—Major-General Loring's division on the right, crossing the Canton road; Major-General Breckenridge's on the left, crossing the New Orleans Railroad; Major-General French's between Breckenridge's and the Clinton road; and Major-General Walker's between that road and Loring's. Brigadier-General Jackson was directed to observe and guard the fords of Pearl River above and below the town with his cavalry.

Instead of attacking as soon as it came up, as we had been hoping, the Federal army intrenched itself, and began to construct batteries.

On the 10th there was spirited skirmishing, with a light cannonade, continuous throughout the day. This was kept up, with varying intensity and but little interruption, until the period of our evacuation. Hills within easy cannon-range, commanding and encircling the town, offered very favorable sites for Federal batteries. A cross-fire of shot and shell reached all parts of the town, showing that the position would be untenable under the fire of a powerful artillery. Such, as it was ascertained, was soon to be brought to bear upon it.

On the 11th, I described to the President, by telegraph, the weakness of the position, and the defects of the intrenched line; and explained that want of supplies, which we had been unable to collect, made it impossible to stand a siege; and therefore, unless the enemy should attack us, we must at the last moment abandon the place; for we could not make a serious attack without exposing ourselves to destruction. Brisk skirmishing was continued until night.

On the 12th, besides the usual skirmishing, there was increased fire of artillery, especially by batteries near the Canton road, and those immediately to the south of that, to Clinton. The missiles fell in all parts of the town. An assault, though not a vigorous one, was made on Breckenridge's front. It was quickly repulsed, however, by the well-directed fire of Slocomb's and Cobb's batteries, and a flank attack by the skirmishers of the First, Third, and Fourth Florida, and Forty-seventh Georgia regiments. The enemy lost about two hundred prisoners, the same number killed, many wounded, and the colors of the Twenty-eighth, Forty-first, and Fifty-third Illinois regiments. The attacking troops did not advance far enough to be exposed to the fire of Breckenridge's *line*.

On the 13th the Federal lines had been so extended that both flanks rested upon Pearl River. Colonel C. A. Fuller, of Lieutenant-General Pemberton's staff, arrived from Vicksburg, and informed us of the terms of the capitulation. The garrison was paroled and permitted to return to the Confederacy, officers retaining their side-arms and personal baggage. He stated, also, that, at the time of surrender, about eighteen thousand men were reported fit for duty in the trenches, and about six thousand sick and wounded in the hospitals. And the estimates for rations to be furnished to the troops of the garrison by the United States commissary department were based on a total of thirty-one thousand men.

On the 14th our scouts reported that a large train, loaded with artillery-ammunition, had left Vicksburg by the Jackson road. The enemy was observed to be actively employed in the construction of batteries on all suitable positions. He was evidently preparing to concentrate upon us the fire of about two hundred pieces of ordnance. This made it certain that the abandonment of Jackson could be deferred little longer. General Jackson was directed, however, to endeavor to intercept and destroy the ammunition-train, to postpone at least the necessity of abandoning the place.

In reporting these things to the President by telegraph on the 15th, I said that the enemy would make no assault, but had begun a siege which we could not resist, and that it would be madness on our part to attack him.

Early in the afternoon of the 16th it was ascertained that the attempt by our cavalry to intercept the ammunition-train from Vicksburg had failed, and that the train was near the Federal camp. This, and the advanced condition of the enemy's batteries, made it probable that the fire of all his artillery would commence next day. The evacuation of Jackson that night was decided on and accomplished before daybreak. All public property, and the sick and wounded, except a few not in condition to bear removal, had been carried to the rear, to Brandon and beyond. The right wing marched on the new, and the left on the old Brandon road, crossing the Pearl River on the bridges prepared for the expedition beyond the Big Black, which had been laid by Captain Lockett, the engineer-officer who constructed them, at the two ferries of the river. They were destroyed by the cavalry rear-guard, after the troops had passed.

By the division reports our loss in Jackson was seventy-one killed, five hundred and four wounded, and twenty-five missing.

At Brandon, where we halted several hours, some of our soldiers who, according to their own accounts, were asleep when the troops left Jackson, rejoined their regiments. They said that they had left the town at seven or eight o'clock, and that, apparently, the enemy had not then discovered its evacuation.

I intended to place the troops in a position near Brandon, and encamp on the nearest stream, but the water was neither good nor sufficiently abundant. The movement eastwardly was therefore resumed on the 18th, and continued at the rate of six or eight miles a day, in search of good camping-ground, until the 20th, when we halted three or four miles west of Morton.

Two divisions of Federal infantry and a body of cavalry, drove our cavalry rear-guard through Brandon on the 19th, and returned to Jackson on the 20th. The object of the expedition seemed to be the destruction of the railroad-bridges and depot, to which the outrage of setting fire to the little town, and burning the greater part of it, was added.

On the 12th I received from Colonel J. L. Logan, commanding a small brigade of cavalry in the southern part of the State, intelligence of the surrender of Port Hudson on the 9th. This report was confirmed by Major Jackson, General Gardner's adjutant-general, who stated that the stock of provisions was exhausted, and but twenty-five hundred of the garrison were fit for duty at the time of surrender.

Federal forces advanced against Yazoo City, both by land and water, on the 13th. The attack by the gunboats was handsomely repulsed by the heavy battery, under the direction of Commander J. N. Brown, Confederate States Navy. The De Kalb, the flag-ship of the United States squadron, an iron-clad, carrying thirteen guns, was sunk by a torpedo. The garrison, commanded by the lieutenant-colonel of the Twenty-ninth North Carolina regiment, offered little, if any, resistance to the enemy's land-forces.

The Federal army remained only five or six days in Jackson, but in that short time it destroyed all of the town so closely built that fire could communicate from house to house; its rear-guard left the place, for Vicksburg, on the 23d.

On that day the following telegram from General Cooper, dated 22d, reached me: " In conformity with your expressed wish, you are relieved from the fur- ther command of the Department of Tennessee, which, as advised by you, is united to that of East Tennessee, so as to extend General Bragg's command over the department of General Buckner."

On the 18th a dispatch, dated 17th, was received from General Bragg, in which he suggested the transfer of his troops to Mississippi, and an effort to defeat the Federal army with our combined forces. It was too late: such a combination might have been advantageous before or during the siege of Vicksburg: but not after its disastrous termination.

It was notorious that, after the events just re- lated, the President censured me very strongly and openly; ascribed the loss of Vicksburg to my mis- conduct, and asserted that, with the means placed by him at my disposal, I could have defeated the besieg- ing army, or, at least, broken the investment of the place.

Telegraphic correspondence with the President and Secretary of War, and the returns of the troops, made by their immediate commanders, informed them accurately of the whole strength of my com- mand.[1] Sickness, and details for various employ- ments out of the ranks, reduced the fighting force of that command to about twenty thousand before it could be equipped for the field.

General Grant's army was estimated at sixty thousand when it crossed the Mississippi, and, imme- diately after the investment of Vicksburg, it began

[1] *See* page 198.

to receive accessions which soon increased it to eighty thousand, according to the reports of our scouts in observation along the Mississippi. It is unlikely that this is an exaggeration; for General Grant had a hundred and thirty thousand men at his disposal for the siege.[1] Before my little force was in condition to take the field, the besiegers were as strongly intrenched as the besieged. And more than half their number, under General Sherman, were charged with the defense of the works covering the operations of the siege against attack from without. General Pemberton's army and mine were nearly equal. His was enabled by its fortifications to repulse all the assaults of the enemy, and Vicksburg was reduced by blockade. It is certain, therefore, that some twenty thousand Confederates could not have stormed intrenchments as strong as those of Vicksburg, and defended by more than twice their number of soldiers. It is equally certain that failure would have brought ruin upon us, for an unfordable river in the rear would have barred retreat.

The opinions of Governor Pettus and four other prominent Southern gentlemen who were in Jackson, and, having the same sources of information, knew as well as the Administration the relative forces of the belligerents in Mississippi, were in full agreement with mine. I give their opinions as expressed by themselves, in a telegram dated Jackson, June 18, 1863:

"PRESIDENT DAVIS: From information derived from the military authorities here, we are convinced

---

[1] Badeau's "Life of General Grant."

that it will require not less than thirty thousand additional troops to relieve Vicksburg. The withdrawal of these troops may possibly involve the surrender of all Middle Tennessee to the enemy. The failure to reënforce to this extent, certainly involves the loss of the entire Mississippi Valley. General Johnston believes that the question should be decided by the Government, and we concur with him. We respectfully submit that Vicksburg, and the country dependent upon it, should be held at every sacrifice, and that you order the requisite number of troops to be sent forward with that view. It is unnecessary to say that time is all important; and that the decision should be promptly made.

"JOHN J. PETTUS,   E. BARKSDALE,
A. G. BROWN,   W. P. HARRIS."
D. F. KENNER,

After all reënforcements had been received, in a dispatch to the President dated June 3d, Governor Pettus had expressed the opinion that our army was too small for the objects to be accomplished; and urged his excellency to "send such reënforcements as would give guarantee of success."

The President said in his reply, dated June 5th: ". . . . I have not the power to comply with the request you make. Had it been otherwise, your application would have been anticipated . . . ." Thus admitting the inadequacy of my forces.

Lieutenant-General Pemberton also confirmed my opinion that my force was inadequate, by warning[1]

---

[1] *See* page 195, message by Captain Saunders.

me that forty thousand was the smallest number of troops with which I should attempt to force the Federal line of circumvallation.

Lieutenant-General Pemberton also maintained that I produced the disasters to our cause in his department—not, however, by failing to attack the besieging army in its intrenchments, according to the expressed desire [1] of the Administration, but by giving him orders that caused the disastrous battle of Baker's Creek, on the 16th of May, and thus led to the siege and capture of Vicksburg. That idea is the foundation of Lieutenant-General Pemberton's defense, in his "Report of the Operations previous to and during the Siege of Vicksburg." This report, dated August 2d, was transmitted to the War Department on the 25th, from Gainesville, Alabama, where the writer then was. This fact came to my knowledge on the 12th of September, and I immediately reminded the War Department that the report should have been made to me, General Pemberton's commander, during the operations to which it related, and requested that it should be transmitted to me. No reply was received. After waiting until the 6th of October, I repeated the request. On the 8th, the War Department promised that, as soon as the reports and sub-reports could be copied, I "should be furnished." As these papers, when published, made a hundred and seventy-five large, closely-printed pages, the copy promised was not received until the end of the month. In this elaborate document, the author makes a mistake, by no

[1] In the telegrams of the Secretary of War, one dated the 16th, and two the 21st of June.

means unusual, that of regarding accusation of me, whom he had selected for an adversary, as defense of himself.

Although this report is probably the longest on record, compared with the operations described, the Secretary of War took the very unusual course of suggesting, as he did [1] in a letter to General Pemberton, dated October 1st, an additional one, to strengthen its weak points, which were indicated. This was made, dated November 10th; and, after General Pemberton had read my report in the war office, he asked and obtained permission to offer a second supplemental one. This is explained by Mr. Seddon, in a letter published with the reports, thus:. "After seeing the report of General Johnston, General Pemberton considered his reply to that letter" (Mr. Seddon's of October 1st) "as not so fully elucidating the points of inquiry as the additional details presented by General Johnston rendered appropriate and necessary. He therefore asked the privilege of making a further reply, 'which, in justice to himself'" (the honorable Secretary naïvely adds), "was accorded." The additional comments upon my conduct thus published, with no opportunity on my part for defense, are almost as long as my whole report. The facts that the Administration, after reading General Pemberton's report, desired him to strengthen his case in a manner which it pointed out, and permitted him, after studying my defense, to reply to it in another supplemental report, show very clearly how little it occupied itself with "justice" to me.

Notwithstanding these advantages on his part,

[1] He says in that letter, "at the suggestion of the President."

who, by his manner of using them, constituted himself my adversary, I should have made no comments
on these publications, but should have limited my
defense to the preceding narrative; because it is dis-
tasteful, even painful to me, although in self-defense,
to write unfavorably of a brother officer, who, no
doubt, served to the best of his ability; the more so,
because that officer was, at the time, severely judged
by the Southern people, who, on the contrary, have
always judged me with their hearts instead of their
minds. But Lieutenant-General Pemberton has recently revived the question, and published, or rather
procured to be published, a longer, more elaborate,
and more uncandid attack upon me than those contained in his official report, and its two supple-
ments.

In these publications, General Pemberton endeavors, by implication, as well as by direct assertion, to fix
upon me the responsibility for the course, on his part,
which led him to defeat at Baker's Creek and the Big
Black River, and caused the capture of Vicksburg and
the gallant army that formed its garrison. I assert, on
the contrary, that, in the short campaign preceding the
siege of Vicksburg, he obeyed none of my orders, and
regarded none of my instructions; and that his disasters were due to his own misapprehension of the
principles of the warfare he was directing. He would
have observed those principles by assailing the Federal troops with at least three divisions, instead of
two or three brigades, on the 1st of May, when they
were divided in the passage of the Mississippi; or,
after that time, by attacking McPherson's and McClernand's corps with all his forces, near Hankinson's

Ferry,[1] where they waited for Sherman's until the 8th;[2] or, having failed to seize those opportunities, by falling upon McClernand's corps on the 12th,[3] when it was between Fourteen-mile Creek and his camp, near Edwards's Depot, and Sherman's and McPherson's corps were at and near Raymond. On all those occasions, the chances of success would have been decidedly in his favor, and the consequences of victory much greater, and of defeat much less, to him than to his adversary.

It was evident, after the 12th, that the Federal army had passed to the east of General Pemberton's position near Edwards's Depot, and, consequently, that that army must defeat General Pemberton's before it could "assault" Vicksburg; so that there was no shadow of reason to keep two divisions in the town. Those two divisions, and four brigades detached, including Gregg's[4] and Walker's, ordered to Jackson, could and should have been in the battle of Baker's Creek, and would have increased the Confederate force on that field to nearly thirty-five thousand men. Such an army, respectably commanded, must have won, for Hovey's division was unsupported[5] till eleven o'clock, when McPherson with his two divisions arrived by the Jackson road. It was at least an hour[6] later when McClernand's corps appeared, coming from Raymond. The advantage of engaging the three fractions of the Federal army successively, would, inevitably, have given General Pemberton the victory; and, as the enemy had abandoned their commu-

---

[1] General Grant's report.

[2] This would have been obedience, too, to my instructions of May 1st and 2d. (*See* page 170.)   [3] General Grant's report.

[4] *See* page 175.   [5] General Grant's report.   [6] Ibid.

nications, such a result would have been more disastrous to them than that of the siege of Vicksburg
was subsequently to the Southern army.

In like manner, when the defense of the Big
Black River was decided upon, all available troops,
including those in Vicksburg, should have been concentrated for the object. The opposite principle that
had been controlling Confederate operations since
the 1st, governed, however, on the 17th. And, instead of strengthening and encouraging the defeated
remnant of his army by bringing two fresh divisions
into it, General Pemberton further discouraged that
disheartened remnant, by leaving one-half in front
of the river to fight, and sending the other behind
it, to bivouac some two miles in rear.

General Pemberton received four orders from me
during this campaign.

The first,[1] dated May 1st, and repeated on the
2d, directed him to attack the Federal army with all
his forces united for the purpose.

The second,[2] dated May 13th, is that by which
he professes to have been instigated to the movement
which entangled him with Federal skirmishers in
the morning of the 16th, and involved him in the
battle which he lost. He was ordered to march
seventeen miles to the east, for the expressed object
of attacking a large *detachment*, in conjunction with
the troops in Jackson, to reopen his communications
and enable coming reënforcements to join him. His
intended movement was to a point nine and a half
miles almost south, for the avowed object of compelling the Federal army to attack him in a position

where our coöperation would have been impossible, and where reënforcements could not have reached him. He was ordered to the east, to take part in a combined attack upon a *detachment.* He moved southward, to fight an *army* in a position where aid could not have reached him. His movement defeated my purpose, distinctly expressed to him, of uniting all the expected reënforcements with his army, a measure necessary to give reasonable hope of success. Yet, in all his publications on the subject, General Pemberton repeats the assertion, that obedience to this order exposed him to attack and led to his defeat—when his design and objects, and mine, were founded on exactly opposite military principles.

But this march of Pemberton's would have involved no other commander in a battle. He moved but three or four miles on the 15th. The presence of the enemy was reported to him that night.[1] It frustrated the intention in such slow course of execution; therefore, he must have felt himself free to return to the " chosen ground "[2] near Edwards's Depot, on which his "matured plans " were to have been executed. His army could have marched to it in about an hour.

Even if he had a right to think himself acting under my order on the 15th, he could not have thought so on the 16th; for at 6.30 A. M.[3] he received my third order, again directing him to march to the east to meet me, that our troops might be united. Obedience was easy, for the engagement did not begin

[1] *See* his second supplemental report.
[2] *See* first supplemental report.
[3] *See* General Pemberton's report, p. 37.

until near mid-day; and in the mean time there was
but a *division* of the enemy before him. Instead of
remaining passive four or five hours, until the Federal army was ready to attack him, he could have
extricated himself in a few minutes from the skirmishers of a force so inferior to his own, and obeyed
the last order. Instead of pursuing this obvious
course, General Pemberton remained inactive while
General Grant was assembling his forces and preparing to attack him.

In discussing this question, Lieutenant-General
Pemberton assumes that the loss of the battle of
Baker's Creek was inevitable. It certainly was made
probable by the complete separation of Gregg's and
Walker's brigades [1] from his army, and his detaching
Vaughn's and Reynold's. The presence of these
four brigades on the field would have added not
less than ten thousand men to his fighting force. It
is not unreasonable to think that such an addition
would have given us the victory; for but three Federal divisions actually fought, while four were held
in check by Loring, or rather, by two of Loring's
three brigades. [2]

In looking for the causes of the Confederate re-
verses in this campaign, it is needless to go beyond
Lieutenant-General Pemberton's startling disclosure,
that his movement from Edwards's Depot [3] in violation of my orders, and in opposition to the opinion
of his council of war, " was made against his judgment, in opposition to his previously-expressed in-

[1] *See* General Pemberton's report, pp. 205, 206.
[2] *See* General Grant's report.
[3] *See* General Pemberton's report, p. 44.

tentions, and to the subversion of his matured plans." The author of such a measure might well regard defeat inevitable in a battle brought on by it.

To be successful in that campaign, it was necessary that the Confederate general should comprehend that he must defeat the invading army in the field, and that Vicksburg must fall if besieged.

The invading army could not be defeated without the concentration of the Confederate forces; but they were always more divided than the much more numerous army of the enemy. And the whole course of the Confederate general indicates a determination, from the beginning, to be besieged in Vicksburg.

Our best opportunity to engage the Federal army was, manifestly, while it was divided in the passage of the Mississippi. Such a force as that which Lieutenant-General Pemberton afterward placed near Edwards's Depot, used for this object, and directed with vigor, would have had all reasonable chance of success. As well convinced of it then as now, I directed Lieutenant-General Pemberton to attack the enemy with all his force, as soon as I was informed, by his dispatch of May 1st, that Major - General Bowen had been attacked by a large body of Federal troops. This order was repeated on the 2d, only to be disregarded. Advantageous opportunities to engage the Federal army were offered continually, until the investment of Vicksburg; for, until then, that army had been united but three or four of the twenty days elapsed since it began to cross the Mississippi.

If Lieutenant-General Pemberton had obeyed either of my orders to march eastwardly from Edwards's, an army of thirty-five thousand men might have been formed. Such a force, properly commanded, would have prevented the siege of Vicksburg.

Being confident that, should Vicksburg be besieged, a Confederate force sufficient to break the investment would not be assembled for the purpose, as well as of the fact that it and Port Hudson had lost their importance since the occupation of the river between them by many Federal vessels-of-war, I directed the evacuation of both places. Port Hudson was invested before the order reached General Gardner, if it ever reached him. It was received by General Pemberton,[1] but set aside, by advice of a council of war; for the extraordinary reason that, "it was impossible to withdraw the army from this position"[2] (Vicksburg) "with such *morale* and material as to be of further service to the Confederacy." This assertion was fully refuted by the courage and constancy with which "the army" faced the dangers and endured the labors and hardships of a long siege.

Lieutenant-General Pemberton dwells much upon his want of cavalry, which he attributes to me; and repeatedly refers to his applications to me for troops of that arm. These applications specified that the troops were required to repel raids in Northern Mississippi. Indeed, General Pemberton's whole correspondence with me in April indicated that he was much more apprehensive of predatory incursions, than of the formidable invasion preparing under his eyes.

[1] This was my fourth order to General Pemberton; *see* p. 181, for this order.
[2] *See* p. 49 of General Pemberton's report.

About the 20th of April, General Bragg was requested by me to send a strong brigade of cavalry into Mississippi. He promptly sent the nearest and strongest, General Roddy's. That brigade encountered the very troops, from Corinth, whose incursions General Pemberton wished to meet; and were contending with threefold odds of those troops, while the Federal army was crossing the Mississippi. They were thus employed in the service for which they were required, in his opinion.

Lieutenant-General Pemberton says: "With a moderate cavalry force at my disposal, I am firmly convinced that the Federal army under General Grant would have been unable to maintain its communications with the Mississippi; and that the attempt to reach Jackson and Vicksburg from that base would have been as signally defeated in May, 1863, as a like attempt, from another base, had, by the employment of cavalry, been defeated in December, 1862."

In its march from Bruinsburg by Port Gibson to Jackson, and thence to Vicksburg, the Federal army drew its supplies from the country; and did not in the least depend on "its communications with the Mississippi." Consequently, cavalry placed on what General Pemberton regarded as "its communications," would have been altogether useless. Major-General Van Dorn's success, referred to, was obtained by the surprise of the garrison of Holly Springs and the destruction of General Grant's military supplies in depot in the town. At the time in question, General Grant had no garrison to be surprised nor depots to be destroyed, in Mississippi; and no disposition

¹ *See* his report, p. 32.

of Confederate cavalry would have been less inconvenient to him than that by which his opponent fancies that he would have been defeated.

Lieutenant-General Pemberton comments thus on my order to him to evacuate Vicksburg: "The evacuation of Vicksburg! It meant the loss of the valuable stores and munitions of war collected for its defense, the fall of Port Hudson, the surrender of the Mississippi River, and the severance of the Confederacy." [1]

Before the 18th of May, when General Pemberton received the order referred to—indeed, before General Grant's army landed in Mississippi—the river had been captured by the Federal fleets, and the "severance of the Confederacy" accomplished. Before the end of April the portion of the river between Vicksburg and Port Hudson was more strongly held by the Federal vessels-of-war than any other. The discovery by the United States naval commanders of the ineffectiveness of our batteries at Vicksburg and Port Hudson, destroyed the illusion that those places were valuable. They were occupied and intrenched to prevent the United States vessels-of-war from passing them. It had been demonstrated that they could not do so. They were valuable on the 18th of May, therefore, only for the munitions of war they contained.

But, without reference to the military value of the place, the army should not have been exposed to investment in it; for the capture of the place was the certain result of a siege. After investment, surrender was a mere question of time; there could be

[1] *See* General Pemberton's report, p. 48.

no reasonable hope of relief. As the Confederate Government had been unable to prevent a siege, it was certain that it could not break one. As the capture of the place could not be prevented, the army should have been saved by leading it away.

If I and the reënforcements sent from Beauregard's department had been ordered to Mississippi in April, in time to join General Pemberton's army, I *could* have directed the Confederate forces, and *would* have been responsible for events; but, by hesitating to transfer troops and send a new commander until too late, the Administration made itself and General Pemberton responsible for consequences, and those consequences were the ruin of our affairs in Tennessee as well as in Mississippi. They were ruined in Mississippi by the long delay of the Administration in sending reënforcements to General Pemberton's army; and in Tennessee, by a draft of eight thousand men from General Bragg's army, whose going to Mississippi was useless, because too late, while it so weakened that army as to enable its antagonist to drive it rapidly across the Cumberland Mountain and Tennessee River.

It would have been much less hazardous to send Longstreet's corps to Mississippi than to weaken the Army of Tennessee, then scarcely strong enough to cope with that of General Rosecrans. The military condition in Virginia seems to have been such in all the spring of 1863, that that corps was not required in General Lee's army, for in all that time it was detached generally in the southern and eastern parts of the State, in some service far less important, certainly, than that which might have been given it near Vicksburg. While it was thus detached, General Lee was able not only to hold the Federal army in check at Fredericksburg, but to gain the victory of Chancellorsville. Until the expedition into Pennsylvania was decided upon, it was engaged in some operations not above secondary. It was well worth delaying an invasion of the Northern States, to preserve the great valley of the Mississippi; and, by sending Longstreet with his corps to that department, we might have been able to repel Grant's invasion, without exposing our armies in Virginia and Tennessee.

During the remainder of the year the operations of the forces of the United States in Mississippi were limited to predatory expeditions, generally by mounted troops. They seemed to have no other object than the infliction of suffering upon the inhabitants of the districts invaded, and the destruction of the few villages and hamlets reached. Our military objects were to defeat such raids, to guard against the destruction, by the enemy, of the railroads and their machinery, and to be in readiness to reënforce the garrison of Mobile.

Most of the predatory warfare was waged by Federal troops stationed on the Memphis and Charleston Railroad, and near it in Mississippi. On the eastern part of that frontier Brigadier-General Ruggles commanded Ferguson's brigade of Confederate cavalry, and ten or twelve field-pieces; and the western was defended by Brigadier-General Chalmers, with his brigade of cavalry and a field-battery; Colonel Logan, with another mounted brigade, operated near Natchez and Port Hudson; and Colonel Power

with his regiment, also mounted, in Northeastern
Louisiana. These dispositions had been made by
Lieutenant-General Pemberton. After the Federal
army, under Major-General Sherman, moved from
Jackson to Vicksburg, General W. H. Jackson's division was advanced to the line from Livingston to
Raymond, to observe the Federal army beyond the
Big Black River, and protect the reconstruction of
the railroad north and south of the town of Jackson; miles of it, in each direction, were destroyed by
the Federal army before its return to Vicksburg.
That the railroad company might repair this important road as soon as possible, military protection
was promised, as well as the necessary laborers and
wagons, which Major L. Mims, who was at the head
of the quartermaster's department in the State, was
instructed to procure by impressment as needed.
The same arrangements were made for the rebuilding of the railroad-bridge at Jackson.

Major-General Maury, who commanded at Mobile,
reported that he had but two thousand infantry, ten
field-pieces, and five hundred mounted troops for the
defense of the works on the land-side of the place.
According to the estimate that accompanied this report, fifteen thousand infantry and four field-batteries
were necessary. The general added that he had just
received intelligence that preparations on a large
scale were in progress at Pensacola and New Orleans,
for a combined attack, by land and water, upon the
batteries and town.

In consequence of these reports, application was
made to Governor Shorter for any considerable part
of the seven thousand troops which the State of Ala-

bama was required to hold ready for such service, that could be furnished for the defense of Mobile. This application was repeated a few days after. The Governor replied that, under the military laws of the Confederacy, he had no power to raise troops; but informed me that he was having negro laborers collected and sent to Mobile, to work on the fortifications.

Lieutenant-General Hardee, transferred from the Army of Tennessee to that of Mississippi, had arrived at Morton. Confidence in that distinguished soldier made me feel at liberty to leave the army. I therefore went to Mobile to complete the examination of its defenses, which had been twice begun (in January and March), and on each occasion interrupted by orders of the Administration, which directed me to repair to General Bragg's headquarters.

These defenses seemed to me very imperfect. They consisted of a little work at Grant's Pass, in which three guns were mounted; Fort Morgan on the east, and an unfinished work on the west side of the entrance to the bay from the gulf, which (the entrance) is three miles wide, and an interior line of batteries to command the channels leading from the bay to the city; the left of this line, however, would have been commanded by batteries placed on the eastern shore of the bay. A line of redoubts from the river-bank north of the city, to the bay-shore southwest of it, promised a sufficient protection on the landside, when finished.

A naval force under Admiral Buchanan was to coöperate with these forts and batteries; but, with capacity to command a squadron, and officers competent to handle its ships, that gallant seaman then had but three little wooden vessels.

Near the end of the month, before leaving Mobile to return to Morton, I received, from an officer to whom it had been intrusted, a letter from the President, ostensibly to correct a misapprehension of mine in relation to the telegram of May 9th, directing me to assume immediate command of the army in Mississippi, but actually commenting very harshly upon much of my military conduct since the previous December. It was not unexpected, for General Wigfall, of the Confederate States Senate, had told me, in recent letters, that a friend of his had twice seen such a paper in preparation in the office of the Secretary of State.

If all the misconduct alleged had been actually committed, the Administration was unjustifiable in keeping me in a position so important as the command of a department. As good-natured weakness was never attributed to Mr. Davis as a fault, it is not easy to reconcile the assertions and tone of this letter with his official course toward me—his not only retaining me in command of a department, but subsequently assigning me to that of the Army of Tennessee after its defeat under General Bragg at Missionary Ridge—the latter being far more important than any other military position in the Confederate service, except that occupied by General Lee.

The accusations of this letter were answered *seriatim*, on my return to my office in Morton, in a letter dated August 8th.

In its next session, and on the 11th of December, Congress called for the " correspondence of the Presi-

dent, Secretary of War, and Adjutant and Inspector
General, with General J. E. Johnston, during the
months of May, June, and July, concerning his command, and the operations in his department." This
was on the motion of Mr. Grimes, of Texas, a devoted
follower of the President.

In his letter to Congress accompanying the correspondence, the President explained: "As the reso
lution fixes definitely the dates within which the
correspondence is desired, I have not deemed it
proper to add any thing which was prior or subsequent to those dates." On that principle, his charges
against me, making much the larger part of his share
of the correspondence, were not accompanied by my
defense. Yet six papers less relevant were included
—an order dated November, 1862, and a correspondence (five dispatches) between the President and
General Bragg. It would have been as consistent
with propriety to transmit my defense with his accusations, and certainly as much so with fairness.
Repeated calls for this paper by Congress, to complete the published correspondence, were unnoticed
by the Executive. This fact gave me the impression,
at the time, that my defense must have been regarded as in some degree effective by those who thus prevented its publication.

As the charges so published were extensively
circulated, I take this occasion to defend myself, and
to present the case fairly by giving both letters.

"RICHMOND, *July* 15, 1863.

"GENERAL: I. Your dispatch of the 5th instant,
stating that you 'considered' your 'assignment to

the immediate command in Mississippi' as giving you 'a new position' and as 'limiting your authority,' being a repetition of a statement which you were informed was a grave error, and being persisted in after your failure to point out, when requested, the letter or dispatch justifying you in such a conclusion, rendered it necessary, as you were informed in my dispatch of 8th instant, that I should make a more extended reply than could be given in a telegram. That there may be no possible room for further mistake in the matter, I am compelled to recapitulate the substance of all orders and instructions given to you, so far as they bear on this question.

II. "On the 24th November last you were assigned, by Special Order No. 275, to a definite geographical command. The description includes a portion of Western North Carolina, and Northern Georgia, the States of Tennessee, Alabama, and Mississippi, and that part of the State of Louisiana east of the Mississippi River. The order concluded in the following language: 'General Johnston will, for the purpose of correspondence and reports, establish his headquarters at Chattanooga, or such other place as in his judgment will best secure communication with the troops within the limits of his command, and will repair in person to any part of said command, whenever his presence may for the time be necessary or desirable.'

III. "This command by its terms embraced the armies under command of General Bragg in Tennessee, of General Pemberton at Vicksburg, as well as those at Port Hudson, Mobile, and the forces in East Tennessee.

IV. "This general order has never been changed nor modified so as to affect your command in a single particular, nor has your control over it been interfered with. I have, as commander-in-chief, given you some orders, which will be hereafter noticed, not one of them, however, indicating in any manner that the general control confided to you was restricted or impaired.

V. "You exercised this command by visiting in person the armies at Murfreesboro', Vicksburg, Mobile, and elsewhere; and on the 22d January I wrote you, directing that you should repair in person to the army at Tullahoma, on account of a reported want of harmony and confidence between General Bragg and his officers and troops. This letter closed with the following passage: 'As that army is part of your command, no order will be necessary to give you authority there, as, whether present or absent, you have a right to direct its operations, and do whatever else belongs to the general commanding.'

VI. "Language cannot be plainer than this, and, although the different armies in your geographical district were ordered to report directly to Richmond, as well as to yourself, this was done solely to avoid the evil that would result from reporting through you, when your headquarters might be, and it was expected frequently would be, so located as to create delays injurious to the public interest.

VII. "While at Tullahoma you did not hesitate to order troops from General Pemberton's army, and, learning that you had ordered the division of cavalry from North Mississippi to Tennessee, I telegraphed you that this order did not change your orders, and, although I thought them injudicious, I refrained from exercising my authority, in deference to your views.

VIII. "When I learned that prejudice and malignity had so undermined the confidence of the troops at Vicksburg as to threaten disaster, I deemed the circumstances such as to present the case foreseen in Special Order No. 275, that you should 'repair in person to any part of said command whenever your presence might for the time be necessary or desirable.'

IX. "You were therefore ordered, on 9th May, to 'proceed at once to Mississippi and the chief command of the forces, giving to those in the field as far as practicable the encouragement and benefit of your personal direction.'

X. "Some details were added about reënforcements, but not a word affecting in the remotest degree your authority to command your geographical district.

XI. "On the 4th June you telegraphed to the Secretary of War in reference to his inquiry, saying, 'My only plan is to relieve Vicksburg; my force is far too small for the purpose; tell me if you can increase it and how much.'

XII. "To which he answered on the 5th: 'I regret inability to promise more troops, as we have drained resources even to the danger of several points. You know best concerning General Bragg's army, but I fear to withdraw more. We are too far outnumbered in Virginia to spare any,' etc., etc.

XIII. "This dispatch shows that, up to the 5th June, the war-office had no knowledge of any impression on your part that you had ceased to control

Bragg's army, but, on the contrary, you were clearly informed that you were considered the proper person to withdraw troops from it, if you deemed it judicious.

XIV. "On the 8th June the Secretary was more explicit, if possible. He said : 'Do you advise more reënforcements from General Bragg? You, as commandant of the department, have power so to order, if you in view of the whole case so determine.'

XV. "On the 10th June you answered that it was for the Government to determine what department could furnish the reënforcements; that you could not know how General Bragg's wants compared with yours, and that the Government could make the comparison.

XVI. "Your statement that the Government in Richmond was better able to judge of the relative necessities of the armies under your command than you were, and the further statement that you could not know how General Bragg's wants compared with yours, were considered extraordinary; but, as they were accompanied by the remark that the Secretary's dispatch had been imperfectly deciphered, no observation was made on them till the receipt of your telegram to the Secretary, of the 12th instant, stating: 'I have not considered myself commanding in Tennessee since assignment here, and should not have felt authorized to take troops from that department after having been informed by the Executive that no more could be spared.'

XVII. "My surprise at these two statements was extreme. You had never been 'assigned' to the Mississippi command, you went there under the cir-

cumstances and orders already quoted, and no justification whatever is perceived for your abandonment
of your duties as commanding general of the geographical district to which you were assigned. Orders as explicit as those under which you were sent
to the West and under which you continued to act
up to the 9th May, when you were directed to repair
in person to Mississippi, can only be impaired or set
aside by subsequent orders equally explicit; and
your announcement that you had ceased to consider
yourself charged with the control of affairs in Tennessee because ordered to repair in person to Mississippi, both places being within the command to
which you were assigned, was too grave to be overlooked; and, when to this was added the assertion
that you should not have felt authorized to draw
troops from that department (Tennessee), after being informed by the 'Executive that no more could
be spared,' I was unable to account for your language, being entirely confident that I had never
given you any such information.

XVIII. "I shall now proceed to separate your
two statements, and begin with that which relates
to your 'not considering yourself commanding in
Tennessee since assignment here,' i. e., in Mississippi.

XIX. "When you received my telegram of 15th
of June, informing you that 'the order to go to Mississippi did not diminish your authority in Tennessee, both being in the country placed under your
command in original assignment,' accompanied by an
inquiry about the information said to have been derived from me restricting your authority to transfer
troops, your answer on the 16th of June was, 'I

meant to tell the Secretary of War that I considered the order directing me to command here as limiting my authority to this department, especially when that order was accompanied by War Department orders transferring troops from Tennessee to Mississippi.'

XX. "This is in substance a repetition of the previous statement, without any reason being given for it. The fact of orders being sent to you to transfer some of the troops in your department from one point to another, to which you were proceeding in person, could give no possible ground for your 'considering' that Special Order No. 275 was rescinded or modified. Your command of your geographical district did not make you independent of my orders as your superior officer, and, when you were directed by me to take troops with you to Mississippi, your control over the district to which you were assigned was in no way involved. But the statement that troops were transferred from Tennessee to Mississippi by order of the War Department, when you were directed to repair to the latter State, gives but half the fact; for, although you were ordered to take with you three thousand good troops, you were told to replace them by a greater number then on their way to Mississippi, and whom you were requested to direct to Tennessee, the purpose being to hasten reënforcements to Pemberton without weakening Bragg. This was in deference to your own opinion that Bragg could not be safely weakened, nay, that he ought even to be reënforced at Pemberton's expense, for you had just ordered troops from Pemberton's command to reënforce Bragg. I differed in opinion from you, and thought Vicksburg far more exposed to danger than Bragg, and was urging forward reënforcements to that point both from Carolina and Virginia, before you were directed to assume command in person in Mississippi.

XXI. "I find nothing, then, either in your dispatch of 16th June, or in any subsequent communication from you, giving a justification for your saying that 'you have not considered yourself commanding in Tennessee since assignment here' (i. e., in Mississippi). Your dispatch of the 5th instant is again a substantial repetition of the same statement, without a word of reason to justify it. You say, 'I considered my assignment to the immediate command in Mississippi as giving me a new position and limiting my authority to this department.' I have characterized this as a grave error, and in view of all the facts cannot otherwise regard it. I must add that a review of your correspondence shows a constant desire on your part, beginning early in January, that I should change the order placing Tennessee and Mississippi in one command and under your direction, and a constant indication on my part whenever I wrote on the subject, that in my judgment the public service required that the two armies should be subject to your control.

XXII. "I now proceed to your second statement in your telegram of 12th June, that 'you should not have felt authorized to take troops from that department' (Tennessee), 'after having been informed by the Executive that no more could be spared.'

XXIII. "To my inquiry for the basis of this

statement, you answered on the 16th by what was in substance a reiteration of it.

XXIV. "I again requested, on the 17th, that you should refer by dates to any such communication as that alleged by you.

XXV. "You answered on 20th June, apologized for carelessness in your first reply, and referred me to a passage from my telegram to you of 28th May, and to one from the Secretary of War of 5th June; and then informed me that you considered 'Executive' as including Secretary of War.

XXVI. "Your telegram of 12th June was addressed to the Secretary of War in the second person; it begins 'your dispatch,' and then speaks of the Executive in the third person, and, on reading it, it was not supposed that the word Executive referred to any one but myself; but, of course, in a matter like this, your explanation of your meaning is conclusive.

XXVII. "The telegram of the Secretary of War of 5th June, followed by that of 8th June, conveyed unmistakably the very reverse of the meaning you attribute to them, and your reference to them as supporting your position is unintelligible. I revert, therefore, to my telegram of 28th May. That telegram was in answer to one from you in which you stated that on the arrival of certain reënforcements, then on the way, you would have about twenty-three thousand; that Pemberton could be saved only by beating Grant; and you added: 'Unless you can promise more troops, we must try with that number. The odds against us will be very great. Can you add seven thousand?'

"My reply was: 'The reënforcements sent to you exceed, by say seven thousand, the estimates of your dispatch of the 27th instant. We have withheld nothing which it was practicable to give you. We cannot hope for numerical equality, and time will probably increase the disparity.'

XXVIII. "It is on this language that you rely to support a statement that I informed you no more troops could be spared from Tennessee, and as restricting your right to draw troops from that department. It bears no such construction. The reënforcements sent you, with an exception presently to be noticed, were from points outside of your department. You had in telegrams of the 1st, 2d, and 7th of May, and others, made repeated applications to have troops withdrawn from other departments to your aid. You were informed that we would give all the aid we possibly could. Of your right to order any change made in the distribution of troops in your own district, no doubt had ever been suggested by yourself nor could they occur to your superiors here, for they had given you the authority.

XXIX. "The reënforcements, which went with you from Tennessee, were (as already explained and as was communicated to you at the time) a mere exchange for other troops sent from Virginia.

XXX. "The troops subsequently sent to you from Bragg were forwarded by him under the following dispatch from me of the 22d of May: 'The vital issue of holding the Mississippi at Vicksburg is dependent on the success of General Johnston in an attack on the investing force. The intelligence from there is discouraging. Can you aid him? If so,

and you are without orders from General Johnston,
act on your judgment.'

XXXI. "The words that I now underscore suf-
fice to show how thoroughly your right of command
of the troops in Tennessee was recognized. I knew
from your own orders that you thought it more advisable to draw troops from Mississippi to reënforce
Bragg, than to send troops from the latter to Pemberton ; and, one of the reasons which induced the instruction to you to proceed to Mississippi was, the
conviction that your views on this point would be
changed on arrival in Mississippi. Still, although
convinced myself that troops might be spared from
Bragg's army, without very great danger, and that
Vicksburg was, on the contrary, in imminent peril, I
was unwilling to overrule your judgment of the
distribution of your troops while you were on the
spot, and therefore simply left to General Bragg the
power to aid you if he could, *and if you had not
given contrary orders.*

XXXII. "The cavalry sent you from Tennessee
was sent you on a similar dispatch from the Secretary
of War to General Bragg, informing him of your
earnest appeal for cavalry, and *asking him if he
could spare any.* Your request was for a regiment
of cavalry to be sent to you from Georgia. My dispatch of 18th May pointed out to you the delay
which a compliance would involve, and suggested
that cavalry could be drawn from ' another part of
your department' as had been previously indicated.

XXXIII. "In no manner, by no act, by no language, either of myself or of the Secretary of War,
has your authority to draw troops from one portion

of your department to another been withdrawn, restricted, or modified.

XXXIV. " Now that Vicksburg has disastrously
fallen, this subject would present no pressing demand
for attention, and its examination would have been
postponed to a future period, had not your dispatch
of the 5th instant, with its persistent repetition of
statements which I had informed you were erroneous,
and without adducing a single fact to sustain them,
induced me to terminate the matter at once by a review of all the facts. The original mistakes in your
telegram of 12th of June would gladly have been
overlooked as accidental, if acknowledged when
pointed out. The perseverance with which they
have been insisted on has not permitted me to pass
them by as mere oversights, or, by refraining from an
answer, to seem to admit the justice of the statements.

     " Very respectfully,
       " Your obedient servant,
  (Signed)   " JEFFERSON DAVIS."

GENERAL J. E. JOHNSTON.

  NOTE.—The paragraphs in the above letter were numbered by me,
for precision of reference.

This letter seems to have been written to prove
that I committed a grave military offense, by regarding the order of May 19th as assigning me to a new
position, and limiting my command to the Department of Mississippi.

Much of it is to prove what those concerned could
not doubt, and never denied: that, on the 24th of
November, 1862, I was assigned to the command of

the armies under General Bragg, and Lieutenant-Generals E. Kirby Smith and Pemberton, in Tennessee and Mississippi. The object of much more of it is to show, to as little purpose, that the order of May 9th annulled no part of that of November 24, 1862.

The President's interpretation of his own orders was conclusive. That in question was interpreted in a telegram dated June 8th, five or six weeks before this letter left his office. This explanation made all arguments and instances useless, and left no occasion for a very long and harsh letter. The fact that General Bragg's department had been formally separated from mine (July 22d) before this letter was dispatched, would have made it useless, if it had not been so before.

I am also accused of having persisted in my error. The only ground of this charge is, that being asked by the President the same question in three distinct telegrams, I replied to them successively, endeavoring to make each reply clearer than the preceding one.

I maintain that, however the order of May 9th may have been intended, it dissolved practically my connection with General Bragg and his army. For it is certain that while commanding one army in Mississippi, in the presence of the much more powerful one of General Grant, it was impossible for me to direct the operations of another far off in Tennessee, also greatly outnumbered by its enemy. That a general should command but one army, and that every army should have its general present with it, are maxims observed by all governments—because the world has produced few men competent to command a large army when present with it, and none capable of directing the operations of one hundreds of miles off; still less one capable of doing both at the same time. My interpretation of the order in question was the only one consistent with the respect I entertained for the President's knowledge of military affairs, and therefore did not make me obnoxious to the rebuke expressed in every part of this letter. My belief that he was incapable of an absurdity too gross to have been committed by the government of any other civilized nation, certainly should not have brought upon me his harsh censure.

I hold now, as I did then, that it was quite immaterial whether or not my lawful authority extended over General Bragg's army when I was in Mississippi; for it was impossible for me to exercise it. I might have drawn troops from Tennessee to Mississippi. But the Executive knew that for months my opinion had been opposed to that, and I knew from the two dispatches of June 5th,[1] one to Governor Pettus, the other[2] to me, that it thought that General Bragg could spare no more men, as I did.

The charge in paragraph XVI., that I abandoned my "duties as commanding general of a military district," is utterly unfounded, unless the *not* doing[3] what both the President and I thought ought *not* to be done constituted failure to discharge my duties.

[1] *See* p. 213.   [2] *See* p. 199.
[3] Transferring troops from Bragg's army to Pemberton's in June.

"MORTON, *August* 8, 1863.

"MR. PRESIDENT: I. Your letter of July 15th was handed to me in Mobile on the 28th, by Colonel Shaller. The want of papers to which it was necessary to refer prevented me from replying sooner.

"II. I respectfully ask your Excellency to reconsider the several allegations of your letter, and especially to consider whether my misapprehension of the order sending me to Mississippi, my having regarded my assignment to the immediate command in that department as having given me a new position and limiting my authority—an opinion which had no practical results, which affected in no way the exercise of my military functions, and which had been removed before you noticed it—was a serious military offense. It affected my military course in no way, because, while commanding on the spot in Mississippi, I could not direct General Bragg's operations in Tennessee, and because I felt that the question of ordering more troops from Bragg, one of great magnitude, involving at least the temporary loss of Tennessee and Mississippi, ought to be decided by the Government, and not by me. This opinion was expressed in my dispatch to the Secretary of War of June 12th, in these words: 'To take from Bragg a force which would make this army fit to oppose that of Grant would involve yielding Tennessee. It is for the Government to decide between this State and Tennessee.' The idea was thus repeated on the 15th: 'Nor is it for me to judge which it is best to hold, Mississippi or Tennessee, that is for the Government to determine; without some great blunder by the

enemy, we cannot hold both.' Had I received a copy
of your orders of May 22d, directing General Bragg
to send troops from his army to Mississippi, my error
would have been corrected then; but it was not sent
to me, and I have its evidence for the first time in
your letter. The dispatch of the Secretary of War,
of June 8th, received on the 10th, removed my misapprehension.

"III. In regard to the repetition and persistence
which you impute to me in the first sentence of your
letter, I cannot feel that my three brief telegrams,
dictated by the respect due from me to you, deserve
to be so characterized; the first and second, being
replies to direct questions in yours of the 15th and
17th, and the third, in reply to yours of the 30th
June, an attempt to say more clearly what had been
carelessly expressed in the first. They are so brief
as to require scarcely more than a minute for reading,
and are respectful in thought and language. You
subsequently characterized my misunderstanding the
order sending me to Mississippi as a grave error.
This error of mine, which was removed by the dispatch of the War Department, dated June 8th, and
which had no effect on my military course, does not
seem to me, I must confess, a grave one.

"IV. In the seventh paragraph of your letter you
write: 'While at Tullahoma you did not hesitate to
order troops from General Pemberton's army, and,
learning that you had ordered the division of cavalry
from Northern Mississippi to Tennessee, I telegraphed
you that this order left Mississippi exposed to cavalry raids without means of checking them. You did
not change your order,' etc. The only order I gave,

sending cavalry from Mississippi to Tennessee, was
early in January, when I was at Jackson, not Tullahoma. I can find but one telegram received from
you on the subject; it is dated April 30th, and in
these words: 'General Pemberton telegraphs that
unless he has more cavalry the approaches to North
Mississippi are almost unprotected, and that he cannot prevent the cavalry raids.' My reply is of the
same date : 'About three thousand of General Bragg's
cavalry, beyond the Tennessee, are employing about
twelve thousand Federal troops from Mississippi.
General Pemberton has been so informed twice.'
The main body of the cavalry of Mississippi was
near Grenada in January, unorganized and unemployed, and from the condition of the country it was
supposed by the officers and intelligent citizens whom
I consulted, including the Governor, that it would
be useless in the State until late in the spring. Grant
had fallen back toward Memphis, and Sherman and
McClernand had been repulsed at Vicksburg, but
Bragg's army had been terribly reduced by the engagements near Murfreesboro'. I therefore directed
Major-General Van Dorn to form about two-thirds of
the cavalry near Grenada into a division, and to join
General Bragg with it. These troops were transferred from a country in which they could not operate,
and a department not threatened, and in which the
enemy had just been repulsed, to one in which they
were greatly needed, where we had just suffered a
reverse and were in danger of another. These troops
and their gallant leader rendered very important
services in Tennessee. They had several engagements with the enemy, to the advantage and honor

of our arms.   Without them we could not have held
the country which, till the latter part of June, furnished food for Bragg's army.   More than two weeks
before your Excellency's dispatch of April 30th, a
brigade of cavalry was sent across the Tennessee to
aid in the protection of Mississippi, and, reports of
large reënforcements to the garrison of Corinth being
received, Brigadier-General Forrest was sent with
another on April 23d.   These two brigades constituted the force referred to in my dispatch of April
30th.   As soon as the falling back of the Federal
army made it practicable, Colonel Roddy was transferred to Mississippi, with about two-thirds of the
joint forces.

"In paragraph XII. you quote the dispatch of the
War Department to me of June 5th, as follows: 'I
regret inability to promise more troops, as we have
drained resources even to the danger of several points.
You know best concerning General Bragg's army,
but I fear to withdraw more.   We are too far outnumbered in Virginia to spare any,' etc., etc.   The
dispatch sent to me reads thus: 'I regret inability to
promise more troops.   Drained resources to the danger of several points.   You know best concerning
General Bragg's army, but I fear to withdraw more.
We are too far outnumbered *in it to spare any.*   You
must rely on what you have and the irregular forces
Mississippi can afford,' etc.   This is one of the dispatches which gave me the impression that the Executive wished no more troops withdrawn from Tennessee.

"V. I did not draw from that telegram the inference which you express in the next paragraph,

but understood the words, 'you know best concerning General Bragg's army,' to refer to the acquaintance with military affairs in Middle Tennessee, that I might be supposed to have acquired.

"VI. In paragraph XVI. your Excellency charges me with abandonment of my duties as commanding general of a geographical district. I respectfully deny the commission of such a military crime. During the month ending June 10th, in which I believed myself to be commanding only the department of Mississippi, it was not possible for me to direct operations in Tennessee also. It is true that I might have drawn troops from it to Mississippi; but my opinion on that subject was expressed to the War Department in my dispatches of June 12th and 15th as follows: 'To take from Bragg a force that would make this army fit to oppose Grant, would involve the yielding Tennessee. It is for the Government to decide between this State and Tennessee. Nor is it for me to judge which it is best to hold, Mississippi or Tennessee; that is for the Government to determine. Without some great blunder by the enemy, we cannot hold both.'

"In paragraph XX. you write: 'This was in deference to your own opinion that Bragg could not be safely weakened—nay, that he ought even to be reenforced at Pemberton's expense; for you had just ordered troops from Pemberton's command to reenforce Bragg.' The time alluded to seems to be the 9th of May, as your reference is to the order of that date. The United States army had then crossed the Mississippi, and defeated a large detachment of ours. To have 'ordered troops from Pemberton's command

to reënforce Bragg,' at that time, would have been
evidence of the grossest incapacity. Your excellency
will therefore pardon me, I am sure, for denying the
existence of such evidence. I have ordered troops
from Mississippi to Tennessee but twice. On both
occasions the condition of affairs was very different
from that existing at the time referred to. The first
order was that given to the cavalry early in January;
it was explained in paragraph IV. The second was
given about the 13th of April, when Lieutenant-General Pemberton informed me that Grant had abandoned operations against Vicksburg, and was moving
his army up the river, he supposed to join Rosecrans.
He had no enemy before him; Vicksburg was no
longer threatened. Bragg, on the other hand, could
not fully cover the country which fed his troops. I
therefore directed a force equal to that sent from
Bragg to Pemberton in December last under your instructions, to be sent from Mississippi to Tennessee;
intending, should Lieutenant-General Pemberton's
surmise prove correct, to continue to draw troops
from his army. But in a few days Lieutenant-General Pemberton reported the United States army
returning; and the troops on the way to Bragg, none
of which had arrived, were ordered back. This was
about the 19th of April, when the Federal army was
on the Mississippi in transports, or on the west side
of the river, and Pemberton's condition far less unfavorable than it was at the time to which you refer,
when the enemy had crossed the river and driven
back his advanced troops.

"In paragraph XXXI., in explaining your orders to General Bragg of May 22d, you say, 'I knew

from your own orders that you thought it more advisable to draw troops from Mississippi to reënforce Bragg than to send troops from the latter to Pemberton.' I have transferred but two bodies of troops from Mississippi to Tennessee—the first a division of cavalry, the other a division of infantry: the first in January, when McClernand and Sherman had abandoned the siege of Vicksburg, and Bragg had not begun to recover from the effects of the battle of Murfreesboro'; the second on the 13th of April, when Grant's army had abandoned Vicksburg. I respectfully submit to your Excellency that these orders do not prove that at a subsequent period, when the relative condition of the two armies was entirely changed, when Pemberton was most threatened, a powerful army having forced the passage of the Mississippi and beaten back his advanced troops, I thought it ' more advisable to draw troops from Mississippi to reënforce Bragg than to send troops from the latter to Pemberton.' But my sending back the division of infantry, employing a division of Bragg's cavalry to aid Pemberton in April, transferring a large brigade of cavalry into Mississippi on the 5th of May, and applying for reënforcements for Pemberton on the 7th, suggesting that the withdrawal of Foster's troops might enable Beauregard to furnish them, prove the contrary.

"In paragraph XXI., your Excellency refers to the constant desire shown in my correspondence, beginning early in January, that you should change the order placing Tennessee and Mississippi in one command under my direction. That desire was founded on the belief that the arrangement was not in accordance with military principles, which require that every army should have its own general, and especially that two armies far apart, having different objects, and opposed to enemies having different objects, should not be under one general. I thought these armies too far apart to reënforce each other in emergencies. Experience has confirmed that opinion. I thought, however, that the troops in Arkansas should coöperate with those of Lieutenant-General Pemberton, for both had the same great object—the defense of the Mississippi Valley; and both were opposed to troops having one object—the possession of the Mississippi: and the main force of these troops was operating on this side of the river.

"Permit me to say that, after careful consideration, I can find nothing in my three brief telegrams which seems to me to call for the animadversions in your last paragraph. They were written in answer to dispatches of yours, and referred to an opinion of mine which had been corrected before your attention was called to it. I had no other object, besides the duty of replying to your dispatches, than to prevent your supposing that the opinion concerning which you questioned me was entirely unfounded. But, whether well founded or unfounded, that opinion was a thing of the past when first brought to your notice, and therefore I cannot feel that the having once entertained it is a military offense, or that the manner in which I attempted to extenuate my misapprehension of the Honorable Secretary's telegram of May

9th, makes me obnoxious to the imputations of your letter, especially those of the concluding paragraph.

"Most respectfully
"Your obedient servant,
(Signed)   "J. E. Johnston,
"*General.*"

(Copy.)

In a letter from the War Department, dated the 6th, the temporary rebuilding of the railroad-bridge at Jackson was suggested to me—the work to be under the direction of the engineer-officers of the army; its object, the bringing off the rolling-stock and a part of the iron of the Mississippi Central Railroad. A part of that rolling-stock, not in daily use, was then at Grenada, where the principal officers of the railroad company had placed it for safety. As the measures already taken seemed to me more proper as well as better than this one, no change was made. If, however, there had been no impediment to the removal of the engines and cars at Grenada, I should not have advocated the measure, for they could not have been carried beyond the Mobile & Ohio Railroad, on which, near Mobile, there was then a very large collection of that kind of property; and I think that it would not have been judicious to collect all the spare engines and cars of the department at one point.

On the 15th it was ascertained that a body of eight or nine hundred Federal cavalry was moving from Yazoo City, by Lexington, toward Grenada; and another, of equal strength, advancing from the vicinity of Grand Junction, as if to meet it. Brig-

adier-General Jackson sent his nearest troops (Whitfield's brigade) in pursuit of the party from Yazoo
City; and Major-General Lee took prompt measures
to unite Chalmers's and Ferguson's brigades with
them.

Brigadier-General Whitfield pressed forward rapidly to Duck Hill; but, having learned there that
the two Federal parties had united at Grenada, he
turned back, and destroyed, in his retreat along the
railroad, all the rolling-stock that was found on it.
The two Federal parties united were at the same
time moving to the north, after burning about a
fourth of the town of Grenada, and the engines and
cars in depot there.

On the 17th an order was received instituting a
court of inquiry to meet in Montgomery on the 15th,
to investigate the management of recent affairs in
Mississippi, and ascertain the causes of our disasters.
Although the purpose of this investigation was to
decide whether Lieutenant-General Pemberton or myself was responsible for those disasters, the arrangement made by the Administration did not make me
a party to it. In a telegram of that date to General
Cooper, I claimed the right to be present for my defense, and on the 21st the War Department conceded that right.

On the 22d the following dispatch, dated Ringgold, August 21st, was received from General Bragg:
"Enemy in force opposite us, and reported in large
force moving on Knoxville. Will need help if he
advances with his troops from Tennessee and Kentucky." I immediately asked the War Department,
by telegraph, if I was authorized to reënforce Gen-

eral Bragg with a part of the troops of the Department of Mississippi, if he should require aid, and informed General Bragg of the inquiry; telling him also that, in the event of an affirmative answer, two divisions would be sent to him. In preparation for the contingency, Major-Generals Breckenridge and W. H. S. Walker were directed to hold their divisions ready to move; and Major Barbour, chief quartermaster, to order the necessary means of railroad transportation. General Cooper's reply, in the affirmative, was received that evening, as well as Major Barbour's report that the railroad trains required were promised at two o'clock P. M. next day. General Bragg was immediately told of this, and informed that the troops would move as soon as the railroad-trains were ready. He was also requested to give the necessary orders at West Point and Atlanta.

All the infantry in the department would have been sent to the assistance of the Army of Tennessee but for the supposed probability of the investment of Mobile by the enemy. According to the estimates of Major-General Maury, and his chief-engineer, Brigadier-General Leadbetter, fifteen thousand infantry would be necessary for the defense of the place on the land-side in the event of a siege. He had but two thousand; and they and the troops remaining in Mississippi, to join the garrison if necessary, amounted to but eleven thousand.

On the 29th Lieutenant-General Hardee was assigned by the Administration to the service of reorganizing the prisoners paroled at Vicksburg and then returning from furlough. He fixed his headquarters at Enterprise, where Hebert's and Baldwin's brigades had been ordered to assemble.

Being summoned by the judge-advocate, Major Barton, to attend the court of inquiry, to be held in Atlanta, in relation to the loss of Vicksburg and Port Hudson, I set out for that place in the evening of the 2d of September, but stopped in Montgomery in consequence of intelligence received there that its time of meeting had been postponed. On the 6th, while still there, I received a dispatch from General Bragg, asking that a division of infantry might be hurried to Atlanta, to save that depot and give him time to defeat the enemy's plans. Lieutenant-General Hardee was immediately requested to send Gregg's and McNair's brigades from Meridian and Enterprise to Atlanta, and to replace them at those points by Featherston's and Adams's. This movement was begun the following night. When it became evident that Atlanta was in no danger, the two brigades sent to defend it were ordered to join General Bragg's army near Chattanooga, and were engaged in the battle of Chickamauga.

Being informed that another day of meeting of the court of inquiry had been appointed (the 9th), I was in attendance in the morning of that day. Those concerned who were present were then informed by Major-General R. Ransom, the president of the court, that the officers composing it were ordered by the Administration to return to their several stations.

At Meridian, where the headquarters of the department were established after my return to Mississippi, a telegram, dated 22d, was received from General Bragg on that day, announcing that " after four days' fighting we had driven the enemy from the State of Georgia, and were still pursuing him; that he had encountered the most obstinate resistance, but the valor of our troops, under great privations, had overcome them all. Under God's providence our loss was severe, but results were commensurate." McNair's and Ector's brigades, the latter substituted for Gregg's, were sent back to Mississippi by General Bragg, after the battle of Chickamauga. The honorable part they bore in that terrible fight had exposed them to very heavy losses.

At Canton, on the 27th, Brigadier-General W. H. Jackson informed me that his scouts on the Mississippi, between Vicksburg and Memphis, reported that sixteen thousand United States troops had passed up the river since the 20th, on their way, it was supposed, to join the army at Chattanooga.

On the 28th, six or eight regiments of Federal cavalry, with a field-battery, advanced toward Canton from the direction of Vernon; but General Jackson, coming from Livingston, interposed Whitfield's brigade of his division, upon which the Federal troops retired.

The following telegram from General Bragg, dated the 29th, came to me in Oxford on that day: "Give us all the assistance you can. Enemy is evidently assembling all his available forces. He is strongly fortified in Chattanooga, but is embarrassed to supply over the mountains. We hold the railroad to Bridgeport. Should he open the route, your cavalry might pass up rear."

I promised, on the same day, to send a body of cavalry under Major-General Lee, to interrupt the railroad communication of the Federal army through Tennessee, and suggested to General Bragg, in that connection, the expediency of adding General Roddy's brigade, belonging to his department, and then near Tuscumbia, to Major-General Lee's detachment.

That officer was instructed to make the expedition as soon as possible, and to select from it about twenty-five hundred of the best cavalry in Northern Mississippi, and his most effective battery, to march by the route on which he would be most likely to escape the observation of the enemy, to the points on the railroad from Nashville to Chattanooga, where most injury could be done to it with least exposure of his troops; and to order Chalmers's brigade to attack the Federal troops stationed along the Mississippi & Charleston Railroad a day or two before his movement began.

Captain Henderson, who directed the service of our scouts, reported that a part of Sherman's (Fifteenth) corps was at Memphis at this time, on its way to join the United States army at Chattanooga.

On the 10th of October, Brigadier-General Chalmers, then at Holly Springs, reported that on the 6th he had driven a detachment of about eight hundred Federal troops from Coldwater, after a slight skirmish, and that on the 8th he had encountered a body of two thousand with six field-pieces, at Salem, and routed it after an engagement of three hours. His loss was three killed and forty-seven wounded. Ten of the enemy were killed, but the number of their wounded could not be ascertained.

On the 12th, at Byhalia, he reported that, after tearing up the rails of the Memphis & Charleston road in four places, he had attacked the Federal forces at Colliersville in their camp, driven them into their intrenchments, burned the camp and a quantity of military property, including thirty wagons, brought off a hundred and four prisoners, five colors, and about twenty wagons. He did not learn the enemy's loss in killed and wounded. His own was fifty. On the approach of fresh Federal troops from Lafayette and Germantown, he retreated to Byhalia.

On the 14th, at Oxford, he reported that eleven regiments of cavalry had followed him to Byhalia and attacked him there; that, after fighting them four hours, he had fallen back, skirmishing, to the Tallahatchie at Wyat, where the assailants were repulsed, and retired, after burning the village. The Confederate baggage and the captured property were preserved.

On the 15th, being still at Oxford, he sent me intelligence (on the authority of his scouts) that some four thousand United States troops, with a hundred wagons, had passed through Holly Springs the day before, going southward. To meet this incursion, Major-General Loring was ordered to hasten to Grenada with his division. Next day, however, another dispatch from General Chalmers, sent from Water Valley, informed me that the Federal party had turned back—"burning in every direction," including the village of Chulahoma.

In the mean time intelligence was received from Canton that two divisions of Federal infantry, a brigade of cavalry, and some artillery, had crossed the Big Black at Messenger's Ferry, and were marching toward Brownsville — very slowly, however, for

General Jackson, with a part of his division, was opposing every step of their progress with character-istic resolution; and with such effect that, in that and the two following days, they advanced but twelve miles. Upon this information, Major-General Loring was directed to join Jackson with his divis-ion, and Ector's and McNair's brigades. Before all of these troops had reached Canton, however, Gen-eral Jackson reported that the enemy had turned back (in the morning of the 18th) seven or eight miles from Livingston, and retired rapidly toward Vicksburg by Bolton's and Edwards's Depots.

Soon after the middle of the month, Major-Gen-eral Lee arrived at the point where he intended to cross the Tennessee River, near the head of the Mus-cle Shoals, with the detachment he had organized for the expedition against the communications of the army at Chattanooga. There he met General Wheel-er with his division, returning from Middle Tennes-see, where he had been operating under General Bragg's orders. His representations of the number of Federal troops in that district of country con-vinced General Lee that he could not operate in it with hope of success, or without great danger of los-ing his detachment, especially as Roddy's brigade had not been put at his disposal. He, therefore, very judiciously abandoned the enterprise.

He found employment for his troops without going far, however; for General Sherman's corps, on its way from Vicksburg *via* Memphis, to the army at Chattanooga, was then between Tuscumbia and Corinth. In a dispatch dated 22d, and received on the 26th, he reported that he was then ten miles west of Tuscumbia, impeding the march of Sherman's corps toward Decatur, encountering Osterhaus's division, which was the leading one. General Sherman's headquarters were at Iuka.

Brigadier-General Chalmers was immediately directed to do his utmost to interrupt the communication of those troops with Memphis, by breaking the railroad in their rear, and otherwise.

In a telegram received on the 26th, General Bragg wrote: "Rosecrans is relieved, and his department merged in Grant's. Thomas commands the army. Grant is here, or soon to be, and this is to be the theatre of future operations."

Major-General Lee, with his twenty-five hundred cavalry, continued to oppose the march of Sherman's troops very effectively for the space of ten days. The contest was terminated at the end of that time, by a change of plan by the Federal commander, who, falling back, crossed the Tennessee below the Muscle Shoals and then resumed his course toward Chattanooga on the north side of the river.

General Bragg, then at Missionary Ridge, informed me by telegraph, on the 4th of November, of the approach of the Fifteenth Corps, and also that General Grant had assumed command of the army confronting him. He added that he should probably be attacked as soon as all the expected reënforcements joined the Federal army, and therefore that he should hope for any troops I could spare from Mobile or Mississippi, but that my " previous generosity forbade him to ask for any thing."

In consequence of this information, two more brigades were immediately ordered to join the Army of Tennessee in front of Chattanooga. They were Quarles's and Baldwin's, the latter composed of Vicksburg troops.

On the 18th the President visited the troops at Demopolis, and on the 20th those at Enterprise. While there he transferred Lieutenant-General Hardee back to the Army of Tennessee, and assigned Lieutenant-General Polk to the position he had occupied in the Department of Mississippi and East Louisiana. With Lieutenant-General Hardee he transferred Pettus's and Moore's brigades, then at Demopolis, to General Bragg's command. All left Demopolis, for the Army of Tennessee, on the 27th.

About that time Brigadier-General Ferguson, who had been detached, by Major-General Lee, with a part of his brigade in pursuit of a party of Federal cavalry on a predatory incursion, in Marion County, Alabama, attacked and routed it, capturing its artillery. It was driven home by this defeat.

On Dec. 18th, a telegram from the President was delivered to me in the camp of General Ross's brigade of Texan cavalry near Bolton's Depot, directing me to transfer the command of the Department of Mississippi and East Louisiana to Lieutenant-General Polk, and to repair to Dalton and assume that of the Army of Tennessee; and promising that I should find *instructions* there.

In obedience to these orders, I transferred my command to Lieutenant-General Polk as soon as possible, proceeded to Dalton without delay, arrived in the evening of the 26th, and assumed the command of the Army of Tennessee on the 27th.

CHAPTER IX.

Find Letter of Instruction from Secretary of War at Dalton.—My Reply.—Letter from the President.—Mine in reply.—Condition of the Army.—General
Hardee ordered to Mississippi to repel General Sherman's Advance.—
Movements of the Enemy in our Front.—Dispositions to meet them.—General Hardee and his Troops return to Dalton.—Correspondence with General Bragg.—Effective Strength of the Army of Tennessee.—Advance of
General Sherman.

I FOUND in Dalton a part of the instructions promised me by the President in his telegram of the 18th
of December, in the following letter from the Secretary of War, Mr. Seddon, dated the 20th:

" GENERAL: You have been instructed by the
President to proceed to Dalton and take command
of the army now under the charge of Lieutenant-
General Hardee. You were also informed that you
would there receive fuller instructions. Such I now
aim, in behalf of this department, to communicate.
" It is apprehended the army may have been, by
recent events, somewhat disheartened, and deprived
of ordnance and material. Your presence, it is hoped,
will do much to reëstablish hope and inspire confidence, and through such influence, as well as by the
active exertions you are recommended to make, men
who have straggled may be recalled to their standards, and others, roused to the dangers to which further successes of the enemy must expose the more

Southern States, may be encouraged to recruit the ranks of your army. It is desired that your early and vigorous efforts be directed to restoring the discipline, prestige, and confidence of the army, and to increasing its numbers; and that at the same time you leave no means unspared to restore and supply its deficiencies in ordnance, munitions, and transportation. It is feared also that under the grave embarrassments to which the commissariat is exposed, both from the deficiencies of supplies in the country, and the impediments which unfortunately the discontents of producers and the opposition of State authorities to the system of impressment established by the law of Congress have caused, you may find deficiences in and have serious difficulties in providing the supplies required for the subsistence of the army. You will use all means in your power to obtain supplies from the productive States around you, and strong confidence is entertained that you may be enabled to rouse among the people and authorities a more willing spirit to part with the means of subsistence for the army that defends them. Meantime the efforts of the Commissary Bureau will be directed to aid in your supply, and General Polk will be instructed to afford from your late department such resources as can be spared.

" The movements of the enemy give no indications of a purpose to attack your army, and it is probable that they may mean to strengthen themselves in the occupation of the portions of Tennessee they have overrun. It is not desirable they should be allowed to do so with impunity, and, as soon as the condition of your forces will allow, it is hoped you will be able to resume the offensive. Inactivity, it is feared, may cause the spirit of despondency to recur, and the practice of desertion and straggling to increase. Should the enemy venture to separate his army, or send off detachments on different expeditions, it is hoped you may be able early to strike them with effect. While, however, these suggestions are ventured, your own experience and judgment are relied on to form and act on your plans of military operations, and there will be the fullest disposition on the part of this department to sustain and coöperate with them. With this view you are invited to communicate freely with the department, and to disclose your conceptions of the military situation, and how the most efficient coöperation may be given you. At the same time it is feared the other imperative claims on the department must confine you almost exclusively to the resources of your present department, and such general aid as it may be in the power of General Polk to render, with whom consultation, as to the general ends to be accomplished by both, is recommended."

Although unable at the time to discover the Honorable Secretary's object in addressing such a letter to one thought competent, apparently, to the second military position in importance in the Confederacy, or to find in it much that was instructive, I replied immediately, and gravely.

"Sir: I had the honor to receive your 'letter of instructions' yesterday. Having perused it carefully more than once, I respectfully inclose it herewith, that you may do me the favor to affix your signature and return it.

"Having arrived but two days ago, I have been able to obtain no information, directly, of the enemy's positions and strength; and the principal officers of the army can give me but little. It is believed by them that the army in our front amounts to about eighty thousand men; occupying Chattanooga, now strongly fortified, Bridgeport, and Stevenson. I find the country unfit for military operations, from the effect of heavy rains. Its condition prevents military exercises—a most important means of discipline.

"The duties of military administration that you point out to me shall be attended to with diligence. The most difficult of them will be the procuring supplies of food. Foreseeing this before leaving Mississippi, I applied for permission to bring Major W. E. Moore with me, to be chief commissary of the army. The reply of the adjutant and inspector general was, that Major Moore had been collecting supplies in Mississippi so long that it was deemed inexpedient to transfer him. General Cooper was mistaken. Major Moore has not served long in Mississippi, nor collected large supplies there. He made his reputation in this army. Major Dameron directs the purchase and impressment of provisions in Mississippi. So that Major Moore's position is not an important one. Therefore Lieutenant-General Polk, from interest in this army, is anxious that he should be its chief commissary. I therefore most respectfully repeat my application.

"This army is now far from being in condition to

'resume the offensive.' It is deficient in numbers, arms, subsistence stores, and field transportation.

"In reference to the subsistence of the army, you direct me to 'use all means in my power to obtain supplies from the productive States around me.' Let me remind you that I have little if any power to procure supplies for the army. The system established last summer deprives generals of any control over the officers of the quartermaster's and subsistence departments detailed to make purchases in the different States. I depend upon three majors in each State, neither of whom owes me obedience. Having no power to procure means of feeding, equipping, and moving the army, I am also released from the corresponding responsibilities. I refer to this matter in no spirit of discontent—for I have no taste, personally, for the duties in question—but to beg you to consider if the responsibility for keeping the army in condition to move and fight ought not to rest upon the general, instead of being divided among a number of officers who have not been thought by the Government competent to the duties of high military grades."

On the 31st I received the following letter from the President, dated 23d. Like that of the Secretary of War, it was ostensibly intended for my instruction.

"GENERAL: This is addressed under the supposition that you have arrived at Dalton, and have assumed command of the forces at that place. The intelligence recently received respecting the condition of that army is encouraging, and induces me to hope that you will soon be able to commence active operations against the enemy.

"The reports concerning the battle at Missionary Ridge show that our loss in killed and wounded was not great, and that the reverse sustained is not attributable to any general demoralization or reluctance to encounter the opposing army. The brilliant stand made by the rear-guard at Ringgold sustains this belief.

"In a letter written to me soon after the battle, General Bragg expressed his unshaken confidence in the courage and *morale* of the troops. He says: 'We can redeem the past. Let us concentrate all our available men, unite them with this little army, still full of zeal, and burning to redeem its lost character and prestige—hurl the whole upon the enemy, and crush him in his power and his glory. I believe it practicable, and that I may be allowed to participate in the struggle which may restore to us the character, the prestige, and the country, we have just lost. This will give us confidence and restore hope to the country and the army, while it will do what is more important, give us subsistence, without which I do not see how we are to remain united.'

"The official reports made to my aide-de-camp, Colonel Ives, who has just returned from Dalton, presented a not unfavorable view of the material of the command.

"The chief of ordnance reported that, notwithstanding the abandonment of a considerable number of guns during the battle, there was still on hand, owing to previous large captures by our troops, as many batteries as were proportionate to the strength of the army, well supplied with horses and equipment; that a large reserve of small-arms was in store at readily-accessible points; and that the supply of ammunition was abundant.

"Comparatively few wagons and ambulances had been lost, and sufficient remained for transportation purposes, if an equal distribution were made throughout the different corps. The teams appeared to be generally in fair condition. The troops were tolerably provided with clothing, and a heavy invoice of shoes and blankets daily expected.

"The returns from the commissary department showed that there were thirty days' provisions on hand.

"Stragglers and convalescents were rapidly coming in, and the morning reports exhibited an effective total, that, added to the two brigades last sent from Mississippi, and the cavalry sent back by Longstreet, would furnish a force exceeding in number that actually engaged in any battle on the Confederate side during the present war. General Hardee telegraphed to me on the 11th instant: 'The army is in good spirits; the artillery reorganized and equipped, and we are now ready to fight.'

"The effective condition of your new command, as thus reported to me, is a matter of much congratulation, and I assure you that nothing shall be wanting on the part of the Government to aid you in your efforts to regain possession of the territory from which we have been driven. You will not need to have it suggested that the imperative demand for prompt and vigorous action arises not only from the importance of restoring the prestige of the army, and averting the injurious and dispiriting results that must attend a season of inactivity, but from the necessity of reoccupying the country, upon the supplies of which the proper subsistence of our armies materially depends.

"Of the immediate measures to be adopted in attaining this end, the full importance of which I am sure you appreciate, you must be the best judge, after due inquiry and consideration on the spot shall have matured an opinion. It is my desire that you should communicate fully and freely with me concerning your proposed plan of action, that all the assistance and coöperation may be most advantageously afforded that it is in the power of the Government to render.

"Trusting that your health may be preserved, and that the arduous and responsible duties you have undertaken may be successfully accomplished, I remain

　　　"Very respectfully and truly yours,
(Signed)　　　　　　"JEFFERSON DAVIS."

I was unable then, as now, to imagine any military object for which this letter could have been written, especially by one whose time was supposed to be devoted to the most important concerns of government. The President could not have thought that I was to be taught the moral and material condition of the army around me by him, from the observations of his aide-de-camp, who had never seen military service, instead of learning them by my own. Nor could he have believed that the army which he so described was competent to recover " the territory from which it had been driven." He had visited it some two months before, and seen that it could make no forward movement for the purpose then, when the opposing Federal army had not been increased by the corps of twenty thousand veterans, led from Mississippi by Sherman; nor ours weakened by the withdrawal from it of Longstreet's corps,[1] and its losses at Missionary Ridge. Those losses must have been severe, for such troops are not easily driven from strong and intrenched positions; still less, easily routed. As I had much better means of information on the subjects of this paper than its author, it could not have been written for my instruction.

The two high executive officers expressed in their letters very different opinions of the effect of its recent defeat, upon the army. The Secretary of War expressed plainly his consciousness of the great losses it had suffered in men, *morale*, and material. The President, on the contrary, regarded " the effective condition " of the army as " a matter of much congratulation." And, to give a distinct idea of its strength, he asserted that " the morning report exhibited an effective total that, added to the two brigades last sent from Mississippi,[2] and the cavalry sent back by Longstreet,[3] would furnish a force exceeding in number that actually engaged in any battle, on the Confederate side, during the present war."

To disprove this assertion, it is not necessary to

[1] About fourteen thousand of the best of the Confederate troops.

[2] Quarles's and Baldwin's brigades, sent back to Mississippi by the President two weeks after.

[3] No cavalry had been sent back by Longstreet; Martin's division, referred to, rejoined us in April following.

go back to the previous years of the war, and the greatest of the Confederate armies—those directed by General Lee against McClellan and Pope. It is enough to refer to the recent history of this very army—the remnant of that which fought at Chicka- mauga and Missionary Ridge. On the first of those occasions a number more than double the " effective total" in question must have been led into battle, for it lost eighteen thousand men then.[1] At least seven thousand were killed, wounded, dispersed, or taken at Missionary Ridge, and in the retreat thence to Dalton, and fifteen thousand five hundred [2] had been sent from it in Longstreet's corps, and Ector's and McNair's brigades. On the other hand, " the two last brigades sent from Mississippi " had an effective total of three thousand, and four thousand of the fugitives of Missionary Ridge had rejoined their regiments at Dalton. According to these fig- ures, forty thousand men had been lost, and seven thousand gained by this army. So that its " effective total " scarcely exceeded half the number that fought on the Confederate side at Chickamauga. Cavalry is not included in the foregoing figures. The number of troops of that arm had been reduced also, and, as Martin's division fought at Chickamauga, its presence at Dalton would not have affected the above state- ment materially, for hard service had told so severely upon its horses that much less than half were effec- tive.

[1] Statement of General Mackall, General Bragg's chief-of-staff.

[2] Longstreet's corps had fourteen thousand infantry and artillery (*see* General Bragg's letter of March, p. 293). Ector's and McNair's brigades numbered about fifteen hundred when they returned to Missis- sippi.

Heavy rains, which were prevailing at the time of my arrival at Dalton, and the consequent deep mud, prevented the immediate bringing out of the troops for inspection, to ascertain their condition. In replying to the President's letter on the 2d of January, I endeavored to avoid erring on the unfavorable side of the case. Fuller information, soon obtained by personal observation, showed that the statements in it relating to the clothing of the troops, and the condition of the horses and mules of the army, were much too favorable. That reply was as follows:

"DALTON, *January* 2, 1864.

"MR. PRESIDENT: I have received the letter which you did me the honor to write to me on the 23d ultimo.

"Having been here but six days, during four of which it rained heavily, I have not been able to observe the condition of the army. I judge, however, from the language of the general officers, that it has not entirely recovered its confidence, and that its discipline is not so thorough as it was last spring. The men are, generally, comfortably clothed; a few shoes and blankets are wanting in each brigade, which the chief quartermaster promises to supply very soon.

"According to the return of December 20th, the effective total of the army (infantry and artillery) is not quite thirty-six thousand; the number present about forty-three thousand; that present and absent about seventy-seven thousand. The reports of the adjutant-general show that about four thousand men have returned to the ranks since the battle of Missionary Ridge. My predecessor estimated the enemy's force at Chattanooga, Bridgeport, and Stevenson, at about eighty thousand.

"Major-General Wheeler reports that about two-thirds of his cavalry is with General Longstreet. He has about sixteen hundred in our front; Major-General Wharton has eight hundred and fifty near Rome, and Brigadier-General Roddy, with his brigade, is supposed to be near Tuscumbia—his strength not reported. I am afraid that this cavalry is not very efficient—that want of harmony among the superior officers causes its discipline to be imperfect. I will endeavor to improve it during the winter.

"The artillery is sufficient for the present strength of the army, but is deficient in discipline and instruction, especially in firing. The horses are not in good condition. It has about two hundred rounds of ammunition. Its organization is very imperfect.

"We have more than one hundred and twenty rounds of infantry ammunition, and no difficulty in obtaining more.

"The chief quartermaster reports that, besides the baggage-wagons of the troops, he has enough to transport eight days' rations, but that will leave no means of transporting forage and other stores of his department. The teams are improving, but are far from being in good condition. One hundred and twenty wagons are expected from the Department of Mississippi, promised by Lieutenant-General Polk.

"The army depends for subsistence upon an officer at Atlanta (Major Cummings), who acts under the orders of the Commissary-General. The chief com-

missary of the army reports that that officer has provided for the next month, but we depend upon the
railroad for bringing supplies to the troops.   As yet
rations for but five days have been accumulated here,
with a supply for three previously placed at Calhoun,
twenty miles to the rear.   We have had no receipts
for two days, for want, it is said, of good fuel on the
road.   The practice of transporting beef-cattle by
railroad has made it impossible to accumulate stores
here.   I propose, as soon as the arrangement can be
made, to have the cattle driven, but the change will
require time.   The men are not entirely satisfied with
the ration, it is said.

"Your Excellency well impresses upon me the
importance of recovering the territory we have lost.
I feel it deeply, but difficulties appear to me in the
way.

"The Secretary of War has informed me that I
must not hope for reënforcements.   To assume the
offensive from this point, we must move either into
Middle or East Tennessee.   To the first, the obstacles
are Chattanooga, now a fortress, the Tennessee River,
the rugged desert of the Cumberland Mountains, and
an army outnumbering ours more than two to one.
The second course would leave the way into Georgia
open.   We have neither subsistence nor field transportation enough for either march.   General Bragg
and Lieutenant-General Hardee, in suggesting the
offensive, proposed to operate with a powerful army
formed upon this as a nucleus.   The former was unable to advance before the arrival of Sherman had
added twenty-five thousand men to the Federal army,
and the march of Longstreet into East Tennessee had

reduced ours by twelve thousand. The latter, in his letter to you of the 17th ultimo, expresses the opinion that this army is too weak to oppose the enemy should he advance.

"There would be much less difficulty, I think, in advancing from Northern Mississippi, avoiding the mountains.

"I can see no other mode of taking the offensive here, than to beat the enemy when he advances, and then move forward. But, to make victory probable, the army must be strengthened. A ready mode of doing this would be by substituting negroes for all the soldiers on detached or daily duty, as well as company cooks, pioneers, and laborers for engineer service. This would give us at once ten or twelve thousand men. And the other armies of the Confederacy might be strengthened in the same proportion. Immediate and judicious legislation would be necessary, however.

"I earnestly ask your Excellency's consideration of this matter. A law authorizing the Government to take negroes for all the duties out of the ranks, for which soldiers are now detailed, giving the slave a portion of the pay, and punishing the master for not returning him if he deserts, would enable us to keep them in service. This is the opinion of the seven or eight ranking officers present.

"My experience in Mississippi was, that impressed negroes run away whenever it is possible, and are frequently encouraged by their masters to do so; and I never knew one to be returned by his master.

"I respectfully suggest the division of this army into three corps, and, should your Excellency adopt that suggestion, the appointment of lieutenant-generals from some other army.

> " Very respectfully,
> "J. E. JOHNSTON."

I supposed, from the information given me by the ranking general officers, that Dalton had not been selected by General Bragg for its value as a defensive position, but that the retreat from Missionary Ridge had ceased at that point, because it was ascertained there that the pursuit had been abandoned by the Federal army. Each division, consequently, was occupying the position it had taken for the encampment of a night, and on it had constructed huts for its winter quarters. These divisions formed two corps: one commanded by Lieutenant-General Hardee, composed of Cheatham's, Breckenridge's, Cleburne's, and Walker's divisions; the other, commanded by Major-General Hindman, was composed of his own, Stevenson's, and Stewart's divisions.

Major-General Wheeler, with such of his cavalry as was fittest for active service, amounting to about sixteen hundred, was at the village of Tunnel Hill, on the railroad, seven miles from Dalton, in the direction of Ringgold; his pickets on Taylor's Ridge, in front, and on the left, but extending to the right beyond the Cleveland road. Cleburne's division occupied the crest of Tunnel Hill, on both sides of the wagon-road from Dalton to Ringgold. Stewart's division had one brigade in front of, one in, and two immediately in rear of Mill-Creek Gap. Breckenridge was between the Gap and Dalton; Hind-

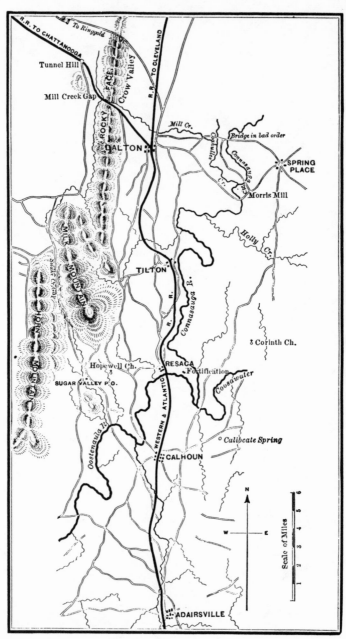

CAMPAIGN IN NORTH GEORGIA. No. 1.

man's, two miles southwest of Dalton, except a brigade on the Cleveland road; Stevenson's, near Hindman's; Walker's, three miles east of Dalton; and
Cheatham's, near and to the south of Walker's.

The Federal army in our front—that by which
ours had been driven from Missionary Ridge to Dalton—was estimated by our principal officers, who
had been confronting it for almost two years, at
eighty thousand men, exclusive of cavalry. This
was undoubtedly an over-estimate.[1] These troops
occupied Chattanooga, Bridgeport, and Stevenson.
Besides them, the Ninth and Twenty-third Corps,
twenty-five or thirty thousand, were at Knoxville.
Longstreet's corps and Martin's cavalry division of
the Army of Tennessee were in observation of these
troops, forty miles from them, toward Virginia.[2]

The position of Dalton had little to recommend
it as a defensive one. It had neither intrinsic
strength nor strategic advantage. It neither fully
covered its own communications nor threatened
those of the enemy. The railroad from Atlanta to
Chattanooga passes through Rocky-Faced Ridge by
Mill-Creek Gap, three miles and a half beyond Dalton, but very obliquely, the course of the road being about thirty degrees west of north, and that of
the ridge about five degrees east of north. As it ter-
minates but three miles north of the gap, it offers
little obstacle to the advance of a superior force

---

[1] This number was estimated to be sixty-five thousand by an officer
who belonged to General Grant's staff at Chattanooga.

[2] Besides these, there were about eight hundred and fifty men under
General Wharton's command, in a sort of camp for broken-down horses,
to the south of Rome, and Brigadier-General Roddy's strong brigade
near Tuscumbia.

from Ringgold to Dalton.   Between Mill-Creek and Snake-Creek Gaps, this ridge protects the road to Atlanta on the west, but at the same time covers any direct approach from Chattanooga to Resaca or Calhoun—points on the route from Dalton to Atlanta—or flank movement in that direction, by an army in front of Mill-Creek Gap.   These considerations would have induced me to draw the troops back to the vicinity of Calhoun, to free our left flank from exposure, but for the earnestness with which the President and Secretary of War, in their letters of instructions, wrote of early assumption of offensive operations and apprehension of the bad effect of a retrograde movement upon the spirit of the Southern people.

An active campaign of six months, half of it in the rugged region between Chattanooga and Dalton, had so much reduced the condition of the horses of the cavalry and artillery, as well as of the mules of the wagon-trains, that most of them were unfit for active service.   The rest they had been allowed at Dalton had not improved their condition materially; for, from want of good fuel, the railroad-trains had not been able to bring up full supplies of forage. This continued until near the end of January, when the management of the railroad had been greatly improved by the intervention of Governor Brown, and a better system introduced in the manner of forwarding military supplies.

This scarcity of food made it necessary to send almost half of the artillery-horses and all the mules not required for camp-service to the valley of the Etowah, where long forage could be found, and the sources of supply of grain were nearer. In that connection, I find, in a letter to the President dated January 15th, this passage: "Since my arrival, very little long forage has been received, and nothing like full rations of corn—that weevil-eaten. The officer commanding the artillery of a division that I inspected to-day reported that his horses had had but thirteen pounds each, of very bad corn, in the last three days."

In the course of the inspection made as soon as practicable, I found the condition of the army much less satisfactory than it had appeared to the President on the 23d of December. There was a great deficiency of blankets; and it was painful to see the number of bare feet in every regiment. In the letter quoted in the last paragraph, the President was informed that two of the four brigades inspected by me that day were not in condition to march, for want of shoes. There was a deficiency, in the infantry, of six thousand small-arms. The artillery-horses were generally still so feeble from long, hard service and scarcity of forage, that it would have been impossible to manœuvre our batteries in action, or to march with them at any ordinary rate on ordinary roads. It was long before they could draw the guns through fields. Early in February, when the supply of forage had become regular, and the face of the country almost dry, after the review of a corps, the teams of the Napoleon guns were unable to draw them up a trifling hill, over which the road to their stables passed.

On the 15th and 16th, Quarles's and Baldwin's brigades, "the last two sent from Mississippi," returned to that department in obedience to orders from the Secretary of War. At the same time Governor Brown transferred two regiments of State troops to the army. They were placed as guards for the protection of the railroad-bridges between Dalton and Atlanta. Intrenchments for this object were then in course of construction, under the direction of the chief-engineer of the army, Brigadier-General Leadbetter.

To supply the great want of effective cavalry, Brigadier-General Roddy was ordered to join the army with his brigade, except one regiment, which he was instructed to leave near Tuscumbia. Soon after his arrival, however, I was directed by the Secretary of War to send him back to his former position. I was taught in this way that my authority over that brigade was ostensible only. About one-third of the brigade, under Colonel Hannon, was retained by me, and served with the army in the campaign of that year.

The time of winter was employed mainly in improving the discipline and instruction of the troops, and attention to their comfort. Before the end of April, more than five thousand absentees had been brought back to their regiments. The establishment of a system which allowed furloughs to all the men in turn, it was thought, contributed greatly to this result. Military operations were confined generally to skirmishing between little scouting-parties of cavalry of our army with pickets of the other. On the 28th of January, however, a strong body of infantry, advancing from Ringgold, drove in our cavalry outposts and approached Tunnel Hill, closely enough to see that it was still occupied. It then returned, as if the object of the expedition had been accomplished.

On the 11th of February, intelligence was received from Lieutenant-General Polk that General Sherman was leading an army of thirty-five thousand infantry and artillery eastwardly from Vicksburg, had crossed Pearl River at Jackson, and was moving along the railroad toward Meridian. Mobile was assumed to be the object of this expedition. Orders by telegraph were received on the same day from the President, directing me to aid Lieutenant-General Polk, either by sending him reënforcements or by joining him myself " with what force I could." The President urged that the enemy should be met before he had established a new base to which supplies and reënforcements might be sent by sea. I replied on the same day, and suggested that it would be impossible for troops from Dalton to meet this Federal army before it reached the Gulf, and therefore asked instructions in that view of the case. This dispatch did not reach the. President's hands, and on the 13th he asked me by telegraph what I could do toward striking at the enemy while in motion, and before he had established a new base. I replied that such an expedition would require two-thirds of the Army of Tennessee and would involve the abandonment of " that line."

On the 16th I was instructed to " detach for temporary service, unless immediately threatened, enough infantry to enable Lieutenant-General Polk to beat the detachment which the enemy had thrown so far into the interior of our country." My reply, on the same day, was to the effect that such a detachment, either marching or transported by railroad, would be too late for the object.

On the 17th the President directed me, by telegraph, to dispatch Lieutenant-General Hardee to Mississippi with Cheatham's, Cleburne's, and Walker's divisions of his corps, with instructions to unite with Lieutenant-General Polk as soon as possible. This order was obeyed as promptly as our means of transportation permitted.

The Federal commanders in Tennessee seem to have anticipated such a detachment, and to have exaggerated its strength; for, on the 14th, General Grant, who, the day before, had instructed Major-General Thomas to move to Knoxville with all the troops that could be spared from Chattanooga, " to coöperate with the Army of the Ohio in driving Longstreet from East Tennessee," countermanded that order, and directed a movement to the immediate front instead, " to gain possession of Dalton, and as far south of that as possible." [1]

On the 22d, intelligence was received from Lieutenant-General Polk's headquarters, at Demopolis, that Sherman's invading column, after passing Meridian, which it destroyed, had turned, and was marching back toward Vicksburg; and Lieutenant-General Hardee's corps, of which only the leading troops had reached that place, were about to return. At night our scouts reported that the Federal army, in marching order, had advanced from Chattanooga to Ringgold that day, and that a large body of infantry and

---

[1] General Thomas's report of March 10, 1864.

artillery, accompanied by Long's [1] brigade of cavalry, had, at the same time, marched from Cleveland to Red Clay.

To meet these movements, Stewart's and Breck-enridge's divisions were posted in the eastern outlet of Mill-Creek Gap, Hindman's in reserve near, and Stevenson's in front of Dalton, on the Cleveland road. This was on the morning of the 23d. The two bodies of Federal troops united in front of Ring-gold in the afternoon, and, advancing upon the Con-federate cavalry, drove it from the village of Tunnel Hill to Cleburne's abandoned camp. After being annoyed by the fire of General Wheeler's artillery from this commanding position, near night, the Fed-eral army drew back three or four miles, and en-camped.

On the 24th the Federal army advanced in three columns, the centre one directed against the Con-federate cavalry. The horse-artillery, by its accurate fire, checked this column until those of the right and left had advanced so far as, by threatening their flanks, to compel General Wheeler's troops to retire. They were led through the gap, and placed in ob-servation in Crow Valley (that lying east of Rocky-Face Ridge), two miles to the north. The Federal army encamped in the valley immediately west of the pass.

In the morning of the 25th the Federal skirmish-ers engaged those of the two divisions in the pass, and desultory firing was maintained during the day.

[1] This officer was instructed to give instant information to General Crufts, if the Confederate troops had abandoned Dalton, that he might promptly advance to the place.

Later, Major-General Wheeler reported that two strong columns had passed around the mountain and were moving down Crow Valley toward us, one following the base of the mountain, and the other the parallel ridge to the east of it. The first was formed by a division and six regiments under General Crufts; the other was General Baird's division. Major-General Hindman was directed to meet this demonstration with Stevenson's division and Clayton's brigade of Stewart's. He chose the best position for this purpose, and disposed his troops in it skillfully: Clayton's and Reynold's brigades on a detached hill near the base of the mountain and in the intermediate pass, and Stevenson's three other brigades (Brown's, Pettus's, and Cummings's) on the opposite height to the east. The skirmishers soon became engaged on both sides of the valley, and the enemy halted. The skirmishing continued, however, with more or less spirit, until near night. Late in the afternoon a sharp attack was made upon Hindman's left, falling principally upon Clayton's brigade, but, after a brisk engagement of half an hour, the assailants were repulsed. The other Federal division retired at the same time, having engaged Stevenson, only with its skirmishers and artillery. In Mill-Creek Gap one threat of serious assault was made by a body of troops which entered it on the north side of the stream, and advanced against Stewart's division; they met, however, the fire of a battery in their front and musketry from the hill above, which drove them back in confusion.

When I returned to Dalton after nightfall, it was reported to me that the guard posted in Dug Gap had been driven from it by a regiment of Federal mounted infantry, and without resistance.   Fortunately, Granberry's "Texas" brigade, the foremost of the returning troops of Hardee's corps, had just arrived at the railroad-station and was leaving the train.   He was directed to march by the Villanow road, which passes through the Dug Gap, to the foot of the mountain, to bivouac there, and at dawn next morning to recover the position.

That gallant officer executed these instructions with the intelligent courage he always exhibited in presence of the enemy.   The appearance of a part of his brigade on the crest of the mountain, at a point commanding the Gap, and that of another in front at the same time, dislodged the Federal troops before sunrise, and they abandoned the ground with a precipitation that amused the Texans greatly.

It was ascertained soon after that the Federal army had retired during the night.

In his report of these operations, dated March 10, 1864, General Thomas wrote: "Being convinced that the rebel army at Dalton largely outnumbered the strength of the four divisions I had opposed to it, and the movement against Johnston being a complete success, inasmuch as it caused the recalling of the reënforcements sent to oppose General Sherman's expedition against Meridian, I concluded to withdraw my troops to the position they occupied before the reconnaissance."   When writing this passage the general had forgotten, apparently, a previous one, in which he stated that this expedition was made by General Grant's order, and for the purpose of occupying Dalton, "and as far south of that as possible." In relation to that object, for which the expedition was ordered, it certainly was not "a success," "complete" or partial. And as to any relation between General Thomas's operations near Mill-Creek Gap, and General Sherman's "against Meridian," the latter was abandoned on the 20th, and the retrograde movement to Vicksburg began on the 21st. In consequence of this, Hardee's troops ("the reënforcements" referred to above), only the foremost of which had reached the Tombigbee, were recalled by the President on the 23d, before General Thomas's designs had been discovered. It is incredible that the skirmishing about Mill-Creek Gap on the 25th and 26th of February could have been intended to "cause the recalling" of Hardee's troops, for they had been on their way back two or three days; or for the relief of Sherman, who was four or five days' march on his return to Vicksburg, while Lieutenant-General Polk's troops were on the Tombigbee. As to being outnumbered, the Federal army had four divisions and six regiments—probably at least seventeen brigades; it encountered seven Confederate brigades on the 25th, and eleven on the 26th.

CHAPTER ·X.

Disposition of the Confederate Troops.—Affair at Dug Gap.—Cavalry Fight at Varnell's Station. — Fighting at Resaca. — General Wheeler encounters Stoneman's Cavalry.—Army withdrawn to Resaca to meet Flanking Movement of the Enemy.

As, since the President's letter of December 23d, no reference had been made to the design of recovering Middle Tennessee, I reminded him of it on the 27th, through General Bragg, who was virtually his chief staff-officer, in the following letter:

" GENERAL: Letters received from the President and Secretary of War, soon after my assignment to this command, gave me the impression that a forward movement by this army was intended to be made in the spring. If I am right in that impression, and the President's intentions are unchanged, I respectfully suggest that much preparation is necessary—large additions to the number of troops, a great quantity of field transportation, subsistence stores, and forage, a bridge-equipage, and fresh artillery-horses, to be procured. Few of those we have are fit for a three days' march, as they have not recovered from the effect of the last campaign. To make our artillery efficient, at least a thousand fresh horses are required, even if we stand on the defensive. Let me suggest that the necessary measures be taken without delay.

"The artillery also wants organization, and especially a competent commander. I therefore respectfully urge that such a one be sent me. I have applied for Colonel Alexander,[1] but General Lee objects that he is too valuable in his present position to be taken from it. His value to the country would be more than doubled, I think, by the promotion and assignment I recommend.

"Should the movement in question be made, Lieutenant-General Longstreet's command would necessarily take part in it. Other troops might be drawn from General Beauregard's and Lieutenant-General Polk's departments. The infantry of the latter is so small a force that what would remain after the formation of proper garrisons for Mobile would be useless in Mississippi, but a valuable addition to the Army of Tennessee. But of these matters you are much better informed than I."

General Bragg replied on the 4th of March:

"General: In reply to yours of the 27th ult., just received, I hasten to inform you that your inference from the letters of the President and Secretary of War is correct and you are desired to have all things in readiness at the earliest practicable moment for the movement indicated.[2] It is hoped but little time will be required to prepare the force now under

[1] Recommending his promotion.
[2] Under rules established by Mr. Seddon, I had no authority to do so.

your command, as the season is at hand, and the time seems propitious.

"Such additional forces will be ordered to you as the exigencies of the service elsewhere will permit, and it is hoped your own efforts will secure many absentees and extra-duty men to the ranks.

"The deficiency you report in artillery-horses seems very large, and so different from the account given by General Hardee on turning over the command, that hopes are entertained that there must be some error on your part. Prompt measures should be taken by you, however, to supply the want, whatever it may be.

"The part of your letter relative to this and field transportation will be referred to the Quartermaster-General.

"Colonel Alexander, applied for by you, as chief of artillery, is deemed necessary by General Lee, in his present position. Brigadier-General W. N. Pendleton, an experienced officer of artillery, has been ordered to your headquarters to inspect that part of your command, and report its condition.

"Should his services be acceptable to you, I am authorized to say you can retain him.

"I am exceedingly anxious to gratify you on this point, for I know the deficiency now existing.

"It is more than probable that such a junction may soon be made as to place Colonel Alexander under your command."

Reply, dated March 12, 1864.

"GENERAL: I had the honor to receive your letter of the 4th instant, in which I am desired to 'have all things in readiness at the earliest practicable moment, for the movement indicated.'

"The last two words quoted give me the impression that some particular plan of operations is referred to. If so, it has not been communicated to me. A knowledge of it and of the forces to be provided for is necessary, to enable me to make proper requisitions. Permit me, in that connection, to remind you that the regulations of the War Department do not leave the preparations referred to to me, but to officers who receive their orders from Richmond — not from my headquarters.

"The defects in the organization of the artillery cannot be remedied without competent superior officers. For them we must depend upon the Government.

"I respectfully beg leave to refer to my letter to the President, dated January 2d, for my opinions on the subject of our operations on this line.

"Is it probable that the enemy's forces will increase during the spring? Or will they diminish in May and June by expiration of terms of service? It seems to me that our policy depends on the answers to these questions. If that to the first is affirmative, we should act promptly. If that to the second is so, we should not, but on the contrary put off action, if possible, until the discharge of many of his soldiers, if any considerable number is to be discharged.

"P. S.—Should Sherman join Thomas, this army would require reënforcement to enable it to hold its ground. Our army that takes the offensive should be our strongest in relation to its enemy."

On the 18th Colonel Sale, General Bragg's military secretary, brought me the following letter from that officer, dated the 12th:

"GENERAL: In previous communications it has been intimated to you that the President desired a forward movement by the forces under your command; and it was suggested that such preparations as are practicable and necessary should be commenced immediately.

"I now desire to lay before you, more in detail, the views of the Department in regard to the proposed operations, and to inform you of the means intended to be placed at your disposal. Of course but a general outline is necessary, as matters of detail must be left to your judgment and discretion.

"It is not deemed advisable to attempt the capture of the enemy's fortified positions by direct attack, but to draw out, and then, if practicable, force him to battle in the open field. To accomplish this object, we should so move as to concentrate our means between the scattered forces of the enemy, and, failing to draw him out for battle, to move upon his lines of communication. The force in Knoxville depends in a great measure on its connection with Chattanooga for support, and both are entirely dependent on regular and rapid communication with Nashville. To separate these two by interposing our main force, and then strike and destroy the railroad from Nashville to Chattanooga, fulfills both conditions.

"To accomplish this, it is proposed that you move as soon as your means and force can be collected, so as to reach the Tennessee River near Kingston, where a crossing can be effected; that Lieutenant-General Longstreet move simultaneously by a route east and south of Knoxville, so as to form a junction with you near this crossing. As soon as you come within supporting distance, Knoxville is isolated, and Chattanooga threatened, with barely a possibility for the enemy to unite. Should he not then offer you battle outside of his intrenched lines, a rapid move across the mountains from Kingston to Sparta (a very practicable and easy route) would place you, with a formidable army, in a country full of resources, where it is supposed, with a good supply of ammunition, you may be entirely self-sustaining. And it is confidently believed that such a move would necessitate the withdrawal of the enemy to the line of the Cumberland.

" At the same time when this move is made, it is proposed to throw a heavy column of cavalry, as a diversion, into West Tennessee; and thence, if practicable, into Middle Tennessee, to operate on the enemy's lines of communication and distract his attention.

" If by a rapid movement, after crossing the mountains, you can precipitate your main force upon Nashville, and capture that place before the enemy can fall back for its defense, you place him in a most precarious position. But in any event, by a movement in rear of Nashville while the Cumberland is low, similar to the one in passing Chattanooga, you isolate that position and compel a retrograde movement of the enemy's main force.

" It is needless, General, for me to impress upon

you the great importance, not to say necessity, of
reclaiming the provision country of Tennessee and
Kentucky; and, from my knowledge of the country
and people, I believe that other great advantages
may accrue, especially in obtaining men to fill your
ranks.

"The following forces, it is believed, will be available, if nothing shall occur to divert them, viz.:

	Infantry.	Artillery.	Cavalry.	Total.
"Your own command.....	33,000	3,000	5,000	41,000
General Martin's cavalry, now *en route* to you ...	....	....	3,000	3,000
From Lieut.-Gen. Polk...	5,000	....	....	5,000
From Gen. Beauregard...	10,000	....	....	10,000
From Gen. Longstreet's command	12,000	2,000	2,000	16,000
	60,000	5,000	10,000	75,000

"It is proposed to hold the reënforcements ready,
and to put them in motion just as soon as you may
be able to use them. To throw them to the front
now, would only impede the accumulation of supplies necessary for your march.

"Measures have been taken to aid in supplying
you with artillery-horses. Additional means of transportation will be furnished as soon as practicable.

"The efficient organization of engineer troops in
your command will supply every want in that department.

"Ammunition in abundance is on hand, subject
to your call; and it is believed that the means of
subsistence are ample in your immediate rear, if
efficient measures are inaugurated to get them forward. On this point you are desired to act at once,

in your own behalf, as the Department here could do no more than refer you to its resources within your reach and control.

"It will give me much pleasure, General, to have your views in full on this subject, in all its bearings, and no effort will be spared in bringing to your assistance the resources of the Government not essential at other points.

"Communicate fully at once, and afterward in detail, as points may arise requiring action."

As invited at the conclusion of this letter, I expressed "my views" both by telegraph and mail, without delay; and still more fully by the intelligent officer who had brought the plan of campaign to me from Richmond.

The telegram, dispatched in an hour or two, was in these words, addressed to General Bragg: "Your letter by Colonel Sale received. Grant is at Nashville; Sherman, by last accounts, at Memphis; where Grant is, we must expect the great Federal effort; we ought, therefore, to be prepared to beat him here; he has not come back to Tennessee to stand on the defensive; his advance, should we be ready for it, will be advantageous for us; to be ready, we must have the *troops you name immediately*, otherwise we might be beaten, which would decide events; give us *those troops*, and if we beat him, we follow; should he not advance, we will then be ready for the offensive; the troops can be fed as easily here as where they now are."

The letter referred to was addressed also to General Bragg on the same day:

"GENERAL: I had the honor to receive your letter of the 12th from Colonel Sale yesterday, and to make a suggestion, by telegraph, on the subject to which it relates.

"Permit me to suggest that the troops intended for the operations you explain should be assembled in this vicinity. The enemy could, without particular effort, prevent their junction near Kingston by attacking one of our armies with his united forces. His interior positions make it easy. There is another reason: Grant's return to Tennessee indicates that he will retain that command, for the present at least. He certainly will not do so to stand on the defensive. I therefore believe that he will advance as soon as he can, with the greatest force he can raise. We cannot estimate the time he will require for preparation, and should, consequently, put ourselves in condition for successful resistance as soon as possible, by assembling here the troops you enumerate. I am doing all I can in other preparations, and do not doubt that abundance of ammunition, food, and forage, will be collected long before we can be supplied with field-transportation. My department is destitute of mules. I must, therefore, depend on the Quartermaster's Department for them.

"It strikes me that we cannot 'isolate' Knoxville in the manner you propose, because we cannot hope to be able to take with us such supplies as would enable us to remain on the line of communication long enough to *incommode* the forces there. We cannot do so unless we can occupy a position from which we can maintain our own communications and interrupt those of Knoxville. Such a position can only be found near Chattanooga.

"The march into Middle Tennessee, via Kingston, would require all the stores we should be able to transport from Dalton., so that we could not reduce Knoxville 'en route.' Would it not be easier to march into Middle Tennessee through North Alabama?

"I believe fully, however, that Grant will be ready to act before we can be; and that, if we are ready to fight him on our own ground, we shall have a very plain course, with every chance of success. For that, we should make exactly such preparations as you indicate for the forward movement, except that I would have the troops assembled here without delay, to repel Grant's attack, and then make our own; or, should the enemy not take the initiative, do it ourselves. Our first object *then* should be, your proposition to bring on a battle on this side of the Tennessee.

"Should not the movement from Mississippi precede any advance from this point so much as to enable those troops to cross the Tennessee before we move? Lieutenant-General Polk thought at the end of February that he could send fifteen thousand cavalry on such an expedition. Even two-thirds of that force might injure the railroads enough to compel the evacuation of Chattanooga. Certainly it could make a powerful diversion.

"I apprehend no difficulty in procuring food (except meat) and forage. This department can furnish nothing. Its officers receive supplies from those of the Subsistence and Quartermaster's Departments at and beyond Atlanta. The efficient head of the Ordnance Department has never permitted us to want any thing that could reasonably be expected from him. I am afraid that the collection of the additional field-transportation will require a good deal of time. None can be obtained within the limits of my authority.

"There has been an unnecessary accumulation of bread-stuffs and corn at Mobile—six months' supply for a much larger force than Major-General Maury's. Half of it will spoil during the summer, if left in Mobile. It would be economical, therefore, as well as convenient, to transfer that portion of it to this army.

"Lieutenant-Colonel Cole, at Augusta, informs me that the artillery-horses required will be furnished by the 1st of May."

Besides the foregoing, other reasons for opposing the plan of operations explained by General Bragg, were committed to Colonel Sale, to be delivered orally—such as: That the interior positions belonged to the enemy, instead of being held by us as was supposed by the military authorities in Richmond; for the Federal army at Knoxville, equally distant from Chattanooga and Dalton, was exactly between Longstreet and our main army—and, to unite near Kingston as proposed, each of our armies would be compelled to march in front of a much greater Federal force, exposed to attack in a column five times as long and not a tenth as strong as its order of battle; that the only manner in which we could "isolate" Knoxville would be by placing our

united forces on the road from that place to Chattanooga, at the point nearest to Dalton, and employing
our cavalry, with its artillery, to close the navigation
of the Tennessee—the army in Chattanooga might
be induced in that way to attack in order to drive
us back and reopen the routes to Knoxville; and
that the attempt to unite the Army of Tennessee and
Longstreet's corps, near Kingston, would be a violation of a sound military rule, never to assemble the
troops that are to act together, in such a manner that
the enemy's army may attack any considerable body
of them before their union.

General Bragg replied on the 21st to my dispatch
of the 18th. His telegram, received on the 22d, indicated that the plan of offensive operations devised
by the Administration was an ultimatum. "Recent
Northern papers report Grant superseded Halleck,
who becomes chief of staff. Sherman takes Grant's
command. Your dispatch of 19th does not indicate
an acceptance of the plan proposed. The troops can
only be drawn from other points for an advance.
Upon your decision of that point further action must
depend."

To correct the misapprehension of my views on
the part of the Administration which General Bragg's
language indicated, I replied immediately:[1]

"In my dispatch of the 18th I expressly accept
taking the offensive. Only differ with you as to details.
I assume that the enemy will be prepared *to advance
before we are*, and will make it to our advantage.
Therefore I propose, as necessary both for the offensive and defensive, to *assemble our troops here* imme-

---

[1] In the original, the words in *italics* were written in cipher.

diately.   Other preparations *for advance* are going on."

No notice was taken of this explanation.

In the mean time our scouts were furnishing evidence of almost daily arrivals of Federal reënforcements, which was punctually communicated to the Administration through General Bragg.   From these indications it was clear that the military authorities of the United States were assembling in our front a much greater force than that which had driven us from Missionary Ridge a few months before.   On the contrary, our army had not recovered from the effects of that defeat—numerically, that is to say.   It was as plain that these Federal preparations were made not for the purpose of holding the ground won from us in the previous campaign, but for the resumption of offensive operations.   On the 25th, therefore, I again urged upon the Government the necessity of strengthening the Army of Tennessee, and suggested that further delay would be dangerous.

On the 3d of April Lieutenant-Colonel A. H. Cole, one of the most efficient officers of the Quartermaster's Department, came to Dalton.   He was instructed, as he informed me, to superintend the procuring the number of artillery-horses and the amount of field-transportation required by the army for an offensive campaign.

The fact that my letter of the 18th and telegram of the 22d of March were not answered made me apprehend that my correspondence with General Bragg in relation to the spring campaign had not been understood by the President.   Colonel B. S. Ewell,

Adjutant-General of the Army of Tennessee, my personal friend, and an officer who had my full confidence, was therefore sent to Richmond on the 8th, to endeavor to remove any misapprehension of the subject that might exist in his Excellency's mind.

He was instructed to show the President that in my correspondence with the Government I had not declined to assume the offensive—as General Bragg charged—but, on the contrary, was eager to move forward whenever the relative forces of the opposing armies should justify me in such a measure; to point out the difference between the plan of operations proposed through General Bragg and that which I advocated, and in that connection to explain that I had been actively engaged in preparations to take the field—those over which I had control being in a satisfactory state of forwardness. But in the important element of field-transportation, the need of which had several times been represented to the Government, and which I had neither means nor authority to collect, nothing had been done, while steps to collect the large number of artillery-horses necessary, had just been taken; and that the surest means of enabling us to go forward was to send the proposed reënforcements to Dalton at once; then, should the enemy take the initiative, as was almost certain, we might defeat him on this side of the Tennessee, where the consequences of defeat would be so much more disastrous to the enemy, and less so to us, than if the battle were fought north of that river.

He was also desired to say that, according to the best information we could obtain, the Federal army opposed to us had been increased, since the battle of Missionary Ridge, by about fifteen thousand men; but that ours was not so strong as on the morning of that battle.

A day or two after Colonel Ewell's departure, General Pendleton, commander of the artillery of General Lee's army, came to Dalton from Richmond. He was sent by the President, to explain his Excellency's wishes in relation to the employment of the Army of Tennessee, and to ascertain if I was willing to assume the offensive with an army weaker by sixteen thousand men than that proposed in General Bragg's letter of March 12th.

The object of Colonel Ewell's mission to Richmond was explained to him, and the instructions given to that officer repeated, as explanations of my military opinions.

Neither General Pendleton's report nor Colonel Ewell's representations led to any action on the part of the Executive—none, at least, that concerned the Army of Tennessee.

This correspondence between the Administration and myself has been given fully, because I have been accused of disobeying the orders of the President and the entreaties of General Bragg to assume the offensive. As there was no other correspondence between the Administration and myself on the subject, the accusation must have this foundation, if any.

In the morning of the 2d May, a close reconnaissance of our outpost at Tunnel Hill was made under the protection of a strong body of infantry, cavalry, and artillery. The reports received on the 1st, 2d, and 4th, indicated that the beginning of an active campaign was imminent. They showed that the enemy was approaching our position, and repairing the railroad from Chattanooga to Ringgold. The intelligence received on each day was immediately transmitted to General Bragg. That officer suggested to me, on the 2d, that I was deceived, probably, by *mere demonstrations*, made for the purpose.

On that day, Mercer's brigade, about fourteen hundred effective infantry, joined the army, from Savannah. It was to be replaced there by J. K. Jackson's, of the Army of Tennessee. The latter was retained, for the present, where it was most needed, for *we* were threatened, and *Savannah* was not.

The effective strength of the Army of Tennessee, as shown by the return of May 1, 1864, was thirty-seven thousand six hundred and fifty-two infantry, twenty-eight hundred and twelve artillery (forty thousand four hundred and sixty-four), and twenty-three hundred and ninety-two cavalry. This was the entire strength of the army, "at and near Dalton," at that time. Canty's brigade (thirteen hundred and ninety-five effectives) is included improperly. It had just arrived at Rome, sent there from the vicinity of Mobile, by Major-General Maury. But, on the other hand, Mercer's was not; nor was Martin's division of cavalry, then near Cartersville, because its horses, worn down by continuous hard service since the beginning of the previous summer, were unfit for the field. It had seventeen hundred men fit for duty, however.

The Federal army which Major-General Sherman was about to lead against us was composed of the troops that fought at Missionary Ridge, under Gen-

MAJOR-GENERAL W. T. SHERMAN

eral Grant, the Sixteenth and Twenty-third Corps, and Hovey's division. The veteran regiments of this army had made a very large number of recruits while on furlough in the previous winter—probably fifteen or eighteen thousand. These men, mixed in the ranks, were little inferior to old soldiers. We had been estimating the cavalry, under General Kilpatrick, at five thousand; but, at the opening of the campaign, Stoneman's, Garrard's, and McCook's divisions arrived—adding, probably, twelve thousand.

Our scouts reported that the Fourth Corps and McCook's division of cavalry were at Cleveland, and the Army of the Ohio at Charleston, on the 2d, both on the way to Chattanooga; and that these troops and the Army of the Cumberland reached Ringgold in the afternoon of the 4th and encamped there.

Our pickets (cavalry) were at the same time pressed back beyond Varnell's Station, on the Cleveland road, and within three miles of Tunnel Hill, on that from Ringgold.

Upon these indications that the enemy was advancing upon us in great force, I again urged the Administration, by telegraph, to put about half of Lieutenant-General Polk's infantry under my control, and ordered Major-General Martin, with his division, from the valley of the Etowah to that of the Oostenaula, to observe it from Resaca to Rome. Brigadier-General Kelly, whose little division of cavalry had just come up from the vicinity of Resaca, was ordered to join the troops of that arm in observation on the Cleveland road.

CHAPTER XI.

Skirmishing at Resaca along our whole Lines.—The Enemy cross the Oostenaula.—Our Army put in Position to meet this Movement.—Causes of leaving Daltor.—The Dispositions there of the Confederate Army.—The Army
at Cassville.—The Position a strong one.—In Line of Battle.—Generals
Hood and Polk urge Abandonment of Positions, stating their Inability
to hold their Ground.—General Hardee remonstrates.—Position abandoned,
and Army crosses the Etowah.—Losses up to Date.—Affairs near New Hope
Church.—Manœuvring of Federal Troops.—Kenesaw.—General Assault.—
Battle of Kenesaw.—Army crosses the Chattahoochee.—Visit of General
Brown.—Relieved from Command of the Army of Tennessee.—Explain my
Plans to General Hood.—Review of the Campaign.—Grounds of my Removal.
—Discussion of them.—General Cobb's Defense of Macon.

On the 5th, the Confederate troops were formed
to receive the enemy: Stewart's and Bate's divisions,
in Mill-Creek Gap, in which they had constructed
some slight defensive works—the former on the right
of the stream, Cheatham's on Stewart's right, occupying about a mile of the crest of the mountain;
Walker's in reserve; Stevenson's across Crow Valley, its left joining Cheatham's right, on the crest of
the mountain; Hindman's, on the right of Stevenson's; and Cleburne's immediately in front of Dalton,
and behind Mill Creek, facing toward Cleveland.

On the same day the Federal army was formed
in order of battle, three miles in front of Tunnel Hill,
and in that position skirmished with our advanced
guard until dark. It was employed all of the next
in selecting and occupying a position just beyond the

range of the field-pieces of the Confederate advanced-guard, on which it halted for the night.

In the evening, a telegram from Lieutenant-General Polk informed me that he had been ordered to join the Army of Tennessee with all his infantry.

At daybreak on the 7th, the Federal army moved forward, annoyed and delayed in its advance by dismounted Confederate cavalry, firing upon it from the cover of successive lines of very slight intrenchments, prepared the day before. Its progress was so slow, that the Confederates were not driven from Tunnel Hill until eleven o'clock A. M., nor to Mill-Creek Gap until three P. M. In the afternoon the Federal army placed itself in front of the Confederate line, its right a little south of Mill-Creek Gap, and its left near the Cleveland road.

In the evening, intelligence was received of the arrival of Canty's brigade at Resaca. It was ordered to halt there, to defend that important position.

On the 8th, the cavalry, which had been driven through Mill-Creek Gap the day before, was divided; Grigsby's (Kentucky) brigade going to the foot of the mountain, near Dug Gap, and the remainder to the ground then occupied by Kelly's troops, in front of our right.

About four o'clock P. M., a division of Hooker's corps, said to be Geary's, assailed our outpost in Dug Gap—two very small regiments of Reynolds's Arkansas brigade, commanded then by Colonel Williamson. They held their ground bravely, and were soon joined by Grigsby's Kentuckians, who, leaving their horses, hastened up the mountain-side, on foot, to their aid. As soon as the musketry was so increased by this accession to our force as to give evidence of a serious attack, Lieutenant-General Hardee was requested to hurry Granberry's (Texan) brigade, which was the nearest, to the assistance of the troops engaged; and, on account of the importance of the position, his own offer to direct its defense was eagerly accepted. The encouragement given to the defenders by that distinguished soldier's arrival among them, made the position secure until the leading Texans came up, at full gallop, on the Kentucky horses they had found a mile from the place of combat, when the contest was terminated and the assailants repulsed.

A sharp attack was also made upon the angle where the Confederate right and centre joined on the crest of the mountain. This point was held by Pettus's brigade, by which the assailants, Newton's division of the Fourth Corps, were quickly and handsomely repulsed. Brown's brigade was then moved from Stevenson's right to the crest of the mountain, joining Pettus's left.

On the 9th another assault was made upon the troops at the angle, including Brown's brigade as well as Pettus's, and much more vigorous than that of the day before, by a larger force advancing in column and exhibiting great determination. It was met, however, with the firmness always displayed where Pettus or Brown commanded, and their troops fought; and the enemy was driven back with a loss proportionate to the determination of their attack. Similar assaults upon Stewart and Bate in the gap, made with the same resolution, were in like manner defeated. The actions of the day, in General Sher

GENERAL JOHN B. HOOD

man's language, "attained the dimensions of a battle."

The Confederate troops suffered little in these engagements, for they fought under the protection of
intrenchments.   But we had reason to believe that
the enemy, who were completely exposed, often at
short range and in close order, sustained heavy
losses.   This belief was strengthened in my mind
by the opinion, long entertained, that the soldiers of
the United States never give way without good
reason.

On the same day Major-General Wheeler, with
Dibrell's and Allen's brigades, encountered a large
body of Federal cavalry near Varnell's Station.
Dismounting all of his troops but two regiments, he
made a combined attack of infantry and cavalry, by
which the enemy was put to flight.   A standard,
many small-arms, and a hundred prisoners, were
captured.   Among the prisoners were Colonel La
Grange, commanding a brigade, three captains, and
five lieutenants.   From information given him by
the colonel, General Wheeler estimated the force he
had just encountered at about five thousand men.

At night Brigadier-General Canty reported that
he had been engaged at Resaca until dark with
troops of the Army of the Tennessee, which was
commanded by Major-General McPherson, and had
held his ground.   As intelligence of the arrival of
that army in Snake-Creek Gap had been received,
Lieutenant-General Hood was ordered to move to
Resaca immediately with three divisions—those of
Hindman, Cleburne, and Walker.

On the 10th that officer reported that the enemy

was retiring; and was recalled, but directed to leave Cleburne's and Walker's divisions near Tilton —one on each road.

Skirmishing, renewed in the morning near Dalton, continued all day, to our advantage—both at the gap and on Stevenson's front. Near night an attack, especially spirited, was made upon Bate's position, on the hill-side facing the gap on the south. It was firmly met, however, and repulsed.

At night reports were received from the scouts in observation near the south end of Rocky Face, to the effect that General McPherson's troops were intrenching their position in Snake-Creek Gap. And on the 11th various reports were received indicating a general movement to their right by the Federal troops, as if to unite with those of McPherson.

On the same day, Brigadier-General Canty again announced that a Federal army was approaching Resaca from the direction of Snake-Creek Gap. But intelligence that Lieutenant-General Polk had reached that point with Loring's division, prevented any immediate apprehension for the place. He was instructed to hold it with the troops then under his command there, and authorized to call Cleburne's and Walker's divisions to him, if necessary. They were within six miles.

In the evening of the same day, Major-General Wheeler was directed to move at dawn of the next, around the north end of Rocky-Face Ridge, toward Tunnel Hill, with all his available cavalry; to ascertain if the movement southward by the Federal army had been a general one; and to learn, also, what forces were still in that vicinity. Major-General

Hindman was instructed to follow this movement with his division, to support the cavalry.

In this movement, made with about twenty-two hundred men, Wheeler encountered what prisoners reported to be Major-General Stoneman's division of United States cavalry, and drove it back; killing, wounding, and capturing a hundred and fifty men. In consequence of the result of this skirmish, the Federal troops burned many of their loaded wagons. According to the reports of the scouts and people of the neighborhood, four hundred were thus destroyed.

This reconnaissance confirmed the impression that the main body of the Federal army was marching toward Snake-Creek Gap, on its way to Resaca. This march was made without exposure, being completely covered by the mountain—Rocky Face.

About one o'clock A. M. on the 13th the Confederate infantry and artillery were withdrawn from the position they had been holding in and near Mill-Creek Gap, and marched to Resaca—the cavalry being ordered to follow after daybreak as rear-guard, and to observe any body of Federal troops that might advance through Dalton.

The Federal army, approaching Resaca on the Snake-Creek Gap road, was met about a mile from the place by Loring's division, and held in check long enough to enable Hardee's and Hood's corps, then just arriving, to occupy their ground undisturbed. As the army was formed (in two lines), Polk's and Hardee's corps were west of the place and railroad, facing to the west; the former on the left, with its left resting on the Oostenaula. Hood's corps extended from Hardee's right across the railroad to the Connesauga, facing to the northwest.

There was brisk skirmishing all the afternoon of May 13th on Polk's front, and that of Hardee's left division—Cheatham's.

The Fourth Corps had been left in front of Mill-Creek Gap, probably to prevent or delay the discovery by us of the withdrawal of the main body of the Federal army. Major-General Wheeler, falling back before that corps, reached Tilton at three o'clock in the afternoon. He received instructions there to do every thing possible to prevent it from passing that point before nightfall, to give Lieutenant-General Hood time to dispose his corps carefully, and make other preparations to hold his ground. For this object his cavalry was reënforced by Brown's brigade. These instructions were executed, and the enemy delayed until night—quite long enough for the object in view.

The skirmishers became engaged along our whole line early in the day (May 14th), beginning on the left. Those of Polk's corps, from some unaccountable mistake, abandoned their ground, which was regained only by great personal efforts on the part of their field-officers, Colonel Conoly and Major J. W. Dawson. A vigorous assault was made upon Hindman's division, but the assailants were handsomely repulsed.

Major-General Wheeler was directed to ascertain the position and formation of the enemy's left. The performance of this service involved him in much desultory fighting, however. The information he obtained indicated circumstances favorable to an attack upon the Federal left, and Lieutenant-General

Hood was directed to make it with Stewart's and Stevenson's divisions by a half-change of front to the
left, that the enemy might be driven to the west; the
two divisions were to be supported by four brigades
drawn from the centre and left.

On the arrival of these brigades, Lieutenant-General Hood put his troops in motion, and engaged the
enemy about six o'clock in the afternoon, gradually
changing front to the west in advancing. Stevenson's
troops, being nearest to the pivot upon which the
wheel was executed, moved upon shorter lines than
those of Stewart's division, and therefore kept somewhat in advance of them; consequently, the larger
share of fighting fell to their lot, but all moved and
fought with admirable precision and vigor, and before dark the Federal left was driven from its ground.
Less resistance was encountered than had been expected; this encouraged me, during the engagement,
to hope that Hood's corps, and the second line of
Polk's and Hardee's, might constitute a force strong
enough to defeat the left of the Federal army, while
its right was held in check by the remaining third
of ours, protected by intrenchments. Lieutenant-
General Hood was accordingly instructed to prepare
to renew the fight at daybreak next morning, and to
let his troops understand it that evening. This announcement, and such success as they had had, elated
them greatly.

On riding from the right to the left, after nightfall,
I learned that Lieutenant-General Polk's advanced
troops had been driven from a hill in front of his
left, which commanded our bridges at short range.
A report from Major-General Martin was received at

the same time, to the effect that Federal forces were crossing the Oostenaula, near Calhoun, by a pontoon-bridge, on which two divisions had already passed. Under such circumstances it was, in my opinion, not only imprudent to weaken our left in the manner intended, but necessary to meet this movement threatening our communications. As a first step, Walker's division, of Hardee's corps, was ordered to march immediately to the point named by Major-General Martin. Lieutenant-General Hood was also informed of the change of plan, and desired to bring back the two divisions that had been engaged, to the position from which they had been advanced; and, to secure an unobstructed passage of the Oostenaula, Lieutenant-Colonel Prestman, the chief-engineer, was directed to make a road during the night, and lay a pontoon-bridge a mile above those now commanded by the enemy's artillery.

On the 15th sharp skirmishing on our whole front commenced early, and continued throughout the day. Several vigorous assaults were made upon Hindman's division; in the last especially the assailants exhibited great resolution, many of them pressing forward to the Confederate intrenchments. All were repelled, however, by the first line alone.

About noon a large body of Federal cavalry captured the hospitals of Hood's corps, which were in an exposed situation east of the Connesauga. Major-General Wheeler, who was sent to the spot with Allen's and Humes's brigades, drove off the enemy and pursued them two miles, taking two standards, and capturing forty prisoners.

An hour or two after noon, intelligence was received from Major-General Walker, near Calhoun, that the report of the passage of the Oostenaula by the enemy was unfounded. So the plan abandoned the evening before was again adopted, and Lieutenant-General Hood was desired to prepare to assail the enemy's left as he had done the day before, and to advance as soon as he should be joined by three brigades ordered to him from Polk's and Hardee's corps.

Major-General Stevenson had, early in the day, and with Lieutenant-General Hood's approval, resumed the position from which he had been recalled the night before. Here he was directed by the Lieutenant-General to place a field-battery in a position some eighty yards in front of his line of infantry. Before the necessary arrangements begun for its protection were completed, he was directed by General Hood to open its fire. This was no sooner done, than so impetuous an attack was made upon it, that the guns could not be drawn back to the main line of the division. After a very sharp contest, the enemy was driven beyond the battery by the well-directed fire of Brown's and Reynolds's brigades, but found shelter in a ravine not far from it. From this position their musketry commanded the position of the battery equally as well as that of the Confederate infantry, so that neither could remove the guns, and they were left between the two armies until night.

Just when Lieutenant-General Hood was about to move forward, a second message from Major-General Walker gave positive information that the right of the Federal army was actually crossing the Oostenaula, near Calhoun. Upon this, the idea of fighting north of the Oostenaula was abandoned at once, and the orders to Lieutenant-General Hood were counter-manded. Stewart's division did not receive the coun-termand from corps headquarters in time to prevent its execution of the previous order, and engaging the enemy, and of course it suffered before being recalled.

The danger that threatened our line of commu-nications made me regard the continued occupation of Resaca as too hazardous. The army was therefore ordered to cross the river about midnight: Polk's and Hardee's corps by the railroad-bridge and one on trestles near it ; and Hood's by the pontoon-bridge laid by Colonel Prestman the night before. After this had been done, Hood's corps took the Spring Place and Adairsville road, and Polk's and Hardee's that to Calhoun.

At that place Lieutenant-General Hardee was directed to move with his corps by the Rome road, to its intersection with that from Snake-Creek Gap to Adairsville, by which the foremost Federal troops were advancing, to hold them in check as long as might be necessary. The other corps halted about a mile and a half south of Calhoun. Hardee's ob-ject was accomplished by sharp skirmishing for sev-eral hours, to our advantage.

The Federal troops, advancing directly from Resaca, were opposed by the Confederate cavalry. That opposition, and the passage of the Oostenaula, delayed them so much, that our soldiers had abun-dant time for rest in the positions in which they had halted.

The preceding narrative shows that the Confed-erate army was dislodged from its first position, that in front of Dalton, by General Sherman's movement to his right through Snake-Creek Gap, threatening our line of communications at Resaca; and from the position taken at Resaca to meet that movement, by a similar one on the part of the Federal general toward Calhoun—the second being covered by the river, as the first had been by the mountain. In both cases, the great numerical superiority of almost three to one enabled him, with little risk, to avail himself of the features of the country, which covered such manœuvres.

The only mode of preventing these operations would have been to defeat the Federal army in its position in front of Tunnel Hill on the 5th. But at that time there were two arguments against such an attempt by us : one, that, in the event of an attack by us, the greater strength of the enemy would have made the chances of battle decidedly against us, and the consequences of defeat would have been disastrous ; the other, that the position of the Federal army indicated clearly the purpose of assailing us. And there was no reasonable doubt of the ability of the Confederate forces to maintain themselves in the position selected for them, and prepared by them, against three times their number.

In his report, General Sherman expresses the opinion that nothing saved the Confederate army from the effects of his first manœuvre "but the impracticable nature of the country, which made the passage of the troops across the valley almost impossible." [1]

This obstacle to a rapid march by the United

[1] From Snake-Creek Gap to Resaca.

States army was not unknown to the Confederates. We had examined the country very minutely; and learned its character thoroughly. We could calculate with sufficient accuracy, therefore, the time that would be required for the march of so great an army from Tunnel Hill to Resaca, through the long defile of Snake-Creek Gap, and by the single road beyond that pass. We knew also in how many hours our comparatively small force, moving without baggage-trains and in three columns, on roads made good by us, would reach the same point from Dalton.

Our course in remaining at Dalton until the night of the 12th was based on such calculations, and the additional consideration that the single road available to the Federal army was closed at Resaca by our intrenched camp. On the 9th of May, when that camp was defended by two brigades, Major-General McPherson, a skillful engineer as well as able general, thought it "too strong to be carried by assault by the Army of the Tennessee," led by him. On the 11th, when General Sherman's march toward Snake-Creek Gap was begun, the place was much more formidable. The defenses had been improved, and the number of defenders increased from two to thirteen brigades,[1] so that on the 11th and 12th its strength, compared with that of the entire Federal army, was much greater than it had been on the 9th, compared with that of the Army of the Tennessee, so that we had no reasonable ground to apprehend that we might be intercepted—cut off from our base —by this manœuvre.

It is true that we did not know certainly, on the

---

[1] Including those of Calhoun and Walker, six miles off.

11th, that the main body of the United States forces
had moved from their camps about Tunnel Hill and
Mill-Creek Gap, and our five divisions near Dalton
were kept in their positions in the lingering hope of
a strong assault upon them. It was easy to march
to Resaca in the night of the 12th, if necessary ; and
it was certain that the Federal army could not reach
that point so soon; consequently there was no serious
danger in the course pursued.

The disposition of the Confederate army about
Dalton was predicated on the belief that the Federal
general would attack it there with his whole force.
For that reason its entire strength was concentrated
there, and the protection of its communications left
to Lieutenant-General Polk's troops, then on their
way from Alabama through Rome to join us. I supposed, from General Sherman's great superiority of
numbers, that he intended to decide the contest by a
battle, and that he would make that battle as near his
own and as far from our base as possible—that is to
say, at Dalton. On general principles, that was his
true policy. It is evident that he did not so act, because he thought as I did—that, in the event of his
assailing us, the chances would have been very strong
in our favor.

My own operations, then and subsequently, were
determined by the relative forces of the armies, and
a higher estimate of the Northern soldiers than our
Southern editors and politicians were accustomed to
express, or even the Administration seemed to entertain. This opinion had been formed in much service
with them against Indians, and four or five battles in
Mexico—such actions, at least, as were then called

battles. Observation of almost twenty years of service of this sort had impressed on my mind the belief that the soldiers of the regular army of the United States — almost all Northern men — were equal, in fighting qualities, to any that had been formed in the wars of Great Britain and France. General Sherman's troops, with whom we were contending, had received a longer training in war than any of those with whom I had served in former times. It was not to be supposed that such troops, under a sagacious and resolute leader, and covered by intrenchments, were to be beaten by greatly inferior numbers. I therefore thought it our policy to stand on the defensive, to spare the blood of our soldiers by fighting under cover habitually, and to attack only when bad position or division of the enemy's forces might give us advantages counterbalancing that of superior numbers. So we held every position occupied until our communications were strongly threatened; then fell back only far enough to secure them, watching for opportunities to attack, keeping near enough to the Federal army to assure the Confederate Administration that Sherman could not send reënforcements to Grant, and hoping to reduce the odds against us by partial engagements. A material reduction of the Federal army might also be reasonably expected before the end of June, by the expiration of the terms of service of the regiments that had not reënlisted. I was confident, too, that the Administration would see the expediency of employing Forrest and his cavalry to break the enemy's railroad communications, by which he could have been defeated.

In crossing the Oostenaula, I hoped to find a good position near Calhoun, covering the several roads leading southward from Snake-Creek Gap and the neighborhood of Resaca. No such were there, however. The large creek, the Oothcaloga, which must have divided any position taken, would have been a great impediment. But it appeared, from the map prepared by our engineer-officers, that, a mile or two north of Adairsville, the valley of this stream was so narrow that our army, formed in order of battle across it, would hold the heights on the right and left with its flanks—the stream being too small to be an obstruction. So, after resting fifteen or eighteen hours where they had halted, the troops marched, early in the morning of the 17th, seven or eight miles, to Adairsville; Polk's and Hood's corps by the Spring Place road, and Hardee's by that from Snake-Creek Gap, on which it had been engaged the day before.

The leading Federal troops appeared in the afternoon, pressing back our cavalry. Lieutenant-General Hardee was desired to send forward a division of his corps to support it, and prevent the near approach of the enemy, that our troops might not be disturbed in their bivouacs. Cheatham's division was detailed, and it and Wheeler's troops together kept the head of the Federal column at a convenient distance, by sharp skirmishing, until nightfall.

During the day the division of cavalry commanded by Brig.-General W. H. Jackson joined the army at Adairsville. It had been ordered to it from Mississippi by Lieutenant-General Polk.

The breadth of the valley here exceeded so much

the front of our army properly formed for battle, that we could obtain no advantage of ground; so, after resting about eighteen hours, the troops were ordered to move to Cassville.

Two roads lead southward from Adairsville—one following the railroad through Kingston, and, like it, turning almost at right angles to the east at that place; the other, quite direct to the Etowah Railroad-bridge, passing through Cassville, where it is met by the first. The probability that the Federal army would divide—a column following each road—gave me a hope of engaging and defeating one of them before it could receive aid from the other. In that connection the intelligent engineer-officer who had surveyed that section, Lieutenant Buchanan, was questioned minutely over the map as to the character of the ground, in the presence of Lieutenant-Generals Polk and Hood, who had been informed of my object. He described the country on the direct road as open, and unusually favorable for attack. It was evident, from the map, that the distance between the two Federal columns would be greatest when that following the railroad should be near Kingston. Lieutenant Buchanan thought that the communications between the columns at this part of their march would be eight or nine miles, by narrow and crooked country roads.

In the morning of the 18th, Hardee's corps marched to Kingston; and Polk's and Hood's, following the direct road, halted within a mile of Cassville—the former deployed in two lines, crossing the road and facing Adairsville; the latter halted on its right. Jackson's division observed the Federal col-

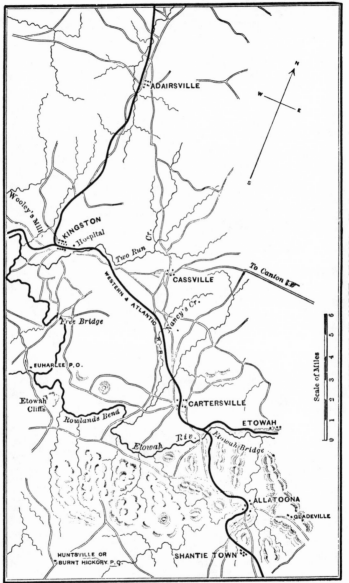

CAMPAIGN IN NORTH GEORGIA. No. 2.

umn on the Kingston road, and Wheeler's troops
that moving toward Cassville. Those two officers
were instructed to keep me accurately informed of
the enemy's progress.

French's division of Polk's corps joined the army
from Mississippi in the afternoon.

Next morning, when Brig.-General Jackson's reports showed that the head of the Federal column
following the railroad was near Kingston, Lieutenant-
General Hood was directed to move with his corps to
a country road about a mile to the east of that from
Adairsville, and parallel to it, and to march north-
ward on that road, right in front. Polk's corps, as
then formed, was to advance to meet and engage the
enemy approaching from Adairsville; and it was
expected that Hood's would be in position to fall
upon the left flank of those troops as soon as Polk
attacked them in front. An order was read to each
regiment, announcing that we were about to give
battle to the enemy. It was received with exulta-
tion.

When General Hood's column had moved two or
three miles, that officer received a report from a member of his staff, to the effect that the enemy was approaching [1] on the Canton road, in rear of the right
of the position from which he had just marched.
Instead of transmitting this report to me, and moving
on in obedience to his orders, he fell back to that
road and formed his corps across it, facing to our

---

[1] The Federal army had been under our unceasing observation for
thirteen days, in the direction of Adairsville and Dalton, and our rear-
guards were then skirmishing with it on that side; so that the report
upon which General Hood acted was manifestly untrue.

right and rear, toward Canton, without informing
me of this strange departure from the instructions
he had received. I heard of this erratic movement
after it had caused such loss of time as to make the
attack intended impracticable; for its success depended on accuracy in timing it. The intention was
therefore abandoned.[1]

The sound of the artillery of the Federal column
following Hardee's corps, and that of the skirmishing of Wheeler's troops with the other, made it evident in an hour that the Federal forces would soon
be united before us, and indicated that an attack by
them was imminent. To be prepared for it, the Confederate army was drawn up in a position that I remember as the best that I saw occupied during the war
—the ridge immediately south of Cassville, with a
broad, open, elevated valley in front of it completely commanded by the fire of troops occupying
its crest.

The eastern end of this ridge is perhaps a mile to
the east of Cassville. Its southwest end is near the railroad, a little to the west of the Cassville Station. Its
length was just sufficient for Hood's and Polk's corps,
and half of Hardee's, formed as usual in two lines,
and in that order from right to left. The other half
of Hardee's troops, prolonging this line, were southwest of the railroad, on undulating ground on which
they had only such advantage as their own labor,
directed by engineering, could give them. They
worked with great spirit, however, and were evidently
full of confidence. This gave me assurance of success on the right and in the centre, where we had
very decided advantage of ground.

[1] *See* General Mackall's letter in note, page 323.

Brigadier-General Shoupe, chief of artillery, had pointed out to me what he thought a weak point near General Polk's right, a space of a hundred and fifty or two hundred yards, which, in his opinion, might be enfiladed by artillery placed on a hill more than a mile off, beyond the front of our right—so far, it seemed to me, as to make the danger trifling. Still, he was requested to instruct the officer commanding there to guard against such a chance by the construction of traverses, and to impress upon him that no attack of infantry could be combined with a fire of distant artillery, and that his infantry might safely occupy some ravines immediately in rear of this position during any such fire of artillery.

The Federal artillery commenced firing upon Hood's and Polk's troops soon after they were formed, and continued the cannonade until night.

On reaching my tent soon after dark, I found in it an invitation to meet the Lieutenant-Generals at General Polk's quarters. General Hood was with him, but not General Hardee. The two officers, General Hood taking the lead,' expressed the opinion

---

[1] In General Hood's *second* report of his operations in Georgia and Tennessee, which was made in Richmond, he contradicts this statement, which was published in my official report.

General Hardee wrote in reference to that contradiction, April 10, 1867: "At Cassville, May 19th, about ten o'clock in the evening, in answer to a summons from you, I found you at General Polk's headquarters, in company with Generals Polk and Hood. You informed me that it was determined to retire across the Etowah. In reply to my exclamation of surprise, General Hood, anticipating you, answered: 'General Polk, if attacked, cannot hold his position three-quarters of an hour; and I cannot hold mine two hours.' Orders were then given for the movement."

On the same subject General W. W. Mackall wrote, April 29, 1873: "I read your report of your operations in Georgia, in Macon, soon

very positively that neither of their corps would be able to hold its position next day; because, they said, a part of each was enfiladed by Federal artillery. The part of General Polk's corps referred to was that of which I had conversed with Brigadier-General Shoupe. On that account they urged me to abandon the ground immediately, and cross the Etowah.

A discussion of more than an hour followed, in which they very earnestly and decidedly expressed the opinion, or conviction rather, that when the Federal artillery opened upon them next day it would render their positions untenable in an hour or two.

Although the position was the best we had occupied, I yielded at last, in the belief that the confidence of the commanders of two of the three corps of the army, of their inability to resist the enemy, would inevitably be communicated to their troops, and produce that inability. Lieutenant-General Hardee, who arrived after this decision, remonstrated against it strongly, and was confident that his corps could hold its ground, although less favorably posted. The error was adhered to, however, and the position abandoned before daybreak.

The army was led to the Etowah,[1] crossed it about

after it was made, and every thing therein stated in regard to General Hood corresponded with my recollections, of the then recent transactions. I was not present in General Polk's quarters when the abandonment of Cassville was proposed, but, being afterward called there by you, I heard General Hood say, to a general officer who entered after me (I think General French), that it was impossible to hold his line."

[1] Near the railroad-bridge.

noon, and bivouacked as near the river as was consistent with the comfort of the troops. The cavalry was placed in observation along the stream—Wheeler's above and Jackson's below the infantry.

Our loss in killed and wounded, not including cavalry, from the commencement of the campaign to the passage of the Etowah, was, as shown by the report of the medical director of the army, Surgeon A. J. Foard:

	Killed.	Wounded.	Total.
In Hardee's corps............	116	850	966
In Hood's corps..............	283	1,564	1,847
In Polk's corps..............	46	529	575
			3,388

As the intervention of the river prevented close observation of the movements of the Federal army, Major-General Wheeler was directed to cross it on the 22d, five or six miles to our right, with all his troops not required for outpost duty, and move toward Cassville, to ascertain in what direction the Federal army was moving. He was instructed, also, to avail himself of all opportunities to inflict harm upon the enemy, by breaking the railroad, and capturing or destroying trains and detachments.

He soon ascertained that the Federal army was moving westward, as if to cross the Etowah near Kingston; and, on the 24th, after defeating the troops guarding a large supply-train, near Cassville, he brought off seventy loaded wagons, with their teams, three hundred equipped horses and mules, and a hundred and eighty-two prisoners, having burned a much greater number of wagons, with their loads, than were brought away.

In the mean time Jackson had given information of General Sherman's march toward the bridges near Stilesboro', and of the crossing of the leading Federal troops there on the 23d. In consequence of this intelligence, Lieutenant-General Hardee was ordered to march that afternoon, by New Hope Church, to the road leading from Stilesboro', through Dallas, to Atlanta; and Lieutenant-General Polk to move to the same road, by a route farther to the left. Lieutenant-General Hood was instructed to follow Hardee on the 24th. Hardee's corps reached the point designated to him that afternoon; Polk's was within four or five miles of it to the east, and Hood's within four miles of New Hope Church, on the road to it from Alatoona. On the 25th the latter reached New Hope Church, early in the day. Intelligence was received from General Jackson's troops soon after, that the Federal army was near—its right at Dallas, and its line extending toward Alatoona.

Lieutenant-General Hood was immediately instructed to form his corps parallel with the road by which he had marched, and west of it, with the centre [1] opposite to the church; Lieutenant-General Polk to place his [2] in line with it, on the left, and Lieutenant-General Hardee to occupy a ridge extending from the ground allotted to Polk's corps, across the road leading from Dallas toward Atlanta—his left division, Bate's, holding that road.

As soon as his troops were in position, Lieutenant-General Hood, to "develop the enemy," sent for-

---

[1] A road from Dallas to Marietta, passing by New Hope Church, at right angles to General Hood's line, was held in this way.

[2] General Polk's corps was about five miles from this position.

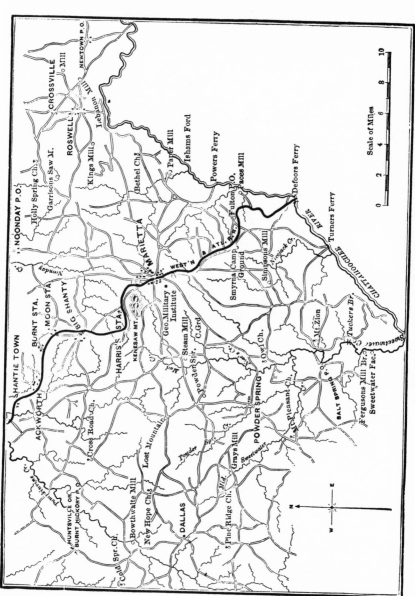

CAMPAIGN IN NORTH GEORGIA. No. 3.

ward Colonel Bush Jones, with his regiment (the united Thirty-second and Fifty-eighth Alabama) and Austin's sharpshooters, in all about three hundred men. After advancing about a mile, this detachment encountered Hooker's (Twentieth) corps. Having the written order of his corps commander to hold his ground after meeting the enemy, Colonel Jones resisted resolutely the attack of the overwhelming Federal forces. But, after a gallant [1] fight, he was, of course, driven back to his division—Stewart's.

An hour and a half before sunset, a brisk cannonade was opened upon Hood's centre division, Stewart's, opposite to New Hope Church. Major-General Stewart regarding this as the harbinger of assault, leaped upon his horse and rode along his line, to instruct the officers and encourage the men. He soon found the latter to be superfluous, from the confident tone in which he was addressed by his soldiers, and urged by them to lay aside all anxiety, and trust, for success, to their courage. Such pledges were well redeemed. The enemy soon appeared—Hooker's corps—in so deep order that it presented a front equal only to that of Stewart's first line—three brigades. After opening their fire, the Federal troops approached gradually but resolutely, under the fire of three brigades and sixteen field-pieces, until within fifty paces of the Confederate line. Here, however, they were compelled first to ·pause, and then to fall back, by the obstinate resistance they encountered.

[1] So gallant a one that the commander of Hooker's leading division thought he was engaged with a brigade, at least. (*See* General Geary's report.)

They were led forward again, advancing as resolutely, and approaching as near to the Confederate
line as before, but were a second time repulsed by
the firmness of their opponents, and their deliberate
fire of canister-shot and musketry. The engagement
was continued in this manner almost two hours,
when the assailants drew off.

In this action a few of the men of Clayton's and
Baker's brigades were partially sheltered by a hasty
arrangement of some fallen timber which they found
near their line. The other brigade engaged, Stovall's,
had no such protection. Nothing entitled to the
term "breastworks" had been constructed by the division.

We found, next morning, that the Federal line
extended much farther to our right than it had done
the day before. Polk's corps was transferred to the
right of Hood's, therefore, covering the road to Acworth. Consequently, all the ground between Hood's
left and the Powder Spring road was guarded by
Hardee's corps. There was little activity apparent
in either army during the day. No other engagements of infantry occurred than attempts by the skirmishers of each army to harass those of the other.
But late in the afternoon a large body of Federal
cavalry, probably feeling for our right flank, encountered Avery's regiment of Georgia cavalry. Although desperately wounded in the onset, Colonel
Avery, supported in his saddle by a soldier, continued to command, and maintained the contest until the arrival of forces capable of holding the
ground.

The Federal troops extended their intrenched

LIEUTENANT-GENERAL A. P. STEWART

line so rapidly to their left, that it was found necessary in the morning of the 27th to transfer Cleburne's division of Hardee's corps to our right, where
it was formed on the prolongation of Polk's line.
Kelly's cavalry, composed of Allen's and Hannon's
Alabama brigades, together less than a thousand
men, occupied the interval, of half a mile, between
Cleburne's right and Little Pumpkin-Vine Creek.
Martin's division (cavalry) guarded the road from
Burnt Hickory to Marietta, two miles farther to the
right; and Humes's the interval between Kelly's
and Martin's divisions.

Between five and six o'clock in the afternoon,
Kelly's skirmishers were driven in by a body of
Federal cavalry, whose advance was supported by the
Fourth Corps. This advance was retarded by the
resistance of Kelly's troops fighting on foot behind
unconnected little heaps of loose stones. As soon
as the noise of this contest revealed to Major-General
Cleburne the manœuvre to turn his right, he brought
the right brigade of his second line, Granberry's, to
Kelly's support, by forming it on the right of his
first line; when the thin line of dismounted cavalry,
that had been bravely resisting masses of infantry
gave place to the Texan brigade.

The Fourth Corps came on in deep order, and assailed the Texans with great vigor, receiving their
close and accurate fire with the fortitude always exhibited by General Sherman's troops in the actions
of this campaign. They had also to endure the fire
of Govan's right,[1] including two pieces of artillery,
on their right flank. At the same time, Kelly's and

---

[1] Originally the right brigade of the first line.

a part of Humes's troops, directed by General Wheeler, met the Federal left, which was following the movement of the main body, and drove back the leading brigade, taking thirty or forty prisoners.[1] The united force continued to press forward, however, but so much delayed by the resistance of Wheeler's troops as to give time for the arrival, on that part of the field, of the Eighth and Ninth Arkansas regiments under Colonel Bancum, detached by General Govan to the assistance of the cavalry. This little body met the foremost of the Federal troops as they were reaching the prolongation of Granberry's line, and, charging gallantly, drove them back, and preserved the Texans from an attack in flank which must have been fatal. Before the Federal left could gather to overwhelm Bancum and his two regiments, Lowry's brigade, hurried by General Cleburne from its position as left of his second line, came to join them, and the two, formed abreast of Granberry's brigade, stopped the advance of the enemy's left, and successfully resisted its subsequent attacks.

The contest of the main body of the Fourth Corps with Granberry's brigade was a very fierce one.[2] The Federal troops approached within a few yards of the Confederates, but at last were forced to give way by their storm of well-directed bullets, and fell back to the shelter of a hollow near and behind them. They left hundreds of corpses within twenty paces of the Confederate line.

When the United States troops paused in their advance, within fifteen paces of the Texan front

---

[1] General Wheeler's report.   [2] General Cleburne's report.

rank, one of their color-bearers planted his colors eight or ten feet in front of his regiment, and was instantly shot dead; a soldier sprang forward to his place, and fell also, as he grasped the color-staff; a second and third followed successively, and each received death as speedily as his predecessors; a fourth, however, seized and bore back the object of soldierly devotion.[1]

About ten o'clock at night, Granberry ascertained that many of the Federal troops were still in the hollow immediately before him, and charged and drove them from it, taking two hundred and thirty-two prisoners, seventy-two of whom were severely wounded.

The Federal dead lying near our line were counted by many persons—officers and soldiers. According to those counts, there were seven hundred of them. The loss in Cleburne's division was eighty-five killed, and three hundred and sixty-three wounded. A similar proportion of dead and wounded in the Fourth Corps would give three thousand five hundred as its loss in killed and wounded. We found about twelve hundred small-arms on the field. I had no report of General Wheeler's loss, nor means of ascertaining that which he inflicted.

In the affair at New Hope Church, two days before, greater forces were engaged—three Confederate brigades with sixteen field-pieces, against the Twentieth Federal corps, which, unless our information was inaccurate, was much stronger than the Fourth. It is reasonable to suppose that greater

[1] This circumstance was related to me on the ground by a number of the nearest Texans.

numbers, exposed at least as long to a much heavier
fire, suffered greater losses. Stewart had, also, the advantage of less uneven ground before him, which
must have greatly increased the effect of his fire
both of musketry and artillery.

The changes of disposition, made in this action
of the 27th, extended our right and the Federal left
to Little Pumpkin-Vine Creek.

Major-General Lovell, whose assignment to the
Army of Tennessee, as a corps commander, I had
earnestly asked in the preceding winter, joined it at
this time as a volunteer, prompted by a zeal in the
cause which made him regardless of the claims of
his rank. He was immediately requested to examine the fords and ferries of the Chattahoochee, and
to dispose the available State troops, including some
artillery, to guard them against any bodies of Federal
cavalry that might attempt to surprise Atlanta, for
the purpose of destroying our depots there.

As circumstances indicated that many troops had
been withdrawn from the intrenchments of the Federal right, in front of Dallas, Major-General Bate,
whose division then formed the left of the Confederate army, was instructed, on the morning of the 28th,
to ascertain, by a forced reconnaissance, if those intrenchments were still held by adequate forces. General Bate determined to seize those works if it should
be found that they were occupied, but only feebly.
He therefore directed the commanders of his three
brigades to form their troops and keep them under
arms, and, if an explained signal should be given, to
advance rapidly against the enemy before them.
General Armstrong, whose brigade of cavalry was

on the left of the infantry, was then directed to approach the extreme right of the Federal line of
works, to learn how it was occupied, if at all. His
brigade was received with a cannonade and fire of
musketry so spirited that each of the two brigade
commanders of the division of infantry supposed
that all of the troops but his own were engaged,
and hastily assailed the field-works before him.
Both, however, were soon convinced of their error
by the reception given them, and drew off, but not
before they had lost some three hundred men killed
and wounded.

When the three lieutenant-generals were together
in my quarters that day, as usual, Lieutenant-General Hood suggested that we should make an attack
upon the Federal army, to commence on its left flank.
The suggestion was accepted, and the three officers
were desired to be ready for battle next morning.
Lieutenant-General Hood was instructed to draw his
corps out of the line to the rear, and to march during the night around our right, and form it facing
the enemy's left flank, somewhat obliquely to his
line, and to assail that flank at dawn next day.
Polk and Hardee were instructed to join in the battle successively, obliquely to the present formation,
when the progress made on the right of each should
enable him to do so.

We waited next morning for the signal agreed upon
—the musketry of Hood's corps—from the appointed
time until about 10 A. M., when a message from the
Lieutenant-General was delivered to me by one of his
aide-de-camps, to the effect that he had found Johnson's division, on the Federal left, thrown back

almost at right angles to the general line, and intrenching; that, under such circumstances, he had
thought it inexpedient to attack, and asked for instructions. I supposed, from the terms of this message,
that Hood's corps was in the presence of the enemy,
and that, his movement and position being known to
them, they would be prepared to repel his assault as
soon as he to make it, after his aide-de-camp's return.
If the attack had been expedient when Lieutenant-
General Hood's message was dispatched, the resulting
delay, by enabling the enemy to reënforce the threatened point and complete the intrenchments begun,
made it no longer so. He was therefore recalled.[1]

The Federal intrenched line was extended daily
toward the railroad, in the direction of Alatoona.
We endeavored to keep pace with this extension, to
prevent being cut off from the railroad and Marietta.
But, from the great inequality of force, two or
three miles of the right of ours was occupied by dismounted cavalry in skirmishing order. The enemy's
demonstrations against this part of our front led to

---

[1] General Hood contradicts this statement, as it appeared in my official report, in his own, referred to in the notes to page 324. (In confirmation of my statement, *see* General Mackall's statement in those notes.)
Lieutenant-General Hardee, in the letter quoted in the note to page
324, wrote: "On the 28th of May, at New Hope Church, instructions
were given the assembled corps commanders, Generals Polk, Hood, and
myself, for a general engagement the next day. General Hood was to
get in position during the night, and attack the left flank of the enemy
the following morning. The attack thus begun was to be joined in by
the rest of the army successively. I was present with you in the forenoon of the 29th, awaiting the attack by General Hood, which was to
signal the general engagement, when a report was received from him
stating that he had found the enemy intrenched, and, deeming it inexpedient to attack, asked instructions. The opportunity had passed.
General Hood was recalled, and the army resumed its defensive attitude."

skirmishing with Wheeler's troops, in which the latter captured above a hundred prisoners between the 1st and 4th of June. The infantry skirmishers of the two armies were incessantly engaged at the same time, from right to left, when there was light enough to distinguish and aim at a man.

At the end of that time it was evident that the great body of the Federal army was moving to its left rear, toward the railroad, the movement being covered by its long line of intrenchment. The Confederate army then marched to a position selected beforehand, and carefully marked out by Colonel Prestman, the chief-engineer. Its left was on Lost Mountain, and its right, composed of cavalry, beyond the railroad and behind Noonday Creek.

According to the report of the medical director of the army, the losses of the three corps in killed and wounded, between the time of the passage of the Etowah and that of the last change of position, were:

	Killed.	Wounded.	Total.
Hardee's Corps	156	879	1,035
Hood's Corps	103	756	859
Polk's Corps	17	94	111
			2,005

That of the cavalry of the right, commanded by Major-General Wheeler, from the 6th to the 31st of May inclusive, was: seventy-three killed, and three hundred and forty-one wounded. In the same period those troops took more than five hundred prisoners, as many horses, and five standards and colors. General Jackson made no report.

Soon after the army was established in the position just described, a large body of Federal cavalry, advancing on the Big Shanty and Marietta road, encountered a part of Wheeler's. After a succession of skirmishes, the Confederates charged and drove the enemy before them several miles beyond Big Shanty. The losses of the two parties were not ascertained, except that of forty-five prisoners by the Federals.

Five or six days elapsed before the enemy approached near enough for the usual skirmishing and partial engagements. The cavalry on both flanks was active, however; especially near the railroad, where it was most numerous.

On the 8th, the body of the Federal army seemed to be near Acworth. Our army was, for that reason, formed to cover the roads leading from that vicinity toward Atlanta: the left of Hardee's corps at Gilgal Church, Bate's division occupying the summit of Pine Mount, a detached hill about three hundred feet high; Polk's right near the Acworth and Marietta road, covered by Noonday Creek; and Hood's massed on the right of that road; Jackson's division on the left, and Wheeler's in front of the right.

On the 11th, the left of the Federal army could be seen from the Confederate signal-station on Kenesaw, intrenched on the high ground beyond Noonday Creek. The centre lay a third or half mile in front of the summit of Pine Mount, and the right extended across the Burnt Hickory and Marietta road.

The cavalry of the Federal right was held in check by Jackson's division, aided by the line of intrenchments constructed by our infantry between Lost Mountain and Gilgal Church; but that of the left

was very active and encountered ours daily, occasionally in large bodies.   According to Major-General
Wheeler's reports, these affairs were always to our
advantage.

In the evening of the 13th, Lieutenant-General
Hardee expressed apprehension that Bate's division,
posted on Pine Mount, might be too far from the line
occupied by his corps, and requested me to visit that
outpost, and decide if it should be maintained.   We
rode to it together next morning, accompanied by
Lieutenant-General Polk, who wished to avail himself of the height to study the ground in front of his
own corps.

Just when we had concluded our examination,
and the abandonment of the hill had been decided
upon, a party of soldiers, that had gathered behind
us from mere curiosity, apparently tempted an artillery officer whose battery was in front, six or seven
hundred yards from us, to open his fire upon them;
at first firing shot very slowly.   Lieutenant-General
Polk, unconsciously exposed by his characteristic in-
sensibility to danger, fell by the third shot, which
passed from left to right through the middle of his
chest.   The death of this eminent Christian and soldier, who had been distinguished in every battle in
which the Army of Tennessee had been engaged,
produced deep sorrow in our troops.   Major-General
Loring, the officer next in rank in the corps, succeeded
temporarily to its command.

Before daybreak of the 15th, the Pine Mount was
abandoned, and Bate's division placed in reserve.
The Confederate skirmishers were vigorously pressed
from right to left.   Loring's, attacked in open ground

and far in front by a full line, were driven in, and their ground held by the enemy.

A division of State militia organized by Governor Brown, under Major-General G. W. Smith, and transferred to the army, was charged about this time with the defense of the bridges and ferries of the Chattahoochee, near Atlanta, to guard against the surprise of the town by the Federal cavalry.

On the 16th a new disposition was made on the left. Hardee's corps changed front to the rear on its right, by which it was placed on the high ground east of Mud Creek, facing to the west. The right of the Federal army made a corresponding movement, and approached Hardee's line, opposed in advancing by Jackson's division, as well as twenty-five hundred men can contend with twenty-five thousand.

This disposition made an angle where Hardee's right joined Loring's left, which was soon found to be a great defect, for it exposed the troops near it to annoyance from enfilade, which should have been foreseen. Another position, including the crest of Kenesaw, was chosen on the 17th, and prepared for occupation under the direction of Colonel Prestman. The troops were placed on this line on the 19th: Hood's corps massed between the railroad and that from Marietta to Canton; Loring's, with a division (his own commanded by Featherston) between the railroad and eastern base of the mountain; and Walthall's and French's along the crest of the short ridge —French's left reaching its southwestern base, and Hardee's from French's left almost due south across the Lost Mountain and Marietta road, to the brow of the high ground immediately north of the branch of Nose's Creek that runs from Marietta—Walker's division on the right, Bate's next, then Cleburne's, and Cheatham's on the left.

Immediately after this new disposition, heavy and long-continued rains made Nose's Creek impassable, and under its cover the Federal line was extended some miles beyond our left toward the Chattahoochee. When the stream subsided, the enemy's right was found to be protected by intrenchments constructed in the mean time.

On the 20th the most considerable cavalry affair of the campaign occurred on our right. The Confederate cavalry on that flank, being attacked by that under General Garrard's command, repulsed the assailants, whom, as they were retiring, Wheeler charged with above a thousand men, and routed, capturing a hundred men and horses, and two standards. Fifty of the enemy's dead were counted on the field. The Confederate loss was fifteen killed and fifty wounded.

As the extension of the Federal army toward the Chattahoochee made a corresponding one necessary on our part, Hood's corps was transferred from the right to the Marietta and Powder-Spring road, his right near and south of Cheatham's left. General Hood was instructed to endeavor to prevent any progress of the Federal right toward the railroad; the course of which was nearly parallel to our left and centre. Our position, consequently, was a very hazardous one.

Next day a sharp but brief fire of musketry on the left, succeeded by that of, apparently, several batteries, announced that Hood's corps, or a large part of it, was engaged. Soon after the firing ceased, General Hood reported that Hindman's and Stevenson's divisions of his corps had been attacked, and that they had not only repulsed the enemy, but had followed them to a line of light intrenchments and driven them from it; but that, being exposed, in this position, to a fire of intrenched artillery, they had been compelled to withdraw.

Subsequent[1] and more minute accounts of this affair, by general and staff officers of the corps, converted the favorable impression made by this report into the belief that, instead of achieving success, we had suffered a reverse. It appeared that our troops had not fallen back merely to escape annoyance, but that, after the Federal infantry had been driven back to and then beyond its line of breastworks, Lieutenant-General Hood determined to capture the intrenched artillery referred to in his brief report. It crowned a high, bare hill, facing the interval between his right and the left of Hardee's corps. To direct his line toward it, a partial change of front to the right was necessary, and that slow operation, performed under the fire of a formidable artillery, subjected his two divisions to a loss so severe that the attempt was soon abandoned—I am uncertain whether by the decision of the commander, or the discretion of the troops themselves; not, however, until they had lost about a thousand men.

An unusually vigorous attack was made upon the skirmishers of Hardee's corps on the 24th. They repelled it unaided, firing from rifle-pits. A similar

---

[1] Since the end of the war.

attack upon Stevenson's skirmishers, the day after, was defeated in like manner.

In the morning of the 27th, after a furious cannonade, the Federal army made a general assault upon the Confederate position, which was received everywhere with firmness, and repelled with a loss to the assailants enormously disproportionate to that which they inflicted. At several points the characteristic fortitude of the Northwestern soldiers held them under a close and destructive fire long after reasonable hope of success was gone. The attack upon Loring's corps was by the Army of the Tennessee; that upon Hardee's by the Army of the Cumberland. The principal efforts of the enemy were directed against Loring's right and left brigades, and the left of Hardee's corps.

The attack upon Loring's right—Scott's brigade of Featherston's division—was by troops of the Seventeenth Corps, advancing in three lines, preceded by skirmishers. They received five or six volleys from Nelson's (Twelfth Louisiana) regiment, deployed as skirmishers, in rifle-pits, six hundred yards in front of the brigade. This regiment held its ground until the first Federal line had approached within twenty-five paces. It then retired to the line of battle. The Federal troops advanced steadily, and two hundred paces from the Confederate line met the fire of Scott's infantry, and received in their flanks that of four batteries. This concentrated fire compelled them to halt. Unable to advance farther, and unwilling to retreat, they remained where they had halted almost an hour, before withdrawing from the shower of missiles.

During this time a single line of Federal infantry was engaged with Wheeler's troops, the skirmishers of Featherston's own, and Adams's brigades, and those of Quarles's brigade of Walthall's division—all in the shelter of rifle-pits. The firing was always within easy, and frequently very short range. A body of the assailants charged into Quarles's rifle-pits, where most of them were killed or captured.

In the assault upon Loring's left (Cockrell's Missouri brigade) the assailants advanced rapidly from the west—their right extending to the south of the Burnt Hickory and Marietta road, and their left encountering the brigade (Sears's) on Cockrell's right. Their right dashed through the skirmishers of Walker's right before they could be reënforced, and took in reverse those on the right and left, while they were attacked in front. In a few minutes about eighty of Walker's men had been bayoneted or captured in their rifle-pits. The Federal troops approaching Walker's line on the south of the road were driven back by the fire of artillery directed against their left flank by Major-General French; but the main body, unchecked by Cockrell's skirmishers, pressed forward steadily under the fire of the brigade, until within twenty or thirty paces of its line. Here it was checked and ultimately repulsed, by the steady courage of the Missourians. The action had continued with spirit for almost an hour, during most of which time fifty field-pieces were playing upon the Confederate troops.

But the most determined and powerful attack fell upon Cheatham's division and the left of Cleburne's. The lines of the two armies were much nearer to each other there; therefore the action was begun at shorter range. The Federal troops were in greater force, and deeper order, too, and pressed forward with the resolution always displayed by the American soldier when properly led. An attempt to turn the left was promptly met and defeated by Cheatham's reserve—Vaughn's brigade. After maintaining the contest for three-quarters of an hour, until more of their best soldiers lay dead and wounded than the number of British veterans that fell in General Jackson's celebrated battle of New Orleans, the foremost dead lying against our breastworks, they retired—unsuccessful—because they had encountered *intrenched* infantry unsurpassed by that of Napoleon's Old Guard, or that which followed Wellington into France, out of Spain. Our losses were:

IN HARDEE'S CORPS.

	Killed.	Wounded.	Missing.	Total.
Cheatham's Division	26	75	94	195
Cleburne's Division	2	9	—	11
Walker's Division		Killed or taken		80
				286

IN LORING'S CORPS.

	Killed.	Wounded.	Missing.	Total.
Featherston's Division	8	13	1	22
French's Division	17	92	77	186
Walthall's Division	6	22	—	28
				522

The comparatively severe loss in French's division was accounted for by its position—on the descending crest of the end of Kenesaw—where it was exposed to the fire of about fifty guns; and by the turning of his line of skirmishers. That of Cheatham's was principally in the reserve, which fought in open ground, unprotected by intrenchments.

From the number[1] of dead counted from his breastworks, Lieutenant-General Hardee estimated the loss of the troops engaged with his corps at five thousand; and in his official report, dated July 30th, Major-General Loring estimated that of the Army of the Tennessee, which assailed his corps, at twenty-five hundred.

I think that the estimate of Northern officers of their killed and wounded on that occasion, "near three thousand," does great injustice to the character of General Sherman's army. Such a loss, in the large force that must have been furnished for a decisive and general attack by an army of almost a hundred thousand men, would have been utterly insignificant —too trifling to discourage, much less defeat brave soldiers, such as composed General Sherman's army. It does injustice to Southern marksmanship, too. The fire of twenty thousand infantry inured to battle, and intrenched, and of fifty field-pieces poured into such columns, frequently within pistol-shot, must have done much greater execution.

On the 29th a truce was agreed to, to permit the Federal soldiers to bury their dead lying near our breastworks.

The reports from the flanks showed that the enemy had much reduced the cavalry of their left, and proportionally increased the strength of that of their right. Major-General Smith was therefore desired to bring forward his division to the support of Jackson's troops. It was done; and the State troops under him rendered good service.

[1] One thousand. The ordinary proportion of one killed to five wounded gives six thousand.

As the Federal commander manifested a strong disposition to operate by his right, which was already nearer to Atlanta than the Confederate left, another position was selected for the army, ten miles south of Marietta, which Colonel Prestman was desired to have prepared for occupation; and Brigadier-General Shoupe was directed to construct a line of redoubts on a plan devised by himself, on a line selected by Major-General Lovell on the high ground near the Chattahoochee, and covering the approaches to the railroad bridge and Turner's Ferry. Negro laborers had been impressed for the work. Some time before, Captain Grant, the engineer-officer who directed the construction of the intrenchments around Atlanta, was instructed to strengthen them in a manner explained to him, and was authorized to impress negro laborers for the work.

The reports of outposts, and observation from the top of Kenesaw on the 1st and 2d of July, showed that General Sherman was transferring strong bodies of troops to his right. The Confederate army was therefore moved to the position prepared for it by Colonel Prestman, which it reached early on the 3d, and occupied in two lines crossing the road to Atlanta almost at right angles—Loring's corps on the right and Hardee's on the left of the road, Hood's on the left of Hardee's, Wheeler's on the right of Loring's corps, and Jackson's, supported by General Smith, on the left of Hood's.

During the twenty-six days in which the two armies confronted each other near Marietta, besides the incessant musketry of skirmishers, the Confederate troops had to endure an almost uninterrupted cannonade—and to endure without returning it; for their supply of artillery-ammunition was so inadequate, that their batteries could be used only to repel assaults, or in serious engagements.

On the 4th, Lieutenant-General Hood's reports indicated that the enemy was turning his left, and that his own forces were insufficient to defeat their design, or hold them in check. Cheatham's division, therefore, was sent to his assistance. In the evening, Major-General Smith reported that the Federal cavalry was pressing on him in such force, that he would be compelled to abandon the ground he had been holding, and retire, before morning, to General Shoupe's line of redoubts. As the position in question covered a very important route to Atlanta, and was nearer than the main body of our army to that place, the necessity of abandoning it involved the taking a new line. The three corps were accordingly brought to the intrenched position just prepared by General Shoupe, which covered both routes to Atlanta, in the morning of the 5th—Major-General Wheeler covering the withdrawal of the right and centre, and General Jackson that of the left. After the infantry and artillery were disposed in the new position, the cavalry was sent to the south bank of the Chattahoochee; Wheeler's to observe the river above, and Jackson's below.

The Federal army approached as cautiously as usual, covering itself by intrenchments as soon as its scouts discovered our line of skirmishers. As soon as these works were strong enough to protect thoroughly the troops occupying them, the passage of the river was commenced by General Sherman above,

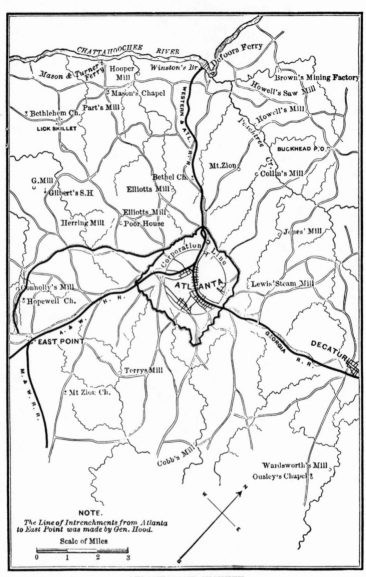

NOTE.
*The Line of Intrenchments from Atlanta
to East Point was made by Gen. Hood.*

Scale of Miles

0   1   2   3

ATLANTA AND VICINITY.

where fords are numerous and broad. On the 8th, two of his corps crossed and intrenched. In consesequence of this, the Confederate army crossed the Chattahoochee in the night of the 9th (each corps had two bridges), and was established two miles from it.

Lieutenant-General Stewart, promoted to the office made vacant by the death of Lieutenant-General Polk, had assumed the command of his corps on the 7th.

As soon as the army passed the Chattahoochee, its engineer-officers joined in the work of strengthening the intrenchments of Atlanta with all the negro laborers that could be collected.[1] Colonel Prestman was instructed to devote his first attention to the works between the Augusta and Marietta roads, as there was no reasonable doubt that the enemy's approach would be on that side.

The character of Peach-Tree Creek, which empties into the Chattahoochee just above the railroad-bridge, and the course of the river, and number of fords above that point, prevented the Confederates from attempting to do more than observe that part of the valley. The broad, deep, and muddy channel of the creek would have been a serious impediment to the passage of troops from right to left, if our line had crossed it; and the course of the river would have put us under the further disadvantage of a concave line.[2] But a position on the high ground looking down into the valley of the creek from the south

---

[1] Captain Grant, who constructed those intrenchments, had been employing a large body of laborers in strengthening them, by my direction, since the beginning of June.

[2] While, on the contrary, the creek and river below its mouth formed a convex one.

was selected for the army; to be occupied when all the Federal forces had crossed the Chattahoochee, and from which to attack it, while divided in the passage of the creek; when I hoped that a favorable opportunity would occur.

On the 14th a division of Federal cavalry crossed the Chattahoochee by Moore's bridge, opposite to Newnan. But Brigadier-General Jackson, who had observed its movement to his left, detached Armstrong's brigade to meet it, which bravely attacked and drove it back.

Just then the army was visited by General Bragg. That officer was directly from Richmond, on his way, he said, to Lieutenant-General S. D. Lee's headquarters, to confer with him and communicate with Lieutenant-General E. Kirby Smith—to ascertain what reënforcements for *me* their departments could furnish. His visit to me was unofficial, he assured me.

At the same time Governor Brown promised to bring ten thousand more State militia into the army; he was confident that it would be done in ten days. The promise gave me great satisfaction, for such a force might be made very valuable in operations about Atlanta.

On the 17th,[1] Major-General Wheeler reported that the whole Federal army had crossed the Chattahoochee, and was near it, between Roswell and Powers's Ferry. At ten o'clock P. M., while Colonel Prestman was with me receiving instructions in relation to his work of the next day on the intrenchments of Atlanta, the following telegram was received from General Cooper, dated July 17th: "Lieutenant-

[1] At night.

General J. B. Hood has been commissioned to the temporary rank of general, under the late law of Congress. I am directed by the Secretary of War to inform you that, as you have failed to arrest the advance of the enemy to the vicinity of Atlanta, far in the interior of Georgia, and express no confidence that you can defeat or repel him, you are hereby relieved from the command of the Army and Department of Tennessee, which you will immediately turn over to General Hood."

Orders transferring the command of the army to General Hood were written and published immediately, and next morning I replied to the Hon. Secretary's telegram: "Your dispatch of yesterday received and obeyed. Command of the Army and Department of Tennessee has been transferred to General Hood. As to the alleged cause of my removal, I assert that Sherman's army is much stronger compared with that of Tennessee, than Grant's compared with that of Northern Virginia. Yet the enemy has been compelled to advance much more slowly to the vicinity of Atlanta, than to that of Richmond and Petersburg; and penetrated much deeper into Virginia than into Georgia.

"Confident language by a military commander is not usually regarded as evidence of competence."

General Hood came to my quarters early in the morning of the 18th, and remained there during the day. Intelligence soon came from Major-Gen. Wheeler, that the Federal army was marching toward Atlanta, and at General Hood's earnest request I continued to give orders through Brigadier-Gen. Mackall, chief of staff,[1] until sunset. By one of them the army was placed in the previously-chosen position covering the roads by which the enemy was approaching.

In transferring the command to General Hood I explained my plans to him.[2] First, I expected an opportunity to engage the enemy on terms of advantage while they were divided in crossing Peach-Tree Creek, trusting to General Wheeler's vigilance for the necessary information. If successful, the great divergence of the Federal line of retreat from the direct route available to us would enable us to secure decisive results ; if unsuccessful, we had a safe place of refuge in our intrenched lines close at hand. Holding it, we could certainly keep back the enemy, as at New Hope Church and in front of Marietta, until the State troops promised by Governor Brown were assembled. Then, I intended to man the works of Atlanta on the side toward Peach-Tree Creek with those troops, and leisurely fall back with the Confederate troops into the town, and, when the Federal army approached, march out with the three corps against one of its flanks. If we were successful, the enemy would be driven against the Chattahoochee where there are no fords, or to the east, away from their communications, as the attack might fall on their right or left. If unsuccessful, the Confederate army had a near and secure place of refuge in Atlanta, which it could hold forever, and so win the campaign, of which that place was the object. The

---

[1] General Mackall was requested to use General Hood's authority, as I had none.

[2] *See* my official report of the campaign, published by the Government.

passage of Peach-Tree Creek may not have given an opportunity to attack; but there is no reason to think that the second and far most promising plan might not have been executed.

Under the control of the Chief of Staff, Brigadier-General Mackall, the administrative departments had been admirably conducted. The condition of the horses of the artillery and mules of the trains, much better on the 18th of July than on the 5th of May, proved the efficiency of the Chief Quartermaster, Colonel McMicken, and the regularity and abundance of the supply of provision to the soldiers, that of Colonel W. E. Moore, Chief Commissary. We were fortunate in depending for the collection of these supplies upon Major J. F. Cummings, one of the most intelligent and zealous agents of the Commissary-general that I encountered during the war.

No material was lost by us in the campaign, but the four field-pieces exposed and abandoned at Resaca by General Hood.[1]

The troops themselves, who had been seventy-four days in the immediate presence of the enemy; laboring and fighting daily; enduring toil and encountering danger with equal cheerfulness; more confident and high-spirited even than when the Federal army presented itself before them at Dalton; and, though I say it, full of devotion to him who had commanded them, and belief of ultimate success in the campaign, were then inferior to none who ever served the Confederacy, or fought on this continent.

At the commencement of this campaign, the army

[1] See p. 232.

I commanded was that defeated under General Bragg at Missionary Ridge, with one brigade added, Mercer's, and two taken from it, Quarles's and Baldwin's. The Federal army opposed to us was Grant's army of Missionary Ridge, then estimated at eighty thousand men by the principal officers of the Army of Tennessee, increased by the Sixteenth and Twenty-third Corps, Hovey's division,[1] and probably twelve or fifteen thousand recruits received during the previous winter; for each regiment that reënlisted received a furlough, and was a recruiting-party while at home. The cavalry of that army amounted to about six thousand on the 1st of May; but it was increased in a few days by at least twelve thousand men in Stoneman's, McCook's, and Garrard's divisions.

The troops received by the Army of Tennessee during the campaign, were those sent and brought to it by Lieutenant-General Polk, and formed the corps of the army which he commanded. Of these, Canty's division of about three thousand effectives, reached Resaca on the 9th of May; Loring's, of five thousand, on the 11th; French's, of four thousand, joined us at Cassville on the 18th; and Quarles's brigade, of twenty-two hundred, at New Hope Church on the 26th.[2]

The effective force of the Confederate cavalry " at and near Dalton," on the 1st of May, was twenty-three hundred and ninety-two. Martin brought three thousand five hundred from the Etowah into the

---

[1] A distinguished officer of the United States army, then on General Grant's staff, estimated the infantry and artillery at sixty-five thousand.

[2] *See* Major Falconer's letter of May 1, 1865, Appendix.

field on the 9th, and Jackson's three thousand nine hundred met us at Adairsville on the 17th; total, nine thousand two hundred and ninety-two. On the 10th of July, the effective total was nine thousand nine hundred and seventy-one. The gradual restoration to condition for service, of the horses broken down in the previous hard campaign, and captures in this, enabled us to remount many dismounted men, and thus more than supply daily losses.

The Federal army received much greater accessions. Our scouts, observing the railroad in its rear, reported several trains filled with troops, passing to it daily, in all the month of May. They were generally garrisons and bridge-guards from Kentucky and Tennessee, relieved by "hundred days' men," to join the army in the field. And the Seventeenth Corps, accompanied by two thousand cavalry, joined it soon after the passage of the Etowah.

General Hood, in his report of his own disastrous operations, accused me of gross official misstatements of the strength of the army and of its losses—asserting that I had "at and near Dalton" an available force of seventy-five thousand men, and that twenty-two thousand five hundred of them were lost in the campaign, including seven thousand prisoners. He recklessly appealed for the truth of these assertions to Major Kinloch Falconer, assistant adjutant-general, by whom the returns of the army were made, which were my authority for the statement attacked by General Hood. At my request, made in consequence of this attack, Major Falconer made another statement[1] from the official data in his possession, which

[1] *See* it in Appendix.

contradicts the appellant. By that statement, the effective strength of this army "at and near Dalton" was forty thousand four hundred and sixty-four infantry and artillery, and twenty-three hundred and ninety cavalry. The prisoners of war taken since the organization of the Army of Tennessee, in 1862, were always borne on its returns. In 1864 there were not quite seven thousand of them. More than two-thirds[1] of the number reported by General Hood; the remainder[2] by General Hardee; none by Polk, whose corps had not belonged to this army before 1864. To swell the list of my losses, General Hood asserted that the prisoners taken by the enemy at Shiloh, Murfreesboro', Chickamauga, Missionary Ridge, and in the intermediate skirmishes, were lost by me in the campaign in Georgia.

The only prisoners taken from us during this campaign, that I heard of, were a company of skirmishers of Hardee's corps, and an outpost of Hood's (some two hundred men), captured about the middle of June, and a few taken from the right of Walker's and left of French's skirmishers on the 27th. As we usually fought in intrenched lines which were always held, the enemy rarely had an opportunity to make prisoners. The fact that those referred to by General Hood belonged to his corps and Hardee's only, which were the old Army of Tennessee, while none were reported in Polk's corps, which had never before belonged to that army, indicates clearly that those prisoners were captured in operations previous to this campaign.

[1] Four thousand eight hundred and thirty-five.
[2] Twenty-one hundred and fifty-nine.

Besides the grounds of my removal alleged in the telegram announcing it, various accusations were made against me subsequently. Some were published in newspapers appearing to have official authority; others were circulated orally, and referred to General Bragg's authority. The principal were:

That I persistently disregarded the President's instructions.

That I would not fight the enemy.

That I refused to defend Atlanta.

That I refused to communicate with General Bragg in relation to the operations of the army.

That I disregarded his entreaties to change my course, and attack the enemy.

And gross exaggerations of the strength and losses of the army.

The President did not give me the benefit of his instructions in the manner of conducting this campaign, further than a brief telegram received early in July, in which he warned me against receiving battle with the Chattahoochee behind the army and near it. But as Lieutenant-General Pemberton's retreat from the Tallahatchie to the Yallobusha, in December, 1862, before an army which he thought not quite double his own; and General Bragg's, first from Murfreesboro' to Tullahoma, then from Tullahoma beyond the Tennessee River, and afterward the rout on Missionary Ridge and flight to Dalton, apparently had not lowered the President's estimate of the military merit of those officers, I supposed that my course would not be disapproved by him; especially as General Lee, by keeping on the defensive, and falling back toward Grant's objective point, under circumstances like mine, was increasing his great fame. I believed then, as firmly as I do now, that the system pursued was the only one at my command that promised success, and that, if adhered to, it would have given us success.

The foregoing narrative shows that the Army of Tennessee did fight, and effectively; and probably inflicted upon the enemy greater injury, in proportion to that it received, than we read of in the history of any other campaign of the war—unless in General Lee's operations in May of the same year.

At Dalton, the great numerical superiority of the Federal army would have made the chances of battle on equal ground much against us, and that army, even if beaten, would have had a secure place of refuge near, in the fortress of Chattanooga; while our nearest, indeed only place of safety in the event of defeat, was Atlanta—a hundred miles off, with three rivers intervening. Therefore, a victory gained by us could not have been decisive, while defeat would have been utterly disastrous. Between Dalton and the Chattahoochee, we could have given battle only by attacking the enemy in intrenchments, unless we had opportunities on the 19th[1] and 28th[2] of May.

The loss of the Confederate army in this campaign, while under my command, was nine thousand nine hundred and seventy-two killed and wounded,[3] not including cavalry. About a third of it occurred near Dalton and at Resaca.

---

[1] *See* page 321.   [2] *See* page 333.
[3] *See* Medical Director's statement, Appendix.

From the observation of our most experienced officers, daily statements of prisoners, and publications which we read in the newspapers of Louisville, Cincinnati, and Chicago, the Federal loss in killed and wounded must have been six times as great as ours. The only occasions on which we had opportunities to estimate it were, the attack on our right by the Fourth Corps, May 27th, and that on our whole army, June 27th. If, as is probable, the proportion of killed to wounded was the ordinary one of one to five, in the Federal army, its losses, on those two occasions, exceeded ours by more than ten to one. The Federal prisoners concurred in saying that their greatest losses occurred in the daily attacks made by them in line of battle upon our skirmishers in their rifle-pits. Whether these attacks were successful or not, they exposed the assailants to heavy losses, and the assailed to almost none. In memoranda of the service of his own corps in this campaign, General Hardee wrote: "But the heaviest losses of the enemy were not in the assaults and partial engagements of the campaign, but in the daily skirmishing. This was kept up continuously for seventy days, during which the two armies never lost their grapple. It soon became customary, in taking up a new position, to intrench the skirmish-line, until it was only less strong than the main one. This line was well manned, and the roar of musketry on it was sometimes scarcely distinguishable from the sound of a general engagement. It was not unfrequently the case that one, two, and even three lines of battle of the enemy were repulsed in an assault upon one of our skirmish-lines." The Federal cemetery at Marietta con-

tains the graves of above ten thousand Federal soldiers who died south of the Etowah. About a thousand of them fell in General Hood's four actions, near
Atlanta and Jonesboro'. Not more than two thousand could have died of disease; for hospitals for the
sick were not near the army. As our loss north of
the Etowah was about half of that south of that
river, it is reasonable to suppose that there was
nearly the same proportion among the Federals; or,
ten thousand killed, while the Confederate army was
under my command, and five times as many wounded.[1] This cemetery completely vindicates General
Sherman's soldiers from the aspersions cast upon
their courage by the under-estimates of their losses
made by their officers.

In the course so strongly condemned by the President, our troops, always fighting under cover, had
losses very trifling compared with those they inflicted; so that it was not unreasonable to suppose
that the numerical superiority of the Federal army
was reduced daily, nor to hope that we might be
able to cope with it on equal ground beyond the
Chattahoochee, where defeat would be its destruction. The Confederate army, on the contrary, if
beaten there, had a place of refuge in Atlanta, too
strong to be taken by assault, and too extensive to
be invested. I also hoped to be able to break, or to
procure the breaking of, the railroad by which the
invading army was supplied, and thus compel it to
assail ours on our own terms, or to a retreat easily
converted into a rout. After the passage of the
Etowah by the Confederate army, five detachments

[1] Five wounded to one killed being the usual proportion.

of cavalry were successively sent to the enemy's rear,
with instructions to destroy as much as possible of
the railroad between that river and Dalton. All
failed, because too weak. We could never spare a
body of cavalry strong enough for such a service;
for its assistance was indispensable in holding every
position defended by the army. Captain Harvey, an
officer of great sagacity and courage, on account of
which he was selected by Brig.-Gen. W. H. Jackson,
was detached, with a hundred men, on the 11th of
June, and remained several weeks near the railroad,
frequently interrupting, but too weak to prevent its
use. Early in the campaign, the accounts of the num
ber of cavalry in Mississippi given by Lieutenant-General Polk, just from the command of that department,
and my correspondence with his successor, Lieutenant-General S. D. Lee, gave me reason to believe that
an adequate force to destroy the railroad communications of the Federal army could be furnished in Mississippi and Alabama, under an officer fully competent to head such an enterprise—General Forrest. I
therefore suggested the measure to the President, directly on the 13th of June and 10th of July; and
through General Bragg on the 3d, 12th, 13th, 16th,
and 26th of June; also, to Lieutenant-General Lee on
the 10th of May, and 3d, 11th, and 16th of June.
That officer promised, on two occasions, to make the
attempt. But, in each case, the troops that were to
have been employed were diverted from that object
to repel a Federal raid into Mississippi. I made
these suggestions in the strong belief that this cavalry would serve the Confederacy far better by contributing to the defeat of a formidable invasion, than

by waiting for and repelling raids. The Confederate Administration seemed to estimate the relative value of the two services differently.

In these efforts, as on all other occasions when he had the power, I was zealously seconded by Governor Brown. This led to the following correspondence between him and the President:

"ATLANTA, *June* 28, 1864.

"HIS EXCELLENCY JEFFERSON DAVIS:

"I need not call your attention to the fact that this place is to the Confederacy almost as important as the heart is to the human body. We must hold it. I have done all in my power to reënforce and strengthen General Johnston's army. As you know, further reënforcements are greatly needed on account of the superior numbers of the enemy. Is it not in your power to send more troops? Could not Forrest or Morgan, or both, do more now for our cause in Sherman's rear than anywhere else? He brings his supplies from Nashville, over nearly three hundred miles of railroad, through a rough country, over a great number of bridges. If these are destroyed, it is impossible for him to subsist his large army, and he must fall back through a broad scope of country destitute of provisions, which he could not do without great loss, if not annihilation. I do not wish to volunteer advice, but so great is our anxiety for the success of our arms, and the defense of the State, that I trust you will excuse what may seem to be an intrusion.

(Signed)   "JOSEPH E. BROWN."

Reply of President Davis, received at Atlanta,
July 4, 1864.

" RICHMOND, *June 29th.*

"To GOVERNOR J. E. BROWN :

"Your dispatch of yesterday received. I fully
appreciate the importance of Atlanta, as evinced by
my past action. I have sent all available reënforcements, detaching troops even from points that remain exposed to the enemy. The disparity of force
between the opposing armies in Northern Georgia is
less, as reported, than at any other point. The cavalry of Morgan is on district service, and may fulfill
your wishes. Forrest's command is now operating
on Sherman's lines of communication and is necessary for other purposes in his present field of service.
I do not see that I can change the disposition of our
forces so as to help General Johnston more effectually than by the present arrangement.

(Signed)   " JEFFERSON DAVIS."

" ATLANTA, *July* 4, 1864.

" HIS EXCELLENCY PRESIDENT DAVIS :

"I received your dispatch last night. I regret
exceedingly that you cannot grant my request, as I
am satisfied Sherman's escape with his army would
be impossible if ten thousand good cavalry under
Forrest were thrown in his rear this side of Chattanooga, and his supplies cut off. The whole country
expects this, though points of less importance
should, for a time, be overrun. Our people believe
that General Johnston is doing all in his power with
the means at his command, and all expect you to

send the necessary force to cut off the enemy's subsistence.   We do not see how Forrest's operations in
Mississippi, or Morgan's raids as conducted in Kentucky, interfere with Sherman's plans in this State,
as his supplies continue to reach him.

" Destroy these, and Atlanta is not only safe, but
the destruction of the army under Sherman opens
up Tennessee and Kentucky to us.   Your information as to the relative strength of the two armies in
North Georgia cannot be from reliable sources.   If
your mistake should result in the loss of Atlanta
and the occupation of other strong points in this
State by the enemy, the blow may be fatal to our
cause and remote posterity may have reason to
mourn over the error.

(Signed)   " Joseph E. Brown."

It can scarcely be doubted that five thousand cavalry directed by Forrest's sagacity, courage, and enterprise, against the Federal railroad communications,
would have been at least so far successful as to prevent as much food as was absolutely necessary for
its subsistence, from reaching the Federal army.
Such a result would have compelled General Sherman to the desperate resource of a decisive battle on
our terms, which involved attacking excellent troops
intrenched, or to that of abandoning his enterprise.
In the first event, the chances of battle would have
been greatly in our favor.   In the second, a rout of
the Federal army could scarcely have been prevented.

The importance to the Confederacy of defeating the enterprise against Atlanta was not to be

measured by military consequences alone. Political considerations were also involved, and added much to the interest of that campaign.

The Northern Democrats had pronounced the management of the war a failure; and declared against its being continued; and the presidential election, soon to occur, was to turn upon the question of immediate peace or continued war. In all the earlier part of the year 1864, the press had been publishing to the Northern people most exaggerated ideas of the military value of Atlanta, and that it was to be taken, and that its capture would terminate the war. If Sherman had been foiled, these teachings would have caused great exaggeration of the consequences of his failure, which would have strengthened the peace party greatly; so much, perhaps, as to have enabled it to carry the presidential election, which would have brought the war to an immediate close.

The proofs that I intended to defend Atlanta, seen by General Bragg and recognized by General Hood are: that under my orders the work of strengthening its defenses, begun several weeks before, was going on vigorously; that I had just brought heavy rifled cannon from Mobile, to mount on the intrenchments; the communication made on the subject to General Hood, and the fact that my family was residing in the town; the removal of the machinery and workmen of the military shops, and prohibition to accumulate large supplies in the town, alleged by General Bragg to be evidence of the intention not to defend it, were measures of common prudence, and no more indicated that it was to be abandoned, than sending the baggage of an army to the rear in time of battle proves a foregone determination to fly from the field.

When General Bragg was at Atlanta, about the middle of July, we had no other conversation concerning the Army of Tennessee than such as I introduced. He asked me no questions regarding its operations, past or future, made no comments upon the one, nor suggestions for the other, and, so far from having reason to suppose that Atlanta would not be defended, he saw the most vigorous preparations for its defense in progress. Supposing that he had been sent by the President to learn and report upon the condition of military affairs there, I described them to him briefly, when he visited me, and proposed to send for the lieutenant-generals, that he might obtain from them such minute information as he desired. He replied that he would be glad to see those officers as friends, but only in that way, as his visit was unofficial. He added that the object of his journey was to confer with Lieutenant-General Lee, and from his headquarters to communicate with Lieutenant-General E. Kirby Smith, to ascertain what reënforcements for *me* could be furnished by their departments. He talked much more of military affairs in Virginia than of those in Georgia, asserting, what I believed, that Sherman's army exceeded Grant's in fighting force; and impressed upon me distinctly that his visit was merely personal. His progress to Lieutenant-General Lee's headquarters terminated in Montgomery; and his communications with the commanders of two departments, concerning military aid to *me*, subsided into a visit to that city.

General Hood asserts in his published report, that the army had become demoralized when he was appointed to command it, and ascribes his invariable defeats partly to that cause. The allegation is disproved by the record of the admirable conduct of those troops on every occasion on which that general sent them to battle—and inevitable disaster. Their courage and discipline were unsubdued by the slaughter to which they were recklessly offered in the four attacks on the Federal army near Atlanta, as they proved in the useless butchery at Franklin[1]—and survived the rout and disorganization at Nashville—as they proved at Bentonville. If, however, such proof is not conclusive, the testimony of the two most distinguished officers of that army—Lieutenant-Generals Hardee and Stewart—is certainly not less than equivalent to General Hood's assertion.

In a letter to me, dated April 20, 1868, Lieutenant-General Hardee testifies:

"GENERAL : In regard to the condition of the 'Army of Tennessee' when, on the 18th of July, 1864, at Atlanta, Georgia, you were relieved of command, I have the honor to say :

"That, in my opinion, the organization, *morale*, and effectiveness of that army, excellent at the opening of the campaign, had not been impaired at its close. There had been nothing in the campaign to produce that effect. It is true that the superior numbers of the enemy, enabling them to cover our front

---

[1] General Hartsuff, General Schofield's Inspector-General, told me in the succeeding spring that the valor and discipline of our troops at Franklin won the highest admiration in the Federal army.

with a part of their forces, and to use the remainder for flanking purposes, rendered our positions successively untenable, and that we lost territory. But the enemy's loss in men and *morale* was more than an equivalent. The continuous skirmishing and sharp partial engagements of the campaign uniformly resulted in success to our arms; and, in the seventy days preceding the 18th of July, we had inflicted upon the enemy a loss probably equal to our whole numbers.

" Our changes of position were deliberate, and without loss, disorder, or other discouragement. The troops were well fed, well cared for, and well handled. When we reached Atlanta, we were nearer to our base, and the enemy farther from his; the disparity in numbers between the two armies had been diminishing daily; our army had suffered no disaster, and the enemy's had gained no advantage; and, altogether, the results of the campaign summed up largely in our favor. Our soldiery were intelligent enough to appreciate this; and in my judgment, then, it was not only a fact, but a natural and logical result of the premises, that the *morale* of the army, so far from being impaired, was improved.

" The troops were in buoyant spirits. They felt that they had been tested in a severe and protracted campaign, and that they had borne the test. They had more confidence in themselves and in their officers; and, especially, they had unwavering and unbounded confidence in the commanding general.

" Speaking for my own corps, I have no hesitancy in saying that I should have led them into action with more confidence at the close than at the beginning of the campaign."

On the 11th of February, 1868, Lieutenant-General Stewart wrote to me on the same subject: " .... You desired my opinion as to the condition of the army when you were relieved from command. I first joined that army a few days before the battle of Shiloh. It was then mostly without discipline, as the battle of Shiloh too sadly evinced. Our stay at Tupelo, Mississippi, after the retreat from Corinth, was improved in drilling and disciplining the army. General Bragg had brought it to a high state of efficiency by the time he set out on his campaign into Kentucky. The army was in a fine condition also when General Bragg retreated from Middle Tennessee, in 1863, and up to the disaster on Missionary Ridge in November of that year. I do not know that its *morale* was ever before equal, certainly never superior, to what it was when the campaign opened in Georgia in 1864, under your command. *You* were the only commander of that army whom *men* and *officers* were disposed to trust and confide in without reserve. While at Dalton, I frequently heard this subject, of the unbounded confidence of the men in ' Old Joe,' discussed among the officers, who seemed but little, if any, exceeded by the rank and file in this respect. The officers seemed to regard this feeling as a great element of strength (as it certainly was), and looked upon it as a part of their duty to cherish and promote it. The army had confidence *in itself*, and had long been wanting a commander in whom they could place reliance. The consequence was, that army *surrendered to you;* they gave you their *love* and *unlimited confidence,* were willing to follow you, advancing or retreating, and you could have led them wherever you chose. At the time of the retreat from Resaca, and perhaps for a few days following, this feeling of *entire trust* in you somewhat abated; but it speedily revived, and was as perfect as ever when you retired. I cannot imagine it possible for an army to entertain more personal affection for a commander, or to place more implicit reliance on one, than that army did for you. I believe the last man of them would have willingly died at your bidding.

" You know how I felt when you showed me the order relieving you—when, after the fall of Atlanta, President Davis visited us at Palmetto Station, he asked me whom the army preferred as its commander. My reply was, in substance, they prefer General Johnston; next to him, of those available for the command, they prefer General Beauregard. He then inquired as to the grounds of their preference for General Johnston. Another officer present advanced the opinion that it was because they believed General Johnston would take care of them and not expose them to danger. I interrupted, and asserted emphatically that such ideas did great injustice to the army; that the true reason of their confidence in General Johnston was, they trusted his skill and judgment, and believed that, whenever he issued an order for battle, they would fight to some purpose. They *would* have engaged the enemy under your command, on the day you left it, with as much cheerfulness and confidence, as on the day the campaign opened. You left on Monday (the 18th, I believe, of July). My own corps showed no demoralization on Wednesday the 20th, on Peach-Tree Creek, and it was *not* either any demoralization on our side, nor the 'electric' effect of General Hooker's presence on his troops, that saved him that day.

"Did not the troops fight well on the 20th and 22d, and everywhere under General Hood, especially at Franklin, Tennessee? Had they then been demoralized? I could say much more on this subject, but perhaps have said enough. . . .

"You are not now, general, at the head of an army, with influence and promotions to award; what may be said cannot be ascribed to interested motives. The Army of Tennessee *loved* you and *confided in you implicitly*, as an army of brave men will love and confide in *skill, pluck*, and *honor*. . . ."

Immediately after my removal from command, I went to Macon, Georgia, to reside; and, soon after doing so, had the pleasure to witness a gallant defense of the place by Major-General Cobb. It was attacked by a division of United States cavalry, with the object, probably, of destroying the valuable workshops which had been established there by the chief of ordnance, General Gorgas. The place had neither intrenchments nor garrison. Fortunately, however, two regiments of the militia promised me while commanding the army, by Governor Brown, were passing on their way to Atlanta. Their officers were serving in the army as privates. So they had none.

With them and as many of the mechanics of the

workshops and volunteers of the town as he could find arms for, in all fifteen or eighteen hundred, General Cobb met the Federal forces on the high ground east of the Ocmulgee; and repelled them after a contest of several hours, by his own courage and judicious disposition, and the excellent conduct of his troops, who heard hostile shot then for the first time.

CHAPTER XII.

Again ordered to the Command of the Army of Tennessee in North Carolina.—Interview with General Beauregard.—Movement of the Federal Forces in North Carolina.—General Bragg attacks the Enemy successfully near Kinston. —General Hardee attacked by two Corps near Averysboro'.—Battle of Bentonville.—Events in Virginia.—Evacuation of Richmond, and Surrender of General Lee's Army.—Negotiations begun with General Sherman.—Details of the Conference.—Armistice and Convention agreed on.—The latter represented by Washington Authorities.— Military Convention. —Farewell Order to the Confederate Troops.

I WAS residing in Lincolnton, North Carolina, in February, 1865, and on the 23d of the month received, by telegraph, instructions from the Administration to report for orders to General Lee, recently appointed general-in-chief. A dispatch from General Lee, in anticipation of such a report from me, was received on the same day. In it he directed me to assume the command of the Army of Tennessee and all troops in the Department of South Carolina, Georgia, and Florida, and to " concentrate all available forces and drive back Sherman."

Before assuming the command thus assigned to me, I visited General Beauregard in Charlotte, where his headquarters then were, to ascertain if he had been consulted on the subject, and if my assignment to this command was agreeable to him. He assured me that the feeble and precarious condition of his health made the arrangement a very desirable one to

him.   He also gave me a copy of a dispatch that he
had addressed to General Lee the day before, in which
the same feeling was expressed.   I therefore accepted
the command, confident of the same loyal and cordial support from that distinguished officer, in the
final operations of the war, that he had given me at
its commencement.   This was done with a full consciousness on my part, however, that we could have
no other object, in continuing the war, than to obtain
fair terms of peace; for the Southern cause must
have appeared hopeless then, to all intelligent and
dispassionate Southern men.   I therefore resumed
the duties of my military grade with no hope beyond
that of contributing to obtain peace on such conditions as, under the circumstances, ought to satisfy
the Southern people and their Government.

The " available forces " were about five thousand
men of the Army of Tennessee, and the troops of
the department, amounting to about eleven thousand.   Two thousand of the former, commanded by
Major-General Stevenson, were near Charlotte.   A
thousand, under Lieutenant-General Stewart, were
near Newberry, approaching Charlotte; and two
thousand, under command of Major-General Cheatham, were between Newberry and Augusta, also
marching toward Charlotte.   The troops of the department, under Lieutenant-General Hardee's command, were moving from Charleston to Cheraw;
eleven hundred of them were South Carolina militia
and reserves, not expected to leave the State.   Major-
General Sherman had seventy thousand men in his
four corps, and about five thousand cavalry in Kilpatrick's division.

After moving along the Columbia and Charlotte Railroad beyond Winnsboro', that army had turned to the right toward Cheraw, and had just crossed the Catawba; consequently, it was near the northern edge of the triangle formed by the points at which the three bodies of Confederate troops assigned to me then were; and, by keeping on its way without losing time, it could prevent their concentration in its front. But, even if united before the powerful Federal army, the Confederate forces were utterly inadequate to the exploit of driving it back, being less than a fourth of its number.

In returning from its disastrous expedition against Nashville, the Army of Tennessee had halted in Northeastern Mississippi. A large proportion of these troops were then furloughed by General Hood, and went to their homes. When General Sherman's army invaded South Carolina, General Beauregard ordered those remaining on duty to repair to that State. The first detachment, under Major-General Stevenson, arrived soon enough to oppose the Federal army in its passage of the Edisto, and at Columbia; and had been directed by General Beauregard to march thence to Charlotte. The second, led by Lieutenant-General Stewart, had reached Newberry at this time; and the third, following it, under Major-General Cheatham, was between the place last named and Augusta. The remaining troops of that army were coming through Georgia in little parties, or individually, unaided by the Government; most of them were united at Augusta afterward, by Lieutenant-General Lee, and conducted by him to the army near Smithfield, N. C. That spirited soldier, although still suffering from a wound received in Tennessee, had taken the field in this extremity. At least two-thirds of the arms of these troops had been lost in Tennessee.[1] They had, therefore, depended on the workshops of Alabama and Georgia for muskets, and had received but a partial supply. But this supply, and the additions that the Ordnance Department had the means of making to it, left almost thirteen hundred of that veteran infantry unarmed, and they remained so until the war ended. These detachments were without artillery and baggage-wagons, and consequently were not in condition to operate far from railroads.

In acknowledging General Lee's order, I gave him the substance of the preceding statement; believing, from the terms of that order, that he was not informed of the numbers or positions of the troops with which he expected me to "drive back Sherman." On assuming command, I found difficulties in the way of prompt movement, besides the dispersed state of the troops. They were due, apparently, to the scarcity of food in General Lee's camps. The officers of the commissariat in North Carolina, upon whom the army in Virginia depended for subsistence, were instructed by the Commissary-General, just then, to permit none of the provisions they collected in that State to be used by the troops serving in it. Similar instructions were sent to me from the War Department. Under them, I was to depend upon the wagons of the army for the collection of provisions during military operations. Such a mode of supplying an army in a thinly-peopled country, made

[1] Lieutenant - General Stewart and Brigadier - General Polk, oral statement.

rapid movements, or even the ordinary rate of marching, impossible.   These orders indicated excessive
caution, at the least; for there were, at that time, rations for sixty thousand men for more than four
months, in the principal railroad-depots between
Charlotte, Danville, and Weldon, inclusive. The fact
was ascertained by taking account of those stores,
which was done under the direction of Colonel W.
E. Moore; and the very zealous and efficient officer,
Major Charles Carrington, who was at the head of
the service of collecting provisions in North Carolina,
for the army, was increasing the quantity rapidly.

As the wagon-train of the Army of Tennessee had
not yet passed through Georgia, on its way from Mississippi, it was perhaps fortunate that so small a part
of the troops had arrived.   Colonel A. H. Cole's excellent system, with the assistance promptly rendered
by Governor Vance, furnished the means of collecting and bringing food to the troops as they arrived,
and subsequently, until their own wagons came up.

General Lee's army had many sick and wounded
in Charlotte and other towns of North Carolina.
There was also an important naval station at Charlotte, containing what we then regarded as large
stores of sugar, coffee, tea, and brandy—articles of
prime necessity to sick and wounded, but almost forgotten in Confederate hospitals.   As we had no
longer a navy, and such articles would have been
very valuable in the military hospitals, I suggested
to the Government their transfer to the army.   The
Administration, however, thought it necessary to
keep them where they were.   Soon after the middle
of April they were scattered by men of the Virginia

army, joined by citizens, but not before the naval officer in command had transferred all that he could control to the military hospital department.

I was equally unsuccessful in an application to the Government for money for the troops, who had received none for many months.

The course of the march of the Federal army from Winnsboro' indicated that it would cross the Cape Fear at Fayetteville, and be joined there by General Schofield, with his forces, believed by us to be at Wilmington. It was a question, on the 1st of March, whether the troops of the department, coming from Charleston, or the Federal army, would reach Cheraw first. The latter, however, was more retarded than the Confederate troops, by the streams, then much swollen by recent heavy rains; for the course of its march crossed the larger streams, while that of the Confederates was parallel to them. Thus General Hardee crossed the Pedee, at Cheraw, on the morning of the 3d, with all the military stores he had the means of transporting—having assembled his forces there on the 2d. His rear-guard was so closely pressed by the leading Federal troops, that it had barely time to destroy the bridge after passing over it. In the march from Winnsboro', the Fifteenth and Seventeenth Corps, which formed General Sherman's right wing, crossed the Catawba at Peay's Ferry; the left wing, consisting of the Fourteenth and Twentieth Corps, after destroying the railroad-track as far as Blackstock, crossed the river at Rocky Mount; the Seventeenth Corps crossed Lynch's Creek by Young's Bridge; the Fifteenth, moving farther to their right, sent detachments to Camden to burn the bridge, railroad-depot, and stores, and marched to Cheraw by Tiller's and Kelly's Bridges. The left wing was detained from the 23d to the 26th, in consequence of the breaking of its pontoon-bridge by a flood in the Catawba; and the right wing seems to have been as much delayed; probably by bad roads, produced by the rains that caused the freshet.

Wheeler's division of Confederate cavalry, about three thousand effectives, and Butler's, about one thousand, all commanded by Lieutenant-General Hampton, observed and as much as possible impeded this march. Just before the Federal army turned to the east, Lieutenant-General Hampton placed Butler's division on its right flank. By the change of direction, Wheeler's division, previously in front, was on the left flank, and Butler's in front, in the march from the Catawba to the Pedee. The service expected of this cavalry was, to retard the enemy's progress, and as much as possible to protect the people of the country from exactions of Federal foraging-parties, and robbery by stragglers.

Having received information, on the evening of the 3d, that Stewart's troops had reached the railroad at Chester, and that Cheatham's were near that point; and feeling confident from Lieutenant-General Hardee's reports of his own movements, and Lieutenant-General Hampton's of those of the enemy, that the former had secured the passage of the Pedee at Cheraw; it seemed to me practicable to unite those troops, Stewart's, Cheatham's, and Stevenson's, near Fayetteville, in time to engage one of the enemy's columns while crossing the Cape Fear. The

order of march of the Federal army by wings frequently a day's march from each other, and the manner in which those wings had crossed the Catawba
and Lynch's Creek, and seemed by their course to be
about to cross the Pedee, justified me in hoping to
find an opportunity to attack one of those columns
in the passage of the Cape Fear when the other was
not within supporting distance.

As it had become certain that the first serious
opposition to General Sherman's progress was to be
in North Carolina, I suggested to the general-in-chief
that it was important that the troops of that department should be added to my command. The suggestion was adopted, and the necessary orders given
without loss of time. General Lee had previously
authorized me to direct the movements of those
troops, should my operations bring me near them.
They were under General Bragg's command near
Goldsboro', and supposed to amount to six or eight
thousand men.

Leaving General Beauregard to protect the line
of railroad from Charlotte to Danville, and to send
the troops of the Army of Tennessee, as they arrived, to Smithfield by railroad, I transferred my
headquarters, on the 4th, from Charlotte to Fayetteville, considering the latter as a better point
to obtain quick intelligence of the enemy's movements, and to direct those of the Confederate
troops.

On the 6th General Bragg, then at Goldsboro',
informed me that the enemy was approaching Kinston in "heavy force," and was then but nine miles
from the place. He suggested that the troops just

arrived at Smithfield from Charlotte could join him
in a few hours, and that such a reënforcement might
enable him to win a victory.   Major-General D. H.
Hill, who commanded the troops referred to, was, for
the object in view, placed under General Bragg's orders.   The troops were united at Kinston on the
7th.   Clayton's division, the remnant of it rather,
which reached Smithfield during the day, was sent
forward also, and joined General Bragg's forces at
Kinston next morning.

After receiving these accessions to his force, together less than two thousand men, General Bragg
attacked the enemy, supposed to be three divisions
under Major-General Cox, with such vigor as to
drive them from the field, three miles during the
afternoon.   Fifteen hundred prisoners and three field-
pieces were captured in the engagement and pursuit.
In reporting this success by telegraph, at night, General Bragg said: "The number of the enemy's dead
and wounded left on the field is large.   Our own
loss, under Providence, is small.   Major-Generals
Hill and Hoke exhibited their usual zeal, energy,
and gallantry."   The two parties skirmished a little
on the 9th, in front of the position taken by the
enemy the evening before, which had been intrenched in the mean time.   On the following morning General Bragg ordered a demonstration in the
enemy's front by one body of his troops, while
another attempted to turn the intrenchments.   He
was unsuccessful.   But, although the failure was attended with little loss, the withdrawal, which became
necessary, impaired greatly the encouragement which
had been given to the troops by their success on the

first day. They fell back to Goldsboro' by General Bragg's order.

While General Sherman was moving from Columbia toward Charlotte, General Beauregard instructed Lieutenant-General Hardee to direct his march toward Greensboro'. As soon as it was ascertained that the Federal army was moving upon Fayetteville, orders were sent to Lieutenant-General Hardee to turn directly to that place; but they were not delivered. Acting under his first instructions, therefore, after crossing the Pedee on the 3d, that officer moved toward Greensboro' as far as Rockingham, which his troops reached on the 4th. The instructions to turn toward Fayetteville, repeated, reached him there, and were immediately observed. He also transmitted similar instructions to Lieutenant-General Hampton. That officer had been compelled, by the swollen condition of the Pedee, to diverge with Wheeler's cavalry, far to the left of his direct route, to the fords near and above the grassy islands, and was unable to complete the passage of the river before the afternoon of the 7th. The Federal army had crossed it two days before—the right at Cheraw, and the left at Sneedsboro'—and was continuing the march to Fayetteville in its former order. General Kilpatrick's division of cavalry was apparently on the left of the army.

On the 8th Lieutenant-General Hampton united his two divisions; and, having discovered and reconnoitred General Kilpatrick's camp in the night of the 9th, he surprised him at daybreak on the 10th, drove the troops into a neighboring swamp, and held possession of their artillery and wagons for some

time; but many of the Confederate troops took advantage of the opportunity to plunder, and carried
off so many of the captured horses and mules that
neither guns nor wagons could be secured. They
were made unserviceable, however, by cutting their
wheels to pieces. After suffering a good deal, especially in officers, by a spirited fire directed at them
by a brigade of infantry or dismounted cavalry, the
Confederate troops were withdrawn. Both Lieutenant-General Hampton and Major-General Wheeler
thought the Federal loss in killed and wounded
much greater than theirs. They brought away five
hundred prisoners, and released a hundred and seventy-three that had been captured by the enemy.

The important object of opening the road to
Fayetteville, blocked by this camp, was gained by
this action; and Lieutenant-General Hampton reached
the place at night with his troops by that road. The
Federal army was then within seven miles of the
town, and Lieutenant-General Hardee's troops in and
around it. The latter crossed the Cape Fear River
soon after the arrival of their cavalry, which followed
next morning, burning the bridge after crossing the
river.

In the march from the Catawba to the Cape Fear,
the cavalry of the two armies rarely met. In all the
encounters that occurred, if all of them came to my
knowledge, the Confederates had the advantage.
They were: at Mount Elon, where Major-General Butler intercepted and drove back a Federal party sent
to destroy the railroad-track near Florence; at Homes-
boro' on the 4th of March, when General Wheeler
attacked the Federal left flank and took fifty prison-

ers; at Rockingham on the 7th, when the same officer defeated another party, killing and capturing
thirty-five; on the 8th, when Lieutenant-General
Hampton attacked and defeated a detachment; that
of the morning of the 10th, just described; and on
the 11th, at Fayetteville, when a large Federal squadron that dashed into the town was routed by Lieutenant-General Hampton with an inferior force.

As it was uncertain whether General Sherman
intended to take the route through Goldsboro' or
that through Raleigh, General Bragg's troops and
those of the Army·of Tennessee were ordered to
Smithfield, about midway between the two places;
and Lieutenant-General Hardee was instructed to follow the road from Fayetteville to Raleigh, which for
thirty miles is also that to Smithfield. On the 11th
he halted on that road, five miles from Fayetteville.
The South Carolina State troops, eleven hundred in
number, being recalled by Governor Magrath, left
the army and returned to the State.

Lieutenant-General Hampton placed Wheeler's
division on the Raleigh road, and Butler's on that to
Goldsboro'. The former was pressed on the 13th,
eight or ten miles from Fayetteville, but held its
ground; and on the 14th, at Silver Creek, where it
was intrenched under General Hampton's direction,
it easily drove off the Federal cavalry that felt its
position.

During this time, the Fayetteville Arsenal, which
had been constructed by the Government of the
United States, was destroyed by the Federal army.
A quantity of valuable machinery, that had been
brought to it from Harper's Ferry, was destroyed

with the buildings. As it was impossible that the
Confederacy could ever recover it, its destruction was,
at the least, injudicious.

On the 15th the Confederate cavalry, on the
Raleigh road, was pressed back by the Fourteenth
and Twentieth Corps, and at seven o'clock next morning Lieutenant-General Hardee was attacked by those
corps in a position four miles south of Averysboro',
that he had intrenched. The enemy compelled him
to abandon it, however, by turning his left; but he
fell back only four hundred yards, to a better position
than that just abandoned. There he was repeatedly
attacked during the day, but repelled the assailants
without difficulty. In the afternoon he was informed,
by Lieutenant-General Hampton, that the enemy had
crossed Black River, at various points below, as if to
turn his left; he therefore abandoned his position in
the night, some hours after the fighting had ceased,
and marched toward Smithfield, to Elevation, which
he reached about noon of the next day.

In his brief report by telegraph, General Hardee
stated that his loss in killed, wounded, and missing,
was about five hundred; prisoners taken next day, said
that theirs was above three thousand; as reported
to General Sherman, it was seventy-seven killed, and
four hundred and seven wounded. That report, if
correct, proves that the soldiers of General Sherman's
army had been demoralized by their course of life
on Southern plantations. Those soldiers, when fighting between Dalton and Atlanta, could not have
been driven back repeatedly by a fourth of their
number, with a loss so utterly insignificant. It is
unaccountable, too, that the party fighting under cover

and holding its ground should have a hundred and eight men killed, and that unsheltered and repulsed, but seventy-seven.

It was ascertained, on the 17th, that the troops with which Lieutenant-General Hardee was engaged the day before were not marching toward Raleigh; but no precise intelligence of the movements of the Federal forces was gathered during the day. General Hardee remained at Elevation to give his men the rest they needed much. At Smithfield, General Bragg had Hoke's excellent division of North Carolinians, four thousand seven hundred and seventy-five effective men; and Lieutenant-General Stewart thirty-nine hundred and fifty of the Army of Tennessee. The value of the latter was much increased by the comparatively great number of distinguished officers serving among them, who had long been the pride and ornaments of that army.

About daybreak, on the 18th, information came to me from General Hampton, that the Federal army was marching toward Goldsboro': the right wing, on the direct road from Fayetteville, had crossed Black River; the left wing, on the road from Averysboro', had not reached that stream, and was more than a day's march from the point in its route opposite to the hamlet of Bentonville, where the two roads, according to the map of North Carolina, were ten or twelve miles apart. The hamlet itself is about two miles from the road and to the north of it, and sixteen from Smithfield. According to the reports of our cavalry, the Federal right wing was about half a day's march in advance of the left; so that there was probably an interval of a day's march between the heads of the two columns.

To be prepared to attack the head of the left Federal column next morning, the troops at Smithfield and at Elevation were ordered to march immediately to Bentonville, and to bivouac that night between the hamlet and the road on which the left Federal column was marching. By the map, the distance from Elevation to Bentonville was but twelve miles; the timely arrival of all the troops seemed to be certain, therefore. The map proved to be very incorrect, and deceived me greatly in relation to the distance between the two roads on which the Federal columns were marching, which it exaggerated very much, and that from Elevation, which it reduced almost as much. General Hardee found it too great for a day's march.

Lieutenant-General Hampton gave all necessary information that night in Bentonville. He described the ground near the road abreast of us as favorable for our purpose. The Federal camp, however, was but four or five miles from that ground, nearer, by several miles, than Hardee's bivouac, and therefore we could not hope for the advantage of attacking the head of a deep column. But Lieutenant-General Hampton had caused some light intrenchments to be thrown up across the road between the Federal camp and the proposed field of battle, by the help of which he expected Butler's division to keep back the enemy until the arrival of Hardee's corps should enable us to attack.

As soon as General Hardee's troops reached Bentonville next morning, we moved by the left flank,

Hoke's division leading, to the ground selected by General Hampton, and adopted from his description. It was the eastern edge of an old plantation, extending a mile and a half to the west, and lying principally on the north side of the road, and surrounded, east, south, and north, by dense thickets of black-jack. As there was but one narrow road through the thicket, the deployment of the troops consumed a weary time. Hoke's division was formed with its centre on the road, its line at right angles to it, on the eastern edge of the plantation, and its left extending some four hundred yards into the thicket to the south. His two batteries, our only artillery, were on his right, commanding the ground in front to the extent of the range of the guns. The troops belonging to the Army of Tennessee were formed on the right of the artillery, their right strongly thrown forward, conforming to the edge of the open ground. In the mean time the leading Federal troops appeared and deployed, and, when so much of the Confederate disposition as has been described had been made, their right attacked Hoke's division vigorously, especially its left—so vigorously, that General Bragg apprehended that Hoke, although slightly intrenched, would be driven from his position. He therefore applied urgently for strong reënforcements. Lieutenant-General Hardee, the head of whose column was then near, was directed, most injudiciously, to send his leading division, McLaws's, to the assistance of the troops assailed; the other, Taliaferro's, moving on to its place on the extreme right. McLaws's division, struggling through the thicket, reached the ground to which it was ordered just in time to see

the repulse of the enemy by Hoke, after a sharp contest of half an hour, at short range. Soon after the
firing on the left ceased, a similar assault was made
upon Stewart, whose troops, like those on their left,
had already constructed breastworks. This attack
was directed mainly against Stewart's own corps,
commanded by Loring, and Clayton's division, by
which it was received as firmly and repelled as
promptly as that just described had been by
Hoke's.

Lieutenant-General Hardee was then directed to
charge with the right wing—Stewart's troops and
Taliaferro's division, as they faced—obliquely to the
left; and General Bragg to join in the movement
with his brigades successively, from right to left,
each making the necessary change of front to the
left in advancing.

As it could be seen that the Federal first line,
except its right, which was hidden by woods, had
thrown up intrenchments like our own, a body
of troops was prepared to strike its flank, to lessen
the danger of failure. It was a needless precaution,
however, for the result of the charge was not for five
minutes doubtful. The Confederates passed over
three hundred yards of the space between the two
lines in quick time, and in excellent order, and the
remaining distance in double quick, without pausing
to fire until their near approach had driven the
enemy from the shelter of their intrenchments, in full
retreat, to their second line. After firing a few
rounds, the Confederates again pressed forward, and,
when they were near the second intrenchment, now
manned by both lines of Federal troops, Lieut.-Gen.

Hardee, after commanding the double-quick, led the charge, and, with his knightly gallantry, dashed over the enemy's breastworks on horseback, in front of his men.   Some distance in the rear there was a very thick wood of young pines, into which the Federal troops were pursued, and in which they rallied and renewed the fight.   But the Confederates continued to advance, driving the enemy back slowly, notwithstanding the advantage given to the party on the defensive by the thicket which made united action by the assailants impossible.   On the extreme left, however, General Bragg's troops were held in check by the Federal right, which had the aid of breastworks and the thicket of black-jack.

The denseness of the thicket through which Hardee's troops were penetrating made it impossible to preserve their order of battle.   They were ordered to halt to reëstablish it.   This pause seemed to be misunderstood by the enemy; for, before the Confederate lines could be re-formed, a very slow process on such ground, they made a partial attempt to assume the offensive, and assailed Stewart's troops, of the Army of Tennessee, directing their greatest efforts against those commanded by Brigadier-General Pettus; but this attack was easily and quickly repulsed.

Having found it impossible to advance in order through so dense a wood, control the movements of troops, or combine their efforts, I determined not to renew the attack, but only to hold the ground won until all the wounded still upon the field should be removed to the temporary hospitals.   When this had been done, some time after nightfall, the Confederate army resumed the position from which it had moved to attack the enemy.

The action really ceased with the repulse of the attack made upon Stewart's corps; but desultory firing was continued until night.

Four pieces of artillery were taken; but, as we had only spare harnessed horses enough to draw off three, one was left on the field.

The impossibility of concentrating the Confederate forces in time to attack the Federal left wing, while in column on the march, made complete success also impossible, from the enemy's great numerical superiority. One important object was gained, however—that of restoring the confidence of our troops, who had either lost it in the defeat at Wilmington, or in those of Tennessee. All were greatly elated by the event.

There was now no object in remaining in presence of the enemy, but that of covering the bearing off of our wounded. The orders necessary for this duty were given without delay; but very bad roads, and the want of comfortable means of transportation, compelled us to devote two days to the operation.

Early in the morning of the 20th Brig.-Gen. Law, temporarily commanding Butler's division, which was observing the Federal right wing, reported that that wing, which had been following the Fayetteville road to Goldsboro', had crossed to that from Averysboro', on which we were, about five miles east of us, and was coming up rapidly upon the rear of Hoke's division. That officer was directed to change front to the left on his right flank, by which his line was formed parallel to and fronting the road, and near enough to command it.   In this position the usual light intrenchments were immediately begun and soon finished. Hampton prolonged this line to the left, to Mill Creek, with Butler's division, and Wheeler's, which had come up from the direction of Averysboro'.

The Federal army was united before us about noon, and made repeated attacks, between that time and sunset, upon Hoke's division; the most spirited of them was the last, made upon Kirkland's brigade. In all, the enemy was so effectually driven back, that our infirmary corps brought in a number of their wounded that had been left on the field, and carried them to our field-hospitals.

It was soon ascertained that our left was very far overlapped by the Federal right.   Lieut.-Gen. Hardee was therefore requested to detach McLaws's division to Hoke's left.   We were so outnumbered, however, that much of the cavalry was deployed as skirmishers on McLaws's left, to show a front equal to that of the enemy.

On the 21st the skirmishing was resumed with spirit by the enemy, with Hoke's and McLaws's divisions, and the cavalry on the left of the latter. To ascertain why our right was unmolested, Stewart's and Taliaferro's skirmishers were thrown forward. They found the Federal troops in their front drawn back and formed obliquely to the general line; the left retired, and intrenched.   During the whole afternoon a very brisk fire was directed against our centre and left.   About four o'clock the cavalry was so pressed that the little infantry reserves and Taliaferro's division were ordered to the left to support it.

LIEUTENANT-GENERAL WADE HAMPTON

A few minutes later Lieutenant-General Hampton reported that the Seventeenth Corps had broken through the mere " skirmish-line " of his left, and was pressing rapidly toward Bentonville, in rear of our centre and on the only route of retreat. Lieutenant-General Hardee was directed to unite the troops then marching to the left, and to oppose this movement with them. But the rapid march of the leading Federal troops, Mower's division, left no time for this union. Fortunately, Lieut.-Gen. Hampton, while leading a cavalry reserve to meet the enemy, saw Cumming's Georgia brigade, commanded by Colonel Henderson, on its way to the left, and directed it toward Bentonville. It reached the point in the road toward which the enemy was marching just as he appeared. Lieut.-Gen. Hardee galloped up at the same time, followed by the Eighth Texas cavalry regiment which he had found on the way. He instantly directed Henderson to charge the enemy in front, and the Texans their left flank; Lieut.-Gen. Hampton coming up on the other side with Young's brigade, commanded at the time by Colonel Wright, threw it against Mower's right flank; and Maj.-Gen. Wheeler, at a considerable distance from this point, assailed the rear of the Federal column in flank with a part of Allen's Alabamians. These simultaneous attacks were so skillfully and bravely made, that in spite of the great disparity of numbers, the enemy was defeated in a few minutes, and driven back along the route by which the column had advanced. In the Eighth Texan regiment, Lieut.-Gen. Hardee's only son, a noble youth of sixteen, charging bravely in the foremost rank, fell mortally wounded.

The firing upon our front was sustained until the return of the Seventeenth Corps to its place in line, when it subsided into desultory skirmishing.

At night all the wounded that could bear trans. portation had been removed; so that we had no object for remaining in a position made very hazard- ous by the stream behind us, rendered unfordable by recent rain. The army was therefore ordered to cross Mill Creek by the bridge [1] at Bentonville before daybreak of the 22d. About eight o'clock they were halted beyond the stream, two miles north of Mill Creek. Soon after Maj.-Gen. Wheeler had posted his rear-guard on our bank of the stream to hold the bridge, the leading Federal troops appeared on the other. They made repeated attempts to force the passage, but failed in all, after brave efforts, in which three color-bearers fell within fifty feet of the Con- federate rear-guard. [2]

At noon the march was resumed, and the troops bivouacked in the evening near Smithfield, but south of the Neuse.

In the action of the 19th, the Confederate force engaged was about fourteen thousand one hundred infantry and artillery. Butler's division of cavalry was employed in observing General Sherman's right column; and Wheeler's, coming from the direction of Averysboro', approached on the north side of Mill Creek, which recent rains had made impassable, so that he could not join in the action as expected, by falling upon the left flank of the enemy. The Fed- eral army exceeded seventy thousand men; about

[1] The only one.   [2] General Wheeler's report.

half of it was present on the 19th, and all of it after noon of the 20th.

The Confederate loss on the 19th, according to the morning reports of the 20th, was one hundred and eighty killed, twelve hundred and twenty wounded, and five hundred and fifteen missing: in all, nineteen hundred and fifteen. On the 20th, it was six killed, ninety wounded, and thirty-one missing; and on the 21st, thirty-seven killed, one hundred and fifty-seven wounded, and one hundred and seven missing: amounting, in the three days, to two hundred and twenty-three killed, fourteen hundred and sixty-seven wounded, and six hundred and fifty-three missing. Most of the latter were captured in rear of the Federal lines, which they passed through in small parties by the intervals caused by the thicket in which the fight ended on the 19th. Several such parties, included in the number of missing reported above, escaped around the flanks of the Federal army, and rejoined their regiments near Smithfield. Our losses were supplied by the arrival, on the 20th and 21st, of about two thousand men of the Army of Tennessee in several detachments. Major-General Cheatham came with one of them.

We captured nine hundred and three prisoners in the three days, but had no means of ascertaining the number of the enemy's killed and wounded; but, as our troops were generally successful, and were covered by intrenchments in a part of the fighting on the 19th, all of that of the 20th, and most of that on the 21st, it must have exceeded ours very much. From the appearance of the field, and the language of Federals, it largely exceeded four thousand.

On the 23d, Major-General Sherman united his own army and that of Major-General Schofield at Goldsboro'. It was uncertain whether his march to Virginia would be through Raleigh, or by the most direct route, that through Weldon. So the Confederate army was placed between the two roads, in order to be able to precede him on either; and, to make the junction of the Army of Northern Virginia with it practicable, should General Lee determine to abandon his intrenchments to fall upon Sherman's army with our united forces. The cavalry was, at the same time placed in close observation of the enemy—Wheeler's division on the north, and Butler's on the west of their camps around Goldsboro'.

We learned, from prisoners captured occasionally, that the United States troops did not expect to resume their march very soon, but to remain in their present camps for some weeks, to rest, and receive such supplies as they needed.

This pause was advantageous to us too; for it gave time for the arrival of several thousand men of the Army of Tennessee coming along the route through Georgia in detachments, to rejoin their corps. Most of them were united into one body in Augusta, by Lieutenant-General S. D. Lee. Many, indeed the greater number of these veterans, were unarmed; and all the exertions of two excellent officers, Lieutenat-Colonel Kennard, chief ordnance-officer, and Captain Vanderford, his assistant, could not procure infantry arms as fast as they were required, the Ordnance Department[1] being unable to furnish the num-

[1] And yet at this time the Confederate Government was so earnest in the scheme of raising negro troops, that I was directed to furnish a

ber, and on the 10th of April thirteen hundred of this admirable infantry were still unarmed. This inaction gave time for conference with the General-in-Chief with reference to the union of our forces against General Sherman's army, and an officer [1] of high rank, the personal friend of both, visited General Lee, for me, on this interesting subject. It also enabled the chief quartermaster and chief commissary to provide for a march by collecting supplies of food and forage.

The press dispatches, received in the morning of April 5th, announced that Richmond was evacuated by the Administration in the night of the 2d. I inferred from this that General Lee was about to abandon the defense of Richmond, to unite our forces. Supposing the Secretary of War to be with the President at Danville, I asked him, in a telegram directed to that place, to give me full information of the movements of the Army of Northern Virginia. This dispatch was acknowledged on the same day by the President, who was unable to give me the information asked for. Telegrams from Brigadier-General H. H. Walker, at Danville, and Colonel Wood, the President's aide-de-camp, at Greensboro', dated the 7th and 8th respectively, were favorable. One from the Secretary of War dated the 9th, at a railroad-station near the Staunton River, was less so. But there was nothing in any one of the three to suggest the idea that General Lee had been *driven* from the position held many months with so much skill and resolution. The last indicated, however, that he was encountering

cavalry officer of ability, General J. T. Morgan, for that service, in Alabama.

[1] Lieutenant-General Holmes.

the difficulties, in attempting to move southward, that he apprehended when corresponding with me on the subject.

On the 9th, Lieutenant-General Hampton informed me that the country people living near the Federal camps reported that the soldiers expected to march toward Raleigh next morning; and early in the morning of the 10th he reported the march begun. The Confederate forces were ordered to march to Raleigh: Hardee's corps, with Butler's division as rearguard, by the Goldsboro' road, which the Federal army was following; and Stewart's and Lee's, with Wheeler's division as rear-guard, by that crossing the Neuse at Battle's Bridge. Near that bridge, where I encamped that night, at one o'clock in the morning a telegram was received from the President, dispatched from Danville the evening before, conveying the intelligence that an unofficial report had just been brought to that place, to the effect that General Lee had surrendered on Sunday, the 9th.

The three corps reached Raleigh early in the afternoon of that day. In a telegram, dated Greensboro', 4.30 P. M., the President directed me to leave the troops under Lieutenant-General Hardee's command, and report to him there.

Taking the first train, about midnight, I reached Greensboro' about eight o'clock in the morning, on the 12th, and was General Beauregard's guest. His quarters were a burden-car near, and in sight of those of the President. The General and myself were summoned to the President's office in an hour or two, and found Messrs. Benjamin, Mallory, and Reagan, with him. We had supposed that we were to be questioned concerning the military resources of our department, in connection with the question of continuing or terminating the war. But the President's object seemed to be to give, not to obtain information; for, addressing the party, he said that in two or theee weeks he would have a large army in the field by bringing back into the ranks those who had abandoned them in less desperate circumstances, and by calling out the enrolled men whom the conscript bureau with its forces had been unable to bring into the army. It was remarked, by the military officers, that men who had left the army when our cause was not desperate, and those who, under the same circumstances, could not be forced into it, would scarcely, in the present desperate condition of our affairs, enter the service upon mere invitation. Neither opinions nor information was asked, and the conference terminated. Before leaving the room we learned that Maj.-Gen. Breckenridge's arrival was expected in the course of the afternoon, and it was not doubted that he would bring certain intelligence of the state of affairs in Virginia.

General Breckenridge came as expected, and confirmed the report of the surrender of the army in Virginia. General Beauregard and myself, conversing together after the intelligence of the great disaster, reviewed the condition of our affairs, and carefully compared the resources of the belligerents, and agreed in the opinion that the Southern Confederacy was overthrown. In conversation with General Breckenridge afterward, I repeated this, and said that the only power of government left in the President's hands was that of terminating the war, and that this power should be exercised without more delay. I also expressed my readiness to suggest to the President the absolute necessity of such action, should an opportunity to do so be given me. General Breckenridge promised to make me this opportunity.

Mr. Mallory came to converse with me on the subject, and showed great anxiety that negotiations to end the war should be commenced, and urged that I was the person who should suggest the measure to the President. I, on the contrary, thought that such a suggestion would come more properly from one of his "constitutional advisers," but told Mr. Mallory of my conversation with General Breckenridge.

That gentleman fulfilled his engagement promptly; and General Beauregard and myself were summoned to the President's office an hour or two after the meeting of his cabinet there, next morning. Being desired by the President to do it, we compared the military forces of the two parties to the war: ours, an army of about twenty thousand infantry and artillery, and five thousand mounted troops; those of the United States, three armies that could be combined against ours, which was insignificant compared with either—Grant's, of a hundred and eighty thousand men; Sherman's, of a hundred and ten thousand, at least, and Canby's of sixty thousand—odds of seventeen or eighteen to one, which in a few weeks could be more than doubled.

I represented that under such circumstances it would be the greatest of human crimes for us to attempt to continue the war; for, having neither money nor credit, nor arms but those in the hands of our soldiers, nor ammunition but that in their cartridge-

boxes, nor shops for repairing arms or fixing ammunition, the effect of our keeping the field would be,
not to harm the enemy, but to complete the devastation of our country and ruin of its people. I therefore urged that the President should exercise at once
the only function of government still in his possession,
and open negotiations for peace.

The members of the cabinet present were then
desired by the President to express their opinions on
the important question. General Breckenridge, Mr.
Mallory, and Mr. Reagan, thought that the war was
decided against us; and that it was absolutely
necessary to make peace. Mr. Benjamin expressed
the contrary opinion. The latter made a speech for
war, much like that of Sempronius in Addison's
play. The President replied to our suggestion as if
somewhat annoyed by it. He said that it was idle
to suggest that he should attempt to negotiate, when
it was certain, from the attempt previously made,
that his authority to treat would not be recognized,
nor any terms that he might offer considered by the
Government of the United States. I reminded him
that it had not been unusual, in such cases, for military commanders to initiate negotiations upon which
treaties of peace were founded; and proposed that
he should allow me to address General Sherman on
the subject. After a few words in opposition to
that idea, Mr. Davis reverted to the first suggestion,
that he should offer terms to the Government of the
United States—which he had put aside; and
sketched a letter appropriate to be sent by me to
General Sherman, proposing a meeting to arrange
the terms of an armistice to enable the civil authori-

ties to agree upon terms of peace. That this course might be adopted at once, I proposed that he should dictate the letter then to Mr. Mallory, who was a good penman, and that I should sign and send it to the Federal commander immediately. The letter, prepared in that way, was sent by me with all dispatch to Lieutenant-General Hampton, near Hillsboro', to be forwarded by him to General Sherman. It was delivered to the latter next day, the 14th, and was in these terms:

"The results of the recent campaign in Virginia have changed the relative military condition of the belligerents. I am therefore induced to address you, in this form, the inquiry whether, in order to stop the further effusion of blood and devastation of property, you are willing to make a temporary suspension of active operations, and to communicate to Lieutenant-General Grant, commanding the armies of the United States, the request that he will take like action in regard to other armies—the object being, to permit the civil authorities to enter into the needful arrangements to terminate the existing war."

Lieutenant-General Hardee directed the march of the Confederate army from Raleigh on the 12th, in two columns—Stewart's and Lee's corps and Butler's division, now commanded by that officer himself, by the Hillsboro' road, and the other, his own corps, and Wheeler's division, by that through Chapel Hill. Lieut.-Gen. Hampton had been desired to take measures to discover any movements of the Federal troops by the Pittsboro' road, and all others by which they could turn directly toward Charlotte or Salisbury.

I left Greensboro' on the evening of the 13th, to

rejoin the army, and, although detained on the way the greater part of the night by one of the accidents then inevitable on the North Carolina Railroad, met Stewart's column at Hillsboro' early in the morning of the 14th, just as it was beginning the day's march. Reports were there given me from Lieutenant-General Hampton to the effect that the instructions to observe all roads by which the enemy could turn to the left, directly toward Charlotte or Salisbury, had been executed, and that no such movement had been discovered.

The right column reached the Haw River Bridge that afternoon, and encamped there. The left crossed the stream at a ford near Ruffin's Mill. The Federal cavalry did not advance beyond Morrisville or its vicinity.

In the morning of the 16th, when the army was within a few miles of Greensboro', a reply [1] to the letter of the 13th was received from General Sherman, signifying his assent to the proposal that we should meet for conference in relation to an armistice. Supposing that the President was waiting in Greensboro' to open negotiations should the armistice be agreed upon, I hastened there to show General Sherman's reply, and to receive any instructions he might have to give. He had quitted the town, however, and was on the way to Charlotte.

Having requested Lieutenant-General Hampton, by telegraph, to arrange the time and place of meeting, I went to his headquarters, two or three miles southeast of Hillsboro'. There General Hampton

---

[1] It was dated the 14th, and should have been received twenty-four hours sooner. The delay was by Federal officers, not ours.

informed me that the conference was to be at noon next day, at a house on the Raleigh road midway between the pickets of the two armies.

General Sherman met me at the time and place appointed—the house being that of a Mr. Bennett. As soon as we were without witnesses in the room assigned to us, General Sherman showed me a telegram from Mr. Stanton, announcing the assassination of the President of the United States. A courier, he told me, had overtaken him with it, after he left the railroad-station from which he had ridden. After reading the dispatch, I told General Sherman that, in my opinion, the event was the greatest possible calamity to the South.

When General Sherman understood what seemed to have escaped him in reading my letter, that my object was to make such an armistice as would give opportunity for negotiation between the "civil authorities" of the two countries, he said that such negotiations were impossible—because the Government of the United States did not acknowledge the existence of a Southern Confederacy; nor, consequently, its civil authorities as such. Therefore he could not receive, for transmission, any proposition addressed to the Government of the United States by those claiming to be the civil authorities of a Southern Confederacy. He added, in a manner that carried conviction of sincerity, expressions of a wish to divert from the South such devastation as the continuance of the war would make inevitable; and, as a means of accomplishing that object, so far as the armies we commanded were concerned, he offered me such terms as those given to General Lee.

I replied that our relative positions were too different from those of the armies in Virginia to justify
me in such a capitulation, but suggested that we
might do more than he proposed: that, instead of
a partial suspension of hostilities, we might, as
other generals had done, arrange the terms of a permanent peace, and among other precedents reminded
him of the preliminaries of Leoben, and the terms
in which Napoleon, then victorious, proposed negotiation to the Archduke Charles; and the sentiment he expressed, that the civic crown earned by
preserving the life of one citizen confers truer glory
than the highest achievement merely military.   General Sherman replied, with heightened color, that he
appreciated such a sentiment, and that to put an end
to further devastation and bloodshed, and restore the
Union, and with it the prosperity of the country,
were to him objects of ambition.   We then entered
into a discussion of the terms that might be given
to the Southern States, on their submission to the
authority of the United States.   General Sherman
seemed to regard the resolutions of Congress and the
declarations of the President of the United States as
conclusive that the restoration of the Union was the
object of the war, and to believe that the soldiers
of the United States had been fighting for that object.   A long official conversation with Mr. Lincoln,
on Southern affairs a very short time before, had
convinced him that the President then adhered to
that view.

In the course of the afternoon we agreed upon
the terms expressed in the memorandum drawn up
on the 18th, except that General Sherman did not

consent to include Mr. Davis and the officers of his cabinet in an otherwise general amnesty.[1] Much of the afternoon was consumed in endeavors to dispose of this part of the question in a manner that would be satisfactory both to the Government of the United States and the Southern people, as well as to the Confederate President; but at sunset no conclusion had been reached, and the conference was suspended, to be resumed at ten o'clock next morning. Thinking it probable that the confidential relations of the Secretary of War with Mr. Davis might enable him to remove the only obstacle to an adjustment, I requested him by telegraph to join me as soon as possible.

General Breckenridge and Mr. Reagan came to General Hampton's quarters together, an hour or two before daybreak. After they had received from me as full an account of the discussion of the day before as my memory enabled me to give, and had learned the terms agreed upon, and the difficulty in the way of full agreement, Mr. Reagan proposed to reduce them to writing, to facilitate reconsideration. In doing so, he included the article for amnesty without exceptions, the only one not fully agreed to. This paper, being unfinished when General Breckenridge and myself set out to the place of meeting, was to be sent to me there.

When we met, I proposed to General Sherman that General Breckenridge should be admitted to

[1] This consideration was mine, of course. General Sherman did not desire the arrest of these gentlemen. He was too acute not to foresee the embarrassment their capture would cause; therefore he wished them to escape.

our discussion, as his personal relations with the President of the Confederacy might enable him to remove the obstacle to agreement that we had encountered the day before. He assented, and that gentleman joined us.

We had conversed on the subject discussed the day before perhaps a half-hour, when the memorandum written by Mr. Reagan was brought. I read this paper to General Sherman, as a basis for terms of peace, pointing out to him that it contained nothing which he had not already accepted, but the language that included the President and cabinet in the terms of amnesty. After listening to General Breckenridge, who addressed him six or eight minutes in advocacy of these conditions of peace, General Sherman wrote very rapidly the memorandum that follows, with the paper presented by me before him. He wrote so rapidly that I thought, at the time, that he must have come to the place prepared to agree to amnesty with no exceptions. His paper differed from mine only in being fuller.

Memorandum, or Basis of Agreement, made this 18th Day of April, A. D. 1865, near Durham's Station, in the State of North Carolina, by and between General Joseph E. Johnston, commanding the Confederate Army, and Major-General William T. Sherman, commanding the Army of the United States in North Carolina, both present.

1. The contending armies now in the field to maintain the *status quo* until notice is given by the commanding general of any one to its opponent, and

reasonable time—say forty-eight (48) hours—allowed.

2. The Confederate armies, now in existence, to be disbanded and conducted to their several State capitals, there to deposit their arms and public property in the State arsenal; and each officer and man to execute and file an agreement to cease from acts of war, and to abide the action of the State and Federal authority. The number of arms and munitions of war to be reported to the Chief of Ordnance at Washington City, subject to the future action of the Congress of the United States, and, in the mean time, to be used solely to maintain peace and order within the borders of the States respectively.

3. The recognition, by the Executive of the United States, of the several State governments, on their officers and Legislatures taking the oaths prescribed by the Constitution of the United States, and, where conflicting State governments have resulted from the war, the legitimacy of all shall be submitted to the Supreme Court of the United States.

4. The reëstablishment of all the Federal courts in the several States, with powers as defined by the Constitution and laws of Congress.

5. The people and inhabitants of all the States to be guaranteed, so far as the Executive can, their political rights and franchises, as well as their rights of person and property, as defined by the Constitution of the United States and of the States respectively.

6. The Executive authority of the Government of the United States not to disturb any of the people by reason of the late war, so long as they live in peace and quiet, abstain from acts of armed hostil-

ity, and obey the laws in existence at the place of their residence.

7. In general terms—the war to cease; a general amnesty, so far as the Executive of the United States can command, on condition of the disband-ment of the Confederate armies, the distribution of the arms, and the resumption of peaceful pursuits by the officers and men hitherto composing said armies.

Not being fully empowered by our respective principals to fulfill these terms, we individually and officially pledge ourselves to promptly obtain the necessary authority, and to carry out the above pro-gramme.

J. E. JOHNSTON,   W. T. SHERMAN,

General commanding Confederate   *Major-General commanding Army*
States Army in N. C.   *of the United States in N. C.*

As soon as the requisite number of copies of this paper was made and duly signed, one was dispatched to each President, and we separated.

The next day General Sherman published the following orders to his troops: [1]

"The general commanding announces to the army a suspension of hostilities, and an agreement with General Johnston and high officials which, when formally ratified, will make peace from the Potomac to the Rio Grande. Until the absolute peace is arranged, a line passing through Tyrrell's Mount, Chapel University, Durham's Station, and West Point, on the Neuse River, will separate the two armies. Each army commander will group his camps entirely with a view to comfort, health, and good police. All the details of military discipline

[1] Special Field Orders, No. 58.

must be maintained, and the General hopes and believes that in a very few days it will be his good fortune to conduct you all to your homes. The fame of this army for courage, industry, and discipline, is admitted all over the world. Then let each officer and man see that it is not stained by any act of vulgarity, rowdyism, and petty crime. The cavalry will patrol the front of the line, General Howard will take charge of the district from Raleigh up to the cavalry, General Slocum to the left of Raleigh, and General Schofield in Raleigh, right and rear. Quartermasters and commissaries will keep their supplies up to a light load for the wagons, and the railroad superintendent will arrange a depot for the convenience of each separate army."

I arrived in Greensboro', near which the Confederate troops were in bivouac, before daybreak on the 19th. Colonel Archer Anderson, adjutant-general of the army, gave me two papers addressed to me by the President. The first directed me to obtain from Mr. J. N. Hendren, treasury agent, thirty-nine thousand dollars in silver, which was in his hands, subject to my order, and to use it as the military chest of the army. The second, received subsequently by Colonel Anderson, directed me to send this money to the President at Charlotte. This order was not obeyed, however. As only the military part of our Government had then any existence, I thought that a fair share of the fund still left should be appropriated to the benefit of the army, especially as the troops had received no pay for many months. This sum (except twelve hundred dollars which Mr. Hendren said that the Commissary-General had taken) was divided among the troops irrespective of rank, each individual receiving the same share.

As there was reason to suppose that the Confederate Executive had a large sum in specie in its possession, I urged it earnestly, in writing, to apply a part of it to the payment of the army. This letter was intrusted to Lieutenant-Colonel Mason, who was instructed to wait for an answer. Its receipt was acknowledged by telegraph, and an answer promised. After waiting several days to no purpose, Colonel Mason returned without one.

During the conference, Major-General Stoneman, who had come from the West with a large body of cavalry, approached the line of railroad in Middle North Carolina. General Sherman sent him notice of the armistice by Confederate officers, and directed him to suspend hostilities. Before these orders were received, if they were ever delivered to General Stoneman, the railroad bridges over the Catawba between Chesterville and Charlotte, and Charlotte and Lincolnton, and the railroad depot at Salisbury, were destroyed by these troops. Pettus's brigade, sent from Greensboro' to protect the railroad bridge over the Yadkin, arrived in time to repel the large party sent to burn it. The arrival of Brigadier-General Echols with Duke's and Vaughn's brigades of cavalry from Southwestern Virginia removed any apprehension of further damage of the kind.

On the 21st, a dispatch was received from Major-General Cobb, announcing the occupation of Macon by Major-General Wilson's cavalry the day before— the Federal commander declining to respect the information of an armistice given by his enemy.

During the military operations preceding the armistice, there were ample supplies of provision and forage for our forces in the railroad-depots of North Carolina. We were forming similar depots in South Carolina, then, and collecting provisions abundantly, in a district that had been thought destitute. Early in March, when the wagons of the Army of Tennessee reached Augusta, their number was so large compared with that of the troops, that the officer in charge of them was directed to employ three hundred in the gaps in the line of railroad across South Carolina; and Colonel W. E. Moore [1] was desired to use one hundred in collecting provisions to form a line of depots between Charlotte, North Carolina, and Washington, Georgia. Before the 20th, Colonel Moore reported that more than seven hundred thousand rations had been collected in those depots.

The meeting between General Sherman and myself, and the armistice that followed, produced great uneasiness in the army. It was very commonly believed among the soldiers that there was to be a surrender, by which they would be prisoners of war, to which they were very averse. This apprehension caused a great number of desertions between the 19th and 24th of April—not less than four thousand in the infantry and artillery, and almost as many from the cavalry; many of them rode off artillery horses, and mules belonging to the baggage-trains.

In the afternoon of the 24th, the President of the Confederacy, then in Charlotte, communicated to me, by telegraph, his approval of the terms of the convention of the 17th and 18th, and, within an hour,

_____
[1] At his own suggestion.

a special messenger from General Hampton brought me two dispatches from General Sherman. In one of them he informed me that the Government of the United States rejected the terms of peace agreed upon by us; and in the other he gave notice of the termination of the armistice in forty-eight hours from noon that day.

The substance of these dispatches was immediately communicated to the Administration by telegraph,[1] instructions asked for, and the disbanding of the army suggested, to prevent further invasion and devastation of the country by the armies of the United States. The reply, dated eleven o'clock P. M., was received early in the morning of the 25th; it suggested that the infantry might be disbanded, with instructions to meet at some appointed place, and directed me to bring off the cavalry, and all other soldiers who could be mounted by taking serviceable beasts from the trains, and a few light field-pieces. I objected, immediately, that this order provided for the performance of but one of the three great duties then devolving upon us—that of securing the safety of the high civil officers of the Confederate Government; but neglected the other two—the safety of the people, and that of the army. I also advised the immediate flight of the high civil functionaries under proper escort.

The belief that impelled me to urge the civil authorities of the Confederacy to make peace, that it would be a great crime to prolong the war, prompted me to disobey these instructions—the last that I received from the Confederate Govern-

[1] At six o'clock P. M.

ment. They would have given the President an escort too heavy for flight, and not strong enough to force a way for him; and would have spread ruin over all the South, by leading the three great invading armies in pursuit. In that belief, I determined to do all in my power to bring about a termination of hostilities. I therefore proposed to General Sherman another armistice and conference, for that purpose, suggesting, as a basis, the clause of the recent convention relating to the army. This was reported to the Confederate Government at once. General Sherman's dispatch, expressing his agreement to a conference, was received soon after sunrise on the 26th; and I set out for the former place of meeting, as soon as practicable, after announcing to the Administration that I was about to do so.

We met at noon in Mr. Bennett's house, as before. I found General Sherman, as he appeared in our previous conversation, anxious to prevent further bloodshed, so we agreed without difficulty upon terms putting an end to the war within the limits of our commands, which happened to be coextensive—terms which we expected to produce a general pacification :

Terms of a Military Convention entered into this twenty-sixth (26th) day of April, 1865, at Bennett's House, near Durham's Station, North Carolina, between General Joseph E. Johnston, commanding the Confederate Army, and Major-General W. T. Sherman, commanding the United States Army in North Carolina.

1. All acts of war on the part of the troops under General Johnston's command, to cease from this date.

2. All arms and public property to be deposited at Greensboro', and delivered to an ordnance-officer of the United States Army. 3. Rolls of all the officers and men to be made in duplicate; one copy to be retained by the commander of the troops, and the other to be given to an officer to be designated by General Sherman. Each officer and man to give his individual obligation in writing, not to take up arms against the Government of the United States, until properly released from this obligation. 4. The side-arms of officers and their private horses and baggage to be retained by them. 5. This being done, all the officers and men will be permitted to return to their homes, not to be disturbed by the United States authorities so long as they observe their obligation, and the laws in force where they may reside.

(Signed)   (Signed)
J. E. JOHNSTON,   W. T. SHERMAN,
General commanding Confederate   *Major-General commanding United*
States Forces in N. C.   *States Forces in N. C.*

Military Convention of April 26, 1865—*Supplemental Terms.*

1. The field transportation to be loaned to the troops for their march to their homes, and for subsequent use in their industrial pursuits. Artillery-horses may be used in field transportation, if necessary.

2. Each brigade or separate body to retain a number of arms equal to *one-seventh* of its effective strength, which, when the troops reach the capitals of their States, will be disposed of as the general commanding the department may direct.

3. Private horses, and other private property of both officers and men, to be retained by them.

4. The commanding general of the Military Division of West Mississippi, Major-General Canby, will be requested to give transportation by water, from Mobile or New Orleans, to the troops from Arkansas and Texas.

5. The obligations of officers and soldiers to be signed by their immediate commanders.

6. Naval forces within the limits of General Johnston's command to be included in the terms of this convention.

(Signed)   (Signed)

J. E. JOHNSTON,   J. M. SCHOFIELD,
General commanding Confederate   *Major-General commanding United*
States Forces in N. C.   *States Forces in N. C.*

General Sherman assured me that he would remove from the department all the troops he had brought into it as soon as practicable, after returning to his headquarters, leaving only those of General Schofield's command, who were thought necessary for the maintenance of law and order. Accordingly, on the 27th (the day after), his order No. 66 of that year was published, announcing a final agreement between us, terminating the war east of the Chattahoochee River; sending his own army to Washington; Major-General Wilson's cavalry back to the Tennessee River, near Decatur; and directing Major-General Stoneman's division to return to East Tennessee.

General Sherman was accompanied on this occasion by several among the most distinguished officers of the United States Army. The impression was made distinctly on my mind that they, and the army generally, desired peace on the conditions of the convention of the 18th, and regretted the rejection of those terms by the President of the United States.

The pacification was announced by me to the States immediately concerned, by the following telegram, addressed to their governors:

"The disaster in Virginia, the capture by the enemy of all our workshops for the preparation of ammunition and repairing of arms, the impossibility of recruiting our little army opposed to more than ten times its number, or of supplying it except by robbing our own citizens, destroyed all hope of successful war. I have made, therefore, a military convention with Major-General Sherman, to terminate hostilities in North and South Carolina, Georgia, and Florida. I made this convention to spare the blood of this gallant little army, to prevent further sufferings of our people by the devastation and ruin inevitable from the marches of invading armies, and to avoid the crime of waging a hopeless war."

It was also published to the Confederate army, in general orders No. 18 of April 27th, as follows:

"By the terms of a military convention made on the 26th instant by Major-General W. T. Sherman, United States Army, and General J. E. Johnston, Confederate States Army, the officers and men of this army are to bind themselves not to take up arms against the United States until properly relieved from that obligation; and shall receive guarantees from the United States officers against molestation by the United States authorities, so long as they observe that obligation and the laws in force where they reside.

"For these objects, duplicate muster-rolls will be made immediately, and, after the distribution of the necessary papers, the troops will march under their officers to their respective States, and there be disbanded; all retaining personal property.

"The object of the convention is pacification, to the extent of the authority of the commanders who made it.

"Events in Virginia, which broke every hope of success by war, imposed on its General the duty of sparing the blood of this gallant army, and of saving our country from further devastation, and our people from ruin."

General Sherman published it to the Federal army, in his field-order No. 66, on the same day:

"Hostilities having ceased, the following changes and dispositions of the troops in the field will be made with as little delay as practicable:

"1. The Tenth and Twenty-third Corps will remain in the Department of North Carolina, and Major-General J. M. Schofield will transfer back to Major-General Gillmore, commanding Department of the South, the two brigades formerly belonging to the division of Brevet Major-General Grover, at Savannah. The Third Division, cavalry corps, Brevet Major-General J. Kilpatrick commanding, is hereby transferred to the Department of North Carolina, and General Kilpatrick will report in person to Major-General Schofield for orders.

" 2. The cavalry command of Major-General George Stoneman will return to East Tennessee, and that of Brevet Major-General J. H. Wilson will be conducted back to the Tennessee River, in the neighborhood of Decatur, Alabama.

" 3. Major-General Howard will conduct the Army of the Tennessee to Richmond, Virginia, following roads substantially by Lewisburg, Warrenton, Lawrenceville, and Petersburg, or to the right of that line. Major-General Slocum will conduct the Army of Georgia to Richmond by roads to the left of the one indicated for General Howard, viz., by Oxford, Boydton, and Nottoway Court-House. These armies will turn in, at this point, the contents of their ordnance-trains, and use the wagons for extra forage and provisions. These columns will be conducted slowly and in the best of order, and aim to be at Richmond, ready to resume the march, by the middle of May.

" 4. The chief quartermaster and commissary of the military division, Generals Easton and Beckwith, after making proper dispositions of their departments here, will proceed to Richmond and make suitable preparations to receive those columns, and provide them for the further journey."

Before the Confederate army came to Greensboro', much of the provisions in depot there had been consumed or wasted by fugitives from the Army of Virginia; still, enough was left for the subsistence of the troops until the end of April. In making the last agreement with General Sherman, I relied upon the depots recently established in

South Carolina, for the subsistence of the troops on the way to their homes. A few days before they marched, however, Colonel Moore informed me that those depots had all been plundered by the crowd of fugitives and country‑people, who thought, apparently, that, as there was no longer a government, they might assume the division of this property. That at Charlotte had either been consumed by our cavalry in the neighborhood or appropriated by individuals. So we had no other means of supplying the troops on their homeward march, than a stock of cotton yarn, and a little cloth, to be used as money by the quartermasters and commissaries. But this was entirely inadequate; and great suffering would have ensued, both of the troops and the people on their routes, if General Sherman, when informed of our condition, had not given us two hundred and fifty thousand rations, on no other condition than my furnishing the means of transporting them by railroad from Morehead City. This averted any danger of suffering or even inconvenience.

The preparation and signature of the necessary papers occupied the officers of the two armies intrusted with that business until the 2d of May. On that day the three corps and three little bodies of cavalry were ordered to march to their destinations, each under its own commander. And my military connection with those matchless soldiers was terminated by the following order:

General Orders No. 22.

"COMRADES: In terminating our official relations, I earnestly exhort you to observe faithfully the terms of pacification agreed upon; and to discharge the obligations of good and peaceful citizens, as well as you have performed the duties of thorough soldiers in the field. By such a course, you will best secure the comfort of your families and kindred, and restore tranquillity to our country.

"You will return to your homes with the admiration of our people, won by the courage and noble devotion you have displayed in this long war. I shall always remember with pride the loyal support and generous confidence you have given me.

"I now part with you with deep regret—and bid you farewell with feelings of cordial friendship; and with earnest wishes that you may have hereafter all the prosperity and happiness to be found in the world.

(Signed)   " J. E. Johnston, *General.*

Official:
(Signed)   "Kinlock Falconer, *A. A. G.*"

The United States troops that remained in the Southern States, on *military* duty, conducted themselves as if they thought that the object of the war had been the restoration of the Union. They treated the people around them as they would have done those of Ohio or New York if stationed among them, as their fellow-citizens.[1] Those people supposed, not unnaturally, that if those who had fought against them were friendly, the great body of the Northern people, who had not fought, must be more so. This idea inspired in them a kindlier feeling to the people of the North and the Government of the

---

[1] This language excludes those of the Freedmen's Bureau.

United States, than that existing ten years before. It created, too, a strong expectation that the Southern States would soon resume their places in the Union. The most despondent apprehended no such "reconstruction" as that subsequently established by Congress.

CHAPTER XIII.

Causes of Failure.—Misapplication of Means.—Inefficient Financial System.—
Bad Impressment Laws.—No Want of Zeal or Patriotism.—Refutation of
Charges against Secretary Floyd.—Facts of the Case.—Deficiency of Small-
Arms at the South.

MUCH has been written and much more said of the
cause of the overthrow of the Confederate States in
their great contest for independence. One class, and
much the largest—for it includes the people who were
victorious in the war, and those Europeans who
watched the struggle with interest, as well as many
of the Southern people—ascribes it to the superior
population and greater resources of the Northern
States. Another, a class of Southern people, attributes our defeat to a want of perseverance, unanimity,
and even of loyalty, on our own part; and the consequent abandonment of the Government of the Confederacy in its efforts, by the people themselves. In
my view, both are far wrong.

The cause of the subjugation of the Southern
States was neither want of wealth and population,
nor of devotion to their own cause on the part of
the people of those States. That people was not
guilty of the high crime of undertaking a war without the means of waging it successfully. They had
ample means, which, unfortunately, were not applied

to the object of equipping great armies, and bringing them into the field.

A full treasury was necessary to defray the ex-
penses of a great war. The South had the means of
making one, in its cotton alone. But its Government
rejected those means, and limited its financial efforts to printing bank-notes, with which the country
was soon flooded. The necessity of actual money in
the treasury, and the mode of raising it, were generally understood in the country. It was that the
Government should take the cotton from the owners
and send it to Europe as fast as possible, to be sold
there. This was easily practicable; for the owners
were ready to accept any terms the Government
might fix; and sending to Europe was easy in all the
first year of the Confederacy's existence. Its Government went into operation early in February. The
blockade of the Southern ports was proclaimed in
May, but not at all effective until the end of the following winter; so that there was a period of about
twelve months for the operation of converting four
or five million bales of cotton into money. The sum
raised in that way would have enabled the War
Department to procure at once arms enough for half
a million of men, and after that expenditure the
Confederate treasury would have been much richer
than that of the United States. By applying the
first money obtained in this way, to the purchase of
arms and military accoutrements, or using for the
purpose the credit which such an amount of property would have given, the War Department would
have been able to equip troops as fast as they could
be assembled and organized. And, as the Southern

people were full of enthusiasm, five hundred thousand men could have been ready and in the field had such a course been pursued, at the time when the first battle was actually fought—the 21st of July, 1861. Such a force placed on the Northern borders of the Confederacy before the United States had brought a fourth of the number into the field, would probably have prevented the very idea of " coercion." Such a disposition of such an army, and the possession of financial means of carrying on war for years, would have secured the success of the Confederacy.

The timely adoption of such a financial system would have secured to us the means of success, even without an extraordinary importation of arms, and the immediate organization of large armies. It would have given the Confederacy a treasury richer than that of the United States. We should thus have had, to the end of the war, the means of paying our soldiers; and that would have enabled such of them as belonged to the laboring class to remain in the ranks. This class, in the Confederacy as in all other countries, formed the body of the army. In all the earlier part of the war, when the Confederate money was not much below that of the United States in value, our troops were paid with some regularity, and the soldiers of the laboring class who had families, fed and clothed them with their pay, as they had formerly done with the wages of their labor. And so long as that state of things continued, the strength of the Confederate armies was little impaired; and those armies were maintained on such a footing as to justify the hope, which was general in the South until the fall of 1864, that we were to win in the contest. But after the Confederate currency had become almost worthless—when a soldier's month's pay would scarcely buy one meal for his family—and that was the case in all the last period of ten or twelve months—those soldiers of the laboring class who had families were compelled to choose between their military service and the strongest obligations men know —their duties to wives and children. They obeyed the strongest of those obligations, left the army, and returned to their homes to support their families.

The wretched impressment laws deprived the army of many valuable men of a class less poor than that just referred to. Those laws required the impressment of all articles of military necessity that could not be purchased. The Government had the power of regulating the prices to be paid by it for all such commodities; and its commissioners appointed for the purpose fixed them much below the market values. No one would sell to the Government, of course, when he could get from his neighbors twice the government price for his horses or grain; consequently the officers of the Government could never purchase, but had always to procure supplies by impressment. No rules for their guidance were prescribed; none at least that were observed by them or known to the public, and they were subjected to no supervision. All the property of Confederate citizens applicable to military purposes was, therefore, under their absolute control. The bad and indifferent officers impressed what they were called upon to furnish, in the manner least inconvenient to themselves, usually on the nearest plantations or farms, or those where opposition was not to be apprehended.

The farms of soldiers were generally under the management of women, and therefore were, not unusually, drawn upon for much more than their proportion. Hence it was not uncommon for a soldier to be written to by his wife, that so much of the food he had provided for herself and his children had been impressed, that it was necessary that he should return to save them from suffering or starvation. Such a summons, it may well be supposed, was never unheeded.

The sufferings of the soldiers themselves, produced by the want of proper clothing, drove many of the least hardy out of the ranks. Want of food also is said to have had the same effect, especially in the army before Richmond, in the last winter of the war.

It was by such causes, all due to an empty treasury, that our armies were so reduced in the last months of the war.

As to the charge of want of loyalty, or zeal in the war, I assert, from as much opportunity for observation as any individual had, that no people ever displayed so much, under such circumstances, and with so little flagging, for so long a time continuously. This was proved by the long service of the troops without pay, and under exposure to such hardships, from the causes above mentioned, as modern troops have rarely endured; by the voluntary contributions of food and clothing sent to the armies from every district that furnished a regiment; by the general and continued submission of the people to the tyranny of the impressment system as practised—such a tyranny, I believe, as no other high-spirited people ever endured—and by the sympathy

and aid given in every house to all professing to belong to the army, or to be on the way to join it. And
this spirit continued not only after all hope of success had died, but after the final confession of defeat
by their military commanders.

But, even if the men of the South had not been
zealous in the cause, the patriotism of their mothers
and wives and sisters would have inspired them with
zeal or shamed them into its manifestation. The
women of the South exhibited that feeling wherever
it could be exercised : in the armies, by distributing
clothing made with their own hands; at the railroad-
stations and their own homes, by feeding the marching soldiers; and, above all, in the hospitals, where
they rivaled Sisters of Charity. I am happy in the
belief that their devoted patriotism and gentle charity are to be richly rewarded.

An error in relation to the state of preparation
for war, of each of the two sections of the country,
in the beginning of 1861, has prevailed in the North
since then. I refer to the belief that, when the
Southern Confederacy was formed, the arms that
had been provided by the Government of the United
States for the common defense were in the possession of the seceded States.

This belief was produced by the most malignant
and industriously circulated slanders by which the
reputation of any public man of the United States
ever suffered—the accusation against John B.
Floyd, of Virginia, that while Secretary of War he
had all the public arms removed from Northern to
Southern arsenals; to disarm the North and arm the
South for the impending war. This accusation was

so extensively circulated as to lead to an investigation by a committee of the House of Representatives, in January, 1861. The chairman of that committee was one of the most respected members of
the Republican party in that House, Mr. Stanton, of
Ohio. The report of that committee completely ex-
onerated Mr. Floyd, and refuted the calumny. Yet
it continued to be circulated and believed—while
the refutation, although by such a body, was unnoticed—and, I believe, is now forgotten.

The facts that were distorted into that calumny
are clearly stated in the report of the committee,
and must be well known by the principal officers of
the United States Ordnance Bureau, and recorded in
that Bureau; for the orders in question were given
through that, the proper channel. They are briefly
these:

Previous to the year 1859, the infantry arms
manufactured under the direction of the War Department had been accumulating in the Springfield
Armory, in consequence of the neglect of an old
rule of the Government which required the distribution of these arms in arsenals constructed for the
purpose, in the different sections of the country. In
the beginning of that year, the accumulation had
filled the places of deposit at Springfield, where the
newly-adopted improved arms were made. To make
room there for the new arms as they were finished,
Mr. Floyd ordered the removal of about a hundred
and five thousand muskets[1] and ten thousand rifles,

---

[1] The chief of ordnance, Colonel Craig, in his report on the subject,
states that but sixty thousand of the arms ordered by Mr. Floyd to be
sent to the South were actually removed.

to empty Southern arsenals, constructed many years before to receive them, under laws of Congress. These were old-fashioned arms that had been discarded by the Government on account of the recent improvements in small-arms, and the adoption by it of the "rifled musket." About four hundred thousand of the old discarded arms, and all of the new and improved, were left in the North. About a year later two thousand rifled muskets were offered for distribution to the States under an act of Congress. Only seven hundred of them went to the South, however, because even then there was so little apprehension of war that several Southern States refused or neglected to take their portions. Mr. Floyd's orders, as I have said, were given before secession had been thought of, or war apprehended, by the people of any part of the United States.

The seceding States, in general, made no preparation for war by procuring arms—none of consequence, that is to say. I believe that Georgia procured twenty thousand old-fashioned muskets, and Virginia had forty thousand, made in a State armory more than forty years before. They had, of course, flint locks. Each of the other Southern States, on seceding, claimed, and, when practicable, took possession of, the military property of the United States within its limits. They obtained, in that way, the arms with which they began the war.

To recapitulate: the Confederate States began the war with one hundred and twenty thousand arms of obsolete models, and seven hundred of the recently adopted weapons, "rifled muskets;" and the United States with about four hundred and fifty thousand of the old and all of the modern arms that had been made since the adoption of the new model, about the middle of General Pierce's administration, when Mr. Davis was at the head of the War Department, except, however, the seven hundred held by the Confederacy. The equipped field-batteries and fixed ammunition of all kinds were in the North, as well as the establishments for the manufacture of arms, and the preparation of ammunition; except that at Harper's Ferry, which, being on the border, was abandoned by the United States, after an attempt to destroy it, which left little besides machinery.

CHAPTER XIV.

Mr. Davis's Unsent Message.—Letters of Governor Humphreys and Major Mims.—Synopsis of Unsent Message.—Reply to Unsent Message.

In the winter of 1866–'67, I learned in Jackson, Mississippi, that a paper had been seen by my three or four friends there, purporting to be a message from the President of the Confederacy to the two Houses of Congress, explaining why his Excellency could not conscientiously restore me to military command. This explanation was, ostensibly, a narrative of my military service to the time of my removal from the command of the Army of Tennessee, with comments.

My friends endeavored, but unsuccessfully, to obtain a copy of the paper for me. They gave me, however, the name of the gentleman to whom they supposed that it had been committed.

When informed of Mr. Davis's address, or rather, how I could send a letter to him, I requested him to instruct the gentleman my friends had named to me, to give me a copy of the document. He replied promptly that, although he had written no such message, he desired the gentleman named, by that mail, to give me a copy of any paper written by him in relation to me, that might be in his possession. In due time that gentleman informed me that he had not the paper, but told me who had it in his keeping. I then wrote to Mr. Davis again, explaining my mistake, and requesting him to instruct the gentleman who really had the message to give me a copy. As Mr. Davis had gone to Mississippi in the mean time, this letter was sent to a gentleman in Jackson, who was his friend as well as mine. In that way I know it was received, although never acknowledged; nor was the copy asked for given; I am therefore compelled to believe that the instructions so promptly received by one who had not the paper described, were not given to him to whom it had been intrusted.

The fact that this document was shown to the only gentlemen of Jackson whom I was well acquainted with, gives me reason to think that it has been exhibited freely, while the care with which it is preserved, and the language of him who has it in his keeping, indicate that it is so preserved for publication. Having waited for that event as long as one at my time of life can afford to do, I now defend myself against these accusations as given in the following synopsis—the only form in which I have been able to see them. I am confident of its accuracy, from the best evidence—that of gentlemen of intelligence and honor, who are well known in Mississippi. It is given in the following letter:

VICKSBURG, MISS., *January* 10, 1870.

" DEAR GENERAL: Your letter of 26th December last was received while I was confined to my bed with catarrh-fever, which is my excuse for the delay in answering it.

" I have carefully read the synopsis (furnished you by a friend and sent to me) of the paper read to me

by General T. J. Wharton, in the Executive Office at
Jackson in 1866, purporting to be a message prepared
by President Davis, to be sent to Congress, giving his
reasons for withholding from you any further command in the Confederate Army. I find it to agree won-
derfully with my recollections of the contents of that
paper.   The synopsis is somewhat meagre in elabora-
tion and detail, but, with some few omissions, it is substantially correct, I think.   First, in the charges stated
in regard to your conduct and course in the Valley
before the battle of Manassas; then of what is said of
your movement from Manassas and preliminary to it;
then the accusations against you at Yorktown, at Seven
Pines, and at Vicksburg; and the alleged misconduct
in Georgia, are all given substantially correct.   As
to the omissions I allude to, I think it is stated in the
original paper that you were ordered to take command
of Bragg's army in January, 1863, if it appeared to
you to be advisable, but that you sustained Bragg, expressed confidence, etc., in him. Then you are taken to
task for remaining in Tennessee instead of going to
Mississippi, where you ought to have been, and where
you did not go until expressly ordered. I think another omission is, that you were charged with the loss of
rolling-stock on the railroad above Big Black, in July,
1863, which could have been saved easily by making
a temporary bridge at Jackson.   I think, if the original paper ever sees daylight, it will show the synopsis
and these omissions to be substantially given as stated.

"Very truly, your sincere friend,
(Signed)   "BENJ. G. HUMPHREYS.
"To General J. E. JOHNSTON,
    "*Savannah, Ga.*"

"SAVANNAH, GA., *October* 8, 1873.

"DEAR GENERAL: I have carefully examined the paper which you submitted to me, claiming to be an abstract of a certain manuscript message purporting to have been prepared by Mr. Davis, during his presidency of the Confederate States, but which was not submitted to the Confederate Congress, in which he gives his reasons for not reinstating you to command after your removal before Atlanta.

"This latter document was in my possession for a while, and I read it very carefully, and according to my recollection the abstract or synopsis in your possession is, as far as it goes, correct. I don't think that the points as stated therein are as strong as made in the original, while some are not embraced in it. Without referring to other omissions, I well remember the original as containing some strictures upon you for failing to provide against the heavy loss of rolling-stock on the railroad about Big Black, in July, 1863, which it was claimed could have been done by building a temporary bridge over Pearl River; and another, your failure to take command of Bragg's army in 1863, as ordered.

"Yours truly,

(Signed) "L. MIMS.

"General J. E. JOHNSTON,

"*Savannah, Ga.*"

1.[1] It is stated in this paper that, at the beginning of the struggle, he (the President) had entire confidence in General Johnston's ability, and as soon as active operations commenced placed him in com-

---

[1] The numbers are mine, for clearness of reference.

mand of the troops covering and defending, as was then thought, the most important strategical point in Virginia—Harper's Ferry; that in his letters that officer fully sustained the opinions of others in regard to this point, and estimated its importance as very great, considered either as a place from which to operate against General McClellan, coming from the West, or Patterson, or McDowell; that suddenly he changed his tactics, and represented that the position was untenable, etc., etc., although it had been fortified; and that, abandoning at Harper's Ferry much valuable machinery, he took a new position at or near Winchester, where for several days, if not weeks, he remained in front of Patterson with the avowed object of crushing him—replying to suggestions and orders from Richmond to reënforce General Beauregard at Manassas, that it was essential that he should keep between McClellan and Patterson, to prevent their junction; and that when, finally, he obeyed an imperative and repeated order from Richmond to reënforce General Beauregard at Manassas, he managed so badly as to arrive barely in time to save General Beauregard from a defeat which would have brought great disaster upon our arms.

2. That, as ranking officer, General Johnston was assigned to the command of the army, and his plan was to assume the defensive, fortify Centreville Heights, and recruit the army there. His communications to the Richmond authorities, made voluntarily, and in reply to questions, indicated perfect satisfaction with the excellence and strength of the position and army, which was further shown by the concentration of a vast amount of stores and material of

war in and about Manassas. But, to the astonishment of the authorities, he indicated an intention to fall back; and when, in their surprise, they desired to know to what point he would retreat and stop, he confessed his total ignorance of the country behind him, and could give no satisfactory answer. Surprised and alarmed at this intelligence, engineer officers were sent from Richmond to sketch the topographical features of the country, to furnish General Johnston with information which, as commanding general of the army, he should have given to the Richmond authorities. The matter was deemed of sufficient importance to call him to Richmond for consultation; and, when he left that place to return to the army, no such thing as a hasty retreat was anticipated; but preparations for a rapid movement by the army, as circumstances might direct, were agreed upon. Suddenly, however, he put the army in motion, after destroying vast quantities of supplies, which should have been removed; and halted only when imperative instructions from Richmond commanded him to do so.

3. McClellan having changed his base to Fort Monroe, it then became necessary to face him at Yorktown, involving long marches, and much suffering, and the occupation of a country in which it was very difficult to procure supplies and feed an army. Here General Johnston's judgment was strongly in favor of his position, the strength of his works, and the qualities of his troops. But, just when public confidence was beginning to be restored, he suddenly evacuated his position, destroying quantities of supplies, and refusing the gage of battle, although the

disparity of numbers did not seem to justify it. To check his retreat short of Richmond, orders were finally sent to him to halt; and the line of the Chickahominy was occupied. As soon as McClellan came up, however, he again broke up his camps, and fell back to Richmond, to whose small natural defensive advantages he added nothing by fortification, although he remained in front of the city several weeks.

4. When McClellan, emboldened by Johnston's want of enterprise, placed a division on his side of the Chickahominy, which a rain, sweeping away the bridges, put completely at his mercy, his dispositions were so faulty, and his knowledge of the country so imperfect, that the combat which followed was barely rendered successful as a feat of arms, and was barren of results, that should have been tangible and important. His wound in this battle having disabled him, it became necessary to intrust the command to another, who had the confidence of the army and people. General Lee was selected. When General Johnston recovered, it was deemed impolitic to remove General Lee at a time when his plans for future operations were maturing, the policy of which was in accordance with the views of the Government, and to substitute one whose plans would have to be matured, and whose dispositions might cause such delay as to seriously threaten the fair prospects of the army and country.

5. Although the President's confidence in General Johnston's ability was somewhat shaken by that officer's conduct, he determined to place him in command of the most important department of the Con-

federacy. Johnston's friends were confident of his ability, and the President thought that his own judgment should not be put in opposition to so many good, judicious, and intelligent men. He was there-fore assigned to the command of the Department of the West; his headquarters at Chattanooga; with full and complete control over the armies operating in Tennessee and Mississippi. After assuming that command, he was directed to go to Tullahoma, to as-certain if General Bragg had so lost the confidence of his troops as to render it expedient to remove him. After reporting in favor of that officer, he re-mained in Tullahoma, instead of returning to Jack-son, where his presence was required by the immi-nence of General Grant's invasion; and, even in such a crisis, he went to Mississippi only in conse-quence of a positive order from the Secretary of War.

On arriving in Jackson, instead of leading his troops to join Lieutenant-General Pemberton's, or going to his headquarters, which was feasible, and assuming command in person, he retired with the troops he had, in the direction of Canton, without striking a blow, or endeavoring to impede the prog-ress of the enemy in any manner whatever; and remained inactive for three weeks, although all the troops that could possibly be sent had been directed to reënforce him, swelling his numbers to a respect-able army, strong enough to have cut through Grant's lines and relieve Pemberton. Finally, he did move; but only in time to reach the banks of the Big Black River to hear of Pemberton's surrender. This caused him to fall back to Jackson; which place he represented to be of importance, and worth defending at all hazards. But after remaining there for —————— he telegraphed to the Government that the works were feeble, badly arranged, etc., and Jackson indefensible; although he had first telegraphed that it was well fortified. Losses of stores, army dispirited, confidence of people weakened, followed the evacuation.

After this, while his troops were unemployed, a brigade of Federal cavalry destroyed the portion of the rolling-stock of the Mississippi Central Railroad kept in Grenada. The loss of these cars and engines was much felt in the latter part of the war, when they would have been very valuable, to transport provisions to Lee's army. Their preservation would have been easy. It would have required nothing more than the construction of a temporary bridge over Pearl River at Jackson.

6. After this the President's confidence in Johnston's ability as a general was so far destroyed, that he determined not to intrust him again with the command of an important army. He remained in command at Morton and Meridian until December, and in his department nothing of importance occurred. After the battle of Missionary Ridge, public clamor and the army demanded a change in the command of the Army of Tennessee. General Bragg's repeated applications to be relieved were finally granted, and, upon the earnest, repeated, and urgent appeals of many of the best and foremost men of the country, the President was induced, contrary to his judgment, to assign General Johnston to that command. That officer was immediately notified of the arrangement

(as soon as made) for a campaign, and also of the troops that would be sent him. A plan of campaign was also transmitted to him by the War Department. To this plan he objected, without proposing a better one, and, while the correspondence was going on, Sherman commenced his movement which induced Johnston to retreat.

7. That, at the opening of the campaign, Johnston had subject to his orders between sixty and seventy thousand men, and the disparity of forces between Sherman and him was so much less than between Lee and Grant, that constant hope was entertained of a great and glorious victory; but he only kept on retreating, refusing all the advantages which an able general would have seized ; that the positions taken up by him were almost impregnable by Nature, and but little art was necessary to make them quite so to Sherman's onward progress; that, as Sherman would extend his flanks to envelop him, instead of concentration and battle, it was a retreat and a new position, and so on until he arrived at Atlanta; that his losses, when he arrived there, amounted to twenty - five thousand; that his army was dispirited and broken down by the immense fatigue they had undergone; and the confidence in his ability to check Sherman's onward progress entirely destroyed.

8. That, upon direct interrogatory as to his ability to hold Atlanta, Johnston failed to impress the Department with the belief that he entertained any hope of doing so. It was then determined to change the tactics of the campaign, and put in command one who not only would command the confidence of the army,

but one who would not surrender territory without disputing its possession.

He (the President) adds that upon no consideration could he be induced, over his own signature, to intrust Johnston again with the command of an army.

1. My opinion of Harper's Ferry was thus expressed in my report to the Administration: "Its garrison was out of position to defend the Valley, or to prevent General McClellan's junction with General Patterson. These were the obvious and important objects to be kept in view. Besides being in position for them, it was necessary to be able, on emergency, to join General Beauregard.

"The occupation of Harper's Ferry by our army perfectly suited the enemy's views. We were bound to a fixed point. His movements were unrestricted. These views were submitted to the military authorities. The continued occupation of the place was, however, deemed by them indispensable.

"The practicable roads from the west and northwest, as well as from Manassas, meet the routes from Pennsylvania and Maryland at Winchester. That was therefore, in my opinion, our best position."

General E. Kirby Smith wrote to me as follows, May 28, 1867: "From the date of assuming command at Harper's Ferry to your evacuation of the place, you always expressed the conviction that, with the force under your command, the position was weak and untenable. . . . My recollection is that, after assuming command, you reported to General Lee against the occupation of Harper's Ferry, and that authority for its evacuation was received about the time the position was abandoned."

It is evident from General Lee's letters,[1] of June 1st and 7th, that mine of May 26th and 28th, and June 6th, expressed opinions decidedly unfavorable to Harper's Ferry as a military position, and proposed its evacuation. General Smith's testimony is direct and positive to the same effect; and the extract above, from my official report of the events in question, is conclusive as to the opinion of the intrinsic strength and strategical value of Harper's Ferry that I expressed to the Administration. And all combine with the narrative, from page 6 to page 16, to prove that, from the first, my language and conduct were consistent, and that I abandoned the place from no sudden change of opinion, but in conformity with that officially expressed in the first two days of my command, and reiterated.

The movement to Winchester was indispensable, and so regarded by the President himself. For, in the first passage quoted from General Cooper's letter[2] of June 13th, he authorized it, as well as the evacuation of Harper's Ferry. That authority had been anticipated, however. But for that movement, the battle of Manassas would have been lost; for, if our troops had escaped capture in Harper's Ferry, they could not have reached that field from it, in time to take part in the action.

The place was not fortified, unless mounting two heavy naval guns in battery on Furnace Ridge made it so. No valuable machinery was left there. Even wood for gunstocks[3] was brought away.

[1] Page 20.   [2] *See* page 24.   [3] *See* page 25.

Between the middle of June, when we moved from Harper's Ferry, to the 18th of July, when we moved from Winchester to Manassas, nine regiments [1] were sent to the army in the Valley, and the President thought more urgently required. If I had been professing to be able to crush Patterson, those regiments would not have been sent to me, nor would the President have explained [2] so earnestly why he did not send more. This when Beauregard needed them greatly.

Not even a suggestion to move to Manassas was sent to me before the telegram of July 17th, received on the 18th. On the contrary, the President's instructions to me in General Cooper's letters of June 13th, 18th, and 19th, and in his own of June 22d, and July 10th and 13th, prove that he had no such thought. And these letters prove that in all the time between the march from Harper's Ferry to Winchester, and that to Manassas, the intended that the army I commanded should be employed in the defense of the Valley. In the letter quoted, General E. K. Smith wrote: " As second in command and your adjutant-general, possessing your confidence, my position was one that made it exceedingly improbable that any orders could have been received at headquarters without my cognizance. No order in my recollection was received, either authorizing or directing you to join General Beauregard, other than that of July 17th, which was promptly complied with."

No imperative and repeated order to reënforce

---

[1] About six thousand effective men.
[2] *See* his letters on pages 29 and 31.

General Beauregard was given to me; no dispatch on the subject came to me but that given on page 33, which is not "imperative." General E. K. Smith testifies that I received no other; and that that one was acted upon promptly.

I am accused of arriving at Manassas barely in time to save General Beauregard from defeat. If the Army of the Shenandoah had actually come upon the field too late, the President would have been responsible, not I. For, instead of giving me information of McDowell's advance on the 16th of July, as should have been done, he dispatched his telegram on the subject in the night of the 17th, after the Federal army had encamped at Centreville, but three and a half miles from Beauregard's line, the Army of the Shenandoah being then at least four days' march, for such undisciplined troops, from that position. The operations so criticised secured the concentration that, for the time, saved the Confederacy, by enabling us to gain the battle of Manassas. At the time, the Government and people of the South were satisfied with the Army of the Shenandoah, because it came upon the field soon enough, and fought manfully after coming upon it. Now, the novel charge is made that it arrived *almost* too late.

2. The two armies were equally on the defensive at the time apparently referred to. The result of the conference[1] at Fairfax Court-House terminated our hope of assuming the offensive, and, in consequence, the army was placed at Centreville and intrenched.

So far from expressing satisfaction with the

[1] *See* pages 75 and 76.

strength and excellence of the army, I urged, at Fairfax Court-House, that it should be increased by at least fifty per cent., and my only letter [1] on the subject expressed the strongest dissatisfaction with the condition in numbers and discipline to which the army was reduced by the interference of the War Department with its interior management. The concentration of a vast amount of stores and material of war in and about Manassas was made by the Government itself against my repeated remonstrances, [2] expressed through my proper staff-officer, Major R. G. Cole, chief commissary. Fifteen days were devoted by the army to the removal of the public property that had been recklessly collected at Manassas. It would have been very dangerous to the public safety to employ it longer in that way; for, on the eve of a formidable invasion, it was of great importance that it should be so placed as to be able to unite promptly with other available forces, to repel this invasion.

I indicated no intention to "fall back" before the "consultation" on the 20th of February. The condition of the country made military operations on a large scale impossible, so that the most timid could have imagined no cause for hasty retreat. And in the "consultation" later, when the country was somewhat less impracticable, I opposed [3] any movement on account of the difficulty, which indicates that I could not have intended one when the difficulties would have been much greater.

[1] *See* those especially of February 1st to the acting Secretary of War, page 91; and March 1st, to the President, page 100.

[2] *See* note page 98, including Colonel Cole's letter of February 7th, 1871, and pages 104 and 105. [3] *See* fifth paragraph, page 106.

I was not ignorant of the country. I had studied it carefully, and had selected and prepared a position for the army behind the Rappahannock. But, if it had been otherwise, I had the usual resource of generals— a good map, which would have shown me by what routes to march, and where to halt.

Engineers were not sent to the army at the time (before the consultation) nor for the object asserted, but in consequence of an application by me, repeated after the consultation,[1] and they reported about the 3d of March, when an attempt by them to make a map of the country would have been absurd, if they had been competent to such work. On that subject, Captain Powhatan Robinson, their commander, wrote to me October 6, 1869: "I reported to you on the 1st or 2d of March. The rest of the topographical corps reported to me afterward. As regards the efficiency of the party, Lieutenant Heinrichs and myself were the only ones who had any experience in sketching topography, and, this being our first essay in the military line, we were ridiculously minute, and consequently very slow. I left Manassas March 3d, on my reconnaissance to the Rappahannock; I taking the upper route, and sending Lieutenant Randolph, who had just reported, by the lower. I reported to you on the 6th, at Centreville; received orders on the 7th to prepare Rappahannock Bridge for the passage of trains. The bridge was completed Tuesday morning (11th), just as the trains came up."

In the consultation, the President seemed to think that the army was exposed, and desired its re-

[1] February 22d.

moval. I thought the object of change of position ought to be, facility of uniting all our forces promptly, when McClellan's designs should be developed. It terminated with informal verbal orders to me to fall back as soon as practicable. Nothing was said of positions or routes—proof that the President had not then discovered my ignorance of the country.

The movement was not "hasty." We were preparing for it fifteen days; in which I wrote to the President five times in relation to those preparations. It would not have been proper to bestow more time upon the preservation of commissary stores. The "vast quantities" (rather more than a sixth of the whole supply) destroyed ought not to have been removed. It would have been too hazardous.

The army was not halted by the President's command. It left Centreville and Bull Run to take position on the south bank of the Rappahannock; and had reached that line before the President knew that it had moved. The position had been prepared by field-works near the railroad-bridge, and a depot of provision. The Chief Commissary was informed early in the winter that, when the army left its present position, its next would be behind the Rappahannock. When the orders to remove public property were given on the 22d of February, the principal staff-officers were informed that the new position of the army would be the south bank of the Rappahannock. The right wing, ordered to Fredericksburg, had taken its position before the main body moved. The President certainly did not stop it.

Colonel A. H. Cole, of the Quartermaster's De-

partment, wrote to me on the 30th of March, 1872:
"In reply to your questions in relation to the withdrawal of the army from Centreville and Bull Run
in March, 1862, I will state that, when you ordered
the removal of the military stores from Manassas,
February 22d, your principal staff-officers were informed that the position of the army would be on
the south side of the Rappahannock, near the railroad-bridge. I accompanied you from Manassas to
this position, and in such official and personal relations to you as to give me full knowledge of your
correspondence, and I am sure that you received no
dispatches from Richmond on the way. You could
have received no telegram, for there was no telegraph-office on our route."

We reached the Rappahannock before noon of
the 11th, and the troops bivouacked immediately.
A telegraph-office was established afterward in a
house near the bridge.[1]

If "imperative instructions" to halt ever came
to me from Richmond, it must have been when the
army was established in its new position; so that
they had no effect, and therefore made no impression
on my memory. The representatives of Northern
Virginia, in Congress, were greatly excited by the
withdrawal of the army from Centreville, and saw
the President on the subject. This may have drawn
from him an order to me to halt—after the fact.

3. The allegations of this paragraph are completely refuted by the narrative, from page 113 to
page 116, the first part of my official report presented

---

[1] The railroad-bridge.

to the Executive, May 19th, and the testimony of Generals Wigfall and Longstreet.

In the report I said: "Before taking command on the Peninsula, I had the honor to express to the President my opinion of the defects of the position then occupied by our troops."

After taking command, I reported that the opinion previously expressed was fully confirmed.

Some of my objections were: that its length was too great for our force; that it [1] prevented offensive movements, except at great disadvantage; and that it would be untenable after the guns of Yorktown should be silenced—a result admitted to be inevitable by all our officers, from the enemy's great superiority in artillery. York River being thus opened, a large fleet of transports and several hundred batteaux [2] would enable him to turn us in a few hours.

General Longstreet wrote to me, March 21, 1867: "I cannot remember, at this late day, the particular reasons that were given for and against the move of the army to Yorktown in 1862, in our council held in Richmond while the move was going on. Mr. Davis, Mr. Benjamin, [3] and General Lee, seemed to favor the move to Yorktown—you to oppose it, and I think, General G. W. Smith.

"The effort to represent you as favoring the move of the army to Yorktown is untrue and unjust, if such an effort is being made."

General Wigfall wrote to me on the 29th of March, 1873: "I know, from conversations at the

---

[1] Being covered by inundations.   [2] Spies reported five hundred.
[3] General Randolph, who had lately succeeded Mr. Benjamin in the War-Office.

time with Mr. Davis, that you *did* propose to him the concentration of all available forces at Richmond, for the purpose of giving battle to McClellan there, instead of concentrating and fighting at Yorktown. These conversations occurred immediately after I learned from you that your plan had been rejected, and when the matter was fresh in my memory. And I found the President fully possessed of your views as previously explained by you to me. I can not give you the precise date. It was the last time I saw you before the battle of Williamsburg, when you were in Richmond on your way from the Rapidan to take command at Yorktown."

These three papers prove that I earnestly maintained opinions precisely opposite to those ascribed to me in the "message."

The movement from Yorktown was not made "suddenly." The President was informed of the determination to make it on the 27th of April. It was begun about midnight of May 3d and 4th. The time of traveling from Richmond was not more than ten hours. So that there was ample time to forbid the measure if it had been disapproved.

No supplies were lost, except some hospital stores left on the wharf at Yorktown by the negligence of a surgeon, who was arrested for the offense, and some intrenching-tools.[1]

In a memorandum on the subject, Colonel R. G. Cole stated: "To sum up, then, the amount of loss sustained by the department, from the withdrawal from Yorktown by the army, I regard as so inconsid-

[1] A manuscript narrative by General Early is my authority.

erable in comparison with the number of troops as to justify me in stating that it was nothing.

We refused no "gage of battle," but were ready to repel the enemy's attack each day of the sixteen during which we confronted him near Yorktown; and fought him successfully at Williamsburg, and drove him out of our way at Barhamsville.

As to disparity of numbers, it was a hundred and thirty-three thousand [1] to fifty thousand; far greater than existed when General Lee took command of that army on the first of June, or than that against us in Mississippi in December, 1862, or in Middle Tennessee in 1863. Yet General Lee was justly sustained by the Administration and people for postponing his attack upon McClellan four weeks, that he might make it with a force adequate to win; and Lieutenant-General Pemberton's course was approved when he refused Grant's "gage of battle," and retired from the Tallahatchie; and General Bragg's when he refused Rosecrans's "gage of battle" in the valley of Duck River, and retreated rapidly across the Cumberland Mountains and Tennessee River.

After the battle of Williamsburg the Federal army did not approach us; although our march thence to the Baltimore cross-roads, thirty-seven miles, occupied five days and we remained there five more. We waited for the enemy in that position because it was a good one—the first we had found not liable to be turned by water, while it was accessible by railroad from Richmond. We halted there

[1] Report of Adjutant-General of the United States Army to committee on conduct of the war.

not only without the President's orders, but without his knowledge. The line of the Chickahominy was not taken, nor would the President's order have compelled me to take it; for, by offering our right flank to the enemy, it would have put us at his mercy.

We did not "fall back to Richmond" because McClellan "came up," but took that position in expectation of his transferring[1] his base to James River. We crossed the Chickahominy on the 15th— he not until the 22d.

I did not add to the fortifications of Richmond, because they were sufficient—planned and constructed by the ablest engineer in the Confederacy, Colonel Andrew Tallcott.

4. McClellan placed not a division, but two corps of his army, "on our side of the Chickahominy." We attacked them, and were successful until night interrupted the action. That the combat was successful is evidence that the dispositions for it were not *very* faulty. "Tangible results" were not secured, because the action was not continued[2] next day, as it would have been, but for my desperate wound. In Alfriend's[3] "Life of Jefferson Davis," there is an elaborate attempt to show that Mr. Davis took an active part in the battle. If so, it could have been in no secondary one, but only as commander. This would make him responsible for the want of results.

General Lee had not acquired the confidence of the army and people, then. His great fame was acquired subsequently, at the head of that army. Mr. Davis can claim no merit for the selection, for Gen-

[1] *See* pages 127, 128.   [2] *See* page 138.   [3] *See* page 408.

eral Lee was the only *general* available; and was then, as he had been previously, in a position inadequate to his rank.

5. When the President assigned me to the command of Generals Bragg, Pemberton, and Kirby Smith, he fixed my headquarters in Tennessee. Before the end of December I transferred them to Mississippi. On the 23d of January he ordered me to Tennessee on special service. When I was returning to Mississippi after having performed it, he ordered[1] me to return to Tullahoma and take personal command of General Bragg's army. This made it officially impossible for me to return to Jackson; so that all my absence from Mississippi, in 1863, was compelled by the President. I went to Mississippi in May "only in consequence of a positive order," because I had been deprived by the President of the power to go without one. On arriving at Jackson, I took the promptest[2] measure to unite the troops in Jackson with those immediately under General Pemberton. The measure was defeated[3] by disobedience of my orders. The troops in Jackson rendered the only service possible, by delaying the approach of the Federal forces long enough to enable Major Mims, chief quartermaster of the department, to save such public property as he had the means of removing. To attempt to strike a blow upon at least two corps,[4] with two brigades, would have been gross folly.

We were not inactive[5] during the siege of Vicksburg, nor were my forces adequate to cut through Grant's lines. General Pemberton, as much inter-

[1] *See* page 163.   [2] *See* page 176.   [3] *See* page 181.
[4] General Grant's report.   [5] *See* pages 191–203.

ested as any one could be in bold measures for the
relief of Vicksburg, thought forty thousand men a
minimum for the attempt.   Governor Pettus, Hon-
orables A. G. Brown, D. F. Kenner, E. Barksdale,
and W. P. Harris,[1] thought thirty thousand more
troops necessary, they being on the spot.   For the
causes of Confederate disasters in Mississippi, the
reader is referred to pages 204–211.

The assertions concerning the little siege of Jackson are contradicted by the very correspondence[2] referred to, and in pages 207 and 208.   On the first
day, July 9th, I telegraphed to Mr. Davis that I
should endeavor to hold the place.   On the 11th:
"It" (the intrenched line) "is very defective; cannot
stand a siege, but improves a bad position against
assault."   On the 13th: "The enemy's rifles (cannon)
reached all parts of the town, showing the weakness
of the position, and its untenableness against a powerful artillery. . . . If the position and works were
not bad, want of stores, which could not be collected,
would make it impossible to stand a siege."   These
were my only dispatches to the President on the
subject.

Stores were not lost, for we had none in Jackson.
We were supplied by the railroad from the East, and
our depot was at its terminus east of Pearl River, so
that its contents were easily saved.   The soldiers
were not dispirited by finding that their lives and
blood were valued; but their confidence in the Government, as well as that of the people of the State,

---

[1] *See* their dispatch, pages 212, 213.
[2] *See* it as published by Confederate Congress, and in **Appendix,**
pages

was weakened by the disasters at Baker's Creek and the Big Black, the loss of Vicksburg, and capture of its brave garrison.

These disasters were caused by the hesitation of the Government to reënforce the Army of the Mississippi. About eighteen thousand men were sent to it from Beauregard's and Bragg's departments between the 12th and the end of May. This could have been done as easily between the middle of April, when General Grant's plan became distinctly known, and the 1st of May, when he crossed the Mississippi. With such an addition to his strength, General Pemberton would certainly have enabled Bowen to meet McClernand's corps, near Bruinsburg, with a superior force, and probably decide the campaign by defeating it.

The only proper measures in my power were taken to rebuild the railroad and bridge at Jackson, after their destruction by the Federal army in July. As many laborers, wagons, and teams, as the engineers of the railroad companies required, were impressed for their use. It was with such assistance that one company repaired its road and the other was repairing its bridge, after their destruction in May by General Grant's orders. As that course was not disapproved in the first case, it was reasonable to follow it in the second; especially as we had not seen Confederate troops employed on such work.

The rolling-stock of the Mississippi Central Railroad Company, referred to, was destroyed partly in Grenada by a Federal raiding-party, and partly at different places near the railroad, by a brigade of Confederate cavalry sent to protect it; but enough for the business of the road escaped. This was not a military loss, however, and was not felt by the transportation department. If the railroad-bridge had not been burnt or had been repaired in a few days, it is very unlikely that the engines and cars of the Mississippi Central Railroad would have been taken from it for use in the East; for there was a gap in each of the two railroad routes through Alabama, as difficult to pass as that I am censured for not having closed. A strong proof of this is the fact that the unused cars and engines of the Mobile & Ohio Railroad, in far greater numbers than the Mississippi Central ever had, lay in the company's places of deposit from the time in question until the end of the war. If such means of transportation had been required in the East by the Government, these would have been taken in preference to those more distant, in Mississippi.

6. I may reasonably claim that the earnest, repeated, and urgent appeals of many of the best and foremost men of the country, furnish respectable evidence for me against the President's very unfavorable judgment. I was notified of arrangements *to be* made, not *made*, and not *immediately*, but about the middle of March,[1] when they should have been completed. The troops referred to were to be sent to Dalton when all preparations for a long march should be concluded. This made it almost certain that we should be attacked at Dalton[2] and probably forced back before the arrival of these reënforce-

---

[1] *See* correspondence, pages 287–300.

[2] It is admitted in the "message" that this occurred: "While the correspondence was going on, Sherman commenced his movement."

ments, and the "plan of campaign" defeated before being begun. That was my first objection to it.[1] I did propose what seemed to me a better one—to assemble at once all the troops promised, that we might defeat the enemy when he should attack us, that attack being inevitable, and then assume the offensive. Instead of sixty or seventy thousand men, I had forty thousand four hundred and sixty four infantry and artillery and two thousand three hundred and ninety-two cavalry fit for service, subject to my orders at the opening of the campaign. This is shown by the only authentic statement on the subject—the return sent to the Confederate War-Office, prepared by Major Kinloch Falconer of the Adjutant-General's Department, from the reports of Lieutenant-Generals Hardee and Hood, and Major-General Wheeler. General Sherman states in his report that he commenced the campaign with above ninety-eight thousand men. But, as three of his four divisions[2] of cavalry, probably not less than twelve thousand men, are not included in his estimate, it is not impossible that some infantry may have been omitted also. The Army of Tennessee was certainly numerically inferior to that of Northern Virginia, and General Bragg asserted[3] that Sherman's was superior in fighting force to Grant's. But if the disparity of force was greater in General Lee's case than in mine, I submit to the Southern people that to condemn me alone of all those who served them in the field, for

[1] For others, *see* pages 297, 298.

[2] Stoneman's, McCooks, and Garrard's. The other, Kilpatrick's, exceeded five thousand; it had been with the army since the previous year.

[3] *See* page 364.

not coming up to their highest standard, is a harsh judgment. If the troops [1] enumerated by General Bragg had reënforced the army at Dalton, the President might have had a right to hope for such a victory as would have opened the way for us into Middle Tennessee. But as the case actually was—odds of almost three to one against that army—he had no reason to entertain such a hope. If the writer was informed of opportunities "refused" by me, he should have named them. As he has not done so, I have a right to claim that he knew of none. If the Federal general gave us favorable opportunities to attack him, they were discovered by no one in our army. We neither occupied nor saw positions almost impregnable. None such are to be found between Dalton and Atlanta. Wherever the two armies confronted each other, the ground occupied by one was as favorable for defense as that held by the other. Both armies depended on intrenchments; not on the natural strength of their positions. General Sherman never extended his flanks in the manner described. As we were able to hold our intrenchments against his greatly superior forces, it was evident that we could not attack those forces in fieldworks equally strong, with reasonable chances of success. We were compelled to abandon Dalton, not by the extension of a flank, but by the march of the Federal army itself toward Resaca—that march being completely covered by the mountain, Rocky-Face. And at Resaca, after intrenching his army so strongly as to make it secure from assault, General Sherman availed himself of the course of the Ooste-

[1] *See* page 293.

naula, almost parallel to our railroad, to extend his line, protected by it, to the neighborhood of Calhoun, which compelled us to pass to the rear of that point, to avoid being cut off from Atlanta. At New-Hope Church, where the armies were parallel to each other almost two weeks, General Sherman gradually extended his intrenchments toward the railroad. When he reached it, we established ourselves in front of Marietta, and held that ground about four weeks until the Federal numbers enabled General Sherman to extend his works parallel to our railroad, and five or six miles beyond our left. This made it necessary to draw back again; to place ourselves nearer than the enemy to Atlanta. In all this, I was sustained by General Lee's similar course in Virginia. The difference between the two campaigns was but that of the characters of the two Federal commanders—General Grant attacked repeatedly, with all his strength, and suffered great losses in battles, but reached his destination in about a month. General Sherman, who was cool and cautious, made one general and several partial attacks— the latter to be followed up if successful—but drew off his forces in each case, when he found his opponents ready and resolute. He sought for weak points in our lines daily, and with that object skirmished incessantly. Those engagements, as he expresses it, occasionally swelling to the dimensions of battles. My part of this campaign continued seventy-four days; the Federal army being two days from Atlanta when I was removed from my command. In comparing the operations in Upper Georgia with those in Virginia, it is to be considered that

Sherman's condition became more hazardous as he approached Atlanta, and that of the Confederate army absolutely safe, when it reached the place, in which, as I have already said,[1] it could neither be assailed nor invested. General Grant, on the contrary, found a secure base on James River. The assertion that the Army of Tennessee lost twenty-five thousand men while under my command is an enormous exaggeration. The only authentic statement of that loss is in the reports of Surgeon A. J. Foard, medical director. According to them,[2] it was nine thousand nine hundred and seventy-two killed and wounded. We had good reason to think the enemy's loss six times as great. It is a calumny to say that the Army of Tennessee was dispirited or broken down. It had never before been in finer condition—the men in a high state of discipline, and full of confidence from uniform success in their engagements with the enemy, and the horses of the cavalry and artillery, and the mules of the trains, in fine order for service—much better than when the campaign was begun. As for fatigue, they but once made more than a half-day's march in one day,[3] and never two half-days' marches in two consecutive days. I was never questioned as to my ability to hold Atlanta. General Bragg, who undoubtedly visited the

[1] Page 358.
[2] Less than a sixth of the number were killed. At Dalton, and thence to the Etowah, four hundred and forty-four were killed, and two thousand eight hundred and twenty-eight wounded. Near New-Hope Church three hundred and nine were killed and one thousand nine hundred and twenty-nine wounded. Thence, to the Chattahoochee, five hundred and thirty-five were killed, and three thousand nine hundred and thirty-five wounded. Cavalry are not included.
[3] From Allatoona to New-Hope Church.

army in that connection, saw the most efficient preparations to hold it in progress—the industrious
strengthening by me of the intrenchments made by
General Gilmer's wise foresight, and the mounting
of heavy rifle-cannon, just brought from Mobile, on
the front toward the enemy.

As to the almost impregnable character of the
available positions; General Hardee wrote in his letter of April 10, 1868, already quoted: "The country
between Dalton and Atlanta is, for the most part,
open, intersected by numerous practicable roads, and
readily penetrable. In some portions it is rugged
and broken, but the ridges and ranges of hills, where
they occur, are neither continuous nor regular enough
to afford material advantage for defense. It offers
no advantage to one side not shared by the other.
There are no strongholds in that section, and no positions effectual for defense against largely superior
numbers." For the manner in which the progress
of the enemy was resisted, the dispirited condition
of the army, and its want of confidence in me, the
reader is referred to General Hardee's testimony in
the letter on pages 365, 366, and General Stewart's
in that on pages 367–369.

Mr. Davis's official course toward me, from the
commencement of the war to the 17th of July, 1864,
strongly contradicts all his statements in the "message." If he had believed, when McDowell was near
Manassas, that I had been exhibiting at Harper's
Ferry, and elsewhere in the Valley, the singular incapacity for war he describes in the first part of this
paper, he could not have ordered me to Manassas to
command in a battle the result of which was to de-

cide the fate of the Confederacy, for the time, at least. If, from the time of that action until the Army of Northern Virginia was ordered to York-town, my conduct had more than confirmed previous bad impressions, it is impossible that the President could have so forgotten his obligations to the country as to leave me in the most important military com-mand of the Confederacy. Still more so, that he could have greatly enlarged that command by add-ing two armies to it, and this when General Lee, whom he regarded (though illegally) as my senior, was in a mere staff-office in Richmond. And if in the fall of 1862 he had thought of my conduct at York-town, and in the battle of Seven Pines, as he wrote of it in 1865, his oath of office would not have per-mitted him to place me in command of the most im-portant department of the Confederacy. And, al-though he terminated this message with an assur-ance to the Confederate Congress that nothing would induce him to assign me to an adequate command, the paper was not sent to Congress, and I was ordered to report to General Lee (who had just been appointed commander-in-chief), and assigned to the command of the second department of the Confeder-acy in importance.

In war, the testimony of an enemy in one's fa-vor is certainly worth more than that of a friend, as he who receives a blow can better estimate the dexterity of the striker than any spectator. I there-fore offer that of one of the most prominent officers of the United States Army, who was conspicuous in this campaign, in the following letter:

"New York City, *October* 21, 1873.

"General M. Lovell:

"My dear General: Your letter of the 15th inst., requesting my professional opinion concerning the conduct of the retreat of the Confederate army in 1864, while commanded by General Joseph E. Johnston, and also of the impression produced in the Union army on being informed of the removal of that officer from his position, was received. I have no possible objection to communicating to you my views on this subject, briefly, of course (as I have not my notes and maps of the campaign near me to refer to), and, besides, I wish it to be understood, in advance, that my opinions on this subject are expressed in no ostentatious manner, but merely to comply with your request, and to do justice, as far as lies in my power, to a brother officer toward whom I have always felt the highest admiration for his superior military accomplishments.

"I was familiar with his services in the Seminole War, and also in our war with Mexico.

"During the campaign to which you refer, I served in the army opposed to him, in command of a corps, on which, as you intimate, much of the heavy work of the campaign devolved—I mean the retreat of the Confederate army from Buzzard's Roost Pass to near Atlanta, Ga., embracing the period from May 6th to July 27th. At the former point Johnston found himself too weak to cope with our army with any prospect of success, and it became his problem to weaken the Union army by drawing it from its base of operations and seeking opportunities in the mean time to attack and destroy it whenever occasions presented themselves to do so advantageously. Our vast superiority in numbers enabled us to divide our army, and turn all his positions without risk from any quarter.

"General Johnston, however, as he abandoned his intrenched positions, conducted his retreat, in my judgment, in a prudent and consummate manner, both in strategy and tactics. All the positions chosen for making a stand were selected with the utmost sagacity and skill, and his defenses were thrown up and strengthened with the exercise of marvelous ingenuity and judgment. This was the case near Dalton, Resaca, Cassville, New-Hope Church, Kenesaw Mountain, Peach-Tree Creek, and other points which I do not now remember. Considering that Johnston's army was on the retreat, I think it remarkable that we found no deserters, no stragglers, no muskets or knapsacks, and no material of war. Johnston's troops also covered and protected the citizens living in the vast district in which we were operating, in carrying off all their property from before us. In fact, it was the cleanest and best-conducted retreat, as was remarked by every one, that we had seen or read of. Wherever we went we encountered a formidable line of battle which all commanders were inclined to respect; I know that this was my feeling, and other officers in command of armies and corps appeared to feel as I did. Indeed, this retreat was so masterly that I regard it as a useful lesson for study for all persons who may hereafter elect for their calling the profession of arms. After having given the subject a good deal of reflection, I unhesitatingly state as my conviction that this retreat was the most prominent feature of the war, and, in my judgment, reflects the highest credit upon its author. The news that General Johnston had been removed from the command of the army opposed to us was received by our officers with universal rejoicing.

".... One of the prominent historians of the Confederacy ascribes the misfortunes of the 'Lost Cause' to the relief of General Johnston; I do not think this, but it certainly contributed materially to hasten its collapse.

"Very respectfully, your obedient servant,

"J. HOOKER,[1] *Major-General.*"

In the Adjutant-General's office in Richmond, in December, 1864, on referring to my report of the campaign of the previous summer in Upper Georgia, I found and read an indorsement on it by the President, to the effect that my narrative differed essentially from statements that he had seen, "contemporaneous" with the events described

I immediately wrote him the following note, through the Adjutant-General, which that officer promised to put into his hands next morning. He also promised to obtain a reply as soon as possible.

"RICHMOND, *December* 21, 1864.

"GENERAL: In referring to my report of October 20th, in your office, I saw and read the President's indorsement upon it.

"I respectfully ask his Excellency to permit the substance, at least, of the communications referred

---

[1] I find this letter in a late circular of the Messrs. Appleton, of New York, announcing the publication, at an early day, of this book.

to by him, to be furnished to me, as well as the names of their authors. My object is to meet, as fully as possible, whatever in those letters differs from the statements in my report.

"I regret the want of fullness in the report, but am gratified to find that the President understands the cause of it.

"Most respectfully, your obedient servant,

"J. E. JOHNSTON, *General.*

"General S. COOPER, *A. & I. General.*"

No reply to this note was ever received, so that I now have no more knowledge of the statements in question than that gained by reading the President's indorsement.

APPENDIX

APPENDIX.

[CONFIDENTIAL.]

HEADQUARTERS ARMY OF THE POTOMAC, }
July 20, 1861. }

SPECIAL ORDER, No. —

THE following order is published for the information of division and brigade commanders :

1st. Brigadier - General Ewell's brigade will march *via* Union Mills Ford, and place itself in position of attack upon the enemy. It will be held in readiness, either to support attack upon Centreville, or to move in the direction of Sangster's Cross-roads, according to circumstances.

The order to advance will be given by the commander-in-chief.

2d. Brigadier-General Jones's brigade, supported by Colonel Early's brigade, will march *via* McLean's Ford to place itself in position of attack on the enemy, or about the Union Mill and Centreville road. It will be held in readiness, either to support the attack on Centreville, or to move in the direction of Fairfax Station, according to circumstances, with its right flank toward the left of Ewell's command, more or less distant according to the nature of the country and attack.

The order to advance will be given by the commander-in-chief.

3d. Brigadier-General Longstreet's brigade, supported by Brigadier-General Jackson's brigade, will march *via* Mc-Lean's Ford, to place itself in position of attack upon the enemy on or about the Union Mill and Centreville road. It will be held in readiness, either to support the attack on

Centreville, or to move in the direction of Fairfax Court-House, according to circumstances, with its right flank toward the left of Jones's command, more or less distant according to the nature of the country.

The order to advance will be given by the commander-in-chief.

4th. Brigadier-General Bonham's brigade, supported by Colonel Barton's brigade, will march *via* Mitchell's Ford to the attack of Centreville, the right wing to the left of the Third Division, more or less distant according to the nature of the country and of the attack.

The order to advance will be given by the commander-in-chief.

5th. Colonel Cocke's brigade, supported by Colonel Elzey's brigade, will march *via* Stone Bridge and the fords on the right, thence to the attack of Centreville, the right wing to the left of the Fourth Division, more or less distant according to the nature of the country and of the attack.

The order to advance will be given by the commander-in-chief.

6th. Brigadier-General Bee's brigade, supported by Colonel Wilcox's brigade, Colonel Stuart's regiment of cavalry, and the whole of Walton's battery, will form the reserve, and will march *via* Mitchell's Ford, to be used according to circumstances.

7th. The light batteries will be distributed as follows:

(1.) To General Ewell's command; Captain Walker's, six pieces.

(2.) To Brigadier-General Jones; Captains Alburtis's and Stannard's batteries, eight pieces.

(3.) To Brigadier-General Longstreet's; Colonel Pendleton's and Captain Imboden's batteries, eight pieces.

(4.) To Brigadier-General Bonham's; Captains Kemper's and Shields's batteries, eight pieces.

(5.) To Colonels Cocke and Hunton; Captains Latham's and Beckham's batteries, twelve pieces.

8th. Colonel Radford, commanding cavalry, will detail to report immediately as follows:

To General Ewell, two companies of cavalry.

To General Jones, two companies of cavalry.

To General Longstreet, two companies of cavalry.

To General Bonham, two companies of cavalry.

To Colonel Cocke the remaining companies of cavalry, except those on special service.

9th. The Fourth and Fifth Divisions, after the fall of Centreville, will advance to the attack of Fairfax Court-House *via* the Braddock and Turnpike roads, to the north of the latter.

The First, Second, and Third Divisions will, if necessary, support the Fourth and Fifth Divisions.

10th. In this movement the First, Second, and Third Divisions will form the command of General Holmes, the Fourth and Fifth Divisions that of the second in command. The reserve will move upon the plains between Mitchell's Ford and Stone Bridge, and together with the Fourth and Fifth Divisions will be under the immediate direction of General Beauregard.

By command of General Beauregard:

(Signed) THOMAS JORDAN,
Assistant Adjutant-General.

SPECIAL ORDER, No. — }
HEADQUARTERS ARMY OF THE POTOMAC. }

The plan of attack given by Brigadier-General Beauregard in the above order is approved, and will be executed accordingly.

(Signed) J. E. JOHNSTON, *General C. S. A.*

EDGEFIELD, *January* 14, 1874.

MY DEAR GENERAL: Your letter of the 15th of April, 1870, as to first Manassas, has been too long unanswered, but circumstances, not necessary here to mention, have caused the delay.

You are substantially correct as to what occurred after five o'clock of the 21st. In obedience to your orders, as delivered by Colonel Lay, with my own brigade and Longstreet's, I moved directly on Centreville, as the best and most practicable route for intercepting the enemy's retreat. Guided by the dust, the enemy fired a shot in the direction of our advance. I sent forward Colonel Lay with an escort of cavalry to reconnoitre. I am not sure whether Major Whiting of your staff, then with me, accompanied Colonel Lay—he probably did. The enemy opened fire with artillery on this party; they reported, on their return, that the enemy were in force in line of battle on the heights of Centreville. In the course of the conference which followed, and upon the state of facts then presented, Major Whiting said, in substance, that as a member of your staff he would suggest—possibly that he would direct—the further pursuit stopped. The views of Major Whiting thus expressed had, justly, great weight with, and possibly ought to have controlled, me; but all the circumstances led me to the same conclusion. I did stop, and deployed the two brigades on the right and left of the road; and Major Whiting went to the junction to report, and sent me from there further instructions for the night.

I made a report after the battle, but did not write the details of Major Whiting's connection with the matter.

General McGowan, of Abbeville, and Judge Aldrich, of Barnwell, then on my staff, remember this matter substantially as stated; and probably others of my staff.

Yours very truly,
M. L. BONHAM.

General J. E. JOHNSTON.

General McDowell's orders for the 21st of July were as follows:

HEADQUARTERS DEPARTMENT ARMY OF EASTERN VIRGINIA,
CENTREVILLE, July 20, 1861.

The enemy has planted a battery on the Warrenton turnpike to defend the passage of Bull Run; has seized the Stone Bridge and made a heavy abattis on the right bank, to oppose our advance in that direction. The ford above the bridge is also guarded, whether with artillery or not is not positively known, but every indication favors the belief that he proposes to defend the passage of the stream. It is intended to turn the position, force the enemy from the road, that it may be reopened, and, if possible, destroy the railroad leading from Manassas to the Valley of Virginia, where the enemy has a large force. As this may be resisted by all the force of the enemy, the troops will be disposed as follows : The First Division (General Tyler), with the exception of Richardson's brigade, will, at half-past two o'clock in the morning precisely, be at the Warrenton turnpike to threaten the passage of the bridge, but will not open fire until full daybreak. The Second Division (Hunter's) will move from its camp at two o'clock in the morning precisely, and, led by Captain Woodbury of the Engineers, will, after passing Cub Run, turn to the right, and pass the Bull Run stream above the ford at Sudley's Spring, and, then turning down to the left, descend the stream and clear away the enemy who may be guarding the lower ford and bridge. It will then bear off to the right, and make room for the succeeding division. The Third Division (Heintzelman's) will march at half-past two in the morning, and will follow the road taken by the Second Division, but will cross at the lower ford, after it has been turned as above ; and then, going to the left, take place between the stream and Second Division. The Fifth Division (Miles's) will take position on the Centreville Heights (Richardson's brigade will for the time form part of the Fifth Division, and will continue in its present position). One brigade will be in the village, and one near the present station of Richardson's brigade. This division will threaten the Blackburn Ford, and remain in reserve at Centreville. The commander will open fire with artillery only, and will bear in mind that it is a demonstration only he is to make. He will cause such defensive works, abattis and earthworks, to be thrown up as will strengthen his position. Lieutenant Prime, of the Engineers, will be charged with this duty. These movements may lead to the gravest results, and commanders of divisions and brigades should bear in mind the immense consequences involved. There must be no failure, and every effort must be made to prevent straggling. No one must be allowed to leave the ranks without special authority. After completing the movements ordered, the troops must be held in order of battle, as they may be attacked at any moment.

By command of

Brigadier-General McDOWELL.

JAMES B. FRY, *Adjutant-General.*

HEADQUARTERS, CENTREVILLE, *January* 28, 1862.

General S. COOPER,

Adjutant Inspector-General.

SIR: I am informed that General Order No. 2 has been distributed to the " war regiments " of the army.

A recent order of the Secretary of War directs me to send to Richmond six thousand of the muskets belonging to our absent sick. This deprives the different regiments of the means of arming their men who return from the hospital even, and of course there are no arms for recruits. I shall not, under such circumstances, permit the expense of recruiting to be incurred, without additional orders.

Very respectfully,

Your obedient servant,

J. E. JOHNSTON, *General.*

HEADQUARTERS, CENTREVILLE, *January* 28, 1862.

Major-General JACKSON,

Commanding Valley District, Winchester.

GENERAL: I have to-day received your letters of 21st and 24th.

I regret to be unable to reënforce you. May not your own cavalry—Colonel Ashby's regiment—be concentrated and used for the purpose for which you apply to me for cavalry ? I am an enemy to much distribution of troops. May not yours be brought together—so posted, that is to say, that you may be able to assemble them all to oppose an enemy coming from Harper's Ferry, Williamsport, or the northwest?

Should the report given by General Hill prove to be correct, it would be imprudent, it seems to me, to keep your troops dispersed as they now are. Do you not think so ? The enemy might not only prevent yours concentrating, but interpose himself between us, which we must never permit.   Most respectfully,

Your obedient servant,

J. E. JOHNSTON, <i>General.</i></div>

HEADQUARTERS DEPARTMENT OF NORTHERN VIRGINIA,
CENTREVILLE, January 29, 1862.

Colonel S. BASSETT FRENCH,
Aide-de-camp of Governor of Virginia.

SIR : Your letter of the 25th inst., in relation to arms, the property of the Commonwealth of Virginia, not in the hands of the troops of this army, and desiring me to take measures for their return to the State authorities so far as they can be found within this Department of the Army of the Confederate States, has been duly received.

I am sorry that I can afford little information and less aid in relation to the important and interesting object of your communication.

The troops under my command have generally come into my department with arms in their hands. I had and have no means of ascertaining by whom the arms were furnished. I understand that Virginia does not wish to reclaim arms now in actual use. As arms have become disposable by the deaths or discharges of soldiers, they have been withdrawn from my control under orders of the War Department of the Confederate States. These orders have been repeatedly issued by the Department and executed by me. Of late they have gone to the length of taking the arms of the sick. When removed from the army, the arms, of course, passed under the direct control of the Department of War.   To that Department I must refer you for the information which you seek of me.

There are no flint-lock muskets in the hands of my soldiers, nor have there been any since I assumed the command here.   There were five hundred such in the depot at Manassas when I arrived here from the Valley.   They were soon afterward sent to Richmond, in accordance with the general practice in such matters above specified.

Do me the favor to express to the Governor my grateful acknowledgments of his kind and patriotic message.   Nothing earthly could afford me higher gratification than the fulfillment of his good wishes by the army striking a great blow for the freedom and independence of Virginia and the South.   Most respectfully,

Your obedient servant,

J. E. JOHNSTON, *General.*

Colonel S. BASSETT FRENCH,
    Aide-de-camp to the Governor of Virginia.

CENTREVILLE, *January* 29, 1862.

Hon. J. P. BENJAMIN, Secretary of War.

SIR : I have just had the honor to receive your letter of the 26th inst., inclosed with one to General Beauregard, assigning him to command at Columbus, Ky.

General Beauregard will be relieved from his present command to-morrow.

I regret very much that it is thought necessary to remove this distinguished officer from this district, especially at the present time, when the recent law granting bounty and furloughs is having a disorganizing effect.   I fear that General Beauregard's removal from the troops he has formed may increase this effect among them.

In this connection, permit me to urge the necessity to this army, of the general officers I have asked for more than once.   Most respectfully,

Your obedient servant,

J. E. JOHNSTON, *General.*

CENTREVILLE, *February* 2, 1862.

General S. COOPER,
          Adjutant and Inspector-General.

SIR: We are beginning to feel the want of the arms recently sent to Richmond under orders from the War Department. One regiment already has twenty-three men returned from hospital, who are without arms. The recruiting directed in General Order No. 2 will give us men who cannot be armed, unless a part at least of the arms referred to can be returned.

Permit me again to remind the War Department that a division and five brigades are without their proper generals. The great number of colonels and other field-officers who are absent sick, makes the want of general officers the more felt.

Several of the colonels of this army are well qualified to be brigadier-generals. Besides Colonels A. P. Hill and Forney, Colonels Hampton, Winder, Garland, and Mott, are fully competent to command brigades.

Most respectfully,
          Your obedient servant,
                    J. E. JOHNSTON, *General.*

HEADQUARTERS DEPARTMENT OF NORTHERN VIRGINIA, }
          January 30, 1862.   }

General S. COOPER,
          Adjutant and Inspector-General.

SIR: The execution of War Department General Order No. 1 will greatly reduce the strength of the "one year" regiments of this army. They constitute about two-thirds of the whole number. I respectfully suggest that men to fill those regiments, say twenty or thirty per company, be sent to us as soon as possible.

The Secretary of War proposed to send unarmed regiments to supply the places of the men furloughed. Such regiments would be of little value for some time, but the men composing them, if distributed among our present troops and mixed with them in companies, would be valuable at once, and soon equal to the old soldiers.

Very respectfully,
Your obedient servant,
J. E. JOHNSTON, <i>General.</i></div>

HEADQUARTERS DEPARTMENT OF NORTHERN VIRGINIA,
CENTREVILLE, <i>February</i> 7, 1862.</div>

To the Hon. J. P. BENJAMIN, Secretary of War.

SIR: I had the honor to receive your letter of the 3d instant by the last mail.

On the 2d instant, I sent Lieutenant-Colonel Harrison, Virginia cavalry, with a proposition to Major-General McClellan for an exchange of prisoners of war. That officer was stopped by the enemy's pickets near Falls Church, and his dispatches carried to Brigadier-General Wadsworth at Arlington. That officer informed Lieutenant-Colonel Harrison that they were promptly forwarded to General McClellan. He waited for the answer until yesterday, when, being informed by Brigadier-General Wadsworth that he could form no opinion as to the time when it might be expected, he returned.

On receiving your letter in reply to mine, in relation to reënlistments, I directed your orders on that subject to be carried into immediate effect; furloughs to be given at the rate of twenty per cent. of the men present for duty.

The order directing recruiting for the war regiments is also in course of execution.

In my opinion, the position of the "Valley Army" ought, if possible, to enable it to coöperate with that of the Potomac, but it must also depend upon that of the enemy and his strength. General Jackson occupied Romney strongly, because the enemy was reported to be concentrating his troops, including those supposed to be near Harper's Ferry, at New Creek. I regret very much that you did not refer this matter to me before ordering General Loring to Winchester, instead of now. I think that orders from me, now conflicting with those you have given, would have an unfortunate effect—that of making the impression that our views do not coincide, and that each of us is pursuing his own plan. This might especially be expected among General Loring's troops, if they are, as represented to me, in a state of discontent little removed from insubordination.

Troops stationed at Moorefield could not well coöperate with those in the northern part of the Valley, as the President remarks.

Let me suggest that, having broken up the dispositions of the military commander, you give whatever other orders may be necessary.

Most respectfully,
Your obedient servant,
J. E. JOHNSTON, *General.*

CENTREVILLE, *February* 9, 1862.

General S. COOPER,
Adjutant and Inspector-General.

SIR: I am informed that a law recently passed authorizes the President to organize a provisional corps of engineers.

Officers and soldiers of that branch of the service are greatly needed by us. If one or two competent engineers, with eight or ten subalterns of those appointed under this law, could be sent to this district soon, their services would be of great value. They should have sappers and pontoniers as soon as practicable. Such an organization would add greatly to our strength, and, in the event of marches, would be essential.

We should have a much larger cavalry force. The greatest objection, or rather difficulty, in increasing it, is said to be the want of proper arms. This can be easily removed by equipping a large body of lancers. These weapons can be furnished easily and soon, and would be formidable—much more so than sabres—in the hands of new troops, especially against the enemy's numerous artillery.

The shafts should be about ten feet long, and the heads seven or eight inches. Those furnished to us are, many of them, of heavy wood, and too short, the heads too thin and unnecessarily broad. Ash is the best wood.

Most respectfully,

Your obedient servant,

J. E. Johnston, *General.*

CENTREVILLE, *February* 11, 1862.

Hon. J. P. Benjamin, Secretary of War.

Sir : On the morning of the 2d instant, I dispatched to Major-General G. B. McClellan a proposition for the general exchange of prisoners of war according to modern usage. He was informed that the proposition was made under authority derived from you.

According to some of the Northern newspapers, this letter was the subject of a cabinet council at which General McClellan assisted.

No answer has been received, and it is now reasonable to suppose that none is intended. Under such circumstances, permit me to suggest the propriety of at least suspending the unprecedented mode of exchange now practised.

Most respectfully,

Your obedient servant,

J. E. Johnston, *General.*

HEADQUARTERS DEPARTMENT OF NORTHERN VIRGINIA, }
CENTREVILLE, *February* 11, 1862. }

General S. Cooper,

Adjutant and Inspector-General.

Sir : An order from the War Department removed two artillery companies which manned four of the heavy batteries at Manassas. I cannot supply their places without taking for the purpose excellent infantry who are ignorant of artillery service. I therefore respectfully ask that two companies may be sent to Manassas to man the batteries in question without delay.   They might be sent without small-arms.

Let me again urge the importance of sending to the army the proper number of general officers.   The great number of sick field-officers makes the want of them felt the more.   Most respectfully,

Your obedient servant,

J. E. JOHNSTON, *General.*

HEADQUARTERS DEPARTMENT OF NORTHERN VIRGINIA,
CENTREVILLE, *February* 14, 1862.

To the Hon. J. P. BENJAMIN, Secretary of War.

SIR: .... In a letter dated February 12th, Major-General Jackson informed me that, since the evacuation of Romney by your orders, the United States troops have returned to it; and that the officer commanding at Moorefield reported that the enemy, three thousand strong, were approaching that place.

The reduction of our force by the operation of the furlough system, makes it impracticable to reënforce the Valley district from that of the Potomac.

Most respectfully,

Your obedient servant,

J. E. JOHNSTON, *General.*

HEADQUARTERS DEPARTMENT OF NORTHERN VIRGINIA,
CENTREVILLE, *February* 16, 1862.

To the Hon. J. P. BENJAMIN, Secretary of War.

SIR: I have the honor to acknowledge your letter of the 11th inst., in relation to Captain Rhett, and that of Captain Dyerle to you, dated February 8th, referred to me.

I think that you were mistaken in regarding General Beauregard as the commander of these troops.   I have been so considered here, and so styled by yourself.

More furloughs have already been granted than the condition of the army will justify.   I hope, therefore, that you will not require a rule published to the army to be broken in the case of Captain Rhett's company.

The army is so much weakened by loss of officers from sickness, and soldiers on furlough, that I am compelled to use every man in the way in which he can serve best. It is essential that this authority should not be taken from me. Captain Dyerle's company is serving as infantry, as it engaged to do, for a year. It would be useless as artillery.

The granting authority to raise artillery companies from our present force of infantry has interfered very much with the object of your order No. 1. Besides the persons having such authority, many others have been induced by their success to attempt to form such companies, and have thereby injured the reorganization of our infantry. The infantry which has been converted into artillery is excellent infantry, but entirely ignorant of artillery. We therefore lose decidedly by the change.

The rules of military correspondence require that letters addressed to you by members of this army should pass through my office. Let me ask, for the sake of discipline, that you have this rule enforced. It will save much time and trouble, and create the belief in the army that I am its commander; and moreover will enable you to see both sides of every case (the military and personal) at once.

I have just received information from General Whiting that the enemy's forces near Evansport have just been considerably increased, both on land and on water. And from General Jackson, that from Moorefield the enemy has a graded road to Strasburg, passing a good deal to the south of Winchester. Most respectfully,

Your obedient servant,

J. E. JOHNSTON, *General.*

HEADQUARTERS, CENTREVILLE, }
February 25, 1862. }

To his Excellency the PRESIDENT:

I respectfully inclose a copy of a report by Major-General Jackson.

Brigadier-General Whiting informs me that Brigadier-General French and Captain Chatard think it impracticable to make the desired movement by water. I submit General French's letter on the subject. The land transportation would, it seems to me, require too much time and labor, even were the roads tolerable. They are not now practicable for our field artillery with their teams of four horses.

The army is crippled, and its discipline greatly impaired, by the want of general officers. The four regiments observing the fords of the lower Occoquan are commanded by a lieutenant-colonel, and a division and five brigades besides are without generals, and at least half the field-officers are absent—generally sick.

The accumulation of subsistence stores at Manassas is now a great evil. The Commissary-General was requested, more than once, to suspend those supplies. A very extensive meat-packing establishment at Thoroughfare is also a great incumbrance. The great quantities of personal property in our camps is a still greater one. Much of both kinds of property must be sacrificed in the contemplated movement.

Most respectfully,

Your obedient servant,

J. E. Johnston, *General*.

Headquarters, Centreville, }
March 3, 1862.   }

His Excellency.

Mr. President: I respectfully submit three notes from Major-General Jackson, and one from Brigadier-General Hill, for the information they contain of the enemy.

Your orders for moving cannot be executed now, on account of the condition of the roads and streams. The removal of public property goes on with painful slowness, because, as the officers employed in it report, a sufficient number of cars and engines cannot be had. It is evident that a large quantity of it must be sacrificed, or your instructions not observed.   I shall adhere to them as closely as possible. In conversation with you, and before the cabinet, I did not exaggerate the difficulties of marching in this region.   The suffering and sickness which would be produced can hardly be exaggerated.   Most respectfully,

Your obedient servant,

J. E. JOHNSTON, *General.*

HEADQUARTERS, CENTREVILLE,
 March 5, 1862.

To His EXCELLENCY.

MR. PRESIDENT: In connection with one of the subjects of my letter of the 1st inst., I respectfully submit herewith a handbill said to be circulating in our camps.   Several such recruiting advertisements have been pointed out to me in the newspapers.   It is said that such cases are common— that many officers profess to have letters from the Honorable Secretary of War authorizing them to raise troops endowed with special privileges, which would render them useless as soldiers, should their generals be weak enough to respect such privileges.

It is easy to perceive how ruinous to the reoganization of our excellent infantry such a system must be, and how it is calculated to produce present discontent and future mutiny.

I have just directed that a citizen should be excluded from the camps who professes to have the privilege, granted by the War Department, of raising troops in this army for local service—in "the Valley."

.   .   .   .

Most respectfully,

Your obedient servant,

J. E. JOHNSTON, *General.*

[MEMORANDUM.]

In regard to supplies lost at Yorktown, it is sufficient that I should call attention to the fact that, after the Army of Northern Virginia arrived at the vicinity of Yorktown, application was made to have stopped the supplies from Richmond, except upon my requisition. Very few stores were at the post of Yorktown, and transports could not with safety reach the post. A portion of the troops drew regularly from Yorktown. Provisions for the regular supply were hauled in wagons from King's-Mill Landing on James River. A few days' supply for a division was kept upon a sloop near Mulberry Island. The reserve for the army was kept at Williamsburg, and issued to the troops as they passed. And the best evidence of no loss at this *main* depot is the fact that the last divisions were unable to get a day's rations. The small depot at Gloucester Point lost little or nothing. The meat from there came to the army at Baltimore Cross-roads. Small amount, at Jamestown Island, not removed, of little value.

To sum up, then: the amount of loss sustained by the department by the withdrawal of the army I regard as so inconsiderable in comparison with the number of troops as to justify me in stating that the loss was nothing.

(Signed)   R. G. COLE.

HEADQUARTERS, BARHAMSVILLE,
May 7, 1862.

GENERAL: The enemy has a large fleet of gunboats (seven iron-clads) and transports at West Point. He has been landing troops and artillery under his guns, but in a position in which we cannot reach him. The want of provision, and of any mode of obtaining it here—still more the dearth of forage—makes it impossible to wait to attack him while landing; the sight of the iron-clad boats makes me apprehensive for Richmond, too—so I move on in two columns, one by the New Kent road, under Major-General Smith; the other by that of the Chickahominy, under Major-General Longstreet. The battle of Williamsburg seems to have prevented the enemy from following from that direction. All the prisoners were of Heintzelman's corps, except a few of the last, who said they belong to Sumner's.

Fresh troops seemed to be arriving upon the field continually during the day. Yours, most respectfully,
(Signed)   J. E. JOHNSTON.
General LEE.

HEADQUARTERS, CROSS-ROADS, NEW KENT COURT-HOUSE,
May 10, 1862, 10.30 P. M.

GENERAL : I have written to you several times on the subject of concentrating near Richmond all the troops within reach. I have ordered Major-General Huger to evacuate Norfolk, and conduct his troops to Richmond, but have no information of his progress. "The Army of the North" must be in the Department of Northern Virginia, but, as I have been informed neither of its location, strength, nor the name of its immediate commander, I must suppose that it is not under my orders. If the President will direct the concentration of all the troops of North Carolina and Eastern Virginia, we may be able to hold Middle Virginia at least. If we permit ourselves to be driven beyond Richmond, we lose the means of maintaining this army.

The enemy is now almost exactly between us and "The Army of the North." That army should, therefore, be drawn back to secure its communication with this one.

A concentration of all our available forces may enable us to fight successfully. Let us try.
Most respectfully,
Your obedient servant,
(Signed)   J. E. JOHNSTON.
General R. E. LEE.

HEADQUARTERS, DEPARTMENT OF NORTHERN VIRGINIA,
May 19, 1862.

SIR : Before taking command in the Peninsula I had the honor to express to the President my opinion of the defects of the position then occupied by our troops there. After taking command, I reported that the opinion previously expressed was fully confirmed.

Some of my objections to the position were, that its length was too great for our force ; that it prevented offensive movements, except at great disadvantage ; and that it was untenable after the guns of Yorktown were silenced—a result admitted to be inevitable by all our officers—from the enemy's great superiority in artillery. York River being thus opened, a large fleet of transports and five or six hundred *batteaux* would enable him to turn us in a few hours.

It seemed to me that there were but two objects in remaining in the Peninsula : the possibility of an advance upon us by the enemy ; and gaining time, in which arms might be received and troops organized. I determined, therefore, to hold the position as long as it could be done without exposing our troops to the fire of the powerful artillery which, I doubted not, would be brought to bear upon them.

I believed that, after silencing our batteries on York River, the enemy would attempt to turn us by moving up to West Point by water.

Circumstances indicating that the enemy's batteries were nearly ready, I directed the troops to move toward Williamsburg on the night of the 3d by the roads from Yorktown and Warwick Court-House. They were assembled about Williamsburg by noon on the 4th, and were ordered to march by the road to Richmond, Major-General Magruder leading.

Early in the afternoon the cavalry rear-guard on the Yorktown road was driven in, and rapidly followed by the enemy. Brigadier-General McLaws was sent with the brigades of Kershaw and Semmes to support the cavalry. He met the enemy near the line of little works constructed by Major-General Magruder's forethought, made his dispositions with prompt courage and skill, and quickly drove the Federal troops from the field, in spite of disparity of numbers. I regret that no report of this handsome affair has been made by General McLaws. Major-General Magruder's. march was too late to permit that of Major-General Smith's the same afternoon. His division moved at daybreak on the 5th, in heavy rain and deep mud.

About sunrise the rear-guard was again attacked. The

action gradually increased in magnitude, until about three o'clock, when General Longstreet, commanding the rear, requested that a part of General Hill's troops might be sent to his aid. Upon this I rode upon the field, but found myself compelled to be a mere spectator; for Longstreet's clear head and brave heart left me no apology for interference. For details of the action, see the accompanying reports.

Our wounded, and many of those of the enemy, were placed in hospitals and residences in Williamsburg. Major-General Smith's division reached Barhamsville, eighteen miles; and Major-General Magruder's (commanded by Brigadier-General D. R. Jones) the Diascund Bridge on the Chickahominy road on that day. Those of Longstreet and Hill marched from Williamsburg, twelve miles, on the 6th. On that evening Major-General Smith reported that the enemy's troops were landing in force on the south side of York River, near West Point. On the following morning the army was concentrated near Barhamsville. In the mean time it had been ascertained that the enemy occupied a thick and extensive wood between Barhamsville and their landing-place. Brigadier-General Whiting was directed by General Smith to dislodge him, which was handsomely done—the brigade of Hood, and part of that of Hampton, performed the service. You are respectfully referred, for details, to the accompanying reports.

Want of means of subsistence compelled the army to move on toward Richmond; the divisions of Smith and Magruder taking the road by New Kent Court-House, those of Longstreet and Hill that along the Chickahominy. On the evening of the 9th the army halted; its left near the Cross-roads on the New Kent Court-House road, and its right near the Long Bridge. In this position the York River Railroad supplied us from Richmond.

On the 15th the attack upon the battery at Drury's Bluff by the enemy's gunboats suggested to me the necessity of so placing the army as to be prepared for the enemy's advance up the river or on the south side, as well as from the direction of West Point. We therefore crossed the

Chickahominy, to take a position six or seven miles from Richmond. That ground being unfavorable, the present position was taken on the 17th. Had the enemy beaten us on the 5th, as he claims to have done, the army would have lost most of its baggage and artillery. We should have been pursued from Williamsburg, and intercepted from West Point. Our troops engaged, leaving Williamsburg on the following morning, marched but twelve miles that day; and the army on its march to the Cross-roads averaged less than ten miles a day. Had not the action of the 5th been, at the least, discouraging to the enemy, we would have been pursued on the road, and turned by way of West Point. About four hundred of our wounded were left in Williamsburg, because they were not in condition to be moved. Nothing else was left which we had horses to draw away. Five pieces, found by the chief quartermaster at the Williamsburg wharf, were abandoned for want of horses and harness. In the three actions above mentioned our troops displayed high courage, and, on the march, endured privations and hardships with admirable cheerfulness.

Most respectfully,
Your obedient servant,

(Signed)   J. E. JOHNSTON, *General.*

General COOPER, Adjutant and Inspector-General.

HEADQUARTERS, HARRISON'S,
May 20, 1862.

GENERAL: I had the honor to write to you on Saturday, expressing the opinion that it is absolutely necessary that the Department of Henrico should be included in my command. Having received no reply, I respectfully repeat the suggestion, and ask the President to have the proper orders in the case given. It is needless to remind either of you of the mischief inevitable from divided command.

Most respectfully,
Your obedient servant,

(Signed)   J. E. JOHNSTON.

General LEE.

[CONFIDENTIAL.]

HEADQUARTERS, HARRISON'S, }
May 28, 1862, 9 A. M. }

GENERAL : If McDowell is approaching, of which there can be no doubt, we must fight very soon. Every man we have should be here. Major-General Holmes's troops should, therefore, be ordered to Richmond forthwith—they may be wanted to-morrow. I have more than once suggested a concentration here of all available forces.

Most respectfully,
Your obedient servant,
(Signed)   J. E. JOHNSTON.
General LEE.

I shall bring up Huger.

RICHMOND, VIRGINIA, }
November 24, 1862. }

General COOPER,
          Adjutant and Inspector-General.

SIR : I had the honor, this afternoon, to receive Special Order No. 225, of this date.

If I have been correctly informed, the forces which it places under my command are greatly inferior in number to those of the enemy's opposed to them, while in the Trans-Mississippi Department our army is very much larger than that of the United States. Our two armies on this side of the Mississippi have the further disadvantage of being separated by the Tennessee River and a Federal army (that of Major-General Grant), larger, probably, than either of them.

Under such circumstances, it seems to me that our best course would be to fall upon Major-General Grant with the troops of Lieutenant-Generals Holmes and Pemberton united for the purpose—those of General Bragg coöperating, if practicable.

The defeat of Major-General Grant would enable us to hold the Mississippi, and permit Lieutenant-General Holmes to move into Missouri. As our troops are now distributed, Vicksburg is in danger.

Most respectfully,
Your obedient servant,
J. E. JOHNSTON, General.

CHATTANOOGA, TENNESSEE,
December 4, 1862.

General S. COOPER,
> Adjutant and Inspector-General.

SIR : I have received, this morning, your telegram of yesterday, informing me that Lieutenant-General Pemberton is falling back before a very superior force ; that Lieutenant-General Holmes has been "peremptorily ordered" to reënforce him ; but that, as General Holmes's troops may be too late, the President urges on me the importance of sending a sufficient force from General Bragg's command to the aid of Lieutenant-General Pemberton.

Three railroad-accidents delayed my journey so much that I did not reach this place until after twelve last night. Consequently, your dispatch was delivered to-day too late for communication with General Bragg before to-morrow, when I shall visit his headquarters.

I do not know General Pemberton's late positions. His march, I suppose, will be toward Vicksburg, where General Holmes's troops must cross the river. His movements, therefore, are facilitating the junction, while they daily render that of General Bragg with him more difficult. The enemy, too, is exactly between the latter and himself. It seems to me, consequently, that the aid of General Holmes can better be relied on than that of General Bragg. I, therefore, respectfully suggest that that officer be urged to the utmost expedition.

Should the enemy get possession of Vicksburg, we cannot dislodge him.

The Tennessee River is a formidable obstacle to the expeditious march of General Bragg's troops into Mississippi. He may, besides, be compelled to take a circuitous route.

Of this, however, I am not fully informed. Nor have I learned the enemy's attitude in Tennessee. It is to be presumed that all such information can be acquired at General Bragg's headquarters, which I shall reach to-morrow.

Most respectfully,

Your obedient servant,

J. E. JOHNSTON, *General.*

[TELEGRAM.]

CHATTANOOGA, TENNESSEE,
December 4, 1862.

General COOPER, Richmond, Virginia:

The map convinces me that General Holmes's troops can reënforce sooner than General Bragg's. Urge him again to press his troops forward. I shall be with Bragg as soon as possible, which will be to-morrow.   J. E. JOHNSTON.

[TELEGRAM.]

CHATTANOOGA, TENNESSEE,
December 4, 1862.

General BRAGG, Murfreesboro:

The enemy is advancing on General Pemberton, who is falling back. Can you delay the advance by throwing cavalry on the enemy's rear? I will join you to-morrow.[1]

J. E. JOHNSTON.

MURFREESBORO, *December* 6, 1862.

General S. COOPER, Adjutant-General:

General Rosecrans has an army of about sixty-five thousand men[2] in and around Nashville, and some thirty-five thousand distributed along the railroad to Louisville and in

---

[1] This dispatch was not received by General Bragg, who took the measure suggested, upon intelligence given him by Lieutenant-General Pemberton.

[2] These were General Bragg's figures.

Kentucky. General Bragg has about forty-two thousand men, besides irregular cavalry, which in a few days will occupy Readyville, this place, and Eagleville. They can cross the Tennessee only by ferrying, a very slow process, which Rosecrans would certainly interrupt. The movement to join General Pemberton would, by any route, require at least a month. From the information given me here, I believe that the country between the Tennessee and General Pemberton could not support the trains our troops would require for a march through it. If I am right in this estimate, the President's object of a speedy reënforcement of the army in Mississippi, cannot be accomplished by sending troops from Tennessee. To send a strong force would be to give up Tennessee, and would, the principal officers here think, disorganize this army. Rosecrans could then move into Virginia, or join Grant, before our troops could reach Pemberton's position; for the Tennessee is no obstacle to them. The passage of the Tennessee is so difficult and slow that we shall be unable to use the same troops on both sides of the river until next summer. Two thousand cavalry will be sent to break up the Louisville and Nashville Railroad, and four thousand will be employed in the same way in West Tennessee and Northern Mississippi. The latter may delay General Grant.

Most respectfully,

Your obedient servant,

J. E. JOHNSTON, *General.*

VICKSBURG, *December* 22, 1862.

MR. PRESIDENT: From such information as I have been able to obtain, I think that we shall require, to hold this department and the Mississippi River, an active army of about forty thousand men, to oppose the troops of Grant and Banks, and for garrisons at Vicksburg and Port Hudson, capable of holding those places against combined attacks until succored by the active army.

Major-General Smith has about five thousand nine hundred artillery and infantry for duty to defend a line of ten miles, exclusive of the position of Snyder's Mill, which requires three of his eight regiments. Should the enemy attack by land as well as by water, which is highly probable —almost certain—we would require at least eight more regiments of five or six hundred men each.

I have not seen Port Hudson, but a map of the ground gives me the opinion that it requires a garrison as strong as that necessary here. It now amounts to about five thousand five hundred of all arms; so that an addition of as many more will be required there—in all, eleven or twelve thousand men. For the active force we have now twenty-one thousand men near the Yallobusha. About nine thousand have been ordered to this department from Lieutenant-General Smith's, and it is supposed that an equal force is on its way from Arkansas.

No more troops can be taken from General Bragg without the danger of enabling Rosecrans to move into Virginia, or to reënforce Grant. Our great object is to hold the Mississippi. The country beyond the river is as much interested in that object as this; and the loss to us of the Mississippi involves that of the country beyond it. The eight or ten thousand men which are essential to its safety ought, therefore, I respectfully suggest, to be taken from Arkansas; to return after the crisis in this department.

I firmly believe, however, that our true system of warfare would be to concentrate the forces of the two departments on this side of the Mississippi, beat the enemy here, and then reconquer the country beyond it which he might have gained in the mean time.

I respectfully ask your Excellency's attention to the accompanying letter of Major-General Smith in relation to the inadequacy of the garrison of Vicksburg, begging you to take his estimate of the force needed instead of mine, as his is based upon accurate calculation.

Most respectfully,

Your obedient servant,

J. E. JOHNSTON, *General.*

JACKSON, *January* 2, 1863.

MR. PRESIDENT: General Pemberton continues to command at Vicksburg. He has asked for all the troops here, after being reënforced by Maury's division, in addition to those brigades agreed upon between us. The line of twelve miles to Snyder's Mills probably requires them all. I fear difficulty of subsisting them, however. A report just handed in by the inspecting officers shows that the supply of provision is much smaller than General Pemberton supposed. The place may be reduced, I fear, in consequence of this; or, should it be invested, we shall not have a sufficient force to break the investment.

Grant is still on the Tallahatchie, so that the remainder of Loring's and Price's troops cannot be withdrawn from Grenada. From his halting I suppose he is repairing the railroad. The force at Grenada (about eleven thousand effectives) is too weak to do more than delay the passage of the river by the enemy. My hope of keeping him back is in Van Dorn, under whom I propose to unite all the available cavalry, when Forrest and Roddy can be found.

Should Grant join Sherman at Vicksburg, it would be very embarrassing, for, as he could reach the place from Memphis as soon as we could learn whether he was embarking or moving along the railroad to Grenada, it could be invested by the combined armies. We could not break the investment with eleven thousand men, but it would be necessary to try.

The necessity of holding the Yazoo, as well as Vicksburg, employs a large force, too widely distributed to be in condition for the offensive.

We have no news from Arkansas, which proves, I think, that we are to get no help from that side of the Mississippi.

The Legislature has done nothing yet.

We require about twenty thousand men, the number you have asked for from Arkansas, to make headway against both Grant and Sherman. Will the great victory at Fredericksburg enable General Lee to spare a part of his force?

Should the enemy's forces be respectably handled, the

task you have set me will be above my ability. But the hand of Almighty God has delivered us in times of great danger! Believing that He is with us, I will not lose hope.

J. E. JOHNSTON, *General.*

JACKSON, *January* 6, 1863.

Colonel B. S. EWELL, Chattanooga:

Ascertain General Bragg's intentions, wants, and condition, compared with that of the enemy. Ask him for full information. The enemy did not follow. Can he not hold a part of the rich country northwest of the mountains and disturb the enemy's foraging with his cavalry? If he wants Roddy, he must take him.

J. E. JOHNSTON, *General.*

JACKSON, *January* 6, 1863.

To the PRESIDENT, Richmond:

Your dispatch of yesterday received. Enemy's troops and transports reported gone up the river from Milliken's Bend. We hear of no movement in *this direction by General Holmes.* Grant's forces are reported distributed at Memphis, Holly Springs, and Corinth. The country said to be impracticable. General Bragg reports he has been checked. I hear indirectly that he has *withdrawn* from Murfreesboro. Should he need help, and there appear no *danger* in Mississippi except by the river, could *E. K. Smith's* men return? The impossibility of my knowing the condition of things in Tennessee shows that I cannot direct both parts of my command at once. I am hoping to hear from General Bragg.

J. E. JOHNSTON, *General.*

JACKSON, *January* 7, 1863.

To the PRESIDENT, Richmond:

General Bragg telegraphs from Winchester that the enemy did not follow in force. I regret his falling back so

far. He wants twenty thousand more men to secure East
Tennessee. Can any large part of it be furnished ? E. K.
Smith's troops here might be spared for a few weeks, unless
Sherman reappears. One of Grant's divisions is at Hum-
boldt. Which is most valuable, Tennessee or the Mississippi ?

J. E. JOHNSTON, *General.*

JACKSON, MISSISSIPPI, *January* 6, 1863.

To General PEMBERTON, Vicksburg :

Please have a message sent across the river to learn if
there are any movements from Arkansas connected with
ours.   J. E. JOHNSTON, *General.*

JACKSON, MISSISSIPPI, *January* 7, 1863.

To the PRESIDENT, Richmond :

The following dispatch was received from General M. L.
Smith : " I am returning from Little Rock. No troops will
be sent."   J. E. JOHNSTON, *General.*

JACKSON, *January* 18, 1863.

To the PRESIDENT, Richmond :

I am much relieved to find our troops are on the Duck
River. Not at Deckered.

J. E. JOHNSTON, *General.*

JACKSON, *January* 9, 1863.

To the PRESIDENT, Richmond, Virginia :

Colonel Ewell informs me, from Chattanooga, that on the
31st General Bragg had *thirty-five thousand,* including
Wharton's cavalry. Lost nine thousand—three thousand
sick since from exposure. We have not force enough here
if the enemy is vigorous. Prisoners tell General Bragg of
Federal reënforcements from West Tennessee.

J. E JOHNSTON, *General.*

Jackson, *January* 11, 1863.

Lieutenant-General Pemberton, Port Hudson :

I want to combine a cavalry expedition in the two departments. Please assign General Van Dorn to the same cavalry, with instructions to report to me.

J. E. Johnston, *General.*

Jackson, *January* 11, 1863.

General Bragg, Tullahoma :

One of Van Dorn's great objects will be to cover your left, by preventing Federal troops from going from West to Middle Tennessee. Roddy will contribute far more to this object under Van Dorn, than separate. This is the only pressure possible by the troops in Mississippi. Please order Roddy to report to Van Dorn. Grant is reported to intend to repair the railroad to Corinth :

J. E. Johnston, *General.*

Jackson, Mississippi, }
January 11, 1863. }

Lieutenant-General Pemberton, Port Gibson.

The object of the expedition under Van Dorn will be to interrupt any movement into Mississippi or Middle Tennessee. J. E. Johnston, *General.*

Jackson, Mississippi, }
January 12, 1863. }

General S. Cooper, Richmond.

Sir : General Bragg thinks twenty thousand more men necessary to enable him to hold Middle Tennessee. Lieutenant-General Smith's force in East Tennessee is not more than sufficient to prevent raids.

Lieutenant-General Pemberton informs me that there are forty-two thousand artillery and infantry in this department ; of which he regards twenty-four thousand as absolutely necessary for the immediate defense of Port Hudson and Vicksburg. Grant's army is estimated at thirty-eight thousand ; that which attacked Vicksburg at thirty thousand; and Banks is supposed to be assembling twenty-five thousand at Baton Rouge. Should a large portion of these forces act upon this river, they may invest our two positions, which would fall in the course of time, unless we have an active army to break the investment.

The condition of the country and the breaking of railroads by our cavalry have compelled Grant to fall back, but we must expect him to advance again as soon as practicable. Should Banks and Sherman move at the same time, we could not oppose such a combination with our present forces.

The country will probably be in its present condition for several months. In the mean time Grant may reënforce Rosecrans.

I make these statements to show how much these three departments need reënforcements, and to ask if there is any.   J. E. JOHNSTON, *General.*

RICHMOND, VIRGINIA, }
January 22, 1863. }

General J. E. JOHNSTON, Chattanooga.

GENERAL : As announced in my telegram, I address this letter to you to explain the purpose for which I desire you to proceed promptly to the headquarters of General Bragg's army. The events connected with the late battle at Murfreesboro', and retreat from that place, have led to criticisms upon the conduct of General Bragg which induced him to call upon the commanders of corps for an expression of opinion, and for information as to the feeling in their commands in regard to the conduct of General Bragg. And also whether he had so far lost the confidence of the army as to impair his usefulness in his present position. The answers I am informed have been but partially given ; but are, so far, indicative of a want of confidence, such as is essential for success. Why General Bragg should have selected that tribunal and invited its judgment upon him is to me unexplained. It manifests, however, a condition of things which seems to me to require your presence. The enemy is said to be preparing to advance and, though my confidence in General Bragg is unshaken, it cannot be doubted that, if he is distrusted by his officers and troops, a disaster may result, which but for that cause would have been avoided. You will, I trust, be able, by conversation with General Bragg and others of his command, to decide what the best interests of the service require, and to give me the advice which I need at this juncture. As that army is a part of your command, no order will be necessary to give you authority there ; as, whether present or absent, you have a right to direct its operations, and do whatever else belongs to the general commanding.

Very respectfully and truly yours,
JEFFERSON DAVIS.

TULLAHOMA, February 2, 1863.

Hon J. A. SEDDON, Secretary of War, Richmond :

I have just read the report of furloughs and discharges at Atlanta—from General Bragg's troops alone, sixty-six discharges, fourteen hundred and eighty-one furloughs in three months preceding January 14th—and respectfully repeat my recommendation that Article 4, General Orders No. 72, be revoked because it is draining the army.

J. E. JOHNSTON, General.

TULLAHOMA, February 3, 1863.

MR. PRESIDENT: Your telegram ordering me to General Bragg's headquarters was received in Mobile, when I was on my way to them. Your letter of January 22d reached me here on the 30th. I have spoken to General Bragg, Lieutenant-Generals Polk and Hardee, and Governor Harris, on the subject of your letter. . . . I respectfully suggest that, should it then appear to you necessary to remove General Bragg, no one in this army, or engaged in this investigation, ought to be his successor.

Most respectfully,
Your obedient servant,
J. E. JOHNSTON, General.

TULLAHOMA, *February* 12, 1863.

Major-General ROSECRANS, United States Army.

GENERAL : I have had the honor to receive your letters of the 18th and 19th ultimo, addressed to me, as I understand, because you find yourself compelled, by a sense of duty to humanity, to decline communicating with General Bragg by flag of truce, etc. Being unable to perceive how the interests of humanity are to be promoted by the suspension of correspondence between the commanders of opposite armies, I very much regret your determination. The more so, because it is not in my power to reëstablish that correspondence. General Bragg is the commander-in-chief of the Army of Tennessee, not I. One of his functions as such is, of course, the conducting of such correspondence as you propose to hold with me. I can assume none of the duties or privileges of the position in which our common superior, the President of the Confederacy, placed him. I gladly avail myself of this opportunity to express to you my appreciation of your humanity exhibited in the case of our wounded who fell into your hands at Murfreesboro'.

> Most respectfully,
> Your obedient servant,
> J. E. JOHNSTON, *General.*

TULLAHOMA, *February* 12, 1863.

MR. PRESIDENT : . . . In Mississippi every thing depends upon the result of the labor opposite to Vicksburg. If Grant should succeed in making a navigable canal, and through it pass Vicksburg and invest Port Hudson with the combined armies, it would be difficult for us to succor the place. Indeed, we have not the means of forming a relieving army. General Pemberton is not communicative. I am told, however, that he is confident that the canal cannot be made. It seems to me to depend upon the condition of the river, whether or not it is too high for work with spades.

I have been told by Lieutenant-Generals Polk and Hardee that they have advised you to remove General Bragg and place me in command of this army. I am sure that you will agree with me that the part that I have borne in this investigation would render it inconsistent with my personal honor to occupy that position. I believe, however, that the interests of the service require that General Bragg should not be removed.

Most respectfully,
Your obedient servant,
J. E. JOHNSTON, General.

CHATTANOOGA, *February* 26, 1863.

Major-General VAN DORN.

GENERAL : Your letter of the 22d inst. is just received. My first object in bringing you into Middle Tennessee was to enable you to take part in a battle in the event of the advance of the Federal army. The second, that you might operate upon his line of communication previous to his moving from Murfreesboro', and up to he time of engagement; or, if it should appear to be expedient—battle being unlikely—that you might move into Kentucky, or farther.

The movement in General Bragg's theatre of operations will be, necessarily, under his control. Those from it and beyond it, I will at least inaugurate.

There should be no attack upon Franklin until full information is obtained of the enemy's strength. If expedient, it will require a considerable addition to your force. I hope to be able to visit you very soon.

Most respectfully.
Your obedient servant,
J. E. JOHNSTON, General.

CHATTANOOGA, *February* 25, 1863.

Hon. J. A. SEDDON, Secretary of War, Richmond :

General Bragg reports reënforcements continue to reach Nashville. Major-General Cox arrived last week with a division from West Virginia, and Major-General Sigel is just in with more troops. Should not our troops in West Virginia follow the movement of the Federals? It seems to me urgent.

J. E. Johnston, *General.*

MOBILE, *March* 12, 1863.

Hon. J. A. Seddon:

I received your dispatch ordering me to Tullahoma here on my way to Mississippi. Shall return as soon as I can.

J. E. Johnston, *General.*

MOBILE, *March* 12, 1863.

Hon. J. A. Seddon:

There are no resources under my control to meet the advance you refer to. On the contrary, I have repeatedly asked for reënforcements for all the departments you mention. As the enemy has certainly sent troops from Virginia to Middle Tennessee, we ought to do the same without delay. Troops will not be likely to move from Corinth until Rosecrans advances.

J. E. Johnston, *General.*

MOBILE, *March* 12, 1863.

Hon. J. A. Seddon, Secretary of War.

SIR: I have had the honor to receive here, being on my way to Lieutenant-General Pemberton's headquarters, two dispatches (telegraphic) from you, by way of Chattanooga, to which I have briefly replied by telegraph.

.   .   .   .

The second asks if I have any resources under my control to meet the advance from Corinth, reported by Lieutenant-General Pemberton; if troops can be spared from Mobile or Mississippi, or from Middle Tennessee, for the purpose—if Van Dorn's cavalry, at least, might not return.

The infantry for defense on the land-side of Mobile, amounts to but twenty-five hundred.

I reported to the President in December that nearly twenty thousand additional troops were required in Mississippi. Since then, Grant's army has been heavily reënforced. Allow me to remind you, also, of what I have said of the length of time necessary for the transfer of troops, in any considerable number, from Mississippi to Tennessee. Those two departments are more distant from each other in time than Eastern Virginia and Middle Tennessee.

In relation to detaching from General Bragg's army, permit me to remind you that I have been, for the last two months, asking the department to strengthen it, and representing it as too weak to oppose the powerful army in front of it with confidence. On that account, Major-General Van Dorn's cavalry was added to it. Dividing that army might be fatal to it.

Major-General Jones reported some time ago that the enemy was sending troops from the Kanawah Valley. Soon after, our friends about Nashville informed General Bragg that Major-General Cox had arrived with his division from Western Virginia, and a little later that Major-General Siegel's division had also joined Rosecrans. I therefore suggested that the troops which had been opposed to those in Virginia should be sent to General Bragg without delay. Allow me to repeat that suggestion.

Most respectfully,

Your obedient servant,

J. E. JOHNSTON, *General.*

TULLAHOMA, *March* 19, 1863.

Hon. J. A. SEDDON, Secretary of War, Richmond:

On account of Mrs. Bragg's critical condition, I shall not now give the order for which I came. The country is becoming practicable. Should the enemy advance, General Bragg will be indispensable here.

J. E. JOHNSTON, *General.*

TULLAHOMA, *March* 28, 1863.

MR. PRESIDENT: I have had the honor to receive your letter of the 20th, and with it a copy of your telegram of the 16th. I fear that my reply to the latter did not express my meaning, from my anxiety to be brief.

At Mobile, in Mississippi, and in Middle Tennessee, we cannot foresee attack long enough beforehand to be able to reënforce the threatened army from either of the others. At the first two, the enemy's appearance may, and probably would be the first indication of his intention to attack. In Middle Tennessee, after he begins to advance, his march may be so delayed as to give us three or four days, but in that time troops could be drawn from East Tennessee only, and that department could furnish but a small force. The transportation of eight or ten thousand infantry (without their wagons) from Jackson to Tullahoma, would require more than three weeks. The wagons and horses would require five. I think, therefore, that it is not practicable to strengthen this army by drawing to it "for temporary use" a portion of the troops of Mississippi or Mobile. At the latter, besides the garrisons of the forts and batteries for water-defense, General Buckner has but three thousand infantry to hold the land-side.

.   .   .   .

Most respectfully,
Your obedient servant,
J. E. JOHNSTON.

TULLAHOMA, *April* 5, 1863.

Lieutenant-General PEMBERTON:

Your dispatch of the 3d received. If you discover that the enemy reënforces Rosecrans, let Stevenson's troops, or an equal number, come here immediately. . . .

J. E. JOHNSTON.

TULLAHOMA, *April* 18, 1863.

Brigadier-General JACKSON, Chattanooga:

Stop all troops from the Department of Mississippi until General Buford receives General Pemberton's orders. Do it at Atlanta, as well as Chattanooga.

J. E. JOHNSTON, *General.*

JACKSON, *May* 13, 1863.

Hon. J. A. SEDDON, Richmond:

I arrived this evening, finding the enemy in force between this place and General Pemberton, cutting off the communication. *I am too late.*

J. E. JOHNSTON, *General.*

JACKSON, *May* 13, 1863.

Lieutenant-General PEMBERTON:

I have lately arrived, and learn that Major-General Sherman is between us, with four divisions, at Clinton. It is important to reëstablish communication that you may be reenforced. If practicable, come up on his rear at once. To beat such a detachment would be of immediate value; the troops here could coöperate.

All the strength you can quickly assemble should be brought. Time is all-important.

Your obedient servant,

J. E. JOHNSTON, *General.*

WAR DEPARTMENT, *May* 27, 1863.

General J. E. JOHNSTON, Commanding, etc.

GENERAL: Brigadier-General G. J. Rains having been detailed for duty in connection with torpedoes and *sub-terra* shells, has been ordered to report to you.

The President has confidence in his inventions, and is desirous that they should be employed both on land and river, if opportunity offers, both at Vicksburg and its vicinity. Should communications allow, you are desired to send him there; but if otherwise, to employ him in his devices against the enemy, where most assailable in that way, elsewhere. All reasonable facilities in the supply of men or material for the fair trial of his torpedoes or shells, are requested on your part. Such means of offense against the enemy are approved and recognized by the Department as legitimate weapons of warfare.

With high esteem,

Very truly yours,

JAMES A. SEDDON,

Secretary of War.

CANTON, *May* 31, 1863.

Lieutenant-General E. KIRBY SMITH,

Commanding Trans-Mississippi Department:

Port Hudson is invested by Major-General Banks, Vicksburg by Major-General Grant. I am preparing to aid Vicksburg, but cannot march to Port Hudson without exposing my little army to destruction. If you can do any thing to succor Port Hudson, I beg you to do it.

Very respectfully,

Your obedient servant,

J. E. JOHNSTON, *General.*

CANTON, *May* 31, 1863.

His Excellency the PRESIDENT, Richmond:

Your dispatch of 30th received. By official returns, troops near Canton, including Gist's and Walker's brigades of Beauregard's army, Ector's and McNair's of Bragg's, and Gregg's of Pemberton's, have effective *nine thousand four hundred.* Troops near Jackson, including Loring's division and Maxey's brigade of Pemberton's troops, and Evans's of Beauregard's, have effective *seven thousand eight hundred.* Major-General Breckenridge reports to-day *five thousand eight hundred.* Brigadier-General Jackson's cavalry, numbering about *sixteen hundred* when I was in Tennessee, not included, nor five field-batteries, probably *four hundred.*

General Cooper informs me that no other reënforcements have been ordered to this department. Major-General Gardner is invested in Port Hudson.

J. E. JOHNSTON, *General.*

CANTON, *June* 5, 1863.

Hon. J. A. SEDDON.

DEAR SIR: I thank you cordially for your kind letter of May 25th, but almost regret that you feel such confidence in me as is expressed in it. From the present condition of affairs, I fear that confidence dooms you to disappointment. Every day gives some new intelligence of the enemy's strength, and of reënforcements on the way to him. My first intention on learning that Lieutenant-General Pemberton was in Vicksburg was to form an army to succor him. I suppose from my telegraphic correspondence with the Government that all the troops to be hoped for have arrived. Our resources seem so small, and those of the enemy so great, that the relief of Vicksburg is beginning to appear impossible to me. Pemberton will undoubtedly make a gallant and obstinate defense, and hold out as long as he can make resistance. But unless we assemble a force strong enough to break Grant's line of investment, the surrender of the place will be a mere question of time. General Grant is receiving reënforcements almost daily. His force, according to the best information to be had, is more than treble that which I command. Our scouts say, too, that he has constructed lines of circumvallation, and has blocked up all roads leading to his position.

The enterprise of forcing the enemy's lines would be a difficult one to a force double that at my disposal. If you are unable to increase that force decidedly, I must try to accomplish something in aid of the besieged garrison; and yet, when considering it, it seems to me desperate.

Your suggestion to General Kirby Smith was promptly dispatched to him. I have no doubt that the time is favorable for attacking Helena.

In replying by telegraph to your letters and telegrams, I

have said that, if you can increase the army, it should be done; if you cannot, nothing is left for us but to struggle manfully with such means as the Government can furnish.

I beg you to consider, in connection with affairs in this department, that I had not only to organize, but to provide means of transportation and supplies of all sorts for an army. The artillery is not yet equipped. All of Lieutenant-General Pemberton's supplies were, of course, with his troops about Vicksburg and Port Hudson.

I found myself, therefore, without subsistence, stores, ammunition, or the means of conveying those indispensables. It has proved more difficult to collect wagons and provisions than I had expected. We have not yet the means of operating for more than four days away from the railroads. That to Vicksburg is destroyed.

We draw our provisions from the northern part of the State. The protection of that country employs about twenty-five hundred irregular cavalry. It is much too small. I am endeavoring to increase it by calling for volunteers, but am by no means sanguine as to the result.

Most respectfully,
Your obedient servant,
J. E. JOHNSTON, General.

RICHMOND, VIRGINIA, June 5, 1863.

General J. E. JOHNSTON :

  .   .   .   .

I regret my inability to promise more troops, as we have drained resources, even to the danger of several points. You know best concerning General Bragg's army, but I fear to withdraw more. We are too far outnumbered in Virginia to spare any. You must rely on what you have, and the irregular forces Mississippi can afford. Your judgment and skill are fully relied on, but I venture the suggestion that, to relieve Vicksburg, speedy action is essential. With the facilities and resources of the enemy, time works against us.   (Signed)   J. A. SEDDON,

Secretary of War.

RICHMOND, *June* 8, 1863.

General J. E. JOHNSTON:

General —— was believed to be peculiarly acceptable to his brigade. What is the objection? Do you advise more reënforcements from General Bragg? You, as commandant of the department, have the power so to order, if you, in view of the whole case, so determine. We cannot send from Virginia or elsewhere, for we stand already not one to two.

(Signed)   J. A. SEDDON,
Secretary of War.

JACKSON, *June* 10, 1863.

Hon. J. A. SEDDON, Secretary of War:

Your dispatch of June 8th, in cipher, received. You do not give orders in regard to the recently-appointed general officers. I have not at my command half the number of troops necessary. It is for the Government to determine what department, if any, can furnish the troops required. I cannot know here General Bragg's wants compared with mine. The Government can make such comparisons. Your dispatch is imperfectly deciphered.   J. E. JOHNSTON.

JACKSON, *June* 12, 1863.

Hon. J. A. SEDDON, Secretary of War:

Your dispatch of the 8th imperfectly deciphered and partially answered on the 10th. I have not considered myself commanding in Tennessee since assignment here; and should not have felt authorized to take troops from that department after having been informed by the Executive that no more could be spared. To take from Bragg a force that would make this army fit to oppose Grant's would involve yielding Tennessee. It is for the Government to decide between this State and Tennessee.

(Signed)   J. E. JOHNSTON.

JACKSON, *June* 15, 1863.

Hon. J. A. SEDDON, Secretary of War:

Your repeated dispatch of the 8th is deciphered. I cannot advise in regard to the points from which troops can best be taken, having no means of knowing. Nor is it for me to judge which it is best to yield, Mississippi or Tennessee. That is for the Government to determine. Without some great blunder by the enemy, we cannot hold both. The odds against me are much greater than those you express. I consider saving Vicksburg hopeless.

(Signed)   J. E. JOHNSTON.

RICHMOND, *June* 15, 1863.

General J. E. JOHNSTON:

Your dispatch of the 12th instant, to the Secretary of War, noted. The order to go to Mississippi did not diminish your authority in Tennessee, both being in the country placed under your command in original assignment. To what do you refer as information from me restricting your authority to transfer troops because no more could be spared? Officers ordered to you for duty generally are, of course, subject to assignment by you.   JEFFERSON DAVIS.

JACKSON, *June* 16, 1863.

To his Excellency the PRESIDENT:

Your dispatch of 15th received. I meant to tell the Secretary of War that I considered the order directing me to command here as limiting my authority to this department, especially as that order was accompanied by War Department orders transferring troops from Tennessee to Mississippi. And, whether commanding there or not, that your reply to my application for more troops, that none could be spared, would have made it improper for me to order more troops from Tennessee. Permit me to repeat that an officer having a task like mine, far above his ability, cannot, in addition, command other remote departments. No general can command separate armies.

I have not yet been able to procure the means of moving these troops. They are too weak to accomplish much. The reënforcements you mention have joined Grant.

(Signed)   J. E. JOHNSTON.

RICHMOND, *June* 17, 1863.

General J. E. JOHNSTON :

I do not find in my letter-book any communication to you containing the expression which you again attribute to me, and cite as a restriction on you against withdrawing troops from Tennessee, and have to repeat my inquiry, To what do you refer? Give date of dispatch or letter.

(Signed)   JEFFERSON DAVIS.

JACKSON, *June* 20, 1863.

To his Excellency the PRESIDENT :

I much regret the carelessness of my reply of the 16th to your telegram of the 15th. In my dispatch of the 12th, to the Secretary of War, I referred to your words, " We have withheld nothing which it was practicable to give," in your telegram of May 28th, and to the telegram of June 5th,[1] except the last sentence. I considered Executive as including the Secretary of War.   J. E. JOHNSTON.

WAR DEPARTMENT, *June* 16, 1863.

General J. E. JOHNSTON :

Your telegram[2] grieves and alarms me. Vicksburg must not be lost without a desperate struggle. The interest and honor of the Confederacy forbid it. I rely on you still to avert the loss. If better resources do not offer, you must hazard attack. It may be made in concert with the garrison, if practicable, but otherwise without, by day or night, as you think best.   JAMES A. SEDDON,

Secretary of War.

[1] From the Secretary of War.   [2] That of June 15th.

JACKSON, *June* 19, 1863.

Hon. J. A. SEDDON:

Dispatch of 16th received. I think that you do not appreciate the difficulties in the course you direct, nor the probabilities in consequence of failure. Grant's position, naturally very strong, is intrenched, and protected by powerful artillery; and the roads are obstructed. His reënforcements have been at least equal to my whole force. The Big Black covers him from attack, and would cut off our retreat if defeated. We cannot combine operations with General Pemberton, from uncertain and slow communication. The defeat of this little army would at once open Mississippi and Alabama to Grant. I will do all I can, without hope of doing more than aid to extricate the garrison.

J. E. JOHNSTON.

RICHMOND, *June* 21, 1863.

General J. E. JOHNSTON:

Yours of the 19th received. Consequences are realized, and difficulties are recognized as very great; but still think, other means failing, the course recommended should be hazarded. The aim, in my judgment, justifies any risk, and all probable consequences. JAMES A. SEDDON,
Secretary of War.

RICHMOND, *June* 21, 1863.

General J. E. JOHNSTON:

Only my conviction (of almost imperative necessity for action) induces the official dispatch I have just sent you. On every ground I have great deference to your superior knowledge of the position, your judgment and military genius; but I feel it right to share, if need be to take, the responsibility, and leave you free to follow the most desperate course the occasion may demand. Rely upon it, the eyes and hopes of the whole Confederacy are upon you, with the full confidence that you will act, and with the sentiment that it were better to fail, nobly daring, than, through prudence even, to be inactive. I look to attack in last resort, but rely on your resources of generalship to suggest less desperate modes of relief. I can scarce dare to suggest, but might it not be possible to strike Banks first, and unite the garrison of Port Hudson with you, or to secure sufficient coöperation from General Smith, or to practically besiege Grant by operations with artillery from the swamps, now dry, on the north side of the Yazoo, below Haynes's Bluff? I rely on you for all possible means to save Vicksburg.

J. A. Seddon.

Canton, June 24, 1863.

Hon. J. A. Seddon:

Your two dispatches of 21st received. There has been no voluntary inaction. When I came, all military materials of the department were in Vicksburg and Port Hudson. Artillery had to be brought from the East—horses for it, and all field transportation, procured in an exhausted country; much from Georgia, and brought over wretched railroads, and provision collected. I have not had the means of moving. We cannot contend with the enemy north of the Yazoo. He can place a large force there in a few hours; we, a small one in ten or twelve days. We cannot relieve Port Hudson without giving up Jackson, by which we should lose Mississippi. . . .   J. E. Johnston.

Richmond, June 30, 1863.

General J. E. Johnston:

After full examination of all the correspondence between you and myself and the War-Office, including the dispatches referred to in your telegram of the 20th instant, I am still at a loss to account for your strange error in stating to the Secretary of War that your right to draw reënforcements from Bragg's army had been restricted by the Executive, or that your command over the Army of Tennessee had been withdrawn.

.   .   .   .

Jefferson Davis.

CAMP ON CANEY CREEK, ⎰
July 5, 1863.   ⎱

To his Excellency the PRESIDENT:

Your dispatch of June 30th received. I considered my assignment to the immediate command in Mississippi as giving me a new position, and limiting my authority to this department. The orders of the War Department transferring three separate bodies of troops from General Bragg's army to this, two of them without my knowledge, and all of them without consulting me, would have convinced me, had I doubted. These orders of the War Department expressed its judgment of the number of troops to be transferred from Tennessee. I could no more control this judgment by increasing the number, than by forbidding the transfers. I regret very much that an impression which seemed to me to be natural, should be regarded by you as a " strange error."

.   .   .   .

J. E. JOHNSTON.

RICHMOND, *July* 9, 1863.

General J. E. JOHNSTON:

Your dispatch of the 5th instant received. The mistakes it contains will be noticed by letter. Your dispatch of the 7th instant to the Secretary of War, announcing the disastrous termination of the siege of Vicksburg, received the same day.

Painfully anxious as to the result, I have remained without information from you as to any plans proposed or attempted to raise the siege. Equally uninformed as to your plans in relation to Port Hudson. I have to request such information in relation thereto as the Government has a right to expect from one of its commanding generals in the field.   JEFFERSON DAVIS.

JACKSON, *July* 9, 1863.

To his Excellency the PRESIDENT:

Your dispatch of to-day received. I have never meant to fail in the duty of reporting to the Executive whatever might interest it in my command. I informed the Secretary of War that my force was much too weak to attempt to raise the siege of Vicksburg, and that to attempt to relieve Port Hudson would be to give up Mississippi, as it would involve the loss of this point, and that want of adequate means of transportation kept me inactive until the end of June. I then moved toward Vicksburg to attempt to extricate the garrison, but could not devise a plan until after reconnoitring, for which I was too late. Without General Pemberton's coöperation, any attempt must have resulted in disaster.

The slowness and difficulty of communication rendered coöperation next to impossible.   J. E. JOHNSTON.

Extract from Lieutenant-General Pemberton's Report of the Battles of Port Gibson, Baker's Creek, and the Siege of Vicksburg.

HEADQUARTERS, GAINESVILLE, ALABAMA,
August 2, 1863.

General S. COOPER,
    Adjutant and Inspector-General, Richmond, Va. :

.   .   .   .

On the 30th of April I received the first information of the landing of the enemy on the east bank of the Mississippi River. General Bowen reported by telegraph that three thousand (3,000) Federal troops were at Bethel Church, ten miles from Port Gibson, at three o'clock on the morning of the 29th, and that they were still landing at Bruinsburg. Brigadier-General Tracey, of Stevenson's division, had reached Grand Gulf with his brigade on the 30th. Lieutenant-Colonel Brown, of the Twentieth Mississippi, with fifty mounted men of his regiment, left Jackson for the same place on the 29th ; and Major J. D. Bradford, a good artillery-officer, was sent to replace the lamented Colonel Wade as chief of artillery.

Between twelve and two o'clock P. M., on the 30th, Brigadier-General Baldwin, with his brigade of Smith's division, had crossed the Big Black at Hankinson's Ferry. At nine o'clock A. M., May 1st, General Bowen informed me by telegraph, his army being then in position three miles south of Port Gibson, that General Baldwin was entering the latter place. On the same day, General Bowen telegraphed me that prisoners taken reported McClernand in command; that three divisions had landed, one of which took the right-hand road from Rodney, and that the enemy's force was estimated at twenty thousand men. He added, however, "I disbelieve the report." At three P. M., the same day, General Bowen advised me that he still held his position, but that he was hard pressed, and concluded by asking when Major-General Loring would arrive. In reply, he was notified by telegram that another brigade from Vicksburg was *en route* to reënforce him, and would probably reach him before Major-General Loring could arrive from Jackson. At half-past five P. M., he informed me that he was falling back across the Bayou Pierre, and that he would endeavor to hold that position until the arrival of reënforcements. On reaching Rocky Springs, about eighteen miles from Grand Gulf, Major-General Loring, learning that Brigadier-General Bowen had fallen back before a large force, from Port Gibson, in the direction of Grand Gulf, directed two regiments and a field-battery of Tilghman's brigade, which had been withdrawn from the Big Black Bridge, to move as rapidly as possible to Grindstone Ford, and hold it at all hazards, to prevent the enemy from flanking Bowen in that direction, and then proceeded himself to the headquarters of General Bowen, near Grand Gulf. Major-General Loring concurring with General Bowen as to the impracticability of holding his position with so small a force, directed its withdrawal across Big Black, at Hankinson's Ferry.

In his official report, Major-General Loring says: "This had hardly been determined upon, when your communication was received, stating that the enemy had fallen back toward Grand Gulf, and ordering it to move at once out of its position, and to cross the Big Black at Hankinson's Ferry." The movement was promptly carried out. Previous to crossing the river, however, Colonel A. W. Reynolds's brigade, of Stevenson's division, had arrived. Not having heard from General Bowen after half-past five P. M., on the 1st instant, I dispatched him, *via* Rocky Springs, on the morning of the 2d, as follows:

"If you are holding your position on the Bayou Pierre, and your communication is open by the Big Black to this place, continue to hold it. I am informed that you have fallen back to Grand Gulf; if this is so, carry out my instructions just sent in cipher."

These instructions were, in case he had fallen back to Grand Gulf, which is a *cul-de-sac*, to destroy his heavy guns and such stores as could not be transported, and endeavor to retire across the Big Black. The last brigade of Major-General Stevenson's division, which had been hurried forward to reënforce Bowen, with the hope of enabling him to hold his position on the Bayou Pierre, or, in case he should be compelled to fall back, to protect his retreat, had not all arrived when the retiring column under Major-General Loring commenced crossing the Big Black at Hankinson's Ferry.

For the details of the battle at Port Gibson, the list of casualties, etc., I beg to refer to the official report of Brigadier-General Bowen, and the reports of his subordinate commanders, which I have the honor to transmit herewith, as also the report of Major-General Loring, who commanded the retreat after the column had been put in motion by Brigadier-General Bowen. Among the slain whom the country deplores, I regret to mention Brigadier-General E. D. Tracy, a brave and skillful officer, who fell, where it is the soldier's pride to fall, at the post of duty and of danger.

Though disastrous in its results, the bloody encounter in front of Port Gibson nobly illustrated the valor and constancy of our troops, and shed additional lustre upon the Confederate arms. Confronted by overwhelming numbers, the heroic Bowen and his gallant officers and men maintained the unequal contest for many hours, with a courage and obstinacy rarely equaled ; and, though they failed to secure a victory, the world will do them the justice to say they deserved it.

With a moderate cavalry force at my disposal, I am firmly convinced that the Federal army under General Grant would have been unable to maintain its communications with the Mississippi River, and that the attempt to reach Jackson and Vicksburg from that base would have been as signally defeated in May, 1863, as a like attempt, from another base, had, by the employment of cavalry, been defeated in December, 1862. The repulse of General Bowen at Port Gibson, and our consequent withdrawal to the north bank of the Big Black, rendered it necessary that I should, as rapidly as possible, concentrate my whole force for the defense of Vicksburg from an attack in the rear by Grant's army, which was hourly swelling its numbers. Orders, therefore, were immediately transmitted to the officers in command at Granada, Columbus, and Jackson, to move all available forces to Vicksburg as rapidly as possible. On the morning of the 3d, two of the enemy's barges, loaded with hospital and commissary stores, were destroyed in attempting to pass the batteries at Vicksburg. On the 5th, I telegraphed General Johnston that six thousand cavalry should be used to keep my communications open, and that the enemy advancing on me was double what I could bring into the field. To the Honorable Secretary of War I sent the following telegram, under date of May 6th: "General Beauregard sends but two brigades, perhaps not five thousand men. This is a very insufficient number. The stake is a great one: I can see nothing so important." On the 7th the President notified me that all the assistance in his power to send should be forwarded, and that it was deemed necessary to hold Port Hudson, as a means of keeping up our communications with the Trans-Mississippi department. Major-General Gardner, who, with Brigadier-General Maxcey and five thousand (5,000) men, had previously been ordered to Jackson to reënforce this army, was immediately directed to send Maxcey's brigade rapidly forward, and to return himself with two thousand (2,000) men to Port Hudson, and hold the place at all hazards. On the 7th indications rendered it probable that the enemy would make a raid on Jackson. The staff departments, therefore, and all valuable stores, were ordered to be removed East. In the mean time, my troops were so disposed as to occupy the Warrenton and Hall's-Ferry road, which afforded great facilities for concentration, and various positions on the Baldwin's Ferry road, and from thence between Bovina and Edwards's Depot, each division being in good supporting distance of the other. Colonel Waul, commanding Fort Pemberton, was directed to leave a garrison of three hundred (300) men at that place, and proceed with the remainder of his force to Snyder's Mills. On the 10th, information was received from a scouting party that visited Cayuga and Utica, where the enemy had recently been, that his cavalry force was about two thousand, and that he was supposed to be moving on Vicksburg. My dispositions were made accordingly, and every effort was used to collect all the cavalry possible. Such as could be obtained were placed under the command of Colonel Wirt Adams, who was directed to harass the enemy on his line of march, cut his communications wherever practicable, patrol the country thoroughly, and to keep Brigadier-General Gregg (who had just arrived with his brigade from Port Hudson, and was then at Raymond) fully advised of the enemy's movements. On the 11th, Brigadier-General John Adams, commanding at Jackson, was directed to hurry forward, as fast as they could arrive, the troops from South Carolina, to reënforce Brigadier-General Gregg, at Raymond. At this time, information was received from Brigadier General Tilghman that the enemy was in force opposite Baldwin's Ferry, and Gregg was notified accordingly, and informed that the enemy's movements were apparently toward the Big Black Bridge, and not, as had been supposed, against Jackson. On the 12th, the following was addressed to Major-General Stevenson:

"From information received, it is evident the enemy is

advancing in force on Edward's Depot and Big Black Bridge; hot skirmishing has been going on all the morning, and the enemy are at Fourteen-Mile Creek. You must move up with your whole division to the support of Loring and Bowen at the bridge, leaving Baldwin's and Moore's brigades to protect your right."

In consequence of this information, Brigadier-General Gregg was ordered not to attack the enemy until he was engaged at Edwards's or the bridge, but to be ready to fall on his rear or flank at any moment, and to be particularly cautious not to allow himself to be flanked or taken in the rear. Thus it will be seen that every measure had been taken to protect Edwards's Depot and Big Black Bridge, and, by offering or accepting battle, to endeavor to preserve my communications with the East. At this juncture, however, the battle of Raymond was fought, by a large body of the enemy's forces, and one brigade of our troops under the command of Brigadier-General Gregg. I have received no official report of that affair, and hence cannot say how it was fought, or by whom the engagement was brought on. Unofficial information represents Brigadier-General Gregg and his small command to have behaved with great gallantry and steadiness, but after an obstinate conflict of several hours they were finally overwhelmed by superior numbers, and compelled to retire. The command was withdrawn in good order, and retired to Jackson. On the 14th, a large bdoy of the enemy made their appearance in front of Jackson, the capital of the State. After some fighting, our troops were withdrawn, and the enemy took possession of the place; but as General Johnston was commanding there in person, his official report, which has doubtless gone forward, will furnish all the information required.

On the 12th, the following telegram was sent to General J. E. Johnston:

"The enemy is apparently moving his heavy force toward Edwards's Depot, on Southern Railroad. With my

limited force I will do all I can to meet him; that will be
the battle-field, if I can carry forward sufficient force, leaving troops enough to secure the safety of this place (Vicksburg). Reënforcements are arriving very slowly, only fifteen hundred having arrived as yet. I urgently ask that
more be sent, also that three thousand cavalry be at once
sent to operate on this line. I urge this as a positive
necessity. The enemy largely outnumber me, and I am
obliged to hold back a large force at the ferries on Big Black,
lest he cross and take this place. I am also compelled to
keep considerable force on either flank of Vicksburg, out of
supporting distance."

The same dispatch was also sent to his Excellency President Davis on the same date. The divisions of Major-Generals Loring and Stevenson moved from the line they had
occupied between Warrenton and Big Black Bridge to Edwards's Depot, General Stevenson being directed to keep well
closed up on the rear of General Loring's column. On the
evening of the 12th I moved my headquarters to Bovina, to
be nearer the scene of active operations. The command
arrived at Edwards's Depot on the 13th, and was placed in
position, covering all approaches from the south and east in
the following order, viz.: Bowen on the right, Loring in
the centre, and Stevenson on the left. This position was
occupied from the night of the 13th until the morning of
the 15th.

On the 13th the following dispatch was sent to General
Johnston:

"General Forney reports, from Vicksburg this morning,
four transports loaded with troops, arrived at Young's Point
this morning. Five regiments and a battery passed down
by Brown and Johnson's. Wagon-trains continue to pass
back and forth. My reënforcements will be very small, and
arrive very slowly. If possible, Port Hudson should be reenforced. I have been forced to draw largely from there.
I have no major-general to command brigades arriving in

Jackson. I am in position with eight brigades near Edwards's Depot."

On the morning of the 14th, while on my way to Edwards's Depot from Bovina, I received the following dispatch, dated May 13th, from General Johnston, then at Jackson :

"I have lately arrived, and learn that Major-General Sherman is between us, with four divisions, at Clinton. It is important to reëstablish communications, that you may be reënforced. If practicable, come up in his rear at once; to beat such a detachment would be of immense value. The troops here could coöperate. All the troops you can quickly assemble should be brought. Time is all-important."

I immediately replied as follows :

" BOVINA, *May* 14, 1863.

" I have the honor to acknowledge receipt of your communication. I moved at once with whole available force, about sixteen thousand, from Edwards's Depot, leaving Vaughan's brigade, about fifteen hundred, at Big Black Bridge ; Tilghman's brigade, fifteen hundred, now at Baldwin's Ferry, I have ordered to bring up the rear of my column ; he will be, however, from fifteen to twenty miles behind it. Baldwin's Ferry will be left, necessarily, unprotected. To hold Vicksburg are Smith's and Forney's divisions, extending from Snyder's Mills to Warrenton, numbering, effective, seven thousand eight hundred men. The men have been marching several days, are much fatigued, and I fear will straggle very much. In directing this move, I do not think you fully comprehend the position that Vicksburg will be left in ; but I comply at once with your order."

The " detachment " General Johnston speaks of in his communication consisted of four divisions of the enemy, constituted an entire army corps, numerically greater than my whole available force in the field ; besides, the enemy had at least an equal force to the south, on my right flank, which would be nearer Vicksburg than myself, in case I should make the movement proposed. I had, moreover, positive information that he was daily increasing his strength. I also learned, on reaching Edwards's Depot, that one division of the enemy (A. J. Smith's) was at or near Dillon's.

This confirmed me in the opinion, previously expressed, that the movement indicated by General Johnston was extremely hazardous. I accordingly called a council of war of all the general officers present, and, placing the subject before them (including General Johnston's dispatch), in every view in which it appeared to me, asked their opinions respectively. A majority of the officers present expressed themselves favorable to the movement indicated by General Johnston. The others, including Major-Generals Loring and Stevenson, preferred a movement by which the army might attempt to cut off the enemy's supplies from the Mississippi River.

My own views were strongly expressed as unfavorable to any advance which would separate me farther from Vicksburg, which was my base. I did not, however, see fit to put my own judgment and opinions so far in opposition as to prevent a movement altogether, but, believing the only possibility of success to be in the plan of cutting the enemy's communications, it was adopted, and the following dispatch was addressed to General Johnston :

"EDWARDS'S DEPOT, *May* 14, 1863.

" I shall move as early to-morrow morning as practicable, with a column of seventeen thousand men, to Dillon's, situated on the main road leading from Raymond to Port Gibson, seven and a half miles below Raymond, and nine and a half miles from Edwards's Depot.

" The object is to cut the enemy's communications, and to force him to attack me, as I do not consider my force sufficient to justify an attack on the enemy in position, or to attempt to cut my way to Jackson. At this point your nearest communication would be through Raymond. I wish very much I could join my reënforcements. Whether it will be most practicable for the reënforcements to come by Raymond (leaving it to the right, if the march cannot be made through Raymond), or to move them west along the line of railroad (leaving it to the left and south of the line of march) to Bolton's Depot or some other point west of it, you must determine. In either movement, I should be advised as to the time and road, so that coöperation may be had to enable the reënforcements to come through. I send you a map of the country, which will furnish you with a correct view of the roads and localities."

Pursuant to the plan laid down in this dispatch, the army was put in motion on the 15th, about 1 P. M., in accordance with the following order, viz. :

"HEADQUARTERS DEPARTMENT MISSISSIPPI AND EAST LOUISIANA, }
              EDWARDS'S DEPOT, *May* 14, 1863.   }

" SPECIAL ORDER, }
     NO. —.   }

" This army will move to-morrow morning, 15th instant, in the direction of Raymond, on the military road, in the following order :

"1. Colonel Wirt Adams's cavalry will form the advance-guard, keeping at least one mile in advance of the head of the column, throwing out one company in front of his column, and a small detachment in its advance, besides the flankers upon his column, when practicable.

"2. Loring's division will constitute the right and the advance in the line of march. He will throw a regiment of infantry, with a section of artillery, at least two hundred yards in his front, with a company of infantry at least seventy-five yards in its advance—all with the necessary detachments and flankers.

"3. Bowen's division will constitute the centre, and will follow the leading division.

"4. Stevenson's division will constitute the left, bringing up the rear of the column.

" 5. The artillery of each brigade will march in the rear of the brigade.

" 6. The ambulances of each brigade will follow in the rear of their brigade.

" 7. The ordnance-wagons of each division will follow in the rear of their division.

" 8. The wagon-train will follow in rear of the entire column.

" 9. Should Tilghman's brigade arrive after the departure of the column, it will constitute, with a field-battery, the rear-guard, following immediately in rear of the wagon-train.

" 10. A company of Wirt Adams's cavalry will close the order of march.

" 11. The wagon-train will follow in the order of division —that is to say, the wagon-train of Loring's division on the right of the train; that of Bowen's in the centre, etc.

" Quartermasters, commissaries, and ordnance-officers, will remain with their trains, unless otherwise ordered. Straggling, always disgraceful in an army, is particularly forbidden. Stringent orders will be issued by the division commanders to prevent this evil; the rear-guard is especially instructed to permit no one to fall to the rear under any circumstances."

A continuous and heavy rain had made Baker's Creek impassable by the ordinary ford on the main Raymond road, where the country-bridge had been washed away by previous freshets; in consequence of this the march was delayed for several hours; but, the water not falling sufficiently to make the creek fordable, the column was directed by the Clinton road, on which was a good bridge, and, after passing the creek, upward of one and a half miles, was filed to the right, along Neighborhood road, so as to strike the Raymond road about three and a half miles from Edwards's Depot. The march was continued until the head of the column had passed Mrs. Elliston's house, where it was halted, and the troops bivouacked in order of march.

I made my headquarters at Mrs. Elliston's, where I found Major-General Loring had established his. The divisions of Generals Stevenson and Bowen having been on the march until past midnight, and the men considerably fatigued; desiring also to receive reports of reconnoissances made in my front before proceeding farther, I did not issue orders to continue the movement at an early hour the following morning.

Immediately on my arrival at Mrs. Elliston's, on the night of the 15th, I sent for Colonel Wirt Adams, commanding the cavalry, and gave him the necessary instructions for picketing all approaches in my front, and directed him to send out scouting-parties to discover the enemy's whereabouts. I also made strenuous efforts to effect the same object through citizens, but without success. Nothing unusual occurred during the night.

On the morning of the 16th, at about six and a half o'clock, Colonel Wirt Adams reported to me that his pickets were skirmishing with the enemy on the Raymond road, some distance in our front. While in conversation with him, a courier arrived, and handed me the following dispatch from General Johnston :

"BENTON ROAD, TEN MILES FROM JACKSON, {
        May 15, 1863, 8.30 A. M.   }

" Our being compelled to leave Jackson makes your plan impracticable. The only mode by which we can unite is by your moving directly to Clinton, and informing me that we may move to that point with about six thousand. I have no means of estimating the enemy's force at Jackson.

" The principal officers here differ very widely, and I fear he will fortify if time is left him. Let me hear from you immediately. General Maxcey was ordered back to Brookhaven. You probably have time to make him join you. Do so before he has time to move away."

I immediately directed a countermarch, or rather a retrograde movement, by reversing the column as it then stood, for the purpose of returning toward Edwards's Depot to take the Brownsville road, and then to proceed toward Clinton by a route north of the railroad. A written reply to General Johnston's instructions, in which I notified him that the countermarch had been ordered, and of the route I should take, was dispatched in haste, and without allowing myself sufficient time to take a copy.

Just as this reverse movement commenced, the enemy drove in Colonel Adams's cavalry-pickets, and opened with artillery, at long range, on the head of my column on the Raymond road; not knowing whether this was an attack in force, or simply an armed reconnoissance, and being anxious to obey the instructions of General Johnston, I directed the continuance of the movement, giving the necessary instructions for securing the safety of the wagon-train. The demonstrations of the enemy soon becoming more serious, orders were sent to division commanders to form in line of battle on the cross-road from the Clinton to the Raymond road— Loring on the right, Bowen in the centre, and Stevenson on the left. Major-General Stevenson was instructed to make the necessary dispositions for the protection of the trains then on the Clinton road and crossing Baker's Creek. The line of battle was quickly formed, without any interference on the part of the enemy; the position selected was naturally a strong one, and all approaches from the front well covered. A short time after the formation of the line, Loring's division was thrown back so as to cover the military road, it being reported that the enemy had appeared in that direction. The enemy made his first demonstration on our right, but, after a lively artillery-duel for an hour or more, this attack was relinquished, and a large force was thrown against our left, where skirmishing became heavy about ten o'clock, and the battle began in earnest along Stevenson's entire front about noon. Just at this time a column of the enemy were seen moving in front of our centre toward the right. Landis's battery, of Bowen's division, opened upon and soon broke this column, and compelled it to retire. I then directed Major-General Loring to move forward and crush the enemy in his front, and directed General Bowen to coöperate with him in the movement. Immediately on the receipt of my message, General Bowen rode up and announced his readiness to execute his part of the movement as soon as Major-General Loring should advance. No movement was made by Major-General Loring, he informing me that the enemy was too strongly posted to be attacked, but that he would seize the first opportunity to assault, if one should offer. The enemy still making strenuous efforts to turn Major-General Stevenson's left flank, compelled him to make a similar movement toward the left, thus extending his own line, and making a gap between his and Bowen's divisions. General Bowen was ordered to keep this interval closed, and the same instructions were sent to General Loring in reference to the interval between his and General Bowen's division. General Stevenson having informed me that, unless reënforced, he would be unable to resist the heavy and repeated attacks along his whole line, Bowen was ordered to send one brigade to his assistance, which was promptly brought forward under Colonel F. M. Cockrell, and in a very short time his remaining brigade, under the command of Brigadier-General Martin E. Green, was put in, and the two together, under their gallant leaders, charged the enemy, and for a time turned the tide of battle in our favor, again displaying the heroic courage which this veteran division has made conspicuous on so many stricken fields. The enemy still continued to move troops from his left to his right, thus increasing his vastly superior forces against Stevenson's and Bowen's divisions. Feeling assured that there was no important force in his front, I dispatched several staff-officers in rapid succession to Major-General Loring, ordering him to move all but one brigade (Tilghman's, which was directed to hold the Raymond road and cover the bridge and ford at Baker's Creek) to the left as rapidly as possible. To the first of these messages, sent about two o'clock P. M., answer was returned by Major-General Loring that the enemy was in strong force in his front, and endeavoring to flank him. Hearing no firing on the right, I repeated my orders to Major-General Loring, explained to him the condition of affairs on the left, and directed him to put his two left brigades into the fight as soon as possible. In the transmission of these various messages to and fro, over a distance of more than a mile, much valuable time was necessarily consumed, which the enemy did not fail to take advantage of.

About four o'clock P. M., a part of Stevenson's division broke badly, and fell back in great disorder, but was partially rallied by the strenuous exertions of myself and staff, and put back under their own officers into the fight; but, observing that large numbers of men were abandoning the field on Stevenson's left, deserting their comrades, who in this moment of greatest trial stood manfully at their posts, I rode up to General Stevenson, and, informing him that I had repeatedly ordered two brigades of General Loring's division to his assistance, and that I was momentarily expecting them, asked him whether he could hold his position. He replied that he could not; that he was fighting from sixty to eighty thousand men. I then told him I would endeavor myself to find General Loring and hasten him up; and started immediately with that object. I presently met Brigadier-General Buford's brigade of Loring's division, on the march and in rear of the right of Bowen's division. Colonel Cockrell, commanding the First Missouri brigade, having, in person, some time previously urgently asked for reënforcements, which (none of Loring's troops having come up) I was then unable to give him, one regiment of Buford's brigade was detached at once, and directed to his support; the remainder of Buford's brigade was moved as rapidly as possible to the assistance of General Stevenson. Finding that the enemy's vastly superior numbers were pressing all my forces engaged steadily back into old fields, where all advantages of position would be in his favor, I felt it to be too late to save the day, even should Brigadier-General Featherston's brigade of Loring's division come up immediately. I could, however, learn nothing of General Loring's whereabouts; several of my staff-officers were in search of him, but it was not until after General Bowen had personally informed me that he could not hold his position longer, and not until after I had ordered the retreat, that General Loring, with Featherston's brigade, moving, as I subsequently learned, by a country-road which was considerably longer than the direct route, reached the position on the left known as Champion's Hill, where he was forming a line of battle when he received my order to cover the retreat. Had the movement in support of the left been promptly made, when first ordered, it is not improbable that I might have maintained my position, and it is possible the enemy might have been driven back, though his vastly superior and constantly-increasing numbers would have rendered it necessary to withdraw during the night to save my communications with Vicksburg.

Early in the day, Major Lockett, Chief Engineer, had been instructed to throw a bridge over Baker's Creek, on the Raymond road. The stream had also fallen sufficiently to render the ford practicable. The retreat was ordered to be conducted by that route, and a staff-officer immediately dispatched to Brigadier-General Tilghman, who was directed to hold the Raymond road at all hazards. It was in the execution of this important duty, which could not have been confided to a fitter man, that the lamented general bravely lost his life. He was struck by a fragment of a shell, and died almost instantly. Although, as before stated, a large number of men had shamefully abandoned their commands and were making their way to the rear, the main body of the troops retired in good order. On reaching the ford and bridge, at Baker's Creek, I directed Brigadier-General Bowen to take position with his division on the west bank, and to hold the crossing until Loring's division, which was directed to bring up the rear, had effected the passage. I then proceeded at once to the intrenched line, covering the wagon and railroad bridges over the Big Black, to make the necessary arrangements for holding that point during the passage of the river.

In his official report, Major-General Stevenson says:

"On my arrival, about sunset, at the ford on Baker's Creek, I found that the enemy had crossed the bridge above, and were advancing artillery in the direction of the road on which we were moving. One battery had already taken position and were playing on the road, but at right angles and at too long a range to prevent the passage of troops. Here I found, on the west side, the brigades of General Green and Colonel Cockrell, of Bowen's division, who had there halted and taken up position to hold the point until Loring's division could cross. I found Colonel Scott, of the Twefth Louisiana regiment, of Loring's division, halted about half a mile from the ford on the east side, and directed him to cross. I then addressed a note to General Loring, informing him of what I had done, telling him of the change I had caused Colonel Scott to make in his position, stating that, with the troops then there, and others that I could collect, I would hold the ford and road until his division could cross, and urging him to hasten the movement. To this note I received no answer, but in a short time Colonel Scott moved off his regiment quickly in the direction of his original position, in obedience, I was informed, to orders from General Loring. Inferring from this that General Loring did not intend to cross at that ford, he having had ample time to commence the movement, I suggested to General Green and Colonel Cockrell to move forward to the railroad-bridge. My command reached that point at about one o'clock that night, and bivouacked near Bovina."

The entire train of the army, under the judicious management of Colonel A. W. Reynolds, commanding Tennessee brigade of Stevenson's division, was crossed without loss, though the movements of the enemy compelled Colonel Reynolds's brigade to cross the Big Black above the railroad-bridge.

On reaching the line of intrenchments occupied by Brigadier-General Vaughan's brigade of East-Tennesseans (Smith's division), he was instructed by myself, in person, to man the trenches from the railroad to the left, his artillery to remain as then posted, and all wagons to cross the river at once. Special instructions were left with Lieutenant J. H. Morrison, aide-de-camp, to be delivered to Generals Loring, Stevenson, and Bowen, as they should arrive, and were delivered to all, except to General Loring, as follows:

"General Stevenson's division to cross the river and proceed to Mount Alban; General Loring's to cross and occupy the west bank; Brigadier-General Bowen's division, as it should arrive, was directed to occupy the trenches to the right and left of Vanghan's, and his artillery to be parked, that it might be available for any point of the lines most threatened."

General Stevenson's division arriving very late in the night, did not move beyond Bovina, and I awaited in vain intelligence of the approach of General Loring. It was necessary to hold the position to enable him to cross the river, should the enemy, which was probable, follow him closely up. For this purpose alone, I continued the troops in position, until it was too late to withdraw them under cover of night. I then determined not to abandon so strong a front while there was yet a hope of his arrival. I have not, up to this time, received General Loring's report of the share taken by his division in the battle of Baker's Creek, nor have I yet been informed of the reason why he failed to rejoin the army under my command.

The Big Black River, where it is crossed by the railroad-bridge, makes a bend somewhat in the shape of a horse-shoe. Across this horseshoe, at its narrowest part, a line of rifle-pits had been constructed, making an excellent cover for infantry, and at proper intervals dispositions were made for field-artillery. The line of pits ran nearly north and south, and was about one mile in length. North of, and for a considerable distance south of the railroad, and of a dirt-road to Edwards's Depot, nearly parallel with it, extended a bayou, which in itself opposed a serious obstacle to an assault upon the pits. This line abutted north on the river and

south upon a cypress-brake which spread itself nearly to
the bank of the river. In addition to the railroad-bridge,
which I had caused to be floored for the passage even of
artillery and wagons, the steamer Dot, from which the machinery had been taken, was converted into a bridge by
placing her fore and aft across the river. Between the
works and the bridge, about three-quarters of a mile, the
country was open, being either clear or cultivated fields,
affording no cover should the troops be driven from the
trenches. East and south of the railroad the topographical
features of the country, over which the enemy must necessarily pass, were similar to those above described; but north
of the railroad, and about three hundred yards in front of
the rifle-pits, a copse of wood extended from the road to the
river. One line was manned on the right by the gallant
Cockrell's Missouri brigade, the extreme left by Brigadier-
General Green's Missouri and Arkansas men, both of Bow-
en's division, and the centre by Brigadier-General Vaughan's brigade of East-Tennesseeans, in all about four thousand
men, as many as could be advantageously employed in defending the line, with about twenty pieces of field-artillery.
So strong was the position, that my greatest—almost only
—apprehension was a flank movement by Bridgeport or
Baldwin's Ferry, which would have endangered my communications with Vicksburg. Yet this position was abandoned by our troops almost without a struggle, and with the
loss of nearly all our artillery. I speak not now of the
propriety or of the necessity of holding this position. I
had, as heretofore noticed, my object in doing so. I considered that object sufficient, and I also deemed the force
employed for the purpose ample.

Brigadier-General Vaughan's brigade had not been engaged at Baker's Creek; his men were fresh and, I believed,
were not demoralized. I knew that the Missouri troops,
under their gallant leaders, could be depended upon. By
whose order the battery-horses were so far removed from
their guns as not to be available, I do not know; it certainly was not by mine. General Bowen, with whom I had

a personal interview in his tent on the night of the 16th, and who received his instructions from my own lips (Lieutenant-Colonel Montgomery, of Lieutenant-General E. Kirby Smith's staff, being then present and acting as my aide-de-camp), I do not believe to be responsible for it; he was too old and too good a soldier. Enough, however, will, I think, be developed in a few words to cover the whole case. Early on the morning of the 17th the enemy opened his artillery at long range, and very soon pressed forward with infantry into the copse of wood north of the railroad; about the same time, he opened on Colonel Cockrell's position with two batteries, and advanced a line of skirmishers, throwing forward a column of infantry, which was quickly driven back by our batteries. Pretty heavy skirmishing was for a while kept up along our whole line, but presently the enemy, who had massed a large force in the woods immediately north of the railroad, advanced at a run, with loud cheers. Our troops in their front did not remain to receive them, but broke and fled precipitately. One portion of the line being broken, it very soon became a matter of *sauve qui peut.* I shall only add, with reference to the affair of Big Black, that a strong position, with an ample force of infantry and artillery to hold it, was shamefully abandoned, almost without resistance.

The troops occupying the centre did not do their duty. With an almost impassable bayou between themselves and the enemy, they fled before the enemy had reached that obstacle.

I have received no report from Brigadier-General Vaughan of the operations of his brigade on this occasion. Colonel Cockrell says, in his official report:

"After a lively skirmish-fire had been kept up for some time along our whole front, I saw the line between the railroad and first skirt of timber north of the railroad beginning to give way and then running in disorder. I watched this disorderly falling back a few minutes, when I saw that the enemy had possession of the trenches north of the railroad, and were rapidly advancing toward the bridge, our only crossing and way of escape; the enemy now being nearer this crossing than my line, I therefore ordered the brigade to fall back, and, moving rapidly, gained the bridge, crossed over, and reformed on the west bank of the river, north of the railroad."

Colonel Gates, commanding second brigade Bowen's division, says in his official report:

"They" (the enemy) "formed their men on the river, in the timber, where we could not see them. They brought their men out by the right flank, in column of four, about one hundred and forty yards in front of my regiment, at a double quick. I then opened a most terrific fire upon them, and kept it up until the brigade had passed out of my sight behind a grove of timber immediately upon my right. They moved so as to strike the trenches occupied by General Vaughan's brigade, so I am informed. I do not know whose troops were there, but it was immediately on the right of Green's brigade. After they had passed me, I listened for our men to open a heavy volley on my right and drive the enemy back. Upon not hearing any firing on the right, I directed Lieutenant-Colonel Law to mount his horse and go to General Green and know whether the centre was holding its position or not. Colonel Law returned in a few minutes and said that General Green ordered me to fall back. I did so at once. After I had got back below the bend of the river, I discovered that they had crossed the ditches, and were between me and the bridge."

In this precipitate retreat but little order was observed, the object with all being to reach the bridge as rapidly as possible. Many were unable to do so, but effected their escape by swimming the river; some were drowned in the attempt. A considerable number, unable to swim, and others too timid to expose themselves to the fire of the enemy by an effort to escape, remained in the trenches and were made prisoners. In this connection I deem it my duty to make the following extract from the report of Colonel Cockrell:

" Captain I. B. Wilson, of the Second infantry, Company G, claiming to have been exhausted, did not go with his company into the battle of Baker's Creek, and, having made his way to Big Black, joined his company in the rifle-pits early on the morning of the 17th instant, and, when his company was ordered to fall back, abandoned his company and remained lying in the rifle-pits, and was captured by the enemy; and, while a prisoner, stated to Colonel Elijah Gates, of the First Missouri cavalry, who was also a prisoner, that he (Captain Wilson) intended to take the oath, and then go to fighting the enemy as a guerrilla. Such conduct merits a dismissal in disgrace, and such an officer should not remain in the way of gallant and efficient officers now commanding his company."

In this opinion I fully concur. Neither Brigadier-General Bowen nor Green had furnished reports of the action on Big Black previous to his death. To the former had been intrusted the defense of the *tête de pont*, and he had received my instructions in person; the latter had been second in command. Brigadier-General Vaughan having failed to render his report, I am dependent for the particulars of the action upon those of Colonels Gates and Cockrell, which are respectfully forwarded herewith. Major Lockett, chief-engineer, was instructed to fire both bridges, after seeing that all the troops had crossed; this was effectually accomplished, under his personal supervision. The guns in position were ample for the defense, but, the infantry failing to support them, they were abandoned; such as were not in position were safely brought from the field, placed in battery on the bluff on the west bank, and, with others already established, and a sufficient force of infantry, held the advancing columns of the enemy effectually in check. It had become painfully apparent to me that the *morale* of my army was not such as to justify an attempt to hold the line of the

Big Black River.   Not only was it greatly weakened by the
absence of General Loring's division, but also by the large
number of stragglers who, having abandoned their commands, were already making their way into Vicksburg.
The enemy, by flank movement on my left by Bridgeport, and on my right by Baldwin's or other ferries, might
reach Vicksburg almost simultaneously with myself, or perhaps might interpose a heavy force between me and that
city.

Under these circumstances, nothing remained but to
retire the army within the defenses of Vicksburg, and to
endeavor, as speedily as possible, to reorganize the depressed
and discomfited troops.   Orders were accordingly issued,
at ten A. M., and Major-General Stevenson directed to conduct the retreat, which was executed without haste and in
good order.   I myself proceeded at once to Vicksburg to
prepare for its defense.

I think it due to myself, in bringing this portion of my
report to a conclusion, to state emphatically that the advance
movement of the army from Edwards's Depot, on the afternoon of the 15th of May, was made against my judgment,
in opposition to my previously-expressed intentions, and to
the subversion of my matured plans.   In one contingency
alone I had determined to move toward Jackson.   The
safety of Vicksburg was of paramount importance ; under
no circumstances could I abandon my communication with
it.   A sufficient force must also be left to defend the river-
front of the city, the approaches by Chickasaw Bayou, by
Snyder's Mills, and Warrenton, against a *coup de main*.
My effective aggregate did not exceed twenty-eight thousand ; at least eight thousand would be required for these
purposes.   It would also be necessary to hold the bridges
across the Big Black, on the line of the Southern Railroad.
With these deductions, my movable army might reach
eighteen thousand five hundred.   I give this number as the
maximum.

In the event, therefore, of the enemy advancing with his
whole force, east of the Mississippi River, against Jackson,

my communications by the shortest line being open, would have enabled me to move upon his rear. General Johnston's forces and my own might have formed a junction, or have attacked simultaneously in front and rear; but I did not think it would be wise to attempt to execute this plan until the arrival of expected reënforcements at or near Jackson, hence I received General Johnston's instructions, on the morning of the 14th, to move to Clinton with all the force I could quickly collect, with great regret, and I well remember that, in the presence of one or more of my staff-officers, I remarked, in substance, "Such a movement will be suicidal." Nevertheless, notifying General Johnston of the fact, I took measures for an advance movement at once, not, it is true, directly toward Clinton, but in the only direction which, from my knowledge of the circumstances surrounding me, I thought offered a possibility of success. Had I moved directly to Clinton, the enemy would not have given me battle in front, but would have interposed a force greater than my own between me and Vicksburg.

It is only necessary to refer to the maps accompanying this report to see how feasible was such a movement. I have already given in the body of this report the two letters of instruction from General Johnston, dated respectively 13th and 15th of May, 1863. In obedience to the injunctions contained in the former, which was received on the morning of the 14th, I lost no time in putting my army in motion in the direction already stated, and for the reasons given.

About seven A. M., on the 16th, I received the letter which reiterated the previous instructions. I had, in no measure, changed my views as to the propriety of the movement therein indicated, but I no longer felt at liberty to deviate from General Johnston's positive orders. He had been made aware of my views, and did not sustain them. The order of march was at once reversed, but the army was hardly in motion before it became necessary to form line of battle to meet the greatly superior forces of the enemy.

About six P. M., on the 16th, while on the retreat, the following communication was handed to me:

"CAMP SEVEN MILES FROM JACKSON,
May 14, 1863.

"GENERAL: The body of troops, mentioned in my note of last night compelled Brigadier-General Gregg and his command to evacuate Jackson about noon to-day; the necessity of taking the Canton road, at right angles to that upon which the enemy approaches, prevented an obstinate defense. A body of troops, reported this morning to have reached Raymond last night, advanced at the same time from that direction.

"Prisoners say that it was McPherson's corps (four divisions) which marched from Clinton. I have certain information of the other; both skirmished very cautiously. Telegrams were dispatched, when the enemy was near, directing General Gist to assemble the approaching troops at a point forty or fifty miles from Jackson, and General Maxcey to return to his wagons and provide for the security of his brigade; for instance, by joining General Gist. That body of troops will be able, I hope, to prevent the enemy in Jackson from drawing provision from the East, and this one may be able to keep him from the country toward Panola. Can he supply himself from the Mississippi? Can you not cut him off from it; and, above all, should he be compelled to fall back for want of supplies, beat him? As soon as the re-enforcements are all up, they must be united to the rest of the army. I am anxious to see a force assembled, that they be able to inflict a heavy blow upon the enemy.

"Would it not be better to place the forces to support Vicksburg between General Loring and that place, and merely observe the ferries, so that you might unite if opportunity to fight presented itself? General Gregg will move toward Canton to-morrow. If prisoners tell the truth, the force at Jackson must be half of Grant's army. It would decide the campaign to beat it, which can only be done by concentrating, especially when the remainder of

the Eastern troops arrive. They are to be twelve or thirteen thousand.

        " Most respectfully,
             " Your obedient servant,
                   " J. E. JOHNSTON."

It will be observed that General Johnston's letter of the
15th, which caused me to reverse my column with the view
of marching to Clinton, was received before the retreat commenced, and about eleven hours earlier than this one of the
14th just presented.

I know nothing of the causes which produced this result,
but I respectfully invite attention to the fact that, in this
letter of the 14th, General Johnston suggests the very movement which I had made, and for the purpose I had indicated. After expressing the hope that certain dispositions
made by himself might prevent the enemy from drawing
provisions from the East or from the country toward Panola,
he says : " Can he supply himself from the Mississippi ? Can
you not cut him off from it ; and, above all, should he be
compelled to fall back for want of supplies, beat him ? "

I have introduced General Johnston's letter entire, that
the context, as well as that portion to which I have particularly called attention, may be considered.

I had resisted the popular clamor for an advance, which
began from the moment the enemy set his polluting foot
upon the eastern bank of the Mississippi River. I had resisted the universal sentiment, I believe, of the army—I
know of my general officers—in its favor, and yielded only
to the orders of my superiors. I was not invited by
General Johnston to submit my plans to him for his consideration ; it is, therefore, unnecessary now to speak of
them.

One of the immediate results of the retreat from Big
Black was the necessity of abandoning our defenses on the
Yazoo at Snyder's Mills ; that position, and the line of
Chickasaw Bayou, were no longer tenable. All stores that
could be transported were ordered to be sent into Vicksburg

as rapidly as possible ; the rest, including heavy guns, to be destroyed.

There was, at this time, a large quantity of corn, probably twenty-five or thirty thousand bushels, on boats, much of which might have been brought in had it been possible to furnish the necessary wagons. The boats were sent up the river. Two companies were directed to remain at Snyder's Mills, making a show of force until the approach of the enemy by land should compel them to retire. To them was intrusted the duty of forwarding all stores possible, and of destroying the remainder. This detachment rejoined its command in Vicksburg on the morning of the 18th. Every precaution was taken to guard the important approaches to the city by Forney's and Smith's divisions, while the troops which had been engaged in the battles of the 16th and 17th were bivouacked in the rear of the intrenchments. During these battles the troops of Major-General Forney's division were disposed as follows : Brigadier-General Hebert's brigade occupied the line along the Yazoo River, from Haines's Bluff to the Mississippi, including the approaches by Chickasaw Bayou ; Brigadier-General Moore's brigade, with the Mississippi State troops, under General Harris, attached (about six hundred), guarded the front at Warrenton and the approaches from the lower ferries on the Big Black River ; Brigadier-General Shoupe's brigade of Major-General Smith's division guarded the river-front of the city. Brigadier-General Baldwin's brigade, with Waul's Legion attached, guarded the approaches to the city from the Hall's Ferry road around to the railroad-bridge on the Big Black ; the heavy artillery at the batteries on the river-front, under Colonel Higgins. Brigadier-General Moore's brigade was drawn in at once from Warrenton, and placed in the intrenchments on either side of Baldwin's Ferry road. Brigadier-General Hebert's brigade arrived before daylight on the 18th, bringing with it all the light pieces, and, in addition, two twenty-pound Parrotts and a Whitworth gun. This brigade immediately occupied the intrenchments on both sides of the Jackson road.

On the morning of the 18th the troops were disposed from right to left as follows : Major-General Stevenson's division of five brigades occupied the line from the Warrenton road, including a portion of the river-front, to the railroad, a distance of about five miles ; Major-General Forney, with two brigades, the line between the railroad and the graveyard road, about two miles ; and Major-General Smith, with three brigades, the Mississippi State troops, and a small detachment from Loring's division, the line from the graveyard road to the river-front, on the north, about one and a quarter miles. Brigadier-General Bowen's division was held in reserve to strengthen any portion of the line most threatened, and Waul's Texas Legion (about five hundred) was in reserve especially to support the right of Moore's or the left of Lee's brigades. On the entire line, one hundred and two pieces of artillery of different calibre, principally field, were placed in position at such points as were deemed most suitable to the character of the gun, changes of location being made when occasion called for it. An engineer-officer, under the supervision of Major Lockett, Chief Engineer of the Department, was assigned to each division, with an assistant to each brigade commander. Daily reports were made, through the proper channel, to Major Lockett, of the operations of the engineer department, and of the progress of the enemy's works. Major Lockett thus kept me constantly informed of all important changes, making himself a daily report.

Instructions had been given from Bovina that all cattle, sheep, and hogs, belonging to private parties, and likely to fall into the hands of the enemy, should be driven within our lines. A large amount of fresh meat was secured in this way. The same instructions were given in regard to corn, and all disposable wagons applied to this end. On the 18th, Colonel Wirt Adams, who had been previously directed to cross to the west bank of the Big Black, with all his cavalry, was notified that Snyder's Mills would be abandoned, and that he was expected to operate on the flank and rear of the enemy, with the view of cutting off his supplies in that direction. Colonel Adams's force was, however, very inadequate to this purpose. During the night of the 17th nothing of importance occurred. Most of the artillery was speedily placed in position on the lines, and immediately measures were taken to arm all men who had either unavoidably lost or who had thrown away their arms on the retreat. General Johnston was notified, on the 17th, of the result of the battles of Baker's Creek and Big Black, and informed that I had, in consequence, been compelled to evacuate Snyder's Mills. About noon of the 18th of May, while engaged in an inspection of the intrenchments with Major Lockett, my chief-engineer, and several of my general officers, the enemy was reported to be advancing by the Jackson road. Just at this moment the following communication was received by courier:

"CAMP BETWEEN LIVINGSTON AND BROWNSVILLE, *May* 17, 1863.

"Lieutenant-General PEMBERTON:

"Your dispatch of to-day, by Captain Henderson was received. If Haines's Bluff is untenable, Vicksburg is of no value, and cannot be held. If, therefore, you are invested in Vicksburg, you must ultimately surrender. Under such circumstances, instead of losing both troops and place, we must, if possible, save the troops. If it is not too late, evacuate Vicksburg and its dependencies, and march to the northeast.   Most respectfully,
                "Your obedient servant,
                          "J. E. JOHNSTON, *General.*"

The evacuation of Vicksburg! It meant the loss of the valuable stores and munitions of war collected for its defense, the fall of Port Hudson, the surrender of the Mississippi River, and the severance of the Confederacy. These were mighty interests, which, had I deemed the evacuation practicable in the sense in which I interpreted General Johnston's instructions, might well have made me hesitate to execute them. I believed it to be in my power to hold

Vicksburg. I knew I appreciated the earnest desire of the Government and the people that it should be held. I knew, perhaps better than any other individual, under all the circumstances, its capacity for defense. As long ago as the 17th of February last, in a letter addressed to his Excellency the President, I had suggested the possibility of the investment of Vicksburg by land and water, and for that reason the necessity of ample supplies of ammunition, as well as of subsistence, to stand a siege. My application met his favorable consideration, and additional ammunition was ordered.

With proper economy of subsistence and ordnance stores, I knew that I could stand a siege. I had a firm reliance in the desire of the President and of General Johnston to do all that could be done to raise a siege. I felt that every effort would be made, and I believed it would be successful. With these convictions on my own mind, I immediately summoned a council of war, composed of all my general officers. I laid before them General Johnston's communication, but desired them to confine the expression of their opinions to the question of practicability. Having obtained their views, the following communication was addressed to General Johnston:

"HEADQUARTERS, DEPARTMENT OF MISSISSIPPI AND EAST LOUISIANA,
VICKSBURG, *May* 18, 1863.

"General JOSEPH E. JOHNSTON.

"GENERAL: I have the honor to acknowledge the receipt of your communication, in reply to mine, by the hands of Captain Henderson. In a subsequent letter, of same date as this latter, I informed you that the men had failed to hold the trenches at Big Black Bridge, and that, as a consequence, Snyder's Mill was directed to be abandoned. On the receipt of your communication, I immediately assembled a council of war of the general officers of this command, and, having laid your instructions before them, asked the free expression of their opinion as to the practicability of carrying them out. The opinion was unanimously expressed that it was impossible to withdraw the army from this position with such *morale* and *matériel* as to be of further service to the Confederacy. While the council of war was assembled, the guns of the enemy opened on the works, and it was at the same time reported that they were crossing the Yazoo River at Brandon's Ferry, above Snyder's Mills. I have decided to hold Vicksburg as long as possible, with the firm hope that the Government may yet be able to assist me in keeping this obstruction to the enemy's free navigation of the Mississippi River. I still conceive it to be the most important point in the Confederacy.

"Very respectfully,

"Your obedient servant,

"J. C. PEMBERTON,

"*Lieutenant-General commanding.*"

CONFEDERATE STATES OF AMERICA, WAR DEPARTMENT,
RICHMOND, *October* 1, 1863.

Lieutenant-General J. C. PEMBERTON,

Richmond, Virginia.

GENERAL : At the suggestion of the President, I would call your attention to several points in your recent report of operations in Mississippi, which it would be gratifying to me to have elucidated or explained.

The first dispatch of General Joseph E. Johnston, from Jackson, instructed you to advance and attack in the rear the corps of the enemy at Clinton, and promised coöperation in such attack, on his part. Clinton was on the railroad between General Johnston and Jackson, and yourself at Edwards's Depot. I understood this direction to instruct you to march toward Clinton at once, and by the direct or nearest route, considering the rear to be the side most remote from him (General Johnston), and nearest you, and not to have contemplated that you should make a *détour* to come around on the rear of the line by which the enemy had advanced toward Clinton. Was a different view entertained by you of the intent of this order?

As the object of the order was to have the corps at Clinton promptly assailed while separate and beyond support, I have supposed it contemplated immediate movement on your part to execute it, and that the distance was not so great but that you might, could you have marched at once, have reached and struck the corps in from twelve to twenty-four hours.

Will you state the distance, and what obstacles prevented movement on your part for some twenty-six hours?

I have deemed it unfortunate that, on receiving this first dispatch from General Johnston, you, knowing that he must necessarily be very imperfectly acquainted with your position and resources, as well as with the movements and forces of the enemy, did not take the responsibility of acting on your better knowledge, and maintain your preconceived plan, or, if unwilling to do that, that you did not at once carry out strictly the order received. It appears to me the more to be regretted that, having written to General Johnston that you would move at once, though against your judgment, in execution of his instructions, you should afterward have so far deviated from them as to resolve to direct your movements toward Raymond instead of toward Clinton. When you came to this resolve, you at once informed General Johnston, but it happened, unfortunately, that, after the receipt of your first order, General Johnston had been compelled to act by the advance of the enemy on Jackson, and to proceed in evacuating, on the supposition that you were executing his first orders, and that you were more easily to be approached by his moving out to the north rather than to the south of the Vicksburg Railroad. Had he known of your purpose to move toward Raymond, the reasonable inference is, he would have directed his movements southward, or more in the direction of your proposed advance. I think it not unlikely misapprehension on this subject prevented his so moving as to have enabled him to have taken part in the battle so soon to be fought by you.

Will you explain more fully the motives for your deviation from the direct execution of the instructions, and the consequences which, in your judgment, would have resulted from pursuing the instructions literally?

Were you acquainted with the movements of the several corps of the enemy, when, as it appears, they were separated into two or more distinct columns, separated by twelve or fifteen miles, and when you were nearer to one, and perhaps to two, than they were to each other, could you not have struck at one separately, and, if so, what reasons induced you to wait till nearly all their several forces concentrated and attacked you on your march in obedience to General Johnston's renewed order?

While I have not approved General Johnston's instructions—as, under the circumstances, I think it would have been better to have left you to the guidance of your superior knowledge of the position, and your own judgment—I confess to have been surprised that, seeing he had taken the responsibility of positive directions with a view to a prompt attack on a separate detachment of the enemy, you had not seized the occasion, while they were severed, to attempt the blow. I consider the essential part of his orders to have been *immediate advance* and *attack on a separate column*, and that, if you could not execute that, you would have been well justified in attempting no other compliance, and falling back on your previous plan. As it was, *neither plan* was pursued, and invaluable time, and the advantage of position, were lost in doubtful movements; so, at least, the case has struck my mind.

On another distinct point I should be pleased to have information. How happened it that General Gregg, with his small force, was so far separate from you, and compelled alone, at Raymond, to encounter the greatly superior forces of the enemy? Had he been placed at such distance as a covering force to Jackson, the capital, or with what view?

To recur again to the battle of Baker's Creek, I should be pleased to know if General Loring had been ordered to attack before General Cummings's brigade gave way; and whether, in your opinion, had Stevenson's division been promptly sustained, the troops with him would have fought with so little tenacity and resolution as a portion of them exhibited? Have you had any explanation of the extraor-

dinary failure of General Loring to comply with your reiterated orders to attack? And do you feel assured your
orders were received by him? His conduct, unless explained by some misapprehension, is incomprehensible to
me.

You will, I trust, general, excuse the frankness with
which I have presented the foregoing subjects of inquiry.
They will doubtless only enable you more fully to explain
the movements made by you, and the reasons inducing them,
to the satisfaction as well of others interested as of

Yours, with esteem,

JAMES A. SEDDON, *Secretary of War.*

RICHMOND, *November* 10, 1863.

Hon. JAMES A. SEDDON, Secretary of War.

SIR: To your communication of the 1st ultimo, I have
the honor to make the following reply, taking the points
presented in order as you have placed them:

The first order from General Johnston was, I conceived,
to move on the rear of the corps of the enemy known by
him to be at Clinton, and I believed his intent to be by the
most direct route; but as he did not in his dispatch indicate
by what route, it was consequently left entirely with my
own judgment and discretion—had I seen fit to move to
Clinton at all—to decide the most advantageous route, under
the circumstances, for the advance.

I deem that to have made the movement to Clinton by
any route, but more especially the "most direct or nearest
route," would have been hazardous in the extreme—yes,
suicidal; for in that case would my flank and rear have
been entirely unprotected, and a large portion of the
enemy's force, of whose position General Johnston seemed
to be entirely ignorant, could have interposed itself between my army and its base of operations, Vicksburg, and
have taken that stronghold almost without a struggle, so
small was the garrison after I had withdrawn all my available force for the field.

The object, no doubt, of the order was, that the detachment of the enemy at Clinton should be promptly assailed, "while separate and beyond support." But was it beyond supporting distance of the other columns? Of the position of the enemy I was not definitely informed, but only knew that the whole of Grant's army (three corps) had taken the general direction northeast toward the railroad. At what point on this they would strike, or the positions of the two corps not mentioned nor seemingly regarded by General Johnston, I was not informed, except inasmuch as I had learned from prisoners that Smith's division was at Dillon's, and the rest of the corps to which he was attached was near him.

Could I make the movement on the one corps at Clinton, irrespective and regardless of the major force of the enemy?—jeopardizing my line of communication and retreat, and giving up Vicksburg an easy capture to the enemy, the retention of which in our posession I knew to be the great aim and object of the Government in the campaign; and for this end all my dispositions of troops had been made and plans arranged—plans now subverted entirely by the order under consideration; for it had not been my intention to make any forward movement from Edwards's Depot, but to have there awaited an attack from the enemy (which must have taken place in forty-eight hours, or he would have been compelled to have sought supplies at his base on the Mississippi River) in a chosen position, with my lines secured, and, if overwhelmed by numbers, a way of retreat open across the Big Black, and which line of defense I would have then held as an obstruction to the enemy's investing Vicksburg. And this disarrangement of my plans caused "the delay for some twenty-six hours." Not having contemplated an advance, all the arrangements had to be made for the movement, all my available troops had to be collected, and great difficulty was caused by the heavy rain which fell in the twenty-four hours succeeding the receipt of the order. My movement, considering the difficulties to be encountered, and the preparations necessary to be made, was, I think, promptly executed, and without "delay," in the usual acceptation of the meaning of that term.

General Johnston not having consulted with me, or in any way asked for my plan or opinion, I had perhaps no right to suppose that he was "imperfectly acquainted with my position and resources, as well as with the movements and forces of the enemy;" but on the contrary, when he ordered my advance, I would have been justified in supposing that he must have been better informed as to the disposition of the forces of the enemy than myself; but, notwithstanding this, had I been upheld by the opinions of my general officers, I would not have advanced beyond Edwards's Depot, as I deemed it very hazardous to make any forward movement, but would there have awaited, on chosen ground, the attack of the enemy.

The interval which elapsed between my communications (informing General Johnston, in the first, that I would obey his instructions at once, though against my own judgment; and, in the second, that I would move in a direction to cut off the supplies of the enemy) was not long enough to change or interfere with any movement of his.

By no possibility could General Johnston have effectually coöperated with me in the movement toward Clinton. He, at that time, having retired before the greatly superior force of the enemy, in the direction of Canton, was some twenty miles distant from Clinton; and, moreover, the enemy would certainly have forced battle from me before I should have reached the latter place. "The consequence which, in my judgment, would have resulted from pursuing the instructions literally," would have been the certain fall of Vicksburg, almost without a blow being struck in its defense, so overwhelming a force could the enemy then have thrown, without opposition, on its small garrison. For further elucidation on this point, I beg leave to refer you to an examination of the positions on the map accompanying my report.

In consequence of my great deficiency in cavalry—the force of that arm in my command being scarcely adequate for the necessary picketing—I was not " acquainted with the movements of the several corps of the enemy," but only knew, as before stated, that the general direction of the whole of Grant's army was to the northeast, from its base on Mississippi River. General Johnston, when he sent me the first instructions for the movement on the detachment at Clinton, was not informed of the position of the other detachments of the enemy; for he writes me on the next morning, the 14th, that another corps of the enemy, he learns, is at Raymond, to which he had not, in any manner, referred in his letter of the 13th.[1]

Having concluded that it would be suicidal to make the direct advance to Clinton, I would have attempted " no other compliance " with the order, had the opinion of my general officers in any manner sustained me in so doing; but, they being all eager for an advance, I made a movement in the shortest possible time to threaten the roads to Raymond and to Dillon, thus to cut off the supplies of the enemy, which a communication previously written (of the 14th) by General Johnston, but not received until after the battle of Baker's Creek, suggested. General Gregg, with his brigade from Port Hudson, having arrived at a point near Jackson, and being without his wagon transportation, was ordered to take position at Raymond (that being an advantageous point for the collection of the troops, either to move on the flank of the enemy advancing on Edwards's Depot, or to retire on Jackson), and on there being joined by the reënforcements which were expected, and daily arriving, at Jackson, including, as I hoped, a force of cavalry, to move on the rear and flank of the enemy, should he attack me in position at Edwards's Depot. To await and draw on this attack I had matured all my plans and arrangements (*see* following telegrams to Generals Gregg and Walker on this point, where it will be seen that, though General Gregg sustained the advance of the enemy nobly and bravely, my orders, however, were for him to retire on Jackson, if attacked by a greatly superior force) :

[1] Raymond is eight miles from Clinton.

VICKSBURG, *May* 11, 1863.

"GENERAL GREGG: From information from General Tilghman, of the enemy being in force opposite the ferry at Baldwin's, it is very probable that the movement toward Jackson is, in reality, on Big Black Bridge, in which case you must be prepared to attack them in rear or on flank.

"J. C. PEMBERTON,
"*Lieutenant-General commanding.*"

"VICKSBURG, *May* 11, 1863.

"Brigadier-General WALKER, Jackson:

"Move immediately with your command to Raymond. General Gregg has been ordered, if the enemy advance on him in too strong force, to fall back on Jackson. You will do likewise, in conjunction with him. If the enemy advance on you in not too strong force, you will meet them. If, instead of advancing on Jackson, they should advance on Big Black Bridge, the command, under direction of the senior officer, will attack them in rear and flank.

"J. C. PEMBERTON,
"*Lieutenant-General.*"

"VICKSBURG, *May* 11, 1863.

"Brigadier-General WALKER, Jackson:

"Enemy is reported advancing in heavy force on Jackson. Hold your command in readiness, and move toward Raymond, either to support General Gregg at that place or to cover his retreat. Telegraph to hurry up reënforcements.

"J. C. PEMBERTON,
"*Lieutenant-General commanding.*"

General Loring had been ordered to attack before General Cummings's brigade gave way, and the order had been again and again repeated; and, in my opinion, "had Stevenson's division been promptly sustained," his troops would have deported themselves gallantly and creditably. I have received no explanation of "the extraordinary failure of

General Loring to comply with my reiterated orders to attack," and I do feel "assured that my orders were received by him."

Hoping, sir, that these explanations may be satisfactory, I am, with respect, your obedient servant,

J. C. Pemberton,
Lieutenant-General commanding.

RICHMOND, *December* 14, 1863.

Hon. James A. Seddon, Secretary of War.

Sir: Having been allowed the opportunity of reading General J. E. Johnston's report of the military operations in the Department of Mississippi and East Louisiana during the months of May, June, and July last, in justice to myself I request to be permitted to make the following additional report:

The first order from General Johnston, dated at Jackson, the 13th of May, was received by me near Bovina, on the morning of the 14th, I think, between nine and ten o'clock. It was in these terms:

"I have lately arrived, and learn that Major-General Sherman is between us, with four divisions, at Clinton. It is important to reëstablish communication that you may be reënforced. If practicable, come up in his rear at once; to beat such a detachment would be of immense value; the troops here could coöperate. All the strength you can quickly assemble should be brought; time is all-important."

In this note General Johnston does not intimate a probable movement of the corps under General Sherman from Clinton upon Jackson, nor does he say how "the troops here" (at Jackson) "*could* coöperate." He only directs me, for purposes named, "if practicable, to come up in his" (enemy's) "rear at once." General Sherman, with his corps of four divisions, was represented by General Johnston to be between him and myself at Clinton. It was not clear to me by what route General Johnston wished me to advance. If the enemy should await my approach at Clinton, and give me battle there, General Johnston would have been in his rear, and might have coöperated ; or, if he advanced upon Jackson, and engaged the small force there, and I could, by any possibility, in obedience to General Johnston's orders, have come up in his rear while so occupied, there would have been coöperation. But, in either event, to unite our troops in this way, it is plain that the enemy, whatever his strength, must be first completely routed. I see no other mode by which a junction could have been effected, unless either General Johnston or myself should pass completely around the position or moving columns of the enemy. I have no reason to suppose he contemplated such a movement when he addressed to me his note of the 13th. In the absence of special instructions as to my route to reach the rear of the enemy at Clinton, I was certainly at liberty to select that which I should deem the most advantageous; time or the distance to be marched being only one element, though a very important one, which should influence my selection. I have no desire, however, to conceal the fact that my understanding of General Johnston's orders was to move as rapidly as possible to attack Sherman's corps at Clinton or wherever I might find it ; and I believed that his instructions were influenced by his supposing that these were the only troops I could encounter, as no reference is made to any other force of the enemy. It will be remembered, now, that I received these instructions between nine and ten o'clock on the morning of the 14th, near Bovina, on the west of the Big Black River. I at first determined to obey them at once, although, in my judgment, fraught with peril and absolute disaster ; and so informed General Johnston. Before leaving Bovina, I gave some necessary instructions to meet this unexpected movement, and, as soon as possible, proceeded to Edwards's Depot, where I arrived at about twelve o'clock, and learned, from prisoners just captured, that a corps of the enemy was on my right flank, with one division of it near Dillon's. It will be observed in General John-

ston's communication of the 14th, given in my report, unfortunately not received until the evening of the 16th, that
he informs me he was compelled to evacuate Jackson about
noon on that day; thus showing that, within less than three
hours of my receipt of his order, he was himself compelled
to leave Jackson, the enemy having moved from Clinton
against that place.

And, in the same communication, he further informs me
that a body of troops, which was reported to have reached
Raymond on the preceding night, advanced at the same
time from that direction. Therefore, had I moved immediately, which I could not have done with more than sixteen
thousand effective men, I should have encountered their
combined forces in my front, had they chosen to give me
battle; while McClernand's corps, upon my right, could
either have interposed between me and Vicksburg, or have
moved at once upon my rear. Nor could I have had much
assistance from the reënforcements referred to by General
Johnston; for, in the same communication, he informs me
that " telegrams were dispatched when the enemy was near,
directing General Gist to assemble the approaching troops
at a point forty or fifty miles from Jackson, and General
Maxcey to return to his wagons and provide for the security
of his brigade, for instance, by joining General Gist;" he
himself having moved on the 14th, with the small force at
Jackson, some seven miles toward Canton, and thus placed
himself not less than fifteen miles, as I am informed, by the
nearest practicable route, from Clinton; and, on the following day, he marched ten and a half miles nearer to Canton
and farther from Clinton.

Let us suppose, therefore, for the moment, that, neglecting all provision for the safety of Vicksburg, and by withdrawing Vaughan's brigade of fifteen hundred men from
the defense of the Big Black Bridge (my direct line of communication with Vicksburg), I had swelled my little army
at Edwards's Depot to seventeen thousand five hundred (it
must be remembered Tilghman's brigade was west of Big
Black guarding the important approach by Baldwin's Ferry,

which was threatened by the whole of McClernand's corps, and he could not, therefore, have joined me earlier than the morning of the 15th), and that I had then pushed hurriedly forward on the direct road to Clinton. I ask any candid mind, What would probably—nay, what must certainly— have been the result? I can see none other than the entire destruction or capture of my army and the immediate fall of Vicksburg. Such were my firm convictions at the time, and I so expressed myself to my general officers in council, and such they are still.

I have explained in my report why, contrary to my own judgment, and to the subversion of all my plans for the defense of Vicksburg, I determined to advance from my position at Edwards's Depot, and thus abandon the line of the Big Black, which (although I had crossed when I learned that the main body of General Grant's army was approaching the Southern Railroad, to protect my communications with the East, and more easily to avail myself of the assistance of my reënforcements which were daily arriving) I was yet in a position to recross readily, by both the bridges at the railroad and by Bridgeport, and thus defend my vital positions at Snyder's Mills and Chickasaw Bayou, if I should find that the enemy was advancing in too heavy force against Edwards's Depot. And I accordingly informed General Johnston, on the 12th May, that the enemy was apparently moving his heavy force toward Edwards's Depot, adding, "That will be the battle-field if I can carry forward sufficient force, leaving troops enough to secure the safety of this place (Vicksburg)."

I was firmly convinced that the enemy's supplies must be very limited, as he moved with but few wagons, and his dependence upon those to be drawn from his distant base at Grand Gulf or Bayou Pierre very precarious. I had good reason, therefore, to believe that he would be forced either to advance immediately upon Edwards's Depot to give me battle (which I should have accepted or avoided, according to circumstances), or to return at once to his base upon the Mississippi River.

On the 7th May, and previous to my movement across
the Big Black, the President of the Confederate States telegraphed me as follows:

"I am anxiously expecting intelligence of your further
active operations. Want of transportation of supplies must
compel the enemy to seek a junction with their fleet, after a
few days' absence from it. To hold both Vicksburg and
Port Hudson is necessary to a connection with trans-Mississippi. You may expect whatever it is in my power to do."

I have now shown how important I considered it not to
advance beyond my direct communication with Vicksburg,
and close proximity to the Big Black. Nor would I have
done so, and I believe that every general officer of my command, who attended the council held at Edwards's Depot,
will sustain me in the assertion (so far as his opinion may
go), but for the orders received from General Johnston on
the morning of the 14th May. They know, one and all, the
loud-voiced public sentiment which urged a forward movement. They also know (there may be an individual exception or two) how eager they themselves were (though they
differed as to the preferable movement) to leave the position in which they had been in line of battle from the 13th
to the morning of the 15th, and to advance upon the enemy;
and they know, further, the feeling of their respective commands on the same subject. I have stated in my official report, and I reiterate here, that "I had resisted the popular
clamor for an advance, which began from the moment the
enemy set his polluting foot upon the eastern bank of the
Mississippi River. I had resisted, I believe, the universal
sentiment of the army—I know of my general officers—in
its favor" (I now add there may have been an exception or
two) "and yielded only to the orders of my superiors."

I do not say, nor have I ever said, that General Johnston ordered me to make the movement I did make. He
did, however, order a forward movement, the consequence
of which would, in my judgment, have been utterly disas-

trous had I attempted literally to execute it. But, when it
was known that General Johnston had ordered an advance,
the weight of his name made the pressure upon me too
heavy to bear. The council was, I think, nearly equally divided in opinion as to the respective advantages of the two
movements; among others, those of most experience and of
highest rank, advocated that which was ultimately adopted
by my accepting what I declared to be, in my judgment,
only the lesser of two evils.

When, on the 28th April, General Bowen informed me
by telegraph that " transports and barges loaded down with
troops were landing at Hard Times, on the west bank," I
made the best arrangements I could, if it became necessary,
to forward to his assistance, as rapidly as possible, all the
troops not, in my opinion, absolutely indispensable to prevent a *coup de main*, should it be attempted, against Vicksburg. It was indispensable to maintain a sufficient force to
hold Snyder's Mills, Chickasaw Bayou, the city front, and
Warrenton—a line of over twenty miles in length.

In addition to his troops at Young's Point (whose
strength I had no means of ascertaining), which constantly
threatened my upper positions, the enemy had, as has already been shown, a large force at Hard Times, and afloat
on transports between Vicksburg and Grand Gulf, which
threatened the latter as well as Warrenton, where a landing,
under cover of his gunboats, might have been easily effected,
and his whole army concentrated there instead of at Bruinsburg; and this movement would have placed him at once
west of the Big Black. It was impossible for me to form an
estimate of his absolute or relative strength at the two points
named.

To concentrate my whole force south and east of Big
Black for the support of General Bowen against a landing
at Grand Gulf, or any other point south of it, not yet even
apparently threatened, would, I think, have been unwise, to
say the least of it. To show that I was not alone in my
opinion, I add a telegram from General Stevenson, then
commanding the troops in and about Vicksburg: " The men

will be ready to move promptly. To cross the Mississippi, both gunboats and transports must pass the batteries at Grand Gulf. An army large enough to defend itself on this side would consume much time in crossing. As it is not known what force has been withdrawn from the front, it is not improbable that the force opposite to Grand Gulf is there to lay waste the country on that side, and a feint to withdraw troops from a main attack here. I venture to express the hope that the troops will not be removed far, until further developments from below render it certain that they will cross in force."

On the 30th of April, I received, by telegraph from General Bowen, the first information of the landing of the enemy at Bruinsburg, and on the following day (May 1st) the battle of Port Gibson was lost by us. In corroboration of the statement made with regard to the threatening aspect of affairs toward Vicksburg and its flank defenses, I beg leave to draw attention to the following dispatches from General Stevenson:

"VICKSBURG, *May* 29, 1863.

. . . . "Eight boats loaded with troops from our front are now moving up Yazoo. The display made in moving them showed a desire to attract our attention."

"VICKSBURG, *May* 30, 1863.

"The enemy have been shelling Snyder's at long range most of the day. Forney thinks that five regiments have landed at Blake's lower quarters."

The only instructions or suggestions received from General Johnston, in reference to the movements at Grand Gulf, are contained in the following dispatches, which were dated and received after the battle of Port Gibson, and when our army, in retreat from that position, was recrossing the Big Black:

"TULLAHOMA, *May* 1, 1863.

"If Grant's army lands on this side of the river, the safety of Mississippi depends on beating it. For that object you should unite your whole force."

"TULLAHOMA, *May* 2, 1863.

" If Grant crosses, unite your whole force to beat him. Success will give back what was abandoned to win it."

The question of supplies, and the necessity of a sufficient cavalry force (without which I was powerless) to protect my communications, in event of a movement south of Big Black, toward Bayou Pierre, has been sufficiently referred to in the body of my report.

I have one more remark to make in reference to cavalry. General Johnston informed me, about the middle of April, that he had ordered a brigade to my assistance. So far as my knowledge extends, it did not enter the limits of my department; for a few days subsequently General Johnston notified me that a strong force of the enemy in front of Roddy prevented his leaving Northern Alabama at that time, and requested me, if possible, to send a force to coöperate with him. To this I replied, under date of April 20th, from Jackson, reminding him that I had but a feeble cavalry force, but that I would certainly give Colonel Roddy all the aid I could, and added : " I have virtually no cavalry from Grand Gulf to Yazoo City, while the enemy is threatening to pass (cross) the river between Vicksburg and Grand Gulf, having twelve vessels below Vicksburg."

In relation to the battle of Baker's Creek, I wish to add a few words, in elucidation of my official report. When I left my position at Edwards's Depot, it was with the expectation of encountering the enemy. I was, therefore, neither surprised nor alarmed when, on the night of the 15th, I learned his close proximity. Nor should I have then desired or attempted to avoid battle, but for my anxiety to comply with General Johnston's instructions of the 15th instant, in which he says : " The only mode by which we can unite is by your moving directly to Clinton, informing me that we may move to that point with about six thousand." The remainder of this dispatch is embodied in my report. I used every exertion to comply implicitly with his directions, but the enemy prevented it. It appears, as will be seen by reference,

that General Johnston supposed the enemy to be still at
Jackson, when he wrote on the 15th; while in his note of
the 14th (received subsequently), the enemy being then also
at Jackson, he informed me that the force under General
Gist, he "hopes, will be able to prevent the enemy in Jackson from drawing provisions from the East. This one
(Gregg's, with which he was present in person) may be able
to keep him from the country toward Panola. Can he supply himself from the Mississippi? Can you not cut him off
from it, and, above all, should he be compelled to fall back
for want of supplies, beat him?" The remainder of this
dispatch is also embodied in my report.

I here insert a dispatch from General Johnston, not
given nor referred to in my report :

"CALHOUN STATION, *May* 16, 1863.

"I have just received a dispatch from Captain Yerger,
informing me that a detachment of his squadron went into
Jackson this morning, just as the enemy was leaving it.
They (the Federals) took the Clinton road. It is matter of
great anxiety to me to add this little force to your army, but
the enemy being exactly between us, and consultation by
correspondence so slow, it is difficult to arrange a meeting.
I will take the route you suggest, however, if I understand
it. We have small means of transportation, however. Send
forward a little cavalry to communicate with me orally. Is
the force between us too strong for you to fight, if it inter-
poses itself?"

The various suggestions and instructions in these dispatches seem to me to evidence a want of clear and well-
defined plans ; and all, however, seem to ignore Vicksburg,
the defense of which I had conceived to be the main purpose of the Government in retaining the army in Mississippi.

I would only further remark that when General Johnston,
on the 13th of May, informed me that Sherman was at Clinton, and ordered me to attack him in the rear, neither he
nor I knew that Sherman was in the act of advancing on

Jackson, which place he entered at twelve o'clock, on the next day; that a corps of the enemy was at Raymond, following Sherman's march upon Jackson, and that another corps was near Dillon's, and consequently that the order to attack Sherman could not be executed. Nor was I myself aware, until several hours after I had received, and promised to obey, the order, that it could not be obeyed without the destruction of my army; but on my arrival at Edwards's Depot, two hours after I received the order, I found a large force of the enemy near Dillon's, on my right flank, and ready to attack me in the flank or rear, if I moved on Clinton. Not being able, therefore, to make the movement, I determined, in consequence of the wish indicated by General Johnston's order for a forward movement on my part, to make the only movement of that description which gave any promise of success; and in so doing I relinquished my own plans for the purpose of carrying out what I supposed to be those of General Johnston. The battle of Baker's Creek, and the entire consequences of my movement, resulted from General Johnston's order, and he is, in part, responsible for them; for if that order had never been given, the battle of Baker's Creek would not have been fought.

In relation to General Johnston's complaint that I had made my report direct to the War Department, instead of to him, I am surprised, inasmuch as General J. had been previously informed by the War Department that I had the right to do so.

In conclusion, I earnestly ask that there may be as little delay as possible in reconvening the court of inquiry directed to investigate the subjects herein referred to.

Very respectfully, your obedient servant,

J. C. PEMBERTON,

Lieutenant-General.

[TELEGRAMS.]

RICHMOND, *July* 9, 1863.

General J. E. JOHNSTON :

If it be true that General Taylor has joined General

Gardner and routed Banks, you will endeavor to draw heavy reënforcements from that army, and delay a general engagement until your junction is effected. Thus, it is hoped, the enemy may yet be crushed, and the late disaster be repaired.

Send by telegraph a list of the general and staff officers who have come out on parole from Vicksburg, so that they may be exchanged immediately. As soon as practicable, let the lists of regiments and other organizations be forwarded for same purpose. General Rains should now apply his invention. JEFFERSON DAVIS.

JACKSON, *July* 9, 1863.

To his Excellency the PRESIDENT:

The enemy is advancing in two columns on Jackson, now about four miles distant. I shall endeavor to hold the place, as the possession of Mississippi depends on it. His force is about double ours. J. E. JOHNSTON.

JACKSON, *July* 10, 1863.

To his Excellency the PRESIDENT:

Your dispatch of yesterday received. No report of General Taylor's junction with Gardner has reached me, as it must have done, if true, for we have twelve hundred cavalry in that vicinity. I have nothing official from Vicksburg.

(A list of paroled Vicksburg officers follows.)

J. E. JOHNSTON.

JACKSON, *July* 11, 1863.

To his Excellency the PRESIDENT:

Under General Pemberton's orders, a line of rifle-pits was constructed from the Canton road, at Colonel Withers's house, a few hundred yards from the railroad-depot, and going to the New Orleans Railroad, a thousand yards south. It is very defective, cannot stand siege, but improves a bad position against assault. I thought that want of water would compel this; but the enemy has made no attempt, but skirmished all day yesterday. Should he not assault, we must attack him or leave the place. Prisoners say these are Ord's and Sherman's corps, and three other divisions. Their right is near the Raymond road, their left on Pearl River, opposite Insane Asylum.

. . . .

J. E. JOHNSTON.

RICHMOND, *July* 11, 1863.

General J. E. JOHNSTON:

Dispatch of this day received, and remarks on intrenched position noted. Though late to attempt improvement, every effort should be made to strengthen the line of defense, and compel the enemy to assault.

. . . .

Beauregard and Bragg are both threatened—the former now engaged with the enemy. We are entitled to discharge of paroled prisoners, and the War Department will spare no effort to promptly secure it.

The importance of your position is apparent, and you will not fail to employ all available means to insure success.

I have too little knowledge of your circumstances to be more definite, and have exhausted my power to aid you.

JEFFERSON DAVIS.

JACKSON, *July* 12, 1863.

To his Excellency President DAVIS:

Your dispatch of 11th received. A heavy cannonade this morning for two hours from batteries east of the Canton and south of the Clinton roads. The enemy's rifles reached all parts of the town, showing the weakness of the position and its untenableness against a powerful artillery.

Breckenridge's front, south of the town, was assaulted this morning, but not vigorously. A party of skirmishers of the First, Third, and Fourth Florida, Forty-seventh Georgia, and Cobb's battery, took the enemy in flank, and captured two hundred prisoners and the colors of the Twenty-eighth, Forty-first, and Fifty-third Illinois regiments. Heavy skirmishing all day yesterday.

J. E. JOHNSTON.

JACKSON, July 13, 1863.

To his Excellency the PRESIDENT:

Your dispatch of the 11th received.

I think Grant will keep the Vicksburg prisoners until operations here are ended. He may be strongly reënforced from Port Hudson. If the position and works were not bad, want of stores, which could not be collected, would make it impossible to stand siege. If the enemy will not attack, we must, or at the last moment withdraw. We cannot attack without seriously risking the army. But it is difficult to yield this vital point without a struggle. In afternoon of 11th the enemy extended his right to Pearl River.

J. E. JOHNSTON.

JACKSON, July 14, 1863.

To his Excellency President DAVIS:

We learn from Vicksburg that a large force lately left that place to turn us on the north. This will compel us to abandon Jackson. The troops before us have been intrenching, and erecting batteries ever since their arrival.

J. E. JOHNSTON.

JACKSON, July 15, 1863.

To President DAVIS:

The enemy will not attack, but has intrenched. Is evidently making a siege, which we cannot resist. It would be madness to attack him. In the beginning it might have been done. But I thought then that want of water would compel him to attack us. It is reported by some of its officers who were here yesterday, and by some gentlemen of Brandon, that the Vicksburg garrison is diminishing rapidly. Incessant but slight cannonading kept up; our loss, in killed and wounded, about three hundred and fifty. The remainder of the army under Grant at Vicksburg is, beyond doubt, on its way to this place.   J. E. JOHNSTON.

JACKSON, *July* 16, 1863.

To his Excellency President DAVIS :

The enemy being strongly reënforced, and able, when he pleases, to cut us off, I shall abandon this place, which it is impossible for us to hold.   J. E. JOHNSTON.

BRANDON, *July* 16, 1863.

To his Excellency President DAVIS :

Jackson was abandoned last night. The troops are now moving through this place to encamp three miles to the east. Those officers who have seen the Vicksburg troops think that they cannot be kept together. General Pemberton thinks the best policy is to furlough them by regiments.
     J. E. JOHNSTON.

RICHMOND, *July* 18, 1863.

General J. E. JOHNSTON :

Your dispatch of yesterday received, informing me of your retreat from Jackson toward the east. I desire to know your ulterior purpose. The enemy may not pursue, but move up the Central road to lay waste the rich country toward Tennessee, and coöperate afterward with Rosecrans. Another column, Eastern Louisiana being abandoned, may be sent from New Orleans to attack Mobile on the land side.

The recommendation to furlough the paroled troops from Vicksburg offers a hard alternative under the pressure of our present condition.   JEFFERSON DAVIS.

SAVANNAH, GEORGIA, *July* 27, 1871.

Immediately after our return to Jackson after its occupation by the forces under General Grant, I was ordered by General Johnston to furnish the Southern Railroad authorities all the means within the power of my department to rebuild the bridge across Pearl River, and repair the railroad-track beyond it. I at once assigned Major George Whitfield, then on duty with me (afterward assigned to the important duty of repairs of railroads destroyed by the enemy), to this special duty. Negroes in large numbers were impressed, sufficient transportation afforded, materials furnished, and mechanics and skilled laborers employed, and placed under control of the railroad authorities. The work was vigorously prosecuted, and would have been completed in a few days but for the occupation by the forces under General Sherman.

L. MIMMS, <i>Major and Chief
Quartermaster of the Department of
Mississippi and East Louisiana.</i>

[MEMORANDUM FOR MAJOR-GENERAL S. D. LEE.]

PONTOTOC, <i>October</i> 2, 1863.

Collect about twenty-five hundred of the best troops of Chalmers's, Ferguson's, and Ross's brigades, with Owens's battery, for the expedition into Middle Tennessee, for which, at Oxford on the 29th ult., you were desired to prepare, to break the railroad in rear of Rosecrans's army. It is important to move as soon as possible—and by the route least likely to meet the enemy—to the points on the railroad where most injury can be done with the least exposure of our troops. The bridges over the branches of Duck River and of the Elk are suggested.

As the fords of the Tennessee are in and above the Muscle Shoals, it would be well to move toward Tuscumbia first, and, in crossing the river and moving forward, to ascertain as many routes as possible by which to return.

Fayetteville would be a point in the route to the part of the railroad between Elk and Duck Rivers.

General Bragg is informed of your intended movement, and has been requested to put Brigadier-General Roddy under your command.

Should circumstances now unforeseen make the enterprise too hazardous, abandon it. Your own judgment must decide if risks do or do not counterbalance the important results to be hoped for from success.

Brigadier-General Chalmers's move to Memphis and Charleston Railroad should precede yours by a day if practicable.

Brigadier-General Jackson was instructed, three or four months ago, to issue the cavalry-arms for which I had applied to the Ordnance Department, so as to convert the best-instructed regiments into cavalry first. Let those instructions be executed. Brigadier-General Jackson is under the misapprehension that you have countermanded them.

J. E. JOHNSTON.

[MEMORANDUM FOR COLONEL BROWNE, AIDE-DE-CAMP.]

DALTON, February 8, 1864.

The effective total of the army (infantry and artillery), thirty-six thousand one hundred and eleven. At the end of December it was thirty-six thousand eight hundred and twenty-six, which, during the month, was reduced by the transfer of Quarles's and Baldwin's brigades (twenty-seven hundred). The present brigades of the army, therefore, were increased by nineteen hundred and eighty-five effectives during January. We have a few unarmed men in each brigade. About half are without bayonets. Many barefooted—the number of the latter increasing rapidly. Thirteen thousand three hundred pairs of shoes are now wanted for infantry and artillery.

The artillery is not efficient, is unorganized, and there are not means of ascertaining if it has officers fit for colonels and lieutenant-colonels. Both these grades should be filled. I am endeavoring to improve the organization. About four hundred artillery-horses are wanting. The chief quartermaster is procuring others. There are one hundred and twelve pieces, sixty of which are present, with teams, incapable of manœuvring them on a field of battle. Forty-eight are near Kingston, to improve their horses. I have applied for the promotion and assignment of Colonel E. P. Alexander to the grade of brigadier-general to command this artillery. It requires such an officer to prepare it for the field. The efficient chief of ordnance supplies us well with every thing pertaining to his department, except bayonets, which it is known cannot be procured. By taking about three hundred baggage-wagons from the troops we have for supply-trains six hundred wagons. Many of their mules require rest and food to make them fit for a campaign. One hundred and thirty wagons are being altered to bear pontoons. Such trains would not carry food and forage for more than three days for this army. Although the performance of the railroads is greatly improved, especially that of the Western & Atlantic, we do not yet receive sufficient supplies of long forage to restore artillery-horses to the condition they lost on Missionary Ridge. The army is composed of two corps. It cannot be manœuvred in battle without forming a third. I have, therefore, so recommended, and beg consideration of that recommendation. The army should be organized, as nearly as practicable, as it is to fight. These troops are very healthy, and in fine spirits. This position is too much advanced. But for fear of effect on the country, I would fall back so that we might not be exposed to be turned by the route leading through Rome.

The written effective total of cavalry is five thousand four hundred and forty-two, but Major-General Wheeler reports that but twenty-three hundred of these have efficient horses. It is necessary to keep about two-thirds of them below Rome, near the Coosa, on account of forage.

At the end of December, the effective total was	.			36,826
"	"	"	total present and absent	77,653
"	"	January, the effective total was	.	36,111
"	"	"	total present and absent	69,514

(Cavalry not included.)

At the end of December, the effective total of cavalry
was[1] 5,613
At the end of December, the total present and absent 13,290
At the end of January, the effective total of cavalry
was[1] 5,442
At the end of January, the total present and absent 12,152

Respectfully submitted:

(Signed) J. E. JOHNSTON, *General.*

[TELEGRAMS.]

NEAR MARIETTA, *June* 12, 1864.

General BRAGG, Richmond:

I have urged General S. D. Lee to send his cavalry at once to break the railroad between Dalton and the Etowah. If you agree with me in the opinion that it can at this time render no service in Mississippi to be compared with this, I suggest that you give him orders.

J. E. JOHNSTON, *General.*

NEAR MARIETTA, *June* 12, 1864.

His Excellency the PRESIDENT, Richmond:

Fearing that a previous telegram may not have reached you, I respectfully recommend the promotion of Brigadier-General Walthall to command the division of Lieutenant-General Polk's troops now under Brigadier-General Canty.

General Polk regards this promotion as important as I do.

J. E. JOHNSTON, *General.*

NOTE.—Bad health makes General Canty unable to serve in the field.

NEAR MARIETTA, *June* 13, 1864.

General BRAGG, Richmond:

I earnestly suggest that Major-General Forrest be ordered to take such parts as he may select of the commands

---

[1] The number of *men* able to serve—two-thirds of their horses, however, were unfit for service, so that the term " effective," applied to them as cavalry, is incorrect.

of Pillow, Chalmers, and Roddy, all in Eastern Alabama, and operate in the enemy's rear between his army and Dalton.   J. E. JOHNSTON, *General.*

NEAR MARIETTA, *June* 28, 1864.

General S. COOPER, Richmond:

I have received your dispatch inquiring why three regiments had not been sent to Savannah in exchange for those of Mercer's brigade.

They have not been sent, because, before Mercer's brigade joined, we were engaged with an enemy more than double our numbers, and ever since have been in his immediate presence.

I considered the fact that the Government [1] reënforced us from the coast afterward proof that my course was right. The three regiments shall be sent as soon as it can be done without danger to our position. They are now, like all this army, within rifle-shot of the enemy.

J. E. JOHNSTON.

NEAR MARIETTA, *June* 29, 1864.

General BRAXTON BRAGG, Richmond:

I recommend the assignment of Major-General Lovell to the command of Stewart's division.

All quiet yesterday.

(Signed)   J. E. JOHNSTON.

NEAR MARIETTA, *June* 29, 1864.

General BRAGG, Richmond:

I respectfully urge the importance of immediate decision on my recommendation of assignment of Lovell to Stewart's division. He is now serving as a volunteer—without command, of course.   J. E. JOHNSTON.

---

[1] Canty's troops.

July 3, 1864.

General B. Bragg, Richmond:

Stewart's division requires a commander immediately. It will be useless unless one is assigned. I again urge, most respectfully, the assignment of Major-General Lovell to it.
(Signed)   J. E. Johnston.

Near Chattahoochee Railroad Bridge,
July 8, 1864.

His Excellency the President, Richmond:

I have received your dispatch of yesterday.

Our falling back has been slow. Every change of position has been reported to General Bragg. We have been forced back by the operations of a siege, which the enemy's extreme caution and greatly superior numbers have made it impossible for me to prevent. I have found no opportunity for battle, except by attacking intrenchments.

. . . .

J. E. Johnston.

Near Atlanta, *July* 11, 1864.

General Bragg, Richmond:

I strongly recommend the distribution of the United States prisoners, now at Andersonville, immediately.

J. E. Johnston.

Near Atlanta, *July* 16, 1864.

His Excellency the President, Richmond:

Your dispatch of to-day received.

The slight change in the enemy's dispositions made since my dispatch of the 14th to General Cooper was reported to General Bragg yesterday. It was a report from General Wheeler that Schofield's corps had advanced eastwardly about three miles from Isham's Ford, and intrenched.

As the enemy has double our numbers, we must be on the defensive. My plan of operations must, therefore, depend upon that of the enemy. It is, mainly, to watch for an opportunity to fight to advantage.

We are trying to put Atlanta in condition to be held for a day or two by the Georgia militia, that army movements may be freer and wider. J. E. JOHNSTON.

NEAR GREENSBORO, NORTH CAROLINA, }
May 1, 1865. }

1. The " effective strength" of the Army of Tennessee, as shown by the tri-monthly return of the 1st of May, 1864, was : Infantry, thirty-seven thousand six hundred and fifty-two ; artillery, two thousand eight hundred and twelve (forty thousand four hundred and sixty-four) ; cavalry, twenty-three hundred and ninety-two. This was the entire strength of the army, " at and near Dalton," at that date.

2. The movement from Dalton began on the 12th of May. On that day Loring's division, Army of the Mississippi, and Canty's division, joined at Resaca, with about eight thousand effectives. French's division, same army, joined near Kingston several days later (about four thousand effectives). Quarles's brigade from Mobile (about twenty-two hundred effectives) joined at New Hope Church on the 26th. The cavalry of the Mississippi Army, which joined near Adairsville, was estimated at three thousand nine hundred effectives ; and Martin's cavalry division, which joined near Resaca, at three thousand five hundred. These were the only reënforcements received while General Johnston had command of the army.

3. There was no return (field) of the army made after May 1st, until June 10th. The return of June 10th gave, as effectives : Infantry, forty-four thousand eight hundred and sixty ; artillery, three thousand eight hundred and seventy-two (forty-eight thousand seven hundred and thirty-two) ; cavalry, ten thousand five hundred and sixteen.

4. The next return was made on the 1st of July. Effectives : Infantry, thirty-nine thousand one hundred and ninety-seven ; artillery, three thousand four hundred and sixty-

nine (forty-two thousand six hundred and sixty-six); cavalry, ten thousand and twenty-three.   On the 3d of July, at Vining's Station, the Fifth and Forty-seventh Georgia regiments (about six hundred effectives) left the army for Savannah, under Brigadier-General J. K. Jackson.

5. The next and last return made under General Johnston was on the 10th of July.   Effectives: Infantry, thirty-six thousand nine hundred and one ; artillery, three thousand seven hundred and fifty-five (forty thousand six hundred and fifty-six) ; cavalry, nine thousand nine hundred and seventy-one (exclusive of escorts serving with infantry).   This was the estimated force turned over by General Johnston to General Hood.

6. The report was made under General Johnston, and signed by General Hood.   On the 18th of July the command was turned over to General Hood.   The first return thereafter was that of August 1st, after the engagements of Peach-tree Creek, on the 21st, and around Atlanta, on the 22d and 28th July.

7. The foregoing figures are taken from the official records kept by me as Assistant Adjutant-General of the Army.

(Signed)   KINLOCH FALCONER,

Assistant Adjutant-General.

In the return of the Army of Tennessee, printed July 10, 1864, opposite to "Hardee's Corps," in the column of remarks, is written : "One hundred and seven officers and two thousand and fifty-two men, prisoners of war, are reported among the ' absent without leave.' "   And, opposite to "Hood's Corps," "two hundred and thirty-eight officers and four thousand five hundred and ninety-seven men, prisoners of war, are reported among the ' absent without leave.' "   Below is written this explanation, in Major Falconer's handwriting : "The officers and soldiers reported ' absent without leave,' and who are ' prisoners of war,' include all captured in the army in all previous engagements, and some of whom have hitherto been incorrectly reported ' absent without leave' or ' absent.' "

COLUMBUS, GEORGIA, }
April 3, 1866. }

Consolidated Summaries in the Armies of Tennessee and Mississippi during the Campaign commencing May 7, 1864, at Dalton, Georgia, and ending after the Engagement with the Enemy at Jonesboro' and the Evacuation at Atlanta, furnished for the Information of General Joseph E. Johnston :

Consolidated Summary of Casualties of the Armies of Tennessee and Mississippi in the Series of Engagements around and from Dalton, Georgia, to the Etowah River, for the Period commencing May 7, and ending May 20, 1864:

Corps.	Killed.	Wounded.	Total.
Hardee's	119	859	978
Hood's	283	1,564	1,847
Polks army, Mississippi	42	405	447
	444	2,828	3,272

Consolidated Summary of Casualties of the Armies of Tennessee and Mississippi in the Series of Engagements around New Hope Church, near Marietta, Georgia:

Corps.	Killed.	Wounded.	Total.
Hardee's	173	1,048	1,221
Hood's	103	679	732
Polk's army, Mississippi	33	194	227
	309	1,921	2,230

Consolidated Summary of Casualties of the Armies of Tennessee and Mississippi in the Series of Engagements around Marietta, Georgia, from June 4 to July 4, 1864:

Corps.	Killed.	Wounded.	Total.
Hardee's	200	1,433	1,633
Hood's	140	1,121	1,261
Polk's army, Mississippi	128	926	1,054
	468	3,480	3,948

Consolidation of the above three reports is as follows:

	Killed.	Wounded.	Total.
Dalton to Etowah River	444	2,828	3,272
New Hope Church	309	1,921	2,230
Around Marietta	468	3,480	3,948
	1,221	8,229	9,450

Consolidated Summary of Casualties of the Army of Tennessee (Army
of Mississippi being merged into it) in the Series of Engagements
around Atlanta, Georgia, commencing July 4, and ending July 31,
1864:

Corps.	Killed.	Wounded.	Total.
Hardee's	523	2,774	3,297
Lee's	351	2,408	2,759
Stewart's	436	2,141	2,577
Wheeler's cavalry	29	156	185
Engineer's	2	21	23
	1,341	7,500	8,841

Consolidated Summary of Casualties in Army of Tennessee in Engagements around Atlanta and Jonesboro' from August 1 to September
1, 1864:

Corps.	Killed.	Wounded.	Total.
Hardee's	141	1,018	1,159
Lee's	248	1,631	1,879
Stewart's	93	574	667
	482	3,223	3,705

Consolidation of which two reports is as follows:

	Killed.	Wounded.	Total.
Around Atlanta, July 4 to July 31, 1864	1,341	7,500	8,841
Atlanta and Jonesboro' August 1 to September 1, 1864	482	3,223	3,705
	1,823	10,723	12,546

I certify that the above reports are from the returns made
to my office, and are in my opinion correct.

(Signed)   A. J. FOARD,
Medical Director late Army of Tennessee.

NOTE.—The Atlanta-Dalton campaign began on May 7th, and ended
on the 1st of September, 1864, and the above reports are exact copies
of those made to the commanding general during its progress, and in
the order in which they here appear.

General Johnston commanded from the commencement of the campaign until the 18th of July, when he was relieved from duty, and General Hood assigned to the command of the army. Hence the casualties
of battle which occurred in the army between the 4th and the 18th of
July belong to the period of General Johnston's command, and are as

follows: killed, sixty-seven; wounded, four hundred and fifty-five; total, five hundred and twenty-two. These figures, added to the total of casualties as reported up to July 4th, viz., killed, twelve hundred and twenty-one, wounded, eight thousand two hundred and twenty-nine, total, nine thousand four hundred and fifty, gives the entire losses (killed and wounded) in battle for the whole army, while under the command of General Johnston, as follows: viz., killed, twelve hundred and eighty-eight; wounded, eight thousand six hundred and eighty-four; total, nine thousand nine hundred and seventy-two. A deduction of the same, viz., killed, sixty-seven, wounded, four hundred and fifty-five, total, five hundred and twenty-two, from the total of casualties reported from July 4th to September 1st, viz., killed, eighteen hundred and twenty-three, wounded, ten thousand seven hundred and twenty-three, total, twelve thousand five hundred and forty-six, gives of killed seventeen hundred and fifty-six, wounded, ten thousand two hundred and sixty-seven; total, twelve thousand twenty-three, as the entire losses in killed and wounded during that period of the campaign when the army was commanded by General Hood, viz., from July 18 to September 1, 1864, when it ended, and the army was then prepared for the campaign into Tennessee.

(Signed)   A. J. FOARD,
                    Medical Director late
                    Army of Tennessee.

Memoranda of the Operations of my Corps, while under the command of General J. E. Johnston, in the Dalton and Atlanta, and North Carolina Campaigns.

[DALTON AND ATLANTA.]

At the beginning of the campaign my corps consisted of Cheatham's, Cleburne's, Walker's, and Bate's divisions (about twenty thousand muskets), and four battalions of artillery.

May 7th.

Cheatham's and Bate's divisions sent to report to Hood, and put in position at and to the right of Mill Creek Gap, where they were constantly skirmishing till night of 12th.

May 8th.

Cleburne's division moved to Dug Gap, and assisted Grigsby's cavalry to repel attack of part of Hooker's corps.

Walker had to be sent to Resaca, and moved subsequently to left front of Calhoun, to meet advance of McPherson.

May 12th.

At night my corps moved to Resaca. Heavy skirmishing and occasional assaults on my line at Resaca 13th, 14th, and 15th May—on 13th principally, on Cheatham's line; on 14th and 15th, on Cleburne's and Bate's lines. A man who assisted to disinter dead at Resaca, after the war, reported finding one hundred and seventy Confederate and seventeen hundred and ninety Federal dead.

May 15th.

Night of 15th moved to Calhoun, where Walker was already skirmishing all next day with McPherson. Polk's brigade of Cleburne's division had a sharp fight with a body of the enemy, and punished them handsomely.

May 16th.

On night of 16th moved to Adairville. Cheatham had a heavy skirmish with enemy on 17th.

May 18th.

Moved to Kingstree and Cross Station.

May 19th.

Formed line of battle on left of army; battle-order read to troops. Enemy in sight, and skirmishing begun. Troops wild with enthusiasm and delight.

LATER.

On account of some movement of Hood, ordered to withdraw, about one and a half mile to Cassville line. Troops in fine spirits, expecting to attack enemy next morning. But Polk and Hood could not "hold their lines," and that night withdrew and crossed Etowah following day.

May 27th.

At New Hope Church, Cleburne's division formed left of army. About four o'clock P. M. attacked by four corps of the enemy. Cleburne, with no advantage save well-chosen positions, repulsed corps after obstinate fight of an hour and a half.

At the close of fight, seven hundred Federal dead, within a dozen paces of Cleburne's line. Four color-bearers successively killed within ten paces of line. Fifth bore off colors. Enemy's loss four thousand; Cleburne's, four hundred and fifty killed and wounded.

May 28th.

Bate's division, on left of army and in front of village of Dallas, ordered to envelop enemy, who not believed to be in force. Bate attacked, and was repulsed with loss of several hundred men.

June 27th.

At Kenesaw Mountain, in general assault by enemy. Cheatham's and Cleburne's divisions attacked by Blair's corps of the Army of the Cumberland; assault of enemy very resolute; at its close, three hundred Federal dead left in front of Cleburne's line, some lying against his works. Cleburne's loss two killed and nine wounded. Enemy in his front over eighteen hundred. On Cheatham's line enemy's loss still more severe. Cheatham's loss some two hundred and fifty. Fighting in front of Walker's, on right of Cleburne's, confined to skirmish-line held by Mercer's brigade, until many of the men bayoneted where they stood. Enemy's loss this day, in my front alone, could not have been less than five thousand.

But the heaviest losses of the enemy were not in the assaults and partial engagements of the campaign, but in the daily skirmishing. This was kept up continuously for seventy days, during which the two armies never lost their grapple. It soon became customary, in taking up a new position, to extend the skirmish-lines until they were only less strong than the main one. This line was well manned, and the roar of musketry on it was sometimes scarcely distinguishable from the sound of a general engagement. It was not unfrequently the case that one, two, or even three, lines of battle were repulsed in an assault upon one of our skirmish-lines.

[NORTH CAROLINA CAMPAIGN.]

At Cheraw, South Carolina, received an order from General J. E. Johnston dated 25th of February, assuming command of the Army of Tennessee and the forces of the Department of South Carolina, Georgia, and Florida.

My orders on leaving Charleston had been to move to Greensboro, North Carolina, *via* Wilmington. Capture of latter place, 21st of February, left route by Cheraw the only practicable one.

Arriving at Cheraw in advance of my troops, I found Sherman had changed his course, hitherto directed to Charlotte, North Carolina, and was marching on Cheraw. His advance was within a few miles of the place. A staff-officer, Major Black, sent out to reconnoitre, was captured, but escaped by a daring act of horsemanship. As fast as my troops came up I pushed them out toward the enemy and held him in check until my transportation and supplies came up and I was ready to resume the march.

Cheraw was the terminus of the railroad, and I sent the accumulated rolling-stock back to the central part of the State or the point least exposed. Two thousand prisoners of war left at Florence when Confederate States prison was removed to Salisbury, North Carolina, were exchanged by a staff-officer sent to Federal commander at Wilmington for that purpose.

As I marched out of Cheraw, the enemy pressed my rear closely and there was a sharp skirmish over the bridge spanning the Great Pedee. Skirmishers and flying artillery opened from the opposite bank upon my rear-guard as it cleared the bridge. Major-General Butler, with a squad of cavalry, charged repeatedly for the head of the bridge and drove back the enemy. He passed the bridge himself after it had been fired in a dozen places. The enemy attempted to extinguish the flames, but were prevented by the First Georgia regulars, under Colonel Wayne, from the opposite bank of the river.

Left Cheraw March 3d, and subsequently received orders from General Johnston to move to Smithfield, North Carolina, by way of Rockingham and Fayetteville.

March 10th.

Hampton and Wheeler, who had been hanging on the

left flank of the enemy, gained a success over Kilpatrick's cavalry only less complete from encountering two brigades of infantry assigned to protect Kilpatrick from the rough usage he had been receiving from the hands of Wheeler.

A handsome little affair occurred at Fayetteville next morning. Infantry had crossed Cape Fear, and cavalry had not come in, when one hundred and fifty of the enemy's cavalry charged into the town, which was full of trains and led horses, but without troops. General Hampton, at the head of a dozen men—staff-officers and couriers—charged the body, killing two with his own hand, capturing some, and driving the remainder out of town.

March 16th.

Arrived in vicinity of Averysboro. Breaking off near here are roads leading to Raleigh, Smith's Lane, and Goldsboro; and, to ascertain whether I was followed by Sherman's whole army, or a part of it, and what was its destination, I determined to make a stand here, to develop numbers and object of enemy. I selected a point where Cape Fear and Black Rivers were contiguous.

My force, two divisions, commanded by McLaws and Taliaferro, small originally, and now reduced by the desertions it had been impossible to prevent in a rapid march, and by the withdrawal of a brigade of South Carolina militia, which Governor Magrath had refused to let go out of the State, footed up *six thousand* effectives, including a brigade of South Carolina reserves. My flank was protected by Wheeler, with a part of his cavalry. The enemy brought against me the Fourteenth and Twentieth Corps infantry, and Kilpatrick's cavalry. Sherman was on the field in person.

My troops, for the most part, had never seen field-service, were organized on the march, etc. Regiments and brigades went into action under disadvantages. But, during the day, they changed position under fire, and repelled all attempts of the enemy to break or turn their position, with the steadiness of veterans. My loss was five hundred killed and wounded; the enemy's, if statement of prisoners subsequently captured may be credited, three thousand.[1] My troops were much cheered and inspirited by this affair.

I lost at Averysboro two guns, of Stewart's battery, I think—not taken by the enemy, but abandoned in one of the several rapid evolutions of the day, after every horse attached to the guns had been killed or disabled.

May 16th.

Received orders from General Johnston to march to Bentonville, some twenty miles distant, and arrived on the ground the morning of the 19th. In the afternoon was placed in command of the Army of Tennessee (four thousand), and Taliaferro's division (fifteen hundred), and ordered to attack on the right, to be followed up by Hoke (four thousand five hundred), McLaws (three thousand) on the left in reserve. Enemy's force on the ground believed to be thirty-five thousand. Moved forward at 3 p. m., carried enemy's temporary works, took three pieces of artillery and a stand of colors, and drove enemy one and a half mile, when at nightfall they were found to be in too great force to make it advisable to press them farther. Occupied at night line of battle in rear of advance position of the day, and next day intrenched.

In afternoon of 21st Cummings's brigade (Georgia infantry), three hundred effectives, commanded by Colonel Henderson, and eight of Terry's Rangers, attacked and

[1] My loss at Averysboro is given on the authority of an entry made in a diary kept by my adjutant-general at the time, which states the loss in round numbers at five hundred. I have no means now of determining the proportion of killed, wounded, and missing, of our number. The estimate of the enemy's loss is made upon the credit of a number of prisoners who were in the fight and captured next day by General Wheeler, and who agreed in stating the loss at about three thousand, strengthened by comparing my loss with the enemy's, who were exposed while my troops were protected, and who were constantly attacking and being repulsed all day.

"GENERAL: I remember that the entry in my diary was a transcript from the official reports of the losses made by division commanders.   T. B. ROY."

drove from the ground two divisions of the Seventeenth
Corps, Federal infantry, commanded by General Mower,
which had broken through the cavalry line which formed
the left of the army, and had penetrated to within a few
hundred yards of and were threatening the bridge over ——
Creek, near the village of Bentonville.

W. J. HARDEE.

HEADQUARTERS, HOOD'S CORPS, }
IN THE FIELD, 1864. }

GENERAL : Agreeable to the direction of the general
commanding, I have the honor to herewith submit the operations of the troops of my command since the 7th of May.
On that day Major-General Stewart, with his division, took
position at Mill Creek Gap in Rocky Face Mountain, three
miles northeast of Dalton, the enemy appearing in his immediate front. In the afternoon Major-General Bate, with
his division, reported to me, and was placed in position on
the left of Stewart, and west of railroad. On the 8th Major-General Cheatham, with his division, reported to me,
one brigade of which was placed in position on the right of
Stewart and along the crest of Rocky Face. On the right
the division of Major-General Stevenson was in position,
extending across Crow Valley, General Hindman occupying
the right of my line. Some skirmishing took place along
the line on the 8th, and on the 9th the enemy made five different attempts to gain the mountains, but were each time
driven back, and foiled in all their designs. After this nothing of very great importance occurred up to the time the
army marched for Resaca. On arriving there I took position on the right of the army, Hindman's division on my
left, Stevenson's in the centre, and Stewart on the right.
On the 14th the enemy made repeated assaults on Hindman's left, but not in very heavy lines. Walthall's brigade,
occupying the left of Hindman, suffered severely from enfilade fire of the enemy's artillery, himself and men displaying conspicuous valor throughout under very adverse
circumstances. Brigadier-General Tucker, commanding bri-

gade in reserve, was severely wounded. About the middle of the day on the 15th, the enemy made assaults upon Stevenson's front and the right of Hindman in several lines of battle, each successive time being repulsed with loss. At four o'clock in the afternoon General Stewart moved forward, from the right, with his division, driving the enemy before him, but was subsequently forced to resume his original position before largely superior numbers. During the attack on General Stevenson, a four-gun battery in position thirty paces in front of his line, the gunners being driven from it, was left in dispute. The army withdrew that night, and the guns, without caissons or limberboxes, were abandoned to the enemy, the loss of life it would have cost to withdraw them being considered worth more than the game. After this the march was continued to the south side of the Etowah *via* Adairsville, and Cassville; some slight skirmishing at the latter place. On the morning of the 24th the march was resumed in the direction of Dallas, and, on the morning of the 25th, with my entire command, I arrived at New Hope Church, four miles east of Dallas. About mid-day the enemy was reported advancing, when my line was forward, Hindman on the left, Stewart in the centre, and Stevenson on the right. At five o'clock P. M. a very determined attack was made upon Stewart, extending along a very small portion of Brown's brigade of Stevenson's division. The engagement continued actively until night closed in, the enemy being repeatedly and handsomely repulsed at all points. Then Hooker's entire corps was driven back by three brigades of Stewart's division; prisoners taken were of that corps. Too much praise cannot be accorded to the artillery under the immediate direction of Colonel Beckham, which did great execution in the enemy's ranks, and added much to their discomfiture.

On the morning of the 26th, the enemy found to be extending their left. Hindman's division was withdrawn from my left, and placed in position on the right, the enemy continuing to extend his left. Major-General Cleburne, with his division, was ordered to report to me, and was massed on Hindman's right. On the morning of the 27th, the enemy known to be extending rapidly to the left, attempting to turn my right as they extended. Cleburne's was deployed to meet them, and, at half-past five p. m., a very stubborn attack was made on his division, extending to the right, where Major-General Wheeler, with his cavalry dismounted, was engaging them. The assault was continued with great determination upon both Cleburne and Wheeler until after night, but every attempt to break their lines was gallantly repulsed. About ten o'clock at night, Brigadier-General Granberry, with his brigade of Texans, made a dashing charge on the enemy, driving them from the field, their killed and wounded being left in our hands. During this engagement two or three hundred prisoners were captured, all belonging to Howard's corps. After the engagement around New Hope Church nothing of very great importance transpired while occupying that line. The enemy changed position to Lost Mountain, my corps in the centre. Afterward I moved to the right near Kenesaw Mountain ; subsequently changed position to the extreme left of the army. However, nothing of importance occurred on my line while in this position, save that, on the 22d of June, the divisions of Stevenson and Hindman attacked the enemy, driving him from two lines of works, and capturing some prisoners belonging to Schofield and Hooker. From here the army changed position to the vicinity of Nickagack Creek, my corps on the left.

We subsequently withdrew from this position, and took up a line on the immediate north bank of the Chattahoochee River. After remaining here for several days, the enemy crossed the river and went into bivouac. For further particulars, I refer you to reports of generals of divisions. I inclose Major-General Cleburne's report, and will forward others as soon as received.

Respectfully,
J. B. Hood,
Lieutenant-General.

General J. E. Johnston, Macon, Georgia.

RICHMOND, *February* 22, 1865.

General J. E. JOHNSTON :

The Secretary of War directs that you report by telegram to General R. E. Lee, Petersburg, Virginia, for orders.

S. COOPER,
Adjutant and Inspector-General.

HEADQUARTERS, *February* 22, 1865.

General J. E. JOHNSTON :

Assume command of the Army of Tennessee and all troops in the Department of South Carolina, Georgia, and Florida. Assign General Beauregard to duty under you as you may select. Concentrate all available forces and drive back Sherman.   R. E. LEE.

LINCOLNTON, NORTH CAROLINA,
February 23, 1865.

General R. E. LEE :

It is too late to expect me to concentrate troops capable of driving back Sherman.

The remnant of the Army of Tennessee is much divided. So are other troops.

I will get information from General Beauregard as soon as practicable.

Is any discretion allowed me ?

I have no staff.   J. E. JOHNSTON.

CHARLOTTE, *February* 28, 1865.

Hon. J. C. BRECKENRIDGE,
                    Secretary of War, Richmond :

I respectfully urge that four months' pay be immediately given to the troops of this department, and a small part in specie to each private, and that the money be sent to Major Deslond.

Four months' pay for twenty thousand men.

J. E. JOHNSTON.

CHARLOTTE, *February* 28, 1865.

Hon. J. C. BRECKENRIDGE,
    Secretary of War, Richmond :

The Navy Department has a quantity of coffee here. It would be very valuable to our troops. I suggest its transfer.   J. E. JOHNSTON.

Report of Hon. L. T. Wigfall in the Senate of the Confederate States, March 18, 1865.

Mr. Wigfall, chairman of the Committee on Military Affairs, returned the correspondence between the President and General Johnston, and recommended that it be printed.

Mr. Wigfall also returned the report of General Hood, and said :

Mr. President : I return the report of General Hood, with a recommendation from the Committee on Military Affairs that it be printed. I am instructed by the committee to say that this recommendation would not have been made had the house not already ordered it to be published. No action of the Senate can now keep the report from the public, however desirable it might be. Indeed, having even been sent to both Houses in open session by the President without any warning as to "its tendency to induce controversy" or cause "prejudice to the public service," as in the case of General Johnston's report, the damage was already done—if damage should result from its contents being made known. The official report of the Secretary of War at the beginning of this Congress contains an attack upon General Johnston. It was sent to us by the President in open session, and published by order of Congress. General Johnston's report, which contained his defense against this attack, was asked for promptly, but was withheld for months. It was finally sent to us *in secret session*, with a protest against its publication. A report of the operations of the Army of Tennessee *while under the command of General Hood* is asked for, and we receive this paper *in open session* as soon as it can be copied. No word of warning as to its character is given.

Much of it is but a repetition of the charges made by the late Secretary of War, and, if they can be sustained, it is manifest that our present disasters are not to be attributed to General Johnston's removal, but to his ever having been appointed. It follows, too, that he should not be continued in his present command. It becomes necessary, therefore, to examine into the correctness of these charges. The Senate did not ask for a review of General Johnston's campaign, but for a report of the operations of the army while under the command of General Hood. Though uncalled for, it is before us and the people, and I propose to give it a fair and calm consideration.

In reviewing the review I shall refer to the *official* "field returns" on file in the Adjutant and Inspector-General's office, made and signed by Colonel Mason, Assistant Adjutant-General, and approved by General Johnston, and not to those with the army, revised and "corrected," which I have never seen. The field returns on file here are, or should be, duplicates of those with the army, which are made up from the returns of the corps commanders. Not having the honor of a personal acquaintance with Colonel Falconer, I do not know what reliance is to be placed on his corrections of official documents. I do know Colonel Mason and General Johnston, and I do not believe either capable of making a false or fraudulent return.

General Hood in his review gives the effective total of General Johnston's army, "at and near Dalton," to be seventy thousand on the 6th of May, 1864. These returns appear to have been made tri-monthly, on the 1st, 10th, and 20th of each month. The last official "field return," previously to the 6th of May, on file in the Adjutant and Inspector-General's office, is of the 1st of May. It shows his effective total to be forty thousand nine hundred and thirteen infantry and artillery, and twenty-nine hundred and seventy-four cavalry, amounting in all to forty-three thousand eight hundred and eighty-seven. This return shows, however, that two brigades of cavalry, under the command of General Johnston, were in the rear recruiting their horses, the effective total of which is not given. General Johnston, in his report, estimates his cavalry at this time at "about four thousand," which would make the effective total of these brigades one thousand and twenty-six, which, added to the twenty-nine hundred and seventy-four "at" Dalton, makes the four thousand. Estimating his cavalry at four thousand, it is obvious that from the official returns he had but forty-four thousand nine hundred and thirteen effective total "at and near" Dalton on the 1st of May, the date of the last return before the 6th of that month. The official records show, then, that General Hood over-estimated General Johnston's forces "at and near Dalton" by twenty-five thousand and eighty-seven men.

If General Hood, by the term "at and near Dalton," refers to the forces after this date received by General Johnston from General Polk, he is again in error as to numbers. It was not till the 4th of May that General Polk was ordered to "move with Loring's division and other available force at your command, to Rome, Georgia, and thence unite with General Johnston." On the 6th, the day on which General Hood says this army "lay at and near Dalton, waiting the advance of the enemy," General Polk telegraphs to General Cooper from *Demopolis:* "My troops are concentrating and moving as directed." On the 10th, at Rome, he telegraphs the President: "The first of Loring's brigade arrived and sent forward to Resaca; the second just in; the third will arrive to-morrow morning. . . . French's brigade was to leave Blue Mountain this morning. The others will follow in succession; Ferguson will be in supporting distance day after to-morrow; Jackson's division is thirty-six hours after." Yet General Hood asserts that, four days before this, the army was "assembled" at and near Dalton, and "within the easy direction of a single commander." The last of these reënforcements joined General Johnston at New Hope Church the 26th of May, nearly three weeks after they were alleged to be "at and near Dalton," and amounted to less than nineteen thousand men. If none were lost by sickness, desertion, or the casualties of battle, which is not probable, General Johnston had at New Hope about sixty-four thousand men on the 26th of May, instead of seventy thousand, at Dalton, on the 6th—a difference of six thousand, not very great, it is admitted, yet it shows General Hood to be not quite accurate in his estimates.

General Hood asserts that General Johnston lost twenty-two thousand seven hundred men in his retreat, and offers to prove that by the record. At New Hope he had about sixty-four thousand men. The field returns of the 10th of July, the last made while the army were under his command, shows, at Atlanta : forty thousand six hundred and fifty-six infantry and artillery, and ten thousand two hundred and seventy-six cavalry—fifty thousand nine hundred and thirty-two—say fifty-one thousand. Deduct this from sixty-four thousand and it leaves thirteen thousand loss in artillery, infantry, and cavalry, instead of twenty-two thousand seven hundred, as alleged by General Hood. General Johnston does not give the losses of his cavalry, for want of reports. He had four thousand at Dalton, and received four thousand (Polk's) at Adairsville on the 17th of May—eight thousand. At Atlanta he had ten thousand two hundred and seventy-six, showing that he had recruited his cavalry twenty-two hundred and seventy-six over and above his losses. Leaving out his cavalry, he had at Atlanta, 10th of July, forty thousand six hundred and fifty-six infantry and artillery. At New Hope he had of all arms sixty-four thousand. Of these, eight thousand were cavalry, supposing it not to have increased by recruiting up to that time. That gives him fifty-six thousand infantry and artillery. At Atlanta he had, of these arms, forty thousand six hundred and fifty-six, which deduct from the fifty-six thousand and it shows his losses to be, in infantry and artillery, fifteen thousand three hundred and forty-four.

Under repeated orders from the War Department, General Johnston had before this time sent off three regiments. Supposing them to average two hundred effective total, they would amount to six hundred each; deduct that amount from the fifteen thousand three hundred and forty-four, and it leaves but fourteen thousand seven hundred and forty-four total loss in killed, wounded, deserters, stragglers, and prisoners, of his infantry and artillery. From this amount deduct ten thousand killed and wounded, and we have four thousand seven hundred and forty-four lost from all other causes in these arms. But it appears that the cavalry had increased twenty-two hundred and seventy-six. Deduct this from the four thousand seven hundred and forty-four, and his losses in all arms, except in killed and wounded, amount to but twenty-four hundred and sixty-eight.

We have, then, a loss by desertion and straggling, and prisoners, of only some two thousand five hundred from the "digging and retreating" policy. The demoralization of the army could not have been as great as General Hood supposes, or its losses from these causes would have been greater. The "working by night and traveling by day" would seem, too, not to be a very bad policy where the army has confidence in its leader.

General Hood asserts that a retreating army must lose more by straggling and desertion, if it does not fight, than it would in killed and wounded if it does. He attempts to show this by what he regards well-established principles, and not by figures. Napier differs from General Hood on this point. In discussing the losses of Massena from the Torres Vedras, he says: " It is *unquestionable* that a *retreating army* should fight *as little as possible*."

General Hood also insists that the army at Atlanta was greatly demoralized by the loss of men and officers, and by constant falling back. I do not recollect any general officer, except General Polk, who was killed while Johnston was in command; there may have been others, but certainly not many. What were his losses in general officers from Atlanta to Nashville? His march from Jonesboro to the Tennessee line was a retreat, and from Nashville to Tupelo; yet he lost by desertion but three hundred, and left the army in fine spirits. The demoralization of Johnston's army cannot be accounted for on this theory. But was it demoralized? It fought well when he first took command. His disasters around Atlanta are not attributed by him to a want of spirit in the men, but to incompetency in the officers. He could not have his orders executed. I incline to the opinion that he is mistaken as much as to his facts as he is in his theory.

General Hood insinuates that General Johnston attempts to dodge an acknowledgment of his full losses by " excluding the idea of prisoners," and charges that his official returns show more than seven thousand under the head of "absent without leave." This is a very grave charge against an officer and a gentleman—General Hood should know that the usual, if not only, mode of stating the loss of prisoners is in a marginal note opposite the column of "absent without leave." It can never be other than an approximate estimate; for no general can know how many of his "absent without leave," after a battle, have gone voluntarily to the enemy, and how many have been captured. General Hood should know also that the absent and prisoners of an army are continued on its rolls from time to time, as the "field-returns" are made out, without reference to a change of commanders, and that it is very possible, therefore, that a part, or even the whole, of the seven thousand prisoners may have been lost when the army was under the command of General Bragg. The rout at Missionary Ridge had occurred before General Johnston took command. This is a matter, however, which especially concerns General Hood. The field return of the 10th of July shows a loss of not quite seven thousand prisoners (six thousand nine hundred and ninety-four). Opposite General Hood's corps is this note: " Two hundred and thirty-eight officers and four thousand five hundred and ninety-seven men, prisoners of war, are reported among the 'absent without leave.'" This shows that, out of not quite seven thousand prisoners of war, nearly five thousand (four thousand eight hundred and thirty-five) were captured from his corps. He knows whether they were lost by him under Johnston, or by some one else, under Bragg. For the accuracy of the statement, he, and not General Johnston, is responsible. The return of the army is only a consolidation of the returns of the corps commanders.

But if there were seven thousand prisoners taken during the retreat from Dalton, how does he account for the fact shown by the official returns that General Johnston had, at Atlanta, on the 10th of July, leaving out his killed and wounded, within twenty-five hundred men of the number put under his command previously? How can this excess of loss in prisoners over his total loss (except in killed and wounded) be explained? Upon no other hypothesis than that his army increased by recruiting more rapidly than it decreased by straggling and loss of prisoners. The *morale* of the army, then, could not have been very bad —at least not as bad as it is supposed by General Hood to have been. Nor could the people of the territory which General Johnston was "abandoning" have lost all confidence in him. It must have been from them that his recruits were gathered.

It is alleged that at Dalton "the enemy was but little superior in numbers, none in organization and discipline, and inferior in spirit and confidence." The army which is described as "inferior in spirit and confidence" to Johnston's was the one which had lately routed it at Missionary Ridge, under Bragg. An army flushed with victory is not usually wanting "in spirit and confidence." Did the presence of Johnston cause them to doubt their future success? What infused "spirit and confidence" into the Army of Tennessee? Was it the consciousness that it, at last, had a commander who, careless of his own blood, was careful of that of his men, who knew when to take them under fire and how to bring them out, and whose thorough soldiership would save them from ever being uselessly slaughtered by being led to battle, except when some good purpose was to be accomplished, or some brilliant victory achieved? If the "discipline and organization" of the army were as perfect as described, who produced it? For four months it had been under the control of Johnston. What evidence has General Hood to sustain his assertion that at Dalton the enemy was but little superior to us in numbers? He relies upon Sherman's statement that he was as strong at Atlanta as when the campaign opened. His army at Missionary Ridge was estimated at eighty thousand. He was afterward reënforced by the army from Knoxville and the troops from North Alabama, besides other. Our scouts reported that he had been reënforced with at least thirty thousand men. General Sherman told General Govan, or said in his presence, that he commenced the campaign with one hundred and ten thousand. I have never heard it estimated at less than ninety thousand infantry and artillery. In July General Wheeler estimated it between sixty - five and seventy thousand. The Northern papers, about that time, admitted his losses to be forty-five thousand. His cavalry was estimated by General Wheeler at not less than fifteen thousand. Johnston in the mean time, under orders of the War Department, sent off two brigades and received one.

General Hood charges that General Johnston did not intend to hold Atlanta. As evidence of this, he says that no officer or soldier believed it, and that General Johnston had thrown up no intrenchments in front of his lines opposite Peach-tree Creek. If General Johnston intended, as he says he did, to strike the head of Sherman's columns, as soon as they appeared across Peach-tree Creek, and before they were intrenched, or had time even to deploy into line of battle, what use had he for field - works? They would have been in his way if erected, and his men would have been uselessly fatigued in constructing them. Not having been present, I cannot speak of the opinion of the army. But, admitting the fact, I submit that the opinion of the army is not always evidence of the intentions of the general. Is it not possible, too, that General Hood may have mistaken his own opinion for that of the army? The evidence that General Johnston did intend to hold the place is given in his report. In addition, it may be added that he held New Hope for a fortnight, and only left it because the enemy left their intrenchments confronting it—moving to the railroad and to the rear. He then held a position in front of Kenesaw for a month, and left that, at last, because, by extending his intrenchments, Sherman had got nearer to Atlanta by several miles than we were. In all the fighting we had been successful, and that in positions frequently prepared for defense in a few hours. Is it probable, then, that General Johnston would not have attempted to hold a place fortified already to his hand under the direction of the Engineer Bureau, and previously inspected by Major-General Gilmer, the chief-engineer of our army? Why had he been strengthening it from the 5th of July, with all the labor he could command, if he did not intend to defend it, in the event of his failing to crush the enemy at Peach-tree Creek? Why was he strengthening it at the very moment of his removal? If the position was as weak as described by General Hood, why did Sherman not attempt to carry it by assault?

The place, in my judgment, could not have been taken either by assault or investment. What are the facts? General Sherman first seized the Augusta road, and held it for six weeks to no purpose. To seize the Macon road he had to let go that to Augusta, which could have supplied our army. In making that movement, he exposed his flank to attack, which blunder was not taken advantage of. His movement was concealed by a curtain of cavalry, and was probably not known to General Hood in time. A large portion of his cavalry under Wheeler was in Sherman's rear, operating on his line of communications. To avoid any such *contre-temps*, General Johnston kept his cavalry in hand to watch the movement of the enemy and avoid being outflanked. But I do not propose to discuss General Hood's campaign, which he says was without fault. My purpose is simply to correct errors into which, in my judgment, he has fallen as to General Johnston's, and to do this General Hood has rendered it necessary to consider somewhat the operations around Atlanta. If he did, as he supposes, really commit no blunder, he is probably the only general, living or dead, who can claim such good fortune. Napier says: "The greatest masters of the art may err; he who wars walks in a mist, through which the keenest eyes cannot always discern the right path." Turenne exclaims: "Speak to me of a general who has made no mistakes in war, and you speak of one who has seldom made war."

General Hood charges as a fault that General Johnston abandoned territory which he ought to have defended. Similar objections were made by the King of Spain to Soult's plan of the campaign of Talavera, to which the Duke of Dalmatia replied: "Under present circumstances, we cannot avoid the sacrifices of some territory. . . . This will not be distressing as it may appear, because the moment we have beaten and dispersed the enemy's masses we shall recover all our ground. . . . I conceive it impossible to finish this war by detachments. It is large masses only, the strongest that you can form, that will succeed."

Had all the scattered forces in Mississippi and Alabama been concentrated upon Sherman's rear when he was one hundred and forty miles in the interior, and his communications been thoroughly cut, what to-day would have been our condition? "All our ground recovered," Sherman's army destroyed, and Johnston's ready to raise the siege of Richmond or cross the Ohio.

Again, it is alleged that the mountainous country of Northern Georgia offered great advantages, which were abandoned. Napier says: "Here it may be well to notice an error relative to the strength of mountain-defiles, common enough even among men who, with some experience, have taken a contracted view of their profession. From such persons it is usual to hear of narrow passes in which the greatest multitudes may be resisted. Now, without stopping to prove that local strength is nothing if the flanks can be turned by other roads, we may be certain that there are few positions so difficult as to render superior numbers of no avail. Where one man can climb, another can, and a good and numerous infantry crowning the acclivities on the right and left of a disputed pass will soon oblige the defenders to retreat or fight upon equal terms. If this takes place at any point of an extended front of defiles, such as those of the Sierra Morena, the dangerous consequences to the whole of the beaten army are obvious. Hence such pases should only be considered as fixed points around which an army should operate freely in defense of more expanded positions; for defiles are doors, the keys of which are the summits of the hills around them. A bridge is a defile, yet troops are posted not in the middle, but behind a bridge, to defend the passage."

Peach-tree Creek offered every advantage which deep rivers and mountain-passes could afford. It was impassable for an army, except at a few points. Johnston expected to fall upon the heads of the enemy's columns as they issued from these crossings, and crush them before they could form. From General Hood's report of his own operations, it seems they were allowed time not only to form, but intrench before they were attacked.

What is called General Johnston's defensive policy is severely criticised. Fewer men are lost by fighting than by retreating, etc.

General Hood does not seem to consider sufficiently the worth of an army, nor the consequences which follow the destruction of one. Napoleon said that the very first duty which a general owed to his country was to preserve his army. After the battles of Ocana and Alba de Tormes, in which Ariazaga lost his army, he was defended upon the ground that the campaign was undertaken by the directions of his government. Napier repudiates such defense. He says: "Ariazaga obeyed the orders of his government! No general is bound to obey orders (at least without remonstrance) which involves the safety of his army; so *that* he should sacrifice *every thing but victory,* and many great commanders have sacrificed even victory rather than *appear to undervalue this vital principle.* . . .

"Sir Arthur Wellesley absolutely refused to coöperate in this short and violent campaign. He remained a quiet spectator of events at the most critical period of the war;

and yet, on paper, the Spanish project promised well. . . . This man, so cautious, so conscious of the enemy's superiority, was laying the foundation of measures that finally carried him triumphant through the Peninsular War. False, then, are the opinions of those who, asserting that Napoleon might have been driven over the Ebro in 1808–'9, blame Sir John Moore's conduct. Such reasons would as certainly have charged the ruin of Spain on Sir Arthur Wellesley, if, at this period, the chances of war had sent him to his grave. *But in all times the wise and brave man's toil has been the sport of fools.*"

The complaint against General Johnston cannot be that he would not fight, for he fought almost every day, killing and wounding forty-five thousand of the enemy, and losing ten thousand himself. It is that he did not stake the cause of his country on a single cast of the dice—that he would not risk all on the issue of a single battle. When urged by the Portuguese regency to a like course in 1810, Lord Wellington replied: "I have little doubt of final success, but I have fought a sufficient number of battles to know that the result of any is not certain, even with the best arrangements." He persisted in his defensive policy, and saved Portugal from subjugation. When he had determined to abandon Spain and retreat through Portugal to Lisbon, he was urged to relieve the garrison of Ciudad Rodrigo, containing five thousand men. Napier says: "This was a trying moment. He had in a manner pledged himself, his army was close at hand, the garrison brave and distressed, and the governor honorably fulfilled his part. To permit such a place to fall without a stroke would be a grievous disaster, and a more grievous dishonor to the British arms. The troops desired the enterprise; the Spaniards demanded it as a proof of good faith; the Portuguese, to keep the war away from their own country; finally, policy seemed to call for this effort, lest the world might deem the promised defense of Portugal a heartless and hollow boast. Lord Wellington refused to venture even a brigade, and thus proved himself a great commander, and of a steadfast mind. It was not a single campaign, but a terrible war that he had undertaken. . . . What would even a momentary success have availed? Five thousand men brought off from Ciudad Rodrigo would have ill supplied the ten or twelve thousand men lost in the battle, and the temporary relief of the fortress would have been a poor compensation *for the loss of Portugal.* . . . Massena, sagacious and well understanding his business, only desired that the attempt should be made. He held back his troops, appeared careless, and, in his proclamations, taunted the English general that he was afraid; that the sails were flapping on the ships prepared to carry him away; that he was a man who, insensible to military honor, permitted his ally's towns to fall without risking a shot to save them, or to redeem his plighted word. But all this subtlety failed. Lord Wellington was unmoved, and abided his own time. ' If thou art a great general, Marius, come down and fight.' ' If thou art a great general, Silo, make me come down and fight!' "

General McCook, United States Army, told several of our officers, made prisoners by him, but rescued by Wheeler, that Sherman said, on hearing the change of commanders of our army, that "heretofore the fighting had been as Johnston pleased, but that hereafter it would be as he pleased." I mention this not in disparagement of General Hood. The removal of Johnston was an order to General Hood to adopt the offensive policy and deliver battle whenever the enemy appeared. It is to be regretted that General Hood has permitted himself to become the advocate of that policy, for which he was in no way responsible.

.   .   .   .

History is always repeating itself! The Portuguese Government, in 1810, became "impatient" of Wellington's delays. Fortunately for the country over which they ruled, he was not under their control. In a dispatch of 7th September, he says: "It appears that the government have lately discovered that we are all wrong; that they have become impatient for the defeat of the enemy; and, in imitation of the central junta, called out for a battle and early success. If I had had the power, I would have prevented the Spanish armies from attending to that call" (alluding to Ariazaga's campaign), " and, if I had, the cause would now have been safe ; and, having the power *now* in *my* hands, I will not lose *the only chance* which remains of saving the cause by paying the smallest attention to the senseless suggestions of the Portuguese Government."

It was in this campaign that Wellington established, beyond all question, his reputation as a soldier, and that by declining battle he destroyed the army of Massena and saved Portugal. For adopting a similar policy, Johnston was removed from his command. The result shows the wisdom of the general, and the folly of the Administration. He was covered with disgrace, but now wears the robe of honor in which popular approval has clothed him. He was superseded by order of the President, and he has been restored to command by General Lee. The President who superseded him has himself been superseded. In the effort to destroy Johnston, the President saved Sherman from destruction.

What good to the cause was expected to result from this attack ? Is it intended again to remove him if the public mind can be prepared for such an event ? Is it desired that the soldiers under him shall have their faith in him shaken ? To avoid either of these results I have felt it my duty to say what I have. I have examined carefully the correspondence between the Executive Department and General Johnston during that eventful campaign, sent to the Senate, and now ordered to be published, and the field-returns, which show the strength of the army.

From the evidence before me, I think that General Hood has failed to make out his case. Others must judge as to correctness of my conclusions.

As to General Hood's defense of himself against General Johnston's supposed strictures on him, I have nothing to say. He could have embodied it, I think, with propriety, in his report, if he preferred to do so, though it would have possibly been more regular and more in accordance with the usage of the service had he sent it as a supplement to his original report, through his superior officer. General Johnston could then have made the correction, if in error; if not, he would have been afforded the opportunity of making such comments as he might think proper.

ORIGIN OF THE CONFEDERATE BATTLE-FLAG.

AFTER the battle of Manassas, in 1861, it was observed by the principal officers of the Army of Northern Virginia that it was difficult to distinguish, in the field, the Confederate from the United States colors. I attempted to get rid of this inconvenience by procuring for each regiment its State colors. In this I was unsuccessful, except as to the Virginia regiments. Governor Letcher had the State colors made for each of them, brought them to the army himself, and delivered them to the troops with his own hands.

After failing in this attempt, I determined to have colors for use before the enemy made for the army, and asked (in the army) for designs. Many were offered, and one of several presented by General Beauregard was selected. I modified it only by making the shape square instead of oblong, and prescribed the different sizes for infantry, artillery, and cavalry.

The proper number was then made under the direction of Major W. L. Cabell, the chief quartermaster of the army, and paid for with the funds in his hands for military purposes.

INDEX

INDEX

Note: Johnston's spelling of some names has been corrected in this index.

Acworth, Ga., 328, 336
Adairsville, Ga., 314, 319-321, 353
Adams, Gen. John, CSA, 255, 342, 520
Adams, Col. Wirt, CSA, 175, 182, 520, 525-528, 543-544
Addison, Joseph, 399
Alabama, 70, 140, 200, 227-228, 231, 296, 317, 359, 374, 395
Alabama, Fourth Inf. Regt., 16, 27, 38, 48
Alabama, Eighth Inf. Regt., 33
Alabama, Ninth Inf. Regt., 33
Alabama, Tenth Inf. Regt., 33
Alabama, Eleventh Inf. Regt., 33
Alba de Torres, battle of, 598
Albatross, USS, 163
Alburtis, Capt. Ephraim G., CSA, 27, 48
Aldie, Va., 37
Alexander, Gen. Edward P., CSA, 42, 288, 289, 570
Alexandria, Va., 70, 110
Alfriend, Frank S., 54, 63, 104, 145, 451
Allatoona, Ga., 326, 334
Alleghany Mountains, 81, 85
Allen, Gen. William W., CSA, 307, 312, 329, 391
Anderson, Col. Archer, CSA, 145, 408
Anderson, Gen. George B., CSA, 135
Anderson, Gen. Joseph R., CSA, 130, 178
Anderson, Gen. Richard H., 85, 120, 121, 135
Anderson, Gen. S. R., CSA, 84

Arkansas, 85, 148, 150, 251, 414
Arkansas Post, Ark., 172
Armstrong, Gen. F. C., CSA, 332-333, 348
Army of the Cumberland, US, 303, 341
Army of Mississippi, CS, 151, 155, 176-177, 185, 454
Army of Northern Virginia, CS, 82, 102, 109, 140, 142, 349, 394-395, 456, 461, 485
Army of the Ohio, US, 282, 303
Army of the Peninsula, CS, 110, 115
Army of the Potomac, CS, 27, 50, 55-56
Army of the Shenandoah, CS, 50, 55, 57, 66, 443
Army of Tennessee, CS, 150, 151, 155, 161, 164, 166, 190, 254, 260, 261, 277, 281, 288, 298, 299, 301, 302, 305, 307, 332, 337, 341, 344, 349, 352, 354, 356, 364, 365, 369, 371, 372, 373, 375, 378, 382, 384, 386, 388, 393, 394, 410, 417, 430, 438, 456, 459, 514, 574, 594
Army of the Tennessee, US, 316
Army, US, 10, 11, 41, 50, 56, 60, 248, 249, 257
Ashby, Gen. Turner, CSA, 16, 79, 80, 474
Ashby's Gap, Va., 35
Atlanta, Ga., 254, 255, 273, 277, 278, 280, 297, 326, 332, 336, 338, 345-350, 355, 356, 358, 360-366, 368, 369, 383, 432, 439, 457, 458-460, 462

605

Augusta, Ga., 13, 297, 347, 372, 373, 394, 410
Austin, Maj. J. E., CSA, 327
Avery, Col. I. W., CSA, 328
Averysborough, N. C., 383, 384, 389, 390, 392

Badeau, Adam, 212
Baird, Gen. Absalom, USA, 284
Baker, Gen. Alpheus, CSA, 328
Baker, Col. Edward D., USA, 80
Baker's Creek, Miss., 178, 181, 182, 184, 186, 189, 214, 216, 217, 220
Baldwin, Gen. William E., CSA, 170, 255, 261, 270n, 279-280, 352
Baldwin's Ferry, Miss., 195, 196
Ball's Bluff, Va., 80
Ball's Ford, Va., 40, 53
Baltimore, Md., 21
Baltimore Crossroads, Va., 127, 450
Baltimore and Ohio Railroad, 25, 27, 28, 29
Bancum, Col. G. F., CSA, 330
Banks, Gen. Nathaniel P., USA, 62, 106, 128, 197, 201, 499, 514, 564
Barbour, Col. W. M., CSA, 123
Barhamsville, Va., 125, 126, 127, 450
Barksdale, E., 213, 453
Barksdale, Gen. William, CSA, 80
Barton, Gen. Seth M., CSA, 182, 183
Bartow, Col. Francis S., CSA, 27, 33, 37, 45
Bate, Gen. William B., CSA, 96, 304, 306, 308, 326, 332, 336, 337, 339
Bath, Va., 87
Baton Rouge, La., 13, 168, 191
Battle's Bridge, N. C., 396
Bear Creek, Ala., 167
Beauregard, Gen. P. G. T., CSA, 21, 24, 29, 33, 36-40, 42, 45-50, 52, 54, 58, 59, 67, 71, 72, 75-78, 81, 90, 172, 175, 176, 189, 199, 225, 250, 288, 293, 368, 371, 373, 378, 380, 396-398, 434, 440, 442, 443, 454, 471, 476, 481, 507, 519, 565, 587, 602

Beckham, Maj. R. F., CSA, 52, 53
Beckwith, Gen. Amos, CSA, 417
Bee, Gen. Barnard E., CSA, 27, 33, 38, 40-42, 45, 46, 48, 49, 56, 57, 66, 470
Belmont, Mo., 85
Benjamin, Judah P., 82, 88-91, 94, 95, 99-101, 229, 396, 399, 444n, 448, 474, 476, 478, 480, 481, 484
Bennett House, 402, 412
Benton, Miss., 191
Bentonville, N. C., 365, 384, 385, 391, 392
Berryville, Va., 23, 32, 35
Bethel, Va., 85
Big Black River, Miss., 171, 184-188, 191, 200, 202, 209, 216, 218, 227, 258, 432, 433
Big Shanty, Ga., 336
Birdsong's Ferry, Miss., 202
Blackburn's Ford, Va., 40
Blackstone, S. C., 376
Blair, Gen. Frank, USA, 180, 182
Blair, Maj. W. B., CSA, 83
Bolton's Depot, Miss., 180, 181, 259, 261
Bondurant, Capt. J. W., CSA, 135
Bonham, Gen. Milledge L., CSA, 40, 41, 47, 49, 51-53, 56, 57, 73, 103, 470-472
Bottom's Bridge, Va., 129, 136, 141
Bovina, Miss., 176, 180, 181, 184, 185
Bowen, Gen. John S., CSA, 169-172, 182-184, 221, 522, 524-534, 536, 537, 543, 559, 560
Bowling Green, Ky., 86
Boydton, Va., 417
Bragg, Gen. Braxton, CSA, 147-151, 155, 156, 158-165, 167, 168, 172, 174, 189, 190n, 192, 198, 199, 211, 223, 225, 228-234, 236, 237, 239, 240, 242-250, 253-257, 259-261, 267, 271n, 274, 276, 287, 288, 291, 294, 297-302, 348, 352, 355, 359, 363, 364, 367, 378-380, 382, 384, 386, 387, 388, 432, 433, 437, 438, 450, 452, 454, 456-459, 491-494, 496-502,

504, 507, 509, 510, 514, 515, 565, 571, 572, 573, 593, 594
Bragg, Mrs. Braxton, 163
Branch, Gen. Lawrence O'B., CSA, 128, 130
Brandon, Miss., 209, 210
Breckinridge, Gen. John C., CSA, 156, 158, 190, 202, 206, 207, 254, 276, 283, 395, 397-399, 404, 405, 507, 565, 587, 588
Brentsville, Va., 103
Bridgeport, Ala., 265, 273, 277
Bridgeport, Miss., 185
Bridgeport, Tenn., 256
Bristol, Tenn., 155
Bristow, Va., 66
Brookhaven, Miss., 168
Brown, Commander Isaac N., CSN, 210
Brown, Gen. John C., CSA, 284, 306, 310, 313
Brown, Gov. Joseph E. (Ga.), 14, 278, 280, 338, 348, 350, 360-362, 369
Brownsville, Miss., 258
Bruinsburg Landing, Miss., 169, 178, 223
Bryan, Col. Goode, CSA, 128
Buchanan, Lt. A. H., 320
Buchanan, Adm. Franklin, CSN, 228
Buckner, Gen. Simon B., CSA, 211
Buell, Gen. Don Carlos, USA, 86
Buford, Gen. Abram, CSA, 166, 183
Bull Run, Va., 38, 40-44, 47, 49, 53, 54, 61, 103, 107, 446, 447, 472
Bunker Hill, Va., 23, 24, 32
Burnside, Gen. Ambrose E., USA, 45, 46
Burnt Hickory, Ga., 329, 336, 342
Burnt Ordinary, Va., 126
Burt, Col. E. R., CSA, 80
Butler, Gen. M. Calvin, CSA, 377, 381, 382, 385, 389, 390, 392, 394, 396, 400
Byhalia, Miss., 257, 258

Calhoun, Ga., 274, 278, 312, 313-315, 319

Calhoun Station, Miss., 178
California, 70
Camden, S. C., 376
Canby, Gen. Edward R. S., USA, 398, 414
Cantey, Gen. James, CSA, 302, 305, 307, 308, 352
Canton, Ga., 321, 322, 338
Canton, Miss., 177, 178, 189-191, 205-207, 256, 258, 259, 437
Cape Fear River, 376-378, 381
Carrington, Maj. Carles, CSA, 375
Carson, Gen. James H., CSA, 29, 35
Carter, Gen. Samuel P., USA, 155
Carter, Col. Thomas H., CSA, 135
Carter, Capt. Welby, USA, 50
Cartersville, Ga., 302
Casey, Gen. Silas, USA, 135, 138, 141
Cash, Col. E. B. C., CSA, 51
Cassville, Ga., 320-322, 325, 352
Catawba, N. C., 373
Catawba River, 376-378, 381, 409
Cedar Run, Va., 104, 108
Centreville, Va., 38-40, 43, 47, 66, 67, 77, 78, 81, 83, 96, 97, 103, 114, 443, 446, 447
Chalmers, Gen. James R., CSA, 226, 253, 257, 258, 260
Chambersburg, Pa., 18-20, 22
Champion's Hill, Miss., 181
Chancellorsville, Va., 62, 226
Chapel Hill, N. C., 400
Chapel University, N. C., 407
Charles City, Va., 133
Charles City Road, 132, 134
Charleston, S. C., 13, 115, 372, 376
Charlotte, N. C., 371-373, 375, 378-380, 400, 401, 408-410, 418
Chattahoochee River, 332, 338, 339, 345-348, 350, 355, 356, 358, 414
Chattanooga, Tenn., 150, 162, 163, 255-257, 259-261, 265, 273, 274, 277, 282, 291, 292, 296-298, 302, 356, 361, 437
Cheatham, Gen. Benjamin F., CSA, 276, 277, 282, 304, 310, 319, 339, 342, 343, 346, 372, 373, 377, 393, 578, 580, 584

Cheraw, S. C., 372, 373, 376, 377, 380
Chester, S. C., 377
Chesterville, N. C., 409
Chicago, Ill., 357
Chickahominy River, 128-134, 136, 137, 141-143, 436, 451
Chickamauga, Ga., 255, 256, 271, 354
Chickasaw Bayou, Miss., 160
Chillicothe, USS, 164
Chisholm, Capt. A. R., CSA, 37
Chulahoma, Miss., 258
Cincinnati, Ohio, 357
Clayton, Gen. H. D., CSA, 284, 328, 379, 387
Cleburne, Gen. Patrick R., CSA, 196, 276, 282, 283, 304, 307, 308, 329-331, 339, 342, 343
Cleveland, Tenn., 276, 277, 283, 303, 305
Clinton, Miss., 176, 178, 179, 181, 182, 185, 206, 207
Cobb, Gen. Howell, CSA, 369, 370, 409
Cocke, Gen. Philip St. G., CSA, 40, 42, 49, 51, 66, 73, 470, 471
Cockrell, Gen. F. M., CSA, 342, 529, 530, 532, 534, 535
Coldwater, Miss., 164, 257
Cole, Col. A. H., CSA, 297, 299, 375, 446
Cole, Col. R. G., CSA, 83, 97, 98, 444, 485
Colliersville, Tenn., 258
Colston, Gen. R. E., CSA, 120, 121, 139
Coltart, Col. J. G., CSA, 158
Columbia, S. C., 373, 380
Columbia, Tenn., 161, 162
Columbus, Ky., 86
Commissary Department, CS, 32, 263, 296
Congress, Confederate, 229-230, 263, 349
Connesauga River, 312
Conoley, Col. J. F., CSA, 310
Cooper, Gen. Samuel, CSA, 24, 26, 33, 38, 70, 72, 150, 151, 211, 230, 253, 254, 265, 272, 348, 441, 442, 465, 474, 477, 479,

480, 489-492, 508, 516, 572, 573, 587, 590
Corinth, Miss., 166, 223, 247, 259, 367
Couch, Gen. Darius N., USA, 123, 135, 143
Cox, Gen. Jacob D., USA, 379
Craig, Col. Henry K., USA, 427n
Crittenden, Gen. George B., CSA, 74
Cross Keys, Va., 146
Cruft, Gen. Charles, USA, 283n, 284
Cullen, Dr. J. S. Dorsey, 124
Culpeper Court House, Va., 33, 34, 83, 97, 98, 104
Cumberland River, 161, 292
Cumming, Gen. Alfred, CSA, 182, 284, 391, 548, 553, 583
Cummings, Col. A. C., CSA, 33
Cummings, Maj. J. F., CSA, 273, 351
Cutts, Col. A. S., CSA, 83, 84

Dallas, Ga., 326, 332
Dalton, Ga., 261, 262, 266, 267, 271, 272, 275-278, 280-285, 296-302, 304, 308, 309, 315-317, 321n, 351-356, 359, 367, 383, 455, 457, 460
Dameron, Maj. William H., CSA, 265
Danville, N. C., 375, 378, 395, 396
Darksville, Va., 30, 32
Davis, Jefferson, 13, 14, 17, 20, 24, 26, 29, 31, 34, 38, 53, 54, 59, 63-65, 70-73, 75-79, 89, 96, 97, 100, 101, 104, 106, 109, 110, 112, 114-116, 118, 127, 128, 139, 140, 145, 149-154, 161-163, 167, 197, 198, 199n, 207, 208, 211-213, 215n, 229, 230, 234, 235, 237, 238, 241-244, 247, 248, 250, 261, 262, 266, 269, 270, 272, 274, 275, 278, 279, 281, 282, 286-288, 290, 291, 299-301, 355, 358-361, 364, 368, 395-399, 401, 404, 405, 407, 408, 410, 412, 429-433, 436-438, 440-454, 457, 460, 461, 464, 465, 479, 482-484,

486, 489, 491, 493-497, 500, 501,
  504-507, 511, 512, 514, 515, 519,
  522, 545, 558, 564-567, 571, 573,
  588, 590, 601
Dawson, Maj. J. W., CSA, 310
Decatur, Ala., 260, 414, 417
Decatur, Miss., 168
De Kalb, USS, 164
Democratic Party, 65
Demopolis, Ala., 261, 282
Department of East Tennessee,
  CS, 95, 211
Department of Mississippi, CS,
  148, 154
Department of Mississippi and
  East Louisiana, CS, 147, 261,
  273
Department of Norfolk, CS, 110,
  116
Department of North Carolina,
  US, 416
Department of Northern Virginia,
  CS, 81, 83, 110, 116
Department of the Peninsula, CS,
  110, 116
Department of the South, US, 416
Department of South Carolina,
  Georgia, and Florida, CS, 371
Department of Tennessee, CS,
  148, 154, 211, 349
Department of Trans-Mississippi,
  CS, 148, 149
Department of the West, CS, 437
Diascund Bridge, Va., 119, 125
Dibrell, Gen. George G., CSA, 307
District of the Acquia, CS, 81, 83,
  84
District of Columbia, 10, 13, 18,
  34, 59, 60, 62, 70
District of the Potomac, CS, 81,
  84
District of the Valley, CS, 81, 83,
  84, 89
Dodge, Gen. Grenville M., USA,
  167, 168
Dranesville, Va., 83
Drayton, Gen. Thomas F., CSA,
  146n
Duck Hill, Miss., 253
Duck River, 159, 163, 450
Duke, Gen. Basil W., CSA, 409

Dumfries, Va., 81, 102, 105
Durham Station, N. C., 405, 407,
  412

Early, Gen. Jubal A., CSA, 47,
  49, 52, 56, 66, 73, 103, 109, 122,
  124, 449n, 469
Easton, Gen. Langdon C., USA,
  417
Eastport, Tenn., 167
Echols, Gen. John, CSA, 409
Ector, Gen. M. D., CSA, 189, 256,
  259, 271
Edisto River, 373
Edward's Depot, Miss., 171, 172,
  174, 176, 179, 180, 181, 185,
  186, 188, 202, 203, 217, 219-222,
  259
Elevation, N. C., 383-385
Eltham's Landing, Va., 126
Elzey, Gen. Arnold, CSA, 27, 51,
  52, 58, 59, 67, 74, 470
Enterprise, Miss., 255, 261
Etowah River, 278, 303, 324, 325,
  335, 352, 353, 358
Evans, Gen. Nathan G., CSA, 40,
  41, 44, 45, 48, 66, 80, 83, 190
Evansport, Va., 74, 77, 96
Ewell, Col. B. S., CSA, 299-301,
  496
Ewell, Gen. Richard S., CSA, 40,
  54, 57, 62, 66, 73, 96, 103, 107,
  108, 110, 128, 129, 146, 469-471

Falconer, Maj. Kinloch, CSA, 353,
  419, 456, 575, 589
Falling Waters, Va., 30
Fairfax Court House, Va., 66, 67,
  69, 75, 77, 114, 443, 444
Fair Oaks, Va., 136-138, 141-145
Farragut, Adm. David G., USN,
  164
Fayetteville, N. C., 13, 376-378,
  380-382, 384, 389
Featherston, Gen. William S.,
  CSA, 80, 183, 255, 338, 341-343,
  530, 531
Ferguson, Gen. Samuel W., CSA,
  226, 253, 261
Fifteenth (XV) Army Corps, US,
  171, 257, 260

Fisher, Col. C. F., CSA, 51, 52, 58
Florence, S. C., 381
Florida, 415
Florida, First Inf. Regt., 207
Florida, Second Inf. Regt., 123
Florida, Third Inf. Regt., 207
Florida, Fourth Inf. Regt., 207
Floyd, Gen. John B., CSA, 85, 426-428
Foard, Surgeon A. J., CSA, 325, 459, 577, 578
Forney, Gen. John H., CSA, 31, 66, 477, 522, 542, 543, 560
Forrest, Gen. Nathan B., CSA, 155, 167, 168, 174, 247, 318, 359-362, 495, 571
Foster, Gen. John G., USA, 250
Fort Donelson, 86
Fort Henry, 86
Fort Pemberton, 164
Fort Magruder, 120-122
Fort Morgan (Mobile, Ala.), 228
Fort Monroe, Va., 101, 102, 109, 113, 435
Fourth (IV) Army Corps, US, 303, 306, 310
France, 318, 343
Franklin, Gen.. William B., USA, 123, 129
Franklin, Tenn., 162, 365, 369
Frederick, Md., 18, 29
Fredericksburg, Va., 12, 98n, 101, 102, 108-110, 128, 130, 132, 226, 446; battle of, 495
Freedmen's Bureau (U.S. Bureau of Refugees, Freedmen, and Abandoned Lands), 419n
Fremont, Gen. John C., USA, 62
French, Gen. Samuel G., CSA, 202, 206, 321, 338, 342, 343, 352, 354, 483, 574
French, Col. S. Bassett, CSA, 475, 476
Front Royal, Va., 129
Fuller, Col. C. A., CSA, 208
Furnace Ridge, Va., 17, 22, 441

Gainesville, Ala., 214
Gainesville, Va., 44
Gardner, Gen. Frank, CSA, 189, 191, 197, 210, 222

Garland, Gen. Samuel, CSA, 132, 135, 477
Garnett, Gen. R. B., CSA, 81
Garrard, Gen. Kenner, USA, 303, 339, 352
Geary, Gen. John W., USA, 79, 305
Georgia, 14, 31, 70, 76, 113, 115, 128, 142, 145, 190, 202, 231, 240, 256, 274, 323n, 349, 354, 360-362, 364, 367, 373-375, 391, 394, 415, 428, 432, 458
Georgia, Seventh Inf. Regt., 22, 27, 37, 38
Georgia, Eighth Inf. Regt., 22, 27, 37, 38
Georgia, Ninth Inf. Regt., 27
Georgia, Eleventh Inf. Regt., 33
Georgia, Forty-seventh Inf. Regt., 207
Georgetown, Miss., 168
Georgetown, Va., 70
Germantown, Tenn., 258
Gettysburg, Pa., 62
Gibbons, Col. S. B., CSA, 23
Gilgal Church, Ga., 336
Gilham, Col. William, CSA, 12, 84
Gillmore, Gen. Q. A., USA, 416
Gilmer, Gen. Jeremy F., CSA, 460, 596
Gist, Gen. S. R., CSA, 48, 176, 177, 189
Gloucester Point, Va., 111, 113, 114, 117
Goldsborough, N. C., 378, 380, 382, 384, 389, 394, 396
Gordonsville, Va., 97, 109, 128, 130
Gorgas, Gen. Josiah, CSA, 267, 297, 369
Gosport, Va., 119
Govan, Gen. D. C., CSA, 329, 330, 595
Grafton, Va., 12
Granbury, Gen. H. B., CSA, 285, 306, 329-331
Grand Gulf, Miss., 168, 169, 171
Grand Junction, Miss., 252
Grant, Capt. L. P., CSA, 345

Grant, Gen. U. S., USA, 86, 148-151, 153, 155, 160, 162, 165, 166, 168-172, 176, 178, 180-182, 184, 196-202, 211, 212, 217, 220, 223, 224, 226, 238, 242, 244, 246, 248-250, 260, 277n, 282, 285, 294-296, 298, 303, 318, 349, 352, 355, 364, 398, 400, 437, 439, 450, 452, 454, 456, 458, 459, 490, 493-499, 501, 504, 507, 508, 510, 512-514, 518, 519, 540, 550, 557, 560, 561, 566, 567

Gray, Peter W[.], 230

Great Britain, 318

Green, Gen. Martin E., CSA, 529, 532, 534, 536, 537

Greenbrier River, 85

Greensborough, N. C., 396, 400, 401, 408, 409, 413, 417

Gregg, Gen. John, CSA, 175, 177n, 178, 189, 217, 220, 255, 256, 520, 521, 540, 548, 552, 553, 562

Grenada, Miss., 153, 160, 246, 252, 253, 258, 438

Grierson, Col. Benjamin H., USA, 168

Grigsby, Col. J. Warren, CSA, 305

Grimes, Mr. [See Peter W. Gray], 230

Grover, Gen. Cuvier, USA, 416

Groves, Capt. R. N., CSA, 27

Gulf of Mexico, 281

Hagerstown, Md., 22

Halleck, Gen. Henry W., USA, 298

Hall's Ferry, Miss., 195

Hampton, Gen. Wade, CSA, 41, 42, 45, 46, 84, 102, 126, 377, 380-386, 390, 391, 396, 400, 401, 404, 411, 477, 488, 582

Hancock, Gen Winfield S., USA, 125

Hankinson's Ferry, Miss., 171, 195, 216

Hannon, Col. Moses W., CSA, 280, 329

Hanover Court House, Va., 130

Hard Times, La., 168-170

Hardee, Gen. William J., CSA, 156, 159, 228, 254, 255, 261, 262, 268, 272-276, 282, 285, 286, 289, 306, 309-314, 319, 320, 322-326, 328, 329, 333, 335-338, 340, 341, 343, 344, 345, 354, 357, 365, 372, 376, 377, 380-387, 456, 460, 500, 502, 575-577, 584

Harper, Gen. Kenton, CSA, 12, 15, 30

Harpers Ferry, Va., 12-15, 17-22, 24, 25, 28, 32, 43, 61, 62, 79, 80, 382, 429, 434, 440-442, 460, 475

Harpeth Shoals, Tenn., 161

Harris, W. P., 213, 453

Harrison, Col. Julian, CSA, 95

Hartford, USS, 163

Hartsville, Tenn., 151

Hartsuff, Gen. George L., USA, 365n

Harney, Capt. James B., CSA, 359

Hatton, Gen. Robert, CSA, 130, 140

Haw River Bridge, N. C., 401

Haynes' Bluff, Miss., 171, 187, 201

Hazelhurst, Miss., 168

Hazen, Gen. William B., USA, 157n, 158

Hebert, Gen. Louis, CSA, 255

Helena, Ark., 148

Heintzelman, Gen. S. P., USA, 44-46, 54, 55, 82, 129, 132, 133, 135, 136, 141, 143, 145, 473, 485

Henderson, Col. R. J., CSA, 391

Henderson, Capt. Samuel, CSA, 185, 257

Hendren, J. N., CS treasury agent, 408

Hill, Gen. Ambrose P., CSA, 16, 22, 25, 120, 121, 130, 131, 475, 477, 483, 488

Hill, Gen. Daniel H., CSA, 83, 85, 102, 103, 109, 117, 119-122, 125-128, 131-136, 139, 140, 144, 145, 379

Hillsborough, N. C., 400, 401

Hindman, Gen. T. C., CSA, 276, 277, 283, 284, 304, 307-310, 312, 340

Hoge, Capt. J. B., USA, 50

Hoke, Gen. Robert F., CSA, 379, 384, 386, 387, 389, 390

Holly Springs, Miss., 148, 154, 223, 257, 258

Holmes, Gen. T. H., CSA, 40, 47, 49, 53, 54, 56, 81, 102, 109, 142, 145, 148-150, 152, 153, 395n, 490-492, 496

Homesborough, S. C., 381

Hood, Gen. John B., CSA, 126, 137, 138, 307, 309, 310-314, 319-328, 333-336, 338-340, 345, 346, 349-351, 353, 354, 358, 363, 365, 369, 373, 456, 488, 575-577, 579, 584, 586, 588-598, 600, 601

Hooker, Gen. Joseph, USA, 77, 102, 123, 305, 327, 369, 464, 578, 585, 586

Howard, Gen. Oliver O., USA, 408, 417, 586

Hovey, Gen. Alvin P., USA, 180-183, 217, 303, 352

Huger, Gen. Benjamin, CSA, 114, 119, 128, 131, 133, 136, 486, 490

Humes, Gen. W. Y. C., CSA, 312, 329, 330

Humphreys, Benjamin G., 432

Hunter, Gen. David, USA, 44

Hunton, Gen. Eppa, CSA, 49, 80

Illinois, Twenty-eighth Inf. Regt., 207

Illinois, Forty-first Inf. Regt., 207

Illinois, Fifty-third Inf. Regt., 207

Imboden, Gen. John D., CSA, 27, 45, 46

Island No. Ten, 86

Iuka, Miss., 260

Ives, Col. J. C., CSA, 267

Jackson, Gen. Andrew, 343

Jackson, Gen. Henry R., CSA, 85

Jackson, Gen. J. K., CSA, 302, 575, 590

Jackson, Gen. Thomas J. ("Stonewall"), CSA, 12, 14-16, 22, 27, 28, 30, 33, 36, 37, 40-42, 45, 46, 48, 49, 56-58, 62, 63, 66, 67, 73, 74, 78, 81, 84, 87-89, 106, 110, 128, 129, 146, 469, 474, 478, 481-483

Jackson, Gen. William H., CSA, 190, 198, 199, 202, 206, 208, 227, 253, 256, 259, 319-321, 325, 326, 336, 338, 344-346, 348, 353, 359

Jackson, Miss., 151-154, 163, 165, 171, 172, 175-181, 184, 187-189, 191, 193, 196, 197, 202, 204, 205, 208-210, 212, 217, 218, 223, 227, 246, 252, 281, 430-432, 437, 438, 452, 453, 495-498, 538-540, 542, 544, 546, 547, 553-556, 562, 563, 566

James River, 111, 125, 127, 451

Johnson, Andrew, 407, 415

Johnson, Col. B. J., CSA, 46

Johnson, Gen. Edward, CSA, 85

Johnson, Gen. R. W., USA, 333-334

Johnston, Gen. Albert S., CSA, 70, 72

Johnston, Gen. Joseph E., CSA, 71, 72, 213, 215, 230, 231, 240, 241, 252, 360, 361, 367, 368, 405, 407, 412-415, 419, 432-440, 462-465, 471, 472, 474-484, 486, 489-494, 496-516, 519, 521-524, 527, 528, 539, 540, 544-549, 551, 552, 554-567, 569, 571-576, 578, 580, 581, 583, 586-602

Jones, Col. Bushrod, CSA, 327

Jones, Gen. David R., CSA, 40, 42, 47, 57, 66, 73, 109, 119, 125, 469-471, 488

Jones, Col. R. T., CSA, 140

Jones, Gen. Samuel, CSA, 59, 66, 74

Jonesborough, Ga., 358

Jordan, Gen. Thomas, CSA, 53

Kearny, Gen. Philip, USA, 121, 123, 135

Kelly, Gen. J. H., CSA, 303, 305, 329

Kelly's Bridge, S. C., 377
Kennard, Col. J. M., CSA, 394
Kenner, D. F., 213, 453
Kenesaw Mtn., Ga., 336, 338, 343, 345
Kentucky, 16, 86, 147, 151, 253, 293, 353, 362, 367
Kernstown, Va., 107
Kershaw, Gen. J. B., CSA, 51, 120, 487
Kersley, Maj., CSA, 32
Keyes, Gen. Erasmus D., USA, 46, 129, 132, 133, 135, 141, 143, 145
Kilpatrick, Gen. Judson, USA, 303, 372, 380, 416
Kingston, Ga., 320, 321, 325
Kingston, Tenn., 292, 295-298
Kinston, N. C., 378, 379
Kirkland, Gen. William W., CSA, 390
Knoxville, Tenn., 253, 277, 282, 291, 292, 296-298

Lafayette, Tenn., 168, 258
La Grange, Col. Oscar H., USA, 307
Lake Station, Miss., 174
Law, Gen. Evander M., CSA, 137, 389
Lawrenceville, Va., 417
Lawton, Gen. Alexander R., CSA, 146n, 289
Lay, Col. John F., CSA, 53
Leadbetter, Gen. Danville, CSA, 254, 280
Lee, Gen. Fitzhugh, CSA, 126
Lee, Col. R. B., CSA, 67
Lee, Gen. Robert Edward, CSA, 12-17, 19, 20, 38, 59, 62, 71, 72, 114, 115, 128, 139, 140, 145, 147, 225, 226, 229, 271, 288, 289, 301, 355, 356, 371, 372, 374, 378, 394-396, 402, 416, 436, 438, 439, 441, 448, 450-452, 456, 458, 460, 486, 489, 490, 495, 587, 601
Lee, Gen. Stephen D., CSA, 160, 253, 256, 257, 259-261, 348, 359, 364, 373, 375, 394, 396, 400, 543, 568, 571, 577

Lee, Capt. S. S., CSN, 119
Leesburg, Va., 29, 66, 80, 83, 102
Leoben, battle of, 403
Letcher, Gov. John (Va.), 12, 14, 15, 21, 22, 108, 602
Lewinsville, Va., 73
Lewisburg, Va., 417
Lexington, Miss., 252
Lincoln, Abraham, 9, 402, 403
Lincolnton, N. C., 371, 409
Little Rock, Ark., 148, 150, 152, 497
Livingston, Miss., 185, 227, 256, 259
Logan, Gen. John A., USA, 182, 183
Logan, Col. J. L., CSA, 210, 226
Lockett, Capt. Samuel H., CSA, 209
Lomax, Col. Tennent, CSA, 140
Long, Gen. Eli, USA, 283
Longstreet, Gen. James, CSA, 40, 42, 47, 53, 57, 62, 66, 73, 74, 77, 103, 110, 113, 114, 115, 117, 119-128, 131, 133-140, 145, 225, 226, 268, 270, 271, 273, 274, 277, 282, 288, 292, 293, 297, 298, 448, 469-471, 485, 488
Loring, Gen. William W., CSA, 84, 87, 88, 153, 164, 171, 182, 183, 184, 186, 189, 191, 202, 206, 220, 258, 259, 308, 309, 337, 338, 341-345, 352, 387, 478, 479, 495, 517, 518, 522, 524-533, 540, 543, 548, 549, 553, 554, 574
Loudon Heights, Va., 22
Louisiana, 227, 231
Louisville, Ky., 357
Louisville and Nashville Railroad, 150
Lovell, Gen. Mansfield, CSA, 332, 345, 462, 572, 573
Lowrey, Gen. M. P., CSA, 330
Lynchburg, Va., 15, 48n
Lynch's Creek, S. C., 376, 378

Mackall, Gen. W. W., CSA, 271n, 322n, 323n, 349, 351
Macon, Ga., 323n, 369, 409

Magrath, Gov. A. G. (S.C.), 382, 582

Magruder, Gen. John B., CSA, 85, 109-112, 114, 117, 119, 125-128, 131, 133, 137-139, 141, 487, 488

Mallory, Stephen R., 396, 398-400

Manassas, Va., 24, 41, 44, 63-65, 102-105, 107, 434, 435, 440, 442-445, 447, 460, 480, 483

Manassas, Battle of, 34, 74, 92, 432, 441, 443, 471, 602

Manassas Gap, Va., 29

Manassas Gap Railroad, 18, 23, 36, 51, 99

Manassas Junction, Va., 12, 18-21, 24, 26, 32, 33, 35, 37, 40, 44, 50, 51, 56, 59, 63, 81, 97, 98, 103

Manassas Station, Va., 53, 58

Maney, Capt. Frank, CSA, 96

Mason, Col. ?, CSA, 409

Mason, James M., 22, 23

Mason's Hill, Va., 69, 74

Marietta, Ga., 329, 334, 336, 338, 339, 342, 345, 347, 350, 357

Martin, Gen. W. T., CSA, 270n, 271, 277, 293, 302, 303, 311, 312, 329, 352

Martinsburg, Va., 17-20, 23-25, 27, 30, 32, 87

Maryland, 16-20, 22, 25, 27, 28, 76, 77, 102, 108, 129, 147, 440

Maryland, Third Inf. Regt. (CS), 27

Maury, Gen. Dabney H., CSA, 227, 254, 297, 302, 495

Maxey, Gen. Samuel B., CSA, 176-178, 190

McClellan, Gen. George B., USA, 18, 22, 24, 70, 74, 75, 77, 94, 96, 102, 106, 110, 112-115, 118, 127, 129, 132, 140, 142, 144, 271, 434, 435, 440, 446, 449-451, 478, 480

McClernand, Gen. John A., USA, 166, 169, 174n, 177, 180, 182-185, 216, 217, 246, 250, 454, 517, 556, 557

McCook, Gen. Alexander M., USA, 600

McCook, Gen. Edward M., USA, 303, 352

McCown, Gen. John P., CSA, 151, 156

McCulloch, Gen. Benjamin, CSA, 85

McDonald, Col. Angus, CSA, 87

McDowell, Gen. Irwin, USA, 18, 19, 32, 39, 42, 44, 47, 51, 55, 57, 65, 66, 128-130, 132, 434, 443, 466, 472, 474, 490

McGavock, Col. Randal, CSA, 175n

McGowan, Gen. Samuel, CSA, 472

McIntosh, Col. W. M., CSA, 85

McLaws, Gen. Lafayette, CSA, 119, 386, 390, 487, 582, 583

McLean, Maj. E. E., CSA, 14

McLean's Ford, Va., 40, 469

McMicken, Col. M. B., CSA, 351

McNair, Gen. Evander, CSA, 189, 255, 259, 271

McPherson, Gen. James B., USA, 166, 175-177, 180, 182-185, 216, 217, 307, 308, 316, 540, 579

Meadow's Bridge, Va., 131, 133

Mechanicsville, Va., 130, 131

Meem, Gen. G. S., CSA, 29, 35

Memphis, Tenn., 159, 162, 165, 146, 256, 257, 259, 260, 294, 495, 496

Memphis and Charleston Railroad, 226, 257

Mercer, Gen. Hugh W., CSA, 302, 352

Meridian, Miss., 255, 281, 282, 285, 286, 438

Messenger's Ferry, Miss., 258

Mexican War, 462

Mexico, 317

Miles, Col. Dixon S., CSA, 43, 57

Military Division of West Mississippi, 414

Mill Creek, N. C., 390, 392

Mill Creek Bridge, Tenn., 161

Milliken's Bend, La., 160, 171

Mims, Maj. L., CSA, 177, 227, 433, 568

Missionary Ridge, Battle of, 229, 270, 271, 272, 276, 277, 299,

301, 302, 352, 354, 355, 367, 438, 570, 593-595

Mississippi, 31, 70, 85, 150, 152, 153, 155, 160, 163, 166, 168, 173, 174, 188, 197, 199, 200, 202, 212, 222-227, 229, 231-237, 240, 242-250, 253-257, 260, 265, 268, 270, 271, 275, 279, 282, 288, 296, 319, 321, 359, 362, 373, 375, 431, 432, 437, 450, 542

Mississippi, Second Inf. Regt., 16, 27, 38

Mississippi, Eleventh Inf. Regt., 16, 27, 38

Mississippi, Thirteenth Inf. Regt., 79, 80

Mississippi, Seventeenth Inf. Regt., 80

Mississippi, Eighteenth Inf. Regt., 79, 80

Mississippi, Nineteenth Inf. Regt., 33, 123

Mississippi Central Railroad, 252, 438, 454, 455

Mississippi, Department of, CS, 241, 254, 255

Mississippi River, 148, 149, 152, 153, 159, 162, 165, 166, 170, 172, 178, 186, 188, 197, 199, 211, 212, 216, 221, 223, 224, 226, 231, 239, 249, 250, 256, 454, 493, 524, 541, 544, 546, 550, 552, 557, 558, 560, 562

Mississippi Springs, Miss., 175, 178

Missouri, 85, 148, 149

Mitchell's Ford, Va., 40, 45

Mobile, Ala., 161, 163, 226-229, 231, 232, 244, 252, 254, 260, 281, 288, 297, 302, 363, 414, 460

Mobile and Ohio Railroad, 252, 455

Montgomery, Ala., 13, 15, 17, 253, 255, 351, 364

Moore, Sir John, 599

Moore, Col. Sydenham, CSA, 140

Moore, Maj. W. E., CSA, 265, 375, 410, 418

Moore's Brigade, CS, 261

Moorefield, Va., 87

Morehead City, N. C., 418

Morgan, Gen. John H., CSA, 151, 360-362

Morgan, Gen. J. T., CSA, 395n

Morrisville, N. C., 401

Morton, Miss., 210, 228, 229, 244, 438

Moulton, Ala., 167

Mount Elon, S. C., 381

Mount Jackson, Va., 106, 107, 110

Mount Vernon, Ala., 13

Mott, Col. Christopher H., CSA, 123, 477

Mower, Gen. Joseph A., USA, 391

Mulberry Point, Va., 117

Munson Hill, Va., 69, 74

Murfreesboro, Tenn., 147, 150, 151, 155, 156, 159, 232, 246, 250, 354, 355

Nashville, Tenn., 147, 155, 156, 161, 257, 291, 292, 294, 360, 365, 373

Natchez, Miss., 226

Nelson, Col. N. L., CSA, 341

Neuse River, 396, 407

New Auburn, Miss., 180

Newberry, S. C., 372, 373

New Bridge, Va., 132, 133

New Carthage, La., 166

New Creek, Va., 25

New Hope Church, Ga., 326, 331, 350, 352

New Kent Court House, Va., 125, 126

New Kent Road, 119

Newman, Ga., 348

New Orleans, La., 227, 414

New Orleans, La., Battle of, War of 1812, 343

New Orleans and Jackson Railroad, 168, 206

Newton, Gen. John, USA, 306

Newton, Miss., 168

New York, 419

Nine Mile Road, Va., 135-137

Ninth (IX) Army Corps, US, 277

Norfolk, Va., 12, 113-115, 119, 134

North Carolina, 70, 76, 109, 113, 142, 145, 231, 374, 375, 378, 384, 405, 409, 410, 412, 415

North Carolina, Fifth Inf. Regt., 125

North Carolina, Sixth Inf. Regt., 33, 51, 58, 97, 137

North Carolina, Twenty-ninth Inf. Regt., 210

North Carolina Railroad, 401

Northrop, Col. Lucius B., CSA, 98, 105, 273, 408, 446, 483

Nottoway Court House, Va., 417

Oakhill, Mo., 85

Ocana, Battle of, 599

Occoquan River, 43, 81, 82, 102

Ocmulgee River, 370

Ohio, 419, 427

Ohio River, 148

Oostenoula River, 303, 309, 312-314, 319

Ordnance Bureau, US, 427

Ordnance Department, CS, 32, 91, 297

Orange Court House, Va., 97, 107, 110

Orange and Alexandria Railroad, 97

Osterhaus, Gen. Peter J., USA, 260

Oxford, Miss., 258, 417

Palmer, Gen. John M., USA, 157n

Palmetto Station, Ga., 368

Paris, Va., 37, 58

Patrick, Maj. William, CSA, 73

Patterson, Gen. Robert, USA, 18-20, 22-25, 27, 30-32, 34, 35, 39, 43, 51, 434, 440, 442

Peachtree Creek, Ga., 347, 350, 351, 369

Pearl River, 168, 205, 206, 208, 209, 287, 433

Pecey's Ferry, N. C., 376

Peck, Gen. John J., USA, 123

Pedee River, 376-378, 380

Pemberton, Gen. John C., CSA, 12, 147-154, 159, 160, 163-165, 167,
169-172, 174-176, 178-185, 187-189, 191-198, 200, 204, 205, 208, 212-225, 227, 231, 232, 236, 238, 240, 243n, 245, 246, 248-251, 253, 355, 437, 450, 452, 490, 491-493, 495, 497, 498, 501, 503, 505-509, 512, 516, 544, 546, 552, 554, 563, 564, 567

Pender, Gen. W. Dorsey, CSA, 97

Pendleton, Lt. Alexander ("Sandie"), CSA, 27

Pendleton, Gen. William N., CSA, 16, 21, 37, 48, 56, 69, 103, 289, 301, 470

Peninsula, the (Va.), 110-113, 115-117, 127, 448

Pennsylvania, 17, 27, 226, 440

Pensacola, Fla., 227

Petersburg, Va., 128, 131, 349, 417

Pettus, Gen. Edward W., CSA, 261, 284, 306, 388, 409

Pettus, Gov. John J. (Miss.), 152, 154, 212, 213, 243, 246, 453

Pickett, Gen. George E., CSA, 120, 121, 139, 145

Piedmont, Va., 57-59, 67

Piedmont Station, Va., 36-38

Pierce, Franklin, 429

Pillow, Gen. Gideon, CSA, 85, 572

Pine Mountain, Ga., 336, 337

Pittsborough, N. C., 400

Point of Rocks, Va., 21, 23

Polk, Gen. Leonidas, CSA, 85, 156-159, 261, 263-265, 273, 281, 282, 286, 288, 293, 296, 303, 305, 308-311, 313, 314, 317, 319, 320-326, 328, 329, 333, 335, 337, 347, 352, 354, 359, 374n, 500, 502, 571, 576, 577, 590-592

Pontotoc, Miss., 168

Pope, Gen. John, USA, 62, 271

Porter, Adm. David, USN, 68, 189

Porter, Gen. Fitz-John, USA, 45, 46, 55, 129, 130

Port Gibson, Miss., 169-172, 175, 179, 181, 223

Port Hudson, Miss., 147, 152, 153, 163, 164, 175, 176, 189-191, 196, 197, 199, 201, 202, 210, 222, 224, 226, 231, 255
Port Republic, Va., 146
Portugal, 599-601
Potomac Creek, 101
Potomac River, 17, 18, 21-23, 25, 30, 43, 61, 64, 70, 74, 76, 77, 79, 80, 85, 87, 95, 101, 102, 105, 108-110, 407
Powder Spring, Ga., 328
Power, Col. ?, CSA, 226, 227
Presstman, Col. S. W., CSA, 312, 314, 335, 338, 345, 347, 348
Preston, Col. J. T. L., CSA, 14
Price, Gen. Sterling, CSA, 85, 495
Pryor, Gen. Roger A., CSA, 120, 121

Quantico River, 81
Quarles, Gen. William A., CSA, 241, 270n, 279, 280, 342, 352
Quartermaster Department, CS, 295-297
Quimby, Gen. Isaac F., USA, 183

Radford, Col. R. C. W., CSA, 53
Rains, Gen. Gabriel J., CSA, 135, 506, 564
Raleigh, N. C., 382-384, 394, 395, 400, 402, 408
Randolph, Gen. George W., CSA, 108, 114, 115, 128, 148, 149, 163, 168, 448
Ransom, Gen. Robert, Jr., CSA, 255
Rapidan River, 107-109, 128
Rappahannock River, 74, 83, 97, 101-103, 107, 108, 110, 445-447
Rappahannock Station, Va., 104
Raymond, Miss., 175-178, 180-182, 184, 186, 188, 217, 227
Reagan, John H., 396, 399, 404, 405
Red Clay, Ga., 283
Republican Party, the, 65
Resaca, Ga., 278, 303, 305, 307-309, 314-317, 319, 351, 356, 368, 457

Reynolds, Gen. A. W., CSA, 220, 284, 305, 313, 518, 532
Rhett, Maj. T. G., CSA, 101
Richardson, Gen. Israel B., USA, 141
Richmond, Va., 9, 12, 13, 16-19, 24, 32, 43, 53, 61, 63, 64, 67, 78, 82, 91, 92, 96, 98n, 101, 102, 108-115, 118, 119, 125, 127-129, 131, 140, 142, 154, 194, 230, 232, 234, 290, 294, 297, 300, 301, 323n, 348, 349, 361, 395, 417, 425, 434-436, 447-450, 476, 477, 485, 486, 488-490
Ringgold, Ga., 253, 267, 276, 278, 280, 282, 283, 302, 303
Rio Grande, 407
Ripley, Gen. Roswell S., CSA, 142, 145n
Robinson, Capt. Powhatan, CSA, 101, 445
Rockingham, N. C., 380, 382
Rocky Mount, S. C., 376
Roddy, Gen. Philip, CSA, 166-168, 247, 257, 259, 273, 277n, 280
Rodes, Gen. Robert E., CSA, 73, 132, 135
Rome, Ga., 167, 273, 277n, 302, 303, 314, 317
Romney, W. Va., 22, 23, 25, 87, 89
Rosecrans, Gen. William S. USA, 147, 148, 150, 155-157, 159, 165, 225, 249, 260, 450, 492-494, 499, 501, 503, 504, 567, 568
Ross, Gen. L. S., CSA, 261
Rosser, Gen. Thomas L., CSA, 73
Rousseau, Gen. Lovell H., USA, 157
Ruffin's Mill, N. C., 401
Ruggles, Gen. Daniel, CSA, 226
Runyon, Gen. Theodore, USA, 43

Sale, Col. John B., CSA, 291, 294, 295, 297
Salem, Miss., 257
Salisbury, N. C., 400, 401, 409
Sanders, Capt. ?, CSA, 195, 213
Santa Rose Island, Fla., 85
Savannah, Ga., 115, 302, 416, 432, 433

Schofield, Gen. John McM., USA, 365, 376, 394, 408, 414, 416, 573, 586

Scott, Gen. Thomas M., CSA, 341

Scott, Gen. Winfield, USA, 40, 43

Sears, Gen. C. W., CSA, 342

Seddon, James A., 197-201, 211, 214, 215, 230, 233, 234, 236, 238, 240, 244, · 245, 250, 252, 262, 264, 266, 270, 274, 278, 280, 287, 288, 349, 437, 502-504, 507-516, 519, 549, 554

Sedgwick, Gen. John, USA, 143, 144

Semmes, Gen. Paul, CSA, 120, 487

Senate, CS, 229

Seminole War, the, 462

Seven Pines, Battle of, 130, 132, 135, 138, 142, 143, 147, 432, 461

Seventeenth (XVII) Army Corps, US, 171, 172

Shaller, Col. ?, CSA, 244

Shoup, Francis A., CSA, 323, 324, 345, 346, 542

Sharpsburg, Md., 62

Shelbyville, Tenn., 159

Shenandoah River, 28, 37, 58

Shenandoah Valley, 17, 20, 27, 66, 67, 128

Shepherdstown, Va., 23

Sherman, Gen. William T., USA, 46, 154, 159, 160, 162, 171, 177, 182, 185, 204, 205, 212, 217, 227, 250, 257, 260, 270, 274, 281, 282, 285, 286, 290, 294, 298, 302, 306, 307, 315-318, 326, 329, 344-346, 349, 358, 360-364, 371-374, 376, 378, 380, 382, 383, 392, 394, 395, 398-405, 407, 409-418, 439, 455n, 456-459, 495, 499, 506, 523, 554, 555, 562, 563, 565, 568, 581, 582, 587, 595-597, 600, 601

Shields, Gen. James, USA, 62, 107

Shiloh, Battle of, 354, 367

Shorter, Gov. John Gill (Ala.), 227

Silver Creek, N. C., 382

Sisters of Charity, 426

Sixteenth (XVI) Army Corps, US, 303

Slocum, Gen. Henry W., USA, 408, 417

Smith, Gen. A. J., USA, 524

Smith, Gen. E. Kirby, CSA, 14, 33, 38, 51, 52, 57, 81, 95, 96, 103, 149, 195, 196, 201, 242, 348, 364, 440-443, 452, 496, 497, 507, 508, 514, 516, 535

Smith, Gen. Gustavus W., CSA, 73-76, 78, 109, 110, 113-115, 117, 119, 120, 125, 126, 128, 130, 131, 133, 134, 136-141, 144, 145, 338, 344-346, 448, 485, 487, 488, 494, 495

Smith, Gen. M. L., CSA, 152, 497, 542, 543, 550

Smith, Gen. William, CSA, 49

Smithfield, Va., 24, 32, 34

Smithfield, N. C., 373, 378, 379, 383-385, 393

Sneedsborough, S. C., 380

Snyder's Mill, Miss., 186, 195

South Carolina, 70, 76, 83, 113, 142, 146, 190, 237, 372, 373, 382, 410, 415, 418

Spain, 343, 599

Sparta, Tenn., 292

Springfield Armory, Mass., 427

Stanard, Capt. P., CSA, 33

Stanton, Edwin M., 402, 427

Staunton, Va., 26, 98n, 395

Stevenson, Gen. Carter L., CSA, 151, 154, 155, 165, 182-186, 276, 277, 283, 284, 304, 306, 308, 311, 313, 340, 341, 372, 373, 377, 516, 518, 520, 522, 524, 525, 527-533, 538, 543, 548, 559, 560, 584, 585

Stevenson, Ala., 265, 273, 277

Stewart, Gen. Alexander P., CSA, 276, 283, 284, 303, 306, 311, 314, 327, 332, 347, 365, 367, 372, 373, 384, 387-390, 396, 401, 460, 572, 577, 583-585

Stewart, Gen. Benjamin F., CSA, 374n

Stilesboro, Ga., 326

Stovall, Gen. M. A., CSA, 328

Strasburg, Va., 23, 28, 34, 106, 107, 129
Streight, Col. Abel D., USA, 167, 168
Stone Bridge, 40, 41, 44, 53
Stoneman, Gen. George, USA, 303, 309, 352, 409, 414, 417
Stone River, 156, 158
Stonewall Brigade, 81
Stuart, Gen. J. E. B., CSA, 16, 30, 32, 34, 35, 37, 50, 52, 53, 69, 73, 83, 103, 107, 108, 132, 470
Sudley, Va., 45, 53
Sudley Ford, Va., 44, 45, 52
Sumner, Gen. E. V., USA, 123, 129, 136, 140, 141, 143-145, 485

Talcott, Col. Andrew, CSA, 451
Tallahatchie, Miss., 164
Tallahatchie River, 148, 164, 258, 355, 450
Taliaferro, Gen. William B., CSA, 84, 386, 387, 390, 582, 583
Tatnall, Commodore Josiah, CSN, 119, 127
Taylor, Gen. Richard, CSA, 194, 195, 197, 563, 564
Tennessee, 85, 130, 140, 150, 155, 159-161, 163, 165, 166, 171, 173, 199, 200, 213, 225, 226, 231, 232, 234-237, 239, 240, 242-244, 246, 248-250, 253, 257, 263, 274, 282, 287, 292-296, 323n, 353, 367, 374, 389, 414, 417, 432, 437, 450, 452
Tennessee River, 149, 225, 246, 247, 259, 260, 274, 292, 296, 298, 355, 414, 417, 450
Tennessee, Second Inf. Regt., 22, 27
Tennessee, Third Inf. Regt., 23, 25, 27
Texas, 70, 230, 414
Texas Brigade, 82
Texas, Eighth Cav. Regt., 391
Texas, troops of, 285
Thirteenth (XIII) Army Corps, US, 171, 172, 174n
Thomas, Col. F. J., CSA, 49

Thomas, Gen. Geo. H., USA, 260, 282, 285, 286, 290
Thoroughfare Gap, Va., 98n, 99, 102, 103, 105
Tilghman, Gen. Lloyd, CSA, 183, 184, 186
Tilton, Ga., 308, 310
Tombigbee River, 286
Toombs, Gen. Robert, CSA, 70, 74
Town Creek, Ala., 167
Tracy, Gen. E. D., CSA, 516, 518
Trimble, Gen. Isaac R., CSA, 74
Tullahoma, Tenn., 159, 163, 172, 232, 245, 246, 255, 437, 452
Tunnel Hill, Ga., 276, 280, 283, 301, 304, 305-317
Tupelo, Miss., 147, 367
Tuscumbia, Ala., 166, 167, 257, 259, 260, 273, 277n, 280
Twenty-third (XXIII) Army Corps, US, 277, 303
Tyler, Gen. E. B., USA, 44, 473
Tyrrell's Mount, N. C., 407

Union Mills, Va., 40, 78

Vance, Gov. Zebulon B. (N. C.), 375
Van Cleve, Gen. Horatio P., USA, 197
Vanderford, Capt. Charles F., CSA, 394
Van Dorn, Gen. Earl, CSA, 73, 77, 82, 90, 154, 160, 162, 174, 223, 246, 495, 498, 502-504
Varnell's Station, Ga., 303, 307
Vaughan, Gen. A. J., CSA, 220, 343
Vaughn, Gen. S. B., CSA, 25
Vaughn, Gen. John C., CSA, 23, 29, 96, 409
Vernon, Miss., 256
Vicksburg, Miss., 147, 149, 152-154, 159, 162, 164-166, 168, 169, 171, 174, 175, 178, 180, 185-194, 196, 197, 199-204, 208-214, 216-218, 221-223, 224, 226, 227, 231-233, 237, 239-241, 246, 249, 250, 254-256, 259, 261, 281, 282, 286, 431, 432, 452-454, 491, 493, 497, 498, 539-

542, 544, 545, 550, 551, 556-561, 564, 566, 567

Vienna, Va., 43

Villanow, Ga., 285

Virginia, 9, 13-15, 17, 18, 31, 59, 60, 62, 65, 70, 81, 84, 95, 101, 109, 143, 199n, 225, 226, 233, 237, 239, 247, 277, 349, 364, 374, 394, 397, 400, 403, 409, 415, 416, 426, 428, 434, 447, 458

Virginia, CSS, 119, 127

Virginia, First Cav. Regt., 16

Virginia, Second Inf. Regt., 16, 27

Virginia, Fourth Inf. Regt., 16, 27

Virginia, Fifth Inf. Regt., 16, 27, 30

Virginia, Eighth Inf. Regt., 79, 80

Virginia, Tenth Inf. Regt., 16, 23, 27

Virginia, Thirteenth Inf. Regt., 16, 23, 25, 27, 73

Virginia, Twenty-fourth Inf. Regt., 125

Virginia, Twenty-seventh Inf. Regt., 16, 27

Virginia, Thirty-third Inf. Regt., 33

Virginia Central Railroad, 64

Virginia Military Institute, 88

Virginia, Valley of, 18, 20, 24, 26, 44, 106

Walker, Gen. James A., CSA, 74

Walker, Gen. John R., CSA, 109

Walker, Gen. H. H., CSA, 395

Walker, Gen. Lindsay, CSA, 53

Walker, Gen. W. H. T., CSA, 175, 177n, 178, 189, 191, 202, 206, 217, 220, 254, 276, 277, 282, 304, 307, 308, 312, 313, 339, 342, 343, 354

Walthall, Gen. E. C., CSA, 338, 342, 343

Ward, Col. G. T., CSA, 123

Warrenton, Miss., 195

Warrenton, Va., 33, 40, 103, 417

Warrenton Junction, Va., 104

Warrenton Springs, Va., 103

Warrenton Turnpike, Va., 44, 78

Warwick, Va., 118

Warwick Creek, Va., 111

Warwick River, 111

Washington, D. C., 10, 13, 18, 34, 59, 60, 62, 70

Washington, Ga., 410, 414

Watauga River Bridge, Tenn., 155

Water Valley, Miss., 258

Weldon, N. C., 375, 394

Wellington, Duke of, 343, 598-601

West Point, Ga., 254

West Point, N. C., 407

West Point, Va., 126, 128

Wharton, Gen. John A., CSA, 273, 277n

Wharton, Gen. T. J., CSA, 432

Wheeler, Gen. Joseph, CSA, 155, 161, 259, 273, 276, 283, 284, 307-310, 312, 319, 321, 322, 325, 330, 331, 335-337, 339, 342, 345, 346, 348, 349, 350, 377, 380-382, 390-392, 394, 396, 400, 456, 570, 573, 577, 582, 586, 595, 596, 600

White Oak Swamp, Va., 136

Whitfield, Gen. John W., CSA, 253, 256

Whiting, Gen. W. H. C., CSA, 14, 15, 17, 29, 36, 59, 66, 102, 111, 126, 482, 483, 488

Wigfall, Gen. Louis T., CSA, 82, 102, 229, 448, 588

Wilcox, Gen. Cadmus M., CSA, 74, 109, 120, 121

Williamsburg, Va., 119-123, 125, 126, 128, 129, 131-134, 136, 144, 449, 450, 485, 487

Williamsburg, Battle of, 124, 450

Williamsburg Road, Va., 141

Williamson, Col. J. A., CSA, 305

Williamson, Col. Thomas H., CSA, 74

Williamsport, Md., 17-20, 23

Willow Spring, Miss., 171

Wilmington, N .C., 376, 389

Wilson, Gen. Jasper H., USA, 409, 414, 417

Winchester, Va., 18, 19, 22, 24, 25, 26, 28, 29, 31, 32, 34-39, 58, 59, 81, 87-89, 106, 107, 129, 434, 440-442
Winchester Railroad, 28
Winder, Gen. Charles S., CSA, 477
Winnsboro, N. C., 373, 376
Withers, Col. W. T., CSA, 183
Woodstock, Va., 107
Wright, Col. G. J., CSA, 391
Wyatt, Miss., 258

Yadkin River, 409
Yallabusha River, 153, 164, 355
Yazoo City, Miss., 164, 191, 204, 210, 252, 253

Yazoo Pass, Miss., 164
Yazoo River, 159, 162, 171, 191, 201-203
Yerger, Maj. William, CSA, 176, 179
Yorktown, Va., 12, 109, 111-114, 117-119, 435, 448-450, 461, 484, 485, 487
Yorktown, Battle of, 432
York River, 111, 112, 118, 124, 126, 448
York River Railroad, 127, 134, 137
Young, Gen. P. M. B., CSA, 391
Young's Branch, Va., 44, 45
Young's Bridge, S. C., 376

Other DACAPO titles of interest

OpenGL®
Programming Guide
Seventh Edition